THE

NEW INDIAN GARDENER,

AND

GUIDE,

TO THE SUCCESSFUL CULTURE

OF THE

KITCHEN AND FRUIT GARDEN

IN

INDIA

THE

NEW INDIAN GARDENER,

AND

GUIDE,

TO THE SUCCESSFUL CULTURE OF THE KITCHEN AND FRUIT GARDEN IN

INDIA

BY

G. T. F. S. BARLOW SPEEDE, M. A. & H. S.

GYAN

Published by

GYAN

Gyan Publishing House
5, Ansari Road
Daryaganj, New Delhi-110002
Phone: 011-47034999, 9811692060
E-mail: books@gyanbooks.com

Distribution Network
gyanbooks.com
India, USA, Canada, UK, Australia, France

ISBN: 978-81-212-8260-4 (PB)
First Published, 1848

2nd Impression 2023

Printed at: Gyan Press, Delhi.

THE NEW INDIAN GARDENER, AND GUIDE, TO THE SUCCESSFUL CULTURE OF THE KITCHEN AND FRUIT GARDEN IN INDIA
Author: G. T. F. S. BARLOW SPEEDE

Frontispiece

THE

NEW INDIAN GARDENER,

AND

GUIDE,

TO THE SUCCESSFUL CULTURE

OF THE

KITCHEN AND FRUIT GARDEN

IN

INDIA,

WITH APPROPRIATE ILLUSTRATIONS;

ALSO

A VOCABULARY OF THE MOST USEFUL TERMS, AND A DIGESTED CATALOGUE OF PLANTS, TREES, ETC. IN THE ENGLISH AND NATIVE, AND NATIVE AND ENGLISH LANGUAGES.

BY

G. T. F. S. BARLOW SPEEDE, M.A. & H.S.,

Author of Chronological Tablets of England, France, &c.—the Hand Book of Gardening—Criminal Statistics of Bengal, &c. &c. &c.

CALCUTTA:

W. THACKER AND CO., ST. ANDREW'S LIBRARY.

1848.

TO

THE PRESIDENT,

VICE PRESIDENTS AND MEMBERS

OF THE

AGRICULTURAL AND HORTICULTURAL SOCIETY

OF

India.

THIS WORK IS

DEDICATED

IN TRIBUTE OF RESPECT

FOR THAT ZEAL AND ENERGY

WHICH HAS SO EMINENTLY ADVANCED THE TRUE INTERESTS

OF HORTICULTURE IN THIS COUNTRY,

BY THEIR FELLOW MEMBER

G. T. F. SPEEDE.

Calcutta, January 1848.

PREFACE.

THE literary success that has attended a former work under the title of the "INDIAN HAND BOOK OF GARDENING," which has passed through two editions, leads to a continuance of the same line of publication, in the present enlarged and improved work, in which, with the view of suiting it to a more extended field, the author has availed himself of very valuable information, placed at his disposal, by a distinguished practical horticulturist in the Upper Provinces; at the same time that he has limited it to Horticulture, strictly so speaking, that is to say, the culture of, and all that relates to the kitchen and fruit garden; considering the growth of flowers and shrubs, a distinct art deserving of a separate work, which is now in hand, under the title of the "INDIAN FLORICULTURIST." The Vocabulary, appended to the present work, will be formed greatly improved, by the addition of many new names of plants, and by its also forming an index to their Botanical, as well as to their popular designations. But the author regrets that in an endeavor to encourage native skill in the noble art of printing, he has so far failed that he feels himself obliged to apologize for the typographical defects of the first part of the volume, on which it was, as will be seen by the illustrations, his wish to have secured, at any expense, the best ability obtainable in this country ; this fault however has been remedied in the second part, containing the vocabulary.

THE

NEW INDIAN GARDENER.

If we are to look on gardening as a mere mechanical art that may be efficiently practised by the most ignorant laborer, manuals or books of instruction will be useless; yet how generally is it only so viewed in this country, and hence we need not wonder at the slow progress hitherto made in the cultivation of such products of the garden as are generally held in estimation by the European portion of the community; and left as these commonly are, to the simple Hindoo *mallee* (or gardener,) it is not surprising, that our bazars want what are justly deemed the more delicate vegetables for the table; and that those we have, are limited within the space of a few months only in the year, we must rather on the contrary wonder then that we have, what we have. This *mallee* estimates that, because he had a good crop of cabbages from a certain spot of ground this year, he shall have an equally fine one from the same spot in the next season; and would not conceive that there could be any causes arising from the production of this year's culture to depreciate the quality, or injure the growth of the like article in successive years. Uninstructed as he is, he looks only on a cabbage, as a cabbage, without reference to any variety of the species, and without imagining that one kind can be more delicately flavored than the other, and hence more worthy of his attention; he supposes that perfection is attained when he brings before you an immense drumhead, that would require a boiler to be made especially for its reception, and he looks at you, while presenting it with an air of triumph, little heeding that your preference would be given rather to the small close early york, or the delicate savoy. At the same time he cannot be blamed for his mistake, since we have never, perhaps, ourselves looked on gardening otherwise than as a mere art, requiring manual labor alone to its perfect production; and, impressed with this idea, have never thought of informing him; that it was rather to be ranked among the sciences, and that some study of the character, the habits, and the natural localities even, of divers plants, must be required to bring gardening to perfection. It is this investigation of the natural habits and properties of plants, that demonstrates how wonderfully they have been formed to answer the wants of man in their multiplication and preservation, and how admirably they answer the purposes assigned them by nature, of ministering to his necessities, or his gratifications. It is the examination and study of these, that forms the science of gardening; and combining with manual labor, constitutes what is necessary to its perfection. It is not, however, the object of a work like this, intended but as a *manual for ready reference*, to go very deeply into the matter, as a science; larger works must do this, of which those of Loudon, and the more scientific works of Sir Humphry Davy, the Rev. P. Keith, and Dr. John Lindley are among the best of the present day; the scientific portion, therefore, will be confined to such short remarks as may facilitate the understanding of the subject, sufficiently to mark the principles of vegetable life and growth. In the present work too, much is added with reference to the Upper Provinces, for which the reader has to thank the Reverend J. C. Proby, who before he left India in 1843, most obligingly placed at disposal of the author a packet of papers, containing notes with reference to that part of India; the result of his own experience, as well as of another practical Horticulturist, Captain Corrie, who aided him in his experiments, (but whose career was unfortunately cut short in the passes, on the retreat from Cabool,) the value of which cannot be denied, nor the great obligation which he has, by such a communication, conferred on the cause of Horticulture in India.

Plants.

THEIR ORGANIC CONSTRUCTION.

The first, and most prominent distinction perceptible in plants, which marks their difference from minerals, and distinguishes all such productions of nature as are endowed with what is commonly understood by the term life, whether active or otherwise, from them, is, that the latter are found with *organs* adapted to fulfil the functions for which they are destined.

Unorganized substances may be increased, or lessened in size, by mechanical, or chemical alterations; that is to say, either by the addition of particles of a similar conformation, or by combination with substances originally dissimilar, but amalgamated by chemical action into one whole; but these possess no power able to convert them absolutely into their own nature. This is the office of the organs, in beings possessing life, however passive; and one of the principal functions these have to perform is nutrition, whereby organized bodies are increased in size by receiving internally particles of matter of a nature differing from their own, assimilating them to their own substance; in other words forming, to use a term more generally confined to active life, the food wherewith they are nourished. Organized beings have also the power of reproducing their own species, varied only by the description of nutrition afforded, or the circumstances under which successful practice of removing even full grown trees.

Roots possess the power of constantly adding new matter to their extremities; whereby they penetrate the earth, and insinuate themselves within the smallest crevices, traversing from place to place in search of the food they most desire; making up for the want of locomotive power in the plant, by continually shifting their mouths, in search of fresh nutriment, although the bodies remain at rest.

They are most readily formed in darkness, aided by moderate moisture; and it is evident, that their production is in some way connected with the leaf buds of the plant, since portions of a stem, not having leaves or leaf buds, seldom produce any roots; or if they do, these soon perish.

But, although the cause of the formation of roots is involved in obscurity, it is apparent that it arises from the elaboration of organisable matter by the leaves, and it is clear that their formation is promoted by the descending sap; whence if a ring of bark be removed from a branch, and the wound wrapped round with wet clay, moss, or tow, as in Chinese grafting, roots will invariably be projected from the upper lip of the wound. The proportion borne by the root to the stem varies much in different plants; in those that perspire freely, these organs are known to be much greater in extension of surface than the circle formed by the branches; but this disproportion diminishes, as the plants advance in age.

Besides the power of feeding, roots have also organs whereby plants deposit their excrementitious matter, or such, as is either superfluous, or deleterious to them; and Dr. Lindley informs us that, "If you poison one-half of the roots of any plant, the other half will throw the poison off again from the system. Hence it follows, that, if roots are so circumstanced that they cannot constantly advance into fresh soil, they will, by degrees, be surrounded by their own excrementitious secretions." And from this is to be deduced the system, and necessity of the rotation of crops; for, as it is clear that what a plant has thus deposited, even if its re-absorption do it no actual injury, must have ceased to afford nourishment to that individual, so the plant, or the species must by a continuance, or repetition on the same soil, become weakened and degenerate.

Roots are either *annual*, living for one season; *biennial*, surviving two seasons; or *perennial*, lasting for an indefinite number of years: they consist of two parts—*caudex*, the stump, is the body of the root whence the trunk or stem ascends, and the fibrous portions spring; *radicula*, the fibres, branching out into the earth. There are several kinds distinguished by botanists from their respective forms—viz. *Radix fibrosa*, the fibrous root; *Radix repens*, the creeping trouble of splitting one open, the skeleton of the young plant reposing in the body of the bean, and making a slight indentation in either side; it will be found situated, not, as might be expected, in the centre of the bean, but at that end by which it was connected with the pod by a short *pedicle*, or branch; this pot being called the eye, or *hilum* of the seed, through which the pedicle conveys nourishment to the embryo plant until the seed is ripe, when the former withering, the seed becomes detached, bearing a small scar at its base.

When placed in the earth, this embryo swells, bursting its outer coat or skin, and then sends forth its root in a downward direction, followed by an upward dilation of the young shoot, which, unfolding its cotyledons, exposes the first leaves, becoming green an expansion, and forming the matter, or nutriment, whereby all the pre-existent but scarcely visible rudiments of the plants are eventually brought to light.

ROOTS, AND THE MOUTH OF PLANTS.

These organs nourish and preserve the plant, and for this purpose the tip of every root fibre contains a small spongy sucker, or, in more familiar term, a mouth; but although, in most plants, we cannot discover any direct opening, it is clearly ascertained that fluids are taken up, or absorbed by these mouths, called *spongelets.* The largest, and most distinguishable are to be found in such trees as grow so near to water as to have their roots exposed to a direct communication with it ; in the roots of beans also, and the extremity of the tap root of the turnip, &c. they may be sometimes observed with the naked eye. Their power of absorption is always proportionate, in healthy plants, to the quantity of food they require ; and hence in the spring, when sap is consumed rapidly by the leaves, the root-fibres more quickly form, and project these spongelets than at other periods ; whilst, as the season advances, and the leaves need a less profuse supply of sap, the roots become more torpid, producing fewer absorbent vessels.

These spongelets communicate with the vessels that branch from the larger fibres of the roots, eventually ascending the stem ; but at the extremities the openings are so small as not to allow access to any fluid in the least dense, or viscous ; hence, although water which has flowed through the manure of a farm yard abounds with particles most nutritive to vegetables, it is often found too thick to enter such minute orifices, unless copiously diluted, cloging and obstructing them until absorption ceases ; the consequence being, that the leaves become yellow and fall off, or, as gardeners term it, are burnt by the heat of the manure.

For the same reason also, lime, pounded bones, or shells, cannot, until dissolved by water, or dissipated by putrefaction, obtain access to the larger vessels; plants are, therefore, very liable to injury from the presence of deleterious matter in the soil; and it is most probable, that, if they ever do reject such matter, it is rather because it does not acquire a sufficient tenuity, than from any power in the absorbing vessels to refuse what is noxious. It is a curious fact, however, that poisonous substances fatal to man are generally speaking equally so to plants; for it has been found that by presenting opium, arsenic, or mercury, or other metallic, or alkaline poison, to the roots, a tree may be destroyed as readily as a human being.

A few partial exceptions to the before mentioned inertness in the selection of food are found; as for instance, it has been discovered, that the pea will not absorb a solution of silex, or flint, which will be eagerly taken up by wheat. The compression, or destruction of the spongelets in transplanting, by depriving the plant of its natural food in that proportion to which it has been accustomed, causes the withering attending that operation, and continuing until these spongelets can be either renewed, or placed in similar freedom in the earth, to what they enjoyed before removal. At the same time this evil, if not carried to too great an extent, becomes the source of benefit to the plants, since, but a discussion of such minute details would burden too heavily the pages of the present work. Leaving the reader, therefore, who may be curious on such points, to ascertain particularly their nature by a reference to more extensive works, it will be only necessary to the general understanding of this subject to furnish the following concise sketch; dividing the matter under the several heads of—Seeds and Germination; Roots, and the mouths of Plants; Trunks, Stems, or Stalks; Leaves, Flowers, and Fruits.

SEEDS AND GERMINATION.

The seed becoming at maturity separated from the parent plant, is capable of producing a distinct vegetable of the same family; but it is to be observed that it will not always yield a produce of the same particular species and variety, or carry with it the peculiarities of the original stock; thus, for instance, though the seed of a ribston pippin is certain to produce a plant of the apple kind, it is very doubtful whether that apple will be a ribston pippin—it may be a crab, or it may be a new species of the apple, good or bad. Of the seed itself, little need be said; the formation of the embryo plant, and its connection with the *cotyledons*, or fleshy lobes of the seed, may be observed, with the naked eye, in the bean, by any one who will be at the after separation from the parent stem, and may be planted, either in the soil, or by insertion in the bark of a kindred species, sending forth their root fibres in the first instance into the earth, and in the second producing wood that unites itself to that with which it has been brought in contact. These leaf buds seldom appear except at the angle where the leaves unite with the stem, called the *axil.*

A bulb is only a larger form of the leaf bud, its identity with which is easily traced by gradually unfolding and comparing a leaf bud from any large tree with the bulb, carefully opened, of a tiger lily.

LEAVES.

The leaf, considered scientifically, is a flattened expansion of the fibres of the bark from which it shoots, connected by a layer of cellular tissue, called the *pabulum*, or aliment, the whole covered with a delicate cuticle, or skin, called the *epidermis*, and formed so as to present a large surface to the atmosphere: plants growing in the shade, or damp, have the epidermis very thin, whilst those in hot, dry, and exposed situations have this cuticle very hard and thick; in either case it is full of pores, called *stomates*, by means of which the plant both breathes, and perspires; these are the most abundant, and the largest, in such vegetable productions as are inhabitants of damp and shady situations; whence this property enables us to judge of the habits of unknown plants, with some degree of accuracy, by an examination of the epidermis: in making these, however, the size of the stomates is to be considered, more than their number, for Dr. Lindley mentions, that "the yucca aloifolia has four times as many stomates as a species of cotyledon in my collection, but those of the latter are about the $\frac{1}{750}$ of an inch in their longer diameter, large and active, while the stomates of the yucca are not more than $\frac{1}{2500}$ of an inch long in the aperture, and comparatively inert. The yucca, therefore, with its numerous stomates, has weaker powers of perspiration, and respiration than the cotyledon." The hue of leaves is generally green, becoming more intense in proportion to their exposure to strong light, but when not green, they are said, in botanical language, to be colored. It is unnecessary here to enumerate the several classes into which leaves are divided by botanists, according to their various forms; suffice it to observe, that one of their most essential functions is to preserve and nourish the leaf buds forming at their *axils*, or angles of conjunction with the stem, and to the performance of this office there is no exception, whatever may be the form that the leaf assumes.

from the seed, a mere point, almost imperceptible, and when first developed by germination is termed the *Plumule;* in this form it derives a part of its nourishment from the store maintained by the seed leaves, until, forming those of its own, it ceases to require assistance from that source. When fully formed, the stem of every plant comprises the following parts: 1. *Wood,* the older portion called the heart wood, and the newer, the *alburnum* ; 2. *Bark,* the inner part being called the *liber* ; 3. *Pith,* the centre channel conveying the ascending sap; 4. *Medullary* rays, connecting this last with the bark, or rind, and keeping up a communication between the centre and the circumference of the stem.

The stem is either simple, as in the lily tribe; or branched, as in most other plants; and as the functions of the root are to absorb nourishment from the soil, and transmit it to the superstructure, so those of the stem are to distribute this nutriment to the several parts of the plant,—leaves, flowers, &c. Its various forms are—1. *Caulis,* the stem properly so called, which bears both leaves and flowers; forming the trunks and branches of all trees and shrubs, as well as of many herbaceous plants; 2. *Culmus,* a stalk or culm, the peculiar stem of grasses, rushes, and similar plants; 3. *Scapus,* a stalk, springing immediately from the root bearing flowers and fruit, but not leaves, as in the primrose and the strawberry; 4. *Peduncculus,* a pedicle or foot stalk, the flower stalk springing from the stem or branch, and bearing flowers and fruit, but not leaves ; 5. *Petiolus*, the leaf stalk, a term applied exclusively to the short stalk, or support of the leaf. There is a point or line separated the stem of the root, called the neck, and which may be considered the seat of vitality ; for, if you cut off the root of a young growing plant it again shoots out and if you cut down the stem it will be renewed, but, if this neck be injured the plant must certainly perish. The vitality of this part also, in delicate plants, is injured by being buried below the surface of the soil in transplanting, equally so by being left exposed, in that operation; hence care should be taken to place plants the same depth in their new situation that they held in the spot they previously occupied : a lodgment of water near a plant frequently also destroys it by the effect it has on this part of the stem.

Linnæus divides plants into two classes, from the mode in which stems spring from their seeds in the process of germination ; these he names from the number of cotyledons, or seed leaves, a name given to that sort of leaf into which the fleshy part of the seed forms itself by germinating, constituting at once a defence and source of nourishment to the young plants ; the classes are, *Monocotyledon*, or bearing one cotyledon, and *Decotyledon*, or twofold. Of the first, are the palm, the cocoanut, corn, &c. ; in the second, the most distinguishable, and doubtless often observed by the reader, are the bean, the pea, the lupine, &c. Mushrooms and other fungi, as also lichens, form a third class, having no cotyledons, and hence denominated *Acotyledons.*

The wood, or hard part of the stem, commences its formation from the time that the first leaf expands, appearing as a small fibrous circle within the circumference of the stem, separating it into two parts, and as it advances, is found to be composed of many layers, extending every year of growth; as does also the bark, though not so perceptibly, because its outer coats, becoming too hard to be distended by the pressure occasioned on the increase of the stem, crack and frequently fall off; these are at the first green, but the last, by increased exposure, become darker and drier. The vital part of the stem appears to be situated between the young layers, or outside of the wood, and the corresponding inner coating of the bark,* since the plant suffers most by injury to that part. When the stem is wounded the cellular formation of the bark proceeds to work, repairing the mischief, by forming granulations that finally unite in one mass. The sap is believed to ascend in the woody matter of the stem, but most actively in the *alburnum*, through which, it mounts in straight lines, a part being afterwards

* Called the *liber*, as the outer is termed the *cortical integument*, or rind; and the young wood next the liber, the *alburnum.*

almost entirely through its taper extremity ;—carrots, radishes, parsnips, &c. are of this class.

Radix præmorsa, the abrupt root, is another form of the foregoing, so called from its abruptly terminating as if broken off or bitten ;—of this class are the scabious, the primrose, &c.

Radix bulbosa, the bulbous root, perhaps improperly so called, because the bulb rather forms the base of the stem, whence the leaves directly spring, for the tufts or fibres pendent from the bulb are in reality the roots ;—of this kind are the amaryllis, the onion &c.

Radix tuberosa, the tuberous or knobbed root, consisting of fleshy knobs connected by common fibres, each knob, or even a portion of each, being capable of reproducing one or more plants ;—of this kind are the potatoe, &c.

Radix granulata, the granulated root, is formed of a cluster of little bulbs or scales, connected by a common fibre ;—of this kind are the saxifrage, or London pride, &c.

TRUNKS, STEMS, OR STALKS.

Every plant has a stem through which the sap circulates, and from which the leaves and flowers spring. This appears, in an infant state, whilst not yet emerged

Proceeding to their general character and parts, the fibres, or, as they are commonly called by the unscientific, the veins, will be found to spread out in various directions, in two divisions, generally communicating with the centre of the stem, and with the liber; the former part keeping up the connection between the leaf and the wood, and the latter that of the leaf with the bark: the upper part being the channel for conveyance of the ascending, and the lower of the descending sap: the under surface of the leaf has the ribs, or fibres, prominent, and is generally, alike from less exposure to light, as from other causes, paler in hue, as well as more hairy than the upper side, finally, this side abounds more in pores than the other. The principal vein generally divides the leaf from the base to the extremity, from which others branch out laterally, and from them again, still smaller ones may be observed to issue. Some suppose that by absorption of moisture from the atmosphere, the leaves become refreshed; and this would appear to be the case in those of the pine-apple, which after a heavy night dew, or sprinkling with a fine rosed watering pot, become sensibly revived, and it must be confessed, that the stomates of the leaves seem in general well formed for such a purpose; but on the other hand it is also maintained, and with some appearance of foundation, that this apparent renovation from sprinkling with water, syringing, or the action of a heavy dew, is to be attributed rather to the diminished perspiration caused by its cooling nature. Both these theories appearing feasible, a combination of the two may very reasonably be supposed to have some share in the effect produced.

The nutritious juices imbibed from the earth and converted into sap, as before noticed, are carried by their appropriate vessels into the substance of the leaves, for the purpose of being acted upon by the air and light, as well as by heat and moisture, to produce that change which is requisite for the evaporation of the necessary secretions, whether odoriferous, resinous, oily, mucilaginous, saccharine, bitter, acid, starchy, or alkaline. No less so for the production of the distinguishing principles of peculiar plants; whether these be narcotic, aromatic, pungent, acrid, astringent, or other: all are, however influenced, both as regards quantity, and quality, by the strength of light to which the plants producing them, may be exposed. The action of solar light on the leaf is known to have the effect of decomposing carbonic acid gas; of extricating nitrogen; as well as of producing perspiration. A leaf exposed to the sun, gives out oxygen by the decomposition of carbonic acid, leaving carbon behind in a solid state in the leaf, and this process may be easily observed by placing a leaf in a vessel of water, and exposing it to the sun, where the released oxygen will be seen forming bubbles on the surface of the leaf ; this will not be the case in the absence of solar heat, but what little is then given off, will be carbonic acid, which is, more or less, exhaled at all times; whilst oxygen, which the leaf when exposed to the sun gave out, will, in the shade, be drawn into the pores. In a healthy plant, this process of decomposing carbonic acid gas by day, and of re-forming it at night, with the inhalation of oxygen is going on continually, and hence the healthiness of most plants is proportionate to the quantity of light received in the day.

This rule, however, is subject to exception in favor of those plants that prefer shade, and are, therefore, so organized as to suit such a position only; but in these it is not that a free decomposition of carbonic acid gas will do them injury, but because under the action of the sun's heat, the epidermis yields too readily to the evaporation of moisture by perspiration.

The fact of the perspiration of plants is easily proved, by placing a plant, well covered with leaves, under a glass vessel, and exposing it to the action of solar rays ;—the sides of the glass will in a few minutes be covered with dew, caused by the condensing of the perspiration exuding from the plant ; perspiration, however, only occurs with plants in the light, there is none in darkness.

The heat of the sun is the cause of the growth, as its light is, of the maturity of plants. Animals will live and thrive without much light, but no plants can exist for any time without the presence of this element, at the same time that the external heat of the air is indispensable to a regular and sufficent flow of the sap; and hence the artificial heat produced in hot-houses in England, serves to forward the growth of plants from tropical climates, and brings them to that maturity they could not otherwise attain; and in like manner the increased activity given to those of colder climes when brought to India, so over poweringly increases the growth, as to exhaust all their power in formation of new shoots; leaving no strength for the formation of flowers and fruit. The want of light deprives leaves of their color, and diminishes their powers of action, and above all, of perspiration, so that a plant thereby retaining an excess of liquid, becomes in fact dropsical; on this principle endive, celery, frequently also the hearts of cabbages, lettuces, &c. are what is called blanched, or rendered white, and less strong in flavor, as well as less woody.

After a certain period of existence in the due performance of its functions, the passages or vessels of the leaf, of its *petiolus*, or stalk, of the branch whence it springs, all become choked, its color then changes; it loses its property of decomposing carbon and, morbid by the consequent excess of oxygen, —it withers;—it dies;—ejected to decay, it is thrown off to make room for the new leaves to which it has given

given life and nourishment,—the common fate of all that is earthly in nature.

The floral leaves, or *bractea,* differ from others only by growing, as their name implies, around the embryo blossom, which they protect and assist—preparing the nutriment necessary for its food.

FLOWERS.

In flowers the *calyx*, or cup, protects the bud before it expands; it consists of several parts, resembling small leaves both in form and color: these are called *sepals*, and are sometimes so united as to form a cup apparently of one piece. Above the calyx rises the *corolla*, or colored part of the flower, consisting of several *petals*, or flower leaves, either distinct or joined together, the point of union being the *nectary*, or receptacle for the sweet fluid, serving to nourish the blossom, whence the bee is said to steal honey; within this, in most plants, is the sexual system, the most important portion being the *pistil*, formed of the seed vessel, or *ovary*, having at its summit a thread-like tube called the *style*, with the *stigma*, or small spongy swelling at its extremity, for the reception, and transmission to the seed vessel, of the dust or *pollen* containing in the *anther*, or case, loosely attached to the extremities of the *stamens*, or thread-like filaments generally observed in blossoms clustering near the foot of the petals ; these are often wholly, or in part, wanting; but the sexes are so essential to the formation of a flower, that none can be botanically so considered in which one or other are not to be found although not aways found together, or in some rare instances, such as the Mangosteen, not even on the same tree. In cultivated plants there is an evident tendency in all these parts to be converted into each other, as the necessity, or caprice of nature dictates; and hence the origin of double blossoms, as well as of many of the abortions, and mal-formations so frequently noticeable in flowers; such are, the not uncommon appearance in the rose, of the sepals and even pistil being converted into leaves; the production of smaller fruit from the extremities of larger ones, &c.; and hence we has arisen the inference, that flowers are but modifications of leaves, and that flower buds bear an analogy to leaf buds. This appears the stronger in fruit trees, because those buds that produce blossoms, and those that give birth only to leaves, differ not in the least from each other in their earlier stages; convertable, by modifications of druning, by great excitement, or by neglect into each other.

The causes of these changes are still in obscurity, but it will be found, that whatever tends to produce excess of excitement in a plant, is unfavorable to the production of flower buds, creating a rapid developement of leaf buds; hence it may be concluded, that the period when a plant begins to flower depends on the secretion and conservation, of a sufficiency of nutritious matter, in excess of its daily wants, to afford nutriment in such quantity, as may yield support to them.

The *pollen* is essential to the fructification of the seeds contained in the seed vessel, which without it, could never attain perfection; and a knowledge of this fact aids the gardener in securing the object of his culture with such plants, as, like the melon, the vegetable marrow, &c. have the seed vessel in one blossom, and the anthers in another; when bringing the two into contact, by the hand, will often secure the production of fruit: by the same means varieties are also produced of the same plant, or a mixture with another species of the same genus, by bringing together the pollen and stigma of divers kinds; the results, in the latter case, being termed *hybrid*, and in the former, simply *cross bred.*

After the flower has performed its office of fructifying the seed, the petals and other organs not destined to become part of the fruit, wither and fall off.

FRUITS.

The seed, when fructified, as above shown, begins to enlarge, and requires, like all other parts of the plant, to be supplied with its peculiar food, for under any relaxation in the flow of its fitting nutriment, it will soon languish and die.

There are two great divisions among fruits, the *superior*, and the *inferior* ; they are said to belong to the former class when the pistil is separate from the floral envelopes, or sepals, and when, on their falling off, the fruit forms by an enlargement of the ovary only, as in the peach ; but they are assigned to the latter class when the pistil, or its ovary, and the floral envelopes all grow together, and when the fruit is consequently, an enlargement of the whole flower growing simultaneously, as occurs in the pomegranite. It has been shewn, when treating of leaves. &c. that the supply of food to a plant, or to any part of it, is regulated by the attractive power of its leaves: it follows then, that the inferior fruit retaining a portion of these during the whole period of its growth or enlargement, is stronger and less liable to fall off before maturition, than the superior fruit.

The following are most common of these two classes, that appear among our ordinary fruits.

Inferior.		*Superior.*	
Pomegranite,	Pear,	Peach,	Shaddock,
Guava,	Rose apple,	Plum,	Lemon,
Quince,	Phalsa,	Grape,	Orange,
Melon,	Loquat,	Strawberry,	
Apple,	Fig	Sweet sop,	

Fruit, in common with leaves, has the power of attracting food to itself from the parts of the plant adjacent to, or surrounding it; and this is more clearly perceptible in the state and action of those individuals, which by accident, or advancement of growth, are more vigorous than their neighbours, from whom they draw a portion of nourishment, to the eminent as evident deterioration, and often to the entire destruction of the weaker. As the principal part of this food has to be supplied by the leaves, deriving their nutriment from the soil, through the roots, any thing that deranges the action of either the roots or the leaves, must have a material effect on the fruit; if the leaves of a plant be placed at too great a distance from the fruit, so that this last cannot with facility derive nourishment from them, it must at least be weakened if not destroyed. This shews why fruit appearing upon naked branches will not grow, and also why the existence of a leaf immediately above the fruit upon a branch, is serviceable to it; it shews, moreover, why the thinning of fruit, from a loaded tree, is beneficial to what is allowed to remain. The food, however, that is thus drawn from the leaves is not, as with them, returned into the bark, for the bark of the fruit stalk has little or no power of carrying off from the fruit what it has conveyed to it besides which the commonest observer may remark a sort of band or ring, separating the one from the other, contributing to the same effect; this, therefore, retains for its own use, nearly all that it has attracted until becoming obstructed altogether, the fruit, if not gathered, will fall. These juices further undergo an alteration by the natural action of the fruit itself, varying according to the species, and resulting chiefly from the united action of light and heat; experience having fully established, that a high temperature, combined with a strong light, will produce saccharine matter, or sugar, where, in their absence, acid would have been predominant. The cause of this is thus explained by Dr. Lindley: "As sugar is more rich in carbon than vegetable acids, and has no free oxygen as they have, the sweetness of pulpy fruits ripened under a bright sunshine, may be understood to arise, from the decomposition of carbonic gas, and the expulsion of oxygen, being greater under sunshine than in the shade. Another cause may be, the greater facility with which vegetable acids enter into combination with gum and starch, and so form sugar, at a high, than at a low temperature."

The watery particles that the fruit attracts through the stem, in the course of maturation, undergo an entire decomposition, and become dissipated; an increased supply of water, by requiring longer time for this operation, will retard the ripening of fruit; and on the other hand, a diminished supply will have the contrary effect. Fruit being chiefly intended for the protection and nourishment of the seed, a large portion of its liquid and nutritive secretions are consumed in effecting this object; and whatever circumstances affect the fruit, will equally influence the seed, as well as the future plant that this seed is to produce, the strength and vigor of which will be in the proportion those qualities prevailed in the parent: the plumpest and most weighty seeds always producing the most luxuriant plants; and these qualities greatly diminish with age, even to the extent, in most seeds, of the entire loss of vitality and power of reproduction. It is a knowledge of this fact that induces the gardener to select old cucumber and melon seed, in which this power is somewhat abated, as the plants of new seed are apt to spread so luxuriantly as to deteriorate the quality, and, by an over-production of leaves and branches, to lessen the quantity of their fruit. Plants, as will be, well understood from the principles above laid down should not be allowed to bear when too young, and should also, occasionally, have a partial or entire rest for a season from the maturation of fruit; for as these are maintained by drawing on the nutriment contained in the leaves, their destruction when young, will allow the latter to create a store of that nutriment which is required for the effective production and support of fruit, against a succeeding season.

HEAT, LIGHT, &c.

The exact extent allowed by the laws of vegetation for the capability of plants in endurance either of heat or cold, is not accurately ascertained; for it is well known that many seeds may be boiled not only without injury, but to the improvement of their vegetative powers; whilst others may be exposed to freezing, and still be capable of reproduction. The number of plants, however, that will bear these extremes is small; and the greatest variety of indigenous vegetable productions are known to exist in a temperature ranging from 32° to 90°. All plants become torpid at a certain degree of temperature, varying according to their constitution; when, however the atmospheric heat rises above this, the cellular tissue, is excited, perspiration commences, arousing the absorbent power of the roots, and vegetation awakes to vigor. But if the temperature required to produce this effect vary in different plants in the same climate, how much greater must be its variation in plants in different climates; and thus we find that our native trees—such as the mango, the guava, the coffee, &c. accustomed to be brought into action only by a high degree of temperature, after but a short period of rest, soon wither, even in the warmest season in England; whilst the apple, the currant, and other English trees, suffer from the too great excitement produced by the high temperature (combined, as it so often is, with humidity) of India, whence they either lose the power of producing flowers, and fruit, or perish altogether; the effect of a high temperature being, if dry, to elaborate the natural secretions of plants more rapidly than the parts destined to receive them can be formed; and, if moist, to cause a rapid production of leaves and branches, without giving the strength required to form flowers. Too cold a temperature, if not so low as to destroy, but just to continue life, is found to have much the same effect as the over excitement before shewn; but this is a state hardly to be dreaded in this climate, except in some parts of the hills, and it is, therefore, unnecessary to enter into further detail on the subject.

Variations of temperature are, to a certain extent, necessary to healthy vegetation; for the excitement of increased temperature and light, during the day, producing perspiration, and stimulating the vitality and natural secretions of plants, is as essential to their well being as the repose of night, when perspiration ceases, and the waste of the day is made good by the attraction of the roots, preparing the plant for the renewed exercise of another day.

From a like cause the alternation of seasons is essential to the healthy growth of all plants; for the extreme excitement produced by the hot weather creates a langor that exhausts the strength of the plant, and causes the leaves to become choked and unfitted either to breathe or to perspire; the vessels get clogged, and worn out, and the whole system, by continued exhalation, is dried up and exhausted. To this succeeds a decrease of temperature, and of the duration of light, until the accession of the cold weather allows

important consideration is—temperature. The soil, the air, the water, are of comparatively little moment, considered with reference to the increase or decrease of heat. In transplanting from a colder to a warmer climate, an elevated situation is desirable, and a sufficiency of water to provide for the more abundant evaporation to which the plant becomes subjected, and this is generally more easily effected than the acclimation of those of the torrid zone to the colder climates of Europe; yet there the operation has been carried to such perfection, that many products of Asiatic origin have become completely naturalized: such are the potatoe, the kidney bean, the cucumber, the nasturtium, the dahlia. It must not be expected, however, that this acclimation can be effected at once,—several generations must often transpire ere the object be effected, or perfection of growth obtained in the new station, and people here should be content to cultivate a plant they desire to naturalize, for the first two or three years at least, with a view only to propagation, not for use.

THE FOOD OF PLANTS.

It has been already shown, under the head of "roots, &c." that the mouths of the root fibres are constructed for the admission of liquid only; water, therefore, becomes indispensable as food to all plants, although it will not, as has often been erroneously asserted, alone serve as nourishment. Another indispensable ingredient in the food of plants is air, especially when held in combination, or mixed with water; whence, the giving water in large quantities, direct to the soil, in cool weather, will generally be less beneficial than if the water were distributed from the fine rose of a watering pot, so that every drop may carry down to the roots a portion of air; in this country, however, fermentation is so rapid, that, expect in cold weather, this addition to the benefits derivable from the free bestowal of water is denied to the gardener, or at least its use made dangerous; as, by distributing the fluid from a fine rosed watering pot, the liquid being scattered, is apt to lodge in the joints of the branches, the folds of the leaves, &c. where, fermenting, it rots and destroys the plant. Whilst, however, it is known on the one hand, that plants cannot live in a soil to all appearance dry; it has also been proved, on the other, that few can exist under an excessive supply of moisture. It becomes, therefore, a subject of some importance to determine the proportion most agreeable to plants in general, as well as that fitted to every different species; and the particular period of vegetable growth, when a greater, or less supply may be called for.

It need hardly be pointed out here, that in the cold season, when, as has been shewn, plants are comparatively in a state of repose, but a small quantity of water is needed, because in a torpid state they seek but little food: some moisture, however, will still be beneficial to perennial plants, even in that state of rest, to enable them to prepare for future vegetation, as shewn under the head of "roots." For absorption still going on, and conveying nutriment to the interior of the plant—provides a store for the support of the young shoots of the succeeding year, which are vigorous or otherwise according as this reserve of food has been more or less in quantity. An exception is of course to be made in favor of marsh or aquatic plants, which ought never to be left dry.

Water stagnating on the ground becomes unwholesome food for plants, chiefly on account of its not having the opportunity of mixing with air; and soils of which the stiff clayey nature, prevents this free circulation, are termed cold or sour; their defect however, is the want of a due supply of air, assisted by a great degree of cold in the soil produced by the lodgment of water.

Although too much wet in a soil is undoubtedly injurious, yet if that be kept in free circulation, and its various particles in contract with the air, (and this in the case of stiff soils may sometimes be effected by the admixture of ashes, sand, and the like, to open their texture) the evil consequences will be lessened; but, without this free combination of water and air, not merely will the process of vegetation commence slowly, but its progress, when began, will be checked, the leaves drooping and becoming flaccid, until, at last, they wither altogether and fall off.

Plants in a state of growth, and especially in the early stages of vegetation, require an abundant supply of moisture, to keep up the great demand made by the commencing perspiration of the young leaves as they burst forth, at which period the perspiratory action is most powerful, the whole epidermis feeling the influence of first exposure to light. As they advance, this *epidermis* hardens, and by degrees, even the *stomates* become choked, and subject, in consequence, to less excitability; hence may be deduced, as a general rule, that, at the first beginning of growth, plants demand a more abundant supply of moisture, in proportion to their size, than when their organization is perfected. This rule is especially applicable to culinary plants of the spinaceous and acetaceous kinds, wherein a large quantity of tender succulent leaves is desired; a free supply of water tending greatly to the increase of that succulency. The size of succulent fruit may also be increased by a continued profuse supply of water during their ripening. But this generally, at the expence of flavor, which will be deteriorated by the accumulation of watery particles; and for this reason the quantity usually given, should always be diminished as the fruit advances to ripeness, otherwise said to thirst for their breakfast; provided, however, that the heat of the season be not such as to cause too profuse a perspiration, and therefore an excess of excitement in the plant, so long as the means of supply continue with consequent relaxation should it fall short.

In this country, where the moisture conveyed by the atmosphere at one season is so excessive, and at another hardly perceptible, little use can be made of its variations in the culture of plants; the following rules laid down by Professor Lindley, as deserving of especial attention, may however assist those who are desirous of trying to effect the acclimation of exotic plants to the plains of India, and may find more extensive application in the Hills.

"1. Most moisture in the air is demanded by plants when they first begin to grow, and least, when their periodical growth is completed." Hence the latter end of the rains may be indicated as the most natural time for raising the more hardy plants.

"2. The quantity of atmospheric moisture required by plants is, *cæteris paribus*, in inverse proportion to the distance from the equator of the countries they naturally inhabit." This is particularly noticeable in the rapid growth of plants during the rainy season.

"3. Plants with annual stems require more than those with ligneous stems.

"4. The amount of moisture in the air most suitable

to plants at rest, is in inverse proportion to the quantity of aqueous matter they at that time contain. (Hence the dryness of the air required by succulent plants when at rest)."

In connection with the subject of the food of plants, is to be considered the heat of the soil into which their roots extend; whereby a degree of stimulus is kept up that balances the excitement given by the sun to the leaves of the plant; which, were they raised by its warmth to a higher degree than could be attained by the roots, would cause a consumption of sap more rapidly than could be renewed by these last, and, at the same time, by the absorption of caloric from the upper part of the plant, chill the roots and more vital parts, to their eminent danger. Besides this, the heat so conveyed through the roots to the stem and branches of the plant, is maintained for a greater length of time, whilst the lowered temperature of the night air is prevented from injuriously affecting plants, the power of the internal warmth obtained from the heated soil acting in opposition to the cooler atmosphere without.

WIND, AIR, ETC.

Wind, it is admitted, has the effect of causing greater dryness of the atmosphere, and hence of adding to the perspiration in vegetables, as well as of increasing the evaporation of the moisture from the soil; and these powers gain strength in a proportion more than adequate to the velocity of its progress: anything, therefore, that checks the rapidity of its progress, has the effect of diminishing its injurious effect, for Professor Daniell has shewn, that " the same surface which, in a calm state of the air, would exhale 100 parts of moisture, would yield 125 in a moderate breeze, and 150 in a high wind."

After this it will be unnecessary to point out the importance of protecting the garden from that quarter whence blow the strongest winds, either by trees, walls, or some description of screen. In this principle too is found a solution of the known utility of a shade to plants, recently placed in the earth, as it not only intercepts the sun's rays, but protects them from those currents of air, that would increase the extent of their perspiration.

It is a mistaken notion to believe that because animals require a constant renewal of air for their support vegetable productions feel a necessity for the same; the former have occasion for this constant supply, because they consume oxygen by respiration, at the same time that they also increase the impurity of the atmosphere by the quantity of carbonic acid gas they give out, whereas the reverse has been shewn to be the case with plants during the day: thus in fact rendering the air in their vicinity more fitted to the support of animal life, only assimilating their demand partially to these last in the night time by the inhaling oxygen at that period. Hence, therefore, ventilation is less required for vegetable than animal life: indeed, it has been found that many plants will grow better in a confined atmosphere, than in that which is frequently changed; ventilation is chiefly requisite for the healthiness of most plants, inasmuch as it dispels dampness, and thus prevents the growth of parasites and fungi, which only flourish in damp air, and at a temperature lower than that found under exposure to the sun's rays.

Another benefit supposed to be derived from ventilation, is but of recent discovery, and that is the motion, communicated to plants by the action of the wind, which has been found to increase the circulation of the sap into healthiness; inducing a ready formation of woody fibre, as well as adding strength to that already formed, and being highly favorable to the development of the secretions that contribute to the formation of flowers and fruit, as well as with production of odor, flavor, &c.

Manures, soils, etc.

The system of apportioning manures is founded upon the study of the component parts of the food of plants in their natural state. These are of various kinds, and to be sought for alike in the animal, the vegetable, and the mineral kingdoms, of which the two former are almost invariably absorbent and retentive of moisture ; and the more the component parts of a soil are intermixed the more each is separated and subdivided into minute portions by culture, the greater thenceforth must be the fertility of the soil. When the soil is well pulverized, it is easier also for the minute fibres, forming the roots of plants, to penetrate, and hence the greater must be the number produced, to the evident benefit of the plant, by the increase of its powers of obtaining nutriment.

FERMENTED MANURE.

When a soil is tenacious, or clayey, it receives heat very slowly, and retains water far too obstinately to be fit, unaided, for vegetable nourishment ; on the other hand, sand is so loose, that, although it soaks up water readily, it soon gets heated, and dried up, thus being unfitted for the support of plants. A mixture, therefore, of loam, sand, and peat, is the best suited to vegetation, the last serving to bind, as well as to afford manure or richness to the other two; whilst the first gives tenacity and retentiveness of moisture, and the second lightness to the mass.

Most kinds of animal and vegetable substances require the process of fermentation to take place before being fitted for manure, thereby forming ammonia, but the best compost is, undoubtdly, that obtained from a fair mixture of animal and vegetable matter, such as is found in an English farm-yard. Hence every garden ought to have a hole, into which should every day be thrown the sweepings of the stable, and especially the urine of horses, itself a most powerful manure by facilitating the formation of humin. It would be well, therefore, to have this hole so placed that all the drainings of the stable, including the water wherewith the horses' feet, &c., have been washed, might be allowed to run into it, adding to the rapidity of the fermenting process, no less than to the richness of the manure. Another hole should be made for the reception of the like gleanings from the cow, or bullock shed, and the sheep pen; cow dung being very good for all kitchen plants, possessing the advantage of requiring no fermentation to fit it for immediate application to the soil. These holes should not be left exposed to the sun, but must be covered to prevent in conjunction with animal manures, unless they be too rich, or it is used merely to prevent noxious effluvia.

CLAY.

This is always a good manure for sandy soils, but if dug from any depth below the surface of the earth, it must be exposed for some time to the action of the air before application to tender plants. In a burnt state it serves to alter the nature of the soil, by rendering it more friable, and is, in England, sometimes used on fallows or turnip land in like manner, and for the same purpose, as the refuse of old buildings, or the dust from brick made roads here.

ALLUVIAL SOILS,

These are the natural deposits of the river under inundation, they form the upper layer also, of the bottoms of some tanks, containing light surface soil, fine sand, and decayed vegetable matter, whence they are good manure for any sandy, clayey, or chalky soil, as well as for the renewal of flower borders.

LIQUID MANURE,

The article so called is called is little known practically in India, but it is often of use for the more delicate plants; it is procured by steeping dung in water, and letting it remain until it has acquired a strong deep color; in which state it is applied to the roots.

1. No soil, however well cultivated, can long nourish the same crops without being exhausted.

2. Every crop impoverishes a soil in proportion as it is more or less restored by the plant cultivated.

3. Perpendicular rooting plants, and such as root horizontally, ought to succeed each other.

4. The same kind of plants should not be repeated too frequently.

5. Two plants favorable to the growth of weeds should not succeed each other.

6. Such plants as are known to exhaust the soil considerably, should only be planted on new land or that which is strong from manuring.

7. Plants that are less exhausting, should succeed those that are more so.

Propagation of Plants.

For the increase of vegetable productions proportionate to the wants of man, means have been provided for the perpetuating and multiplying the species. The most simple and natural of these methods is by the first of these following.

SEED.

The process of maturing which has been already described. When it has reached maturity it detaches itself from the parent plant; and, unless removed by the gardener, drops into the soil, where it germinates and takes root, springing up a new individual to replenish its kind. In a state of nature these seeds are distributed by various means, for this purpose she has provided some seeds even, with down, or wings, to facilitate their transport; such are the thistle, the geranium, the maple, &c. To give growth to this embryo, heat, water, air, and darkness have been shewn to be indispensable: the first gives development to the nourishment contained in the lobes: whence in cold climates, and during the cold season here, seeds remain long in the earth without germinating, and in like manner sprout too quickly in the hot weather; the second, by its moisture, softens these lobes, fitting of loam as to counteract their natural adhesiveness, whilst the loam prevents the moisture passing off too rapidly through the interstices of the sand and peat.

The depth that the seeds are placed, must be regulated by experience; but it will be evident that small seeds must, in proportion to their size, bear but a slight covering of soil, their germs having less strength to force a way through the opposing weight of earth, than those that are larger: very small seeds are often mixed with sand and thus sown, with the two-fold purpose of lightly covering, and of separating them so as not to be choaked; as if too close, they will either destroy each other, or it will be necessary to remove a part to give space and strength to the rest.

Seeds getting weak by long keeping, or from other causes, lose their power of decomposing water, but still preserving their capability of absorption, the water thus taken up produces rot. The best mode of preventing this evil, next to carefulness in only using the freshest seed, is to withhold water until the plants have fully germinated, and even then to give it with moderation, leaving it to depend for nourishment rather on the natural moisture of the earth. When a seed is in a hard shell, the shell may be filed, to permit it to burst the more easily; and when seeds are healthy, but for any reason it be desired to accelerate the extrication of the embryo, soaking them in tepid water, until germination becomes visible, may be resorted to.

Late years have introduced the idea of boiling seeds to make them grow, as was, some time since, brought to the notice of our Horticultural Society by Dr. Wallich. The Gardener's Magazine, of February 1832, contains, what is supposed to be, the first mention of this process, in a letter from Mr. J. Bowie, of the Cape of Good Hope; in which he states, that nearly the whole of the seeds of plants of the order Leguminosæ thrive better by having water heated to 200°, or even to the boiling point of Fahrenheit, poured over them, and allowed to cool for twenty-four hours.

A solution of chlorine has, from its tendency to set oxygen at liberty, and to decompose water, been tried as a germinator of seeds with some success; as has also diluted oxalic; the former of these was used by the author, in 1836, to some seeds of the Brussels sprouts, which had failed in the open ground as well as in a hot bed, but germinated pretty freely after being steeped in the solution for a couple of hours.

It may be useful to observe, that some seeds will continue a long time in the earth without germinating; sometimes even, for two or three years, and then, at last unexpectedly spring up, but there are generally those defended by a hard shell.

knurs or eyes, and it is from this principle of reproduction that many of the existing modes of propagating plants have ben adopted ; the only plants, however, in producing which it has been directly applied are, the vine, the potatoe, and other tubers, including the large family of yams, sweet potatoes, arrow root, &c. The success of this mode of propagation depends on some portion of the tuber, or alburnum of the eye, remaining with it, to give nutriment to the shoot; though if the proportion of this be too great, the plant will be weakened by too free a developement of stems and leaves—and the productiveness thereby lessened.

SLIPS AND CUTTINGS.

On the same principle as in the foregoing, the eye produces roots; a series of leaf-buds on a small twig or branch will form for themselves, at the base of the cutting or slip root fibres, and thus become an independent plant; and as the younger twigs of most plants and shrubs will continue to live, if put into the earth, until the leaf-buds that are below the surface put forth roots; many plants, as the rose, the mulberry, &c. may be thus multiplied as easily as by the sowing of seed, with this additional advantage, that they bear blossoms or fruit much sooner. The success of this process depends on the end of the slip, or cutting, not being too young or soft, otherwise it will become gorged with moisture, and rot, at the same time, that if it be too old and hard, it will not take up sufficient water to keep it alive. It is to be remembered, also, that the root fibres will always spring from the foot of a leaf-bud, and it is therefore desirable to cut the branch selected as a cutting, with a slope on the side opposite to the bud, whereby the formation of the new fibre is much facilitated, especially in such plants as are woody and close grained.

Neither a very dry, nor a very moist soil will answer for this operation, and a considerable mixture of sand is preferable for delicate plants, even to the extent of two-thirds sand to one-third of rotten dung and vegetable mould, in equal proportions, to which must be added frequent gentle waterings; or what is yet better, placing the pot in a saucer kept constantly filled with water, so as not to gorge or rot them. They should not have too much light, and ought to be closely trimmed from leaves, except at the upper end of the cutting, where they may be left to keep up perspiration, and assist in the active preparation of the required food, above all, flower-buds must be removed, as these serve to exhaust, by making so great a demand on the strength of the cuttting as to allow it no time for forming root fibres.

In making cuttings, it is well to observe that

under a leaf-bud or joint, and then the cut part must be fixed, a little under the ground, with a small hooked peg, or by a weight placed on it, and carefully covered over, in such position as will best prevent the return of the main stream of sap from the layer into the principal stem, without entirely stopping the communication; in a few days root fibres will form, and after some time the layer may be separated from the parent plant and removed elsewhere. This is the best mode of propagating carnations and choice pinks, and succeeds with almost every kind of shrub and evergreen.

CHINESE GRAFTING.

What is so called, is performed on the same principle, the branch being prepared in the manner for making a layer, or, what is better, by ringing the bark,—that is to say, removing it to the extent of about a quarter of an inch all round the branch; but instead of placing it in the ground, it is surrounded by a large ball of clay and cow dung, well kneaded together, over which a piece of canvas is carefully, but not too tightly, tied. To keep up a constant but moderate supply of moisture to this ball of earth, a small pan, or *handee* of water is suspended over it, perforated at the bottom, and this, being kept constantly filled, allows the water to drip on the graft; six weeks, or two months being generally sufficient to cause the root fibres to sprout into the ball of earth, when the branch may be separated and planted out.

LEAVES.

Some few plants may be propagated by their leaves, which, if inserted in the earth produce roots, and eventually young shoots: many ferns do this, as will also the water cress, but the most easy of production, in such a manner, are the hoya, the arum, and the air plant, as it is called.

GRAFTING AND BUDDING.

When particular sorts of shrubs, or trees, cannot be procured from seed; when seedlings would be uncertain in their produce, or be a number of years in blossoming and fruiting; cuttings or even buds, termed *scions*, of the sorts required, are taken off and fitted to a slit made in another suitable tree or shrub, called the *stock*, by an operation denominated grafting.

The principle on which the union of the grafts and the

stock takes place is, that the sap that would in the ground serve to form root fibres, descends from the scion to its junction with the stock, where being excluded from air and light, it forms woody fibres instead of roots, while at the same time the sap from the stock rises into the scion, whose leaves return it to the bark, in regular course, as with a distinct and fully formed plant. In budding, a small portion of wood must be left with the bud, to give it support until a complete junction be formed.

Whip grafting is the most usual mode practised; in performing it the stock is headed down, one side of it is pared for about an inch, and cut down obliquely at the upper part towards the pith; the scion must also be pared, so as to correspond as closely as possible with the stock, and a cut should be made near the upper end of the slice, forming a tongue which is forced into the corresponding nick in the stock, taking care to adjust the junction of the bark of the two as accurately as possible, and to tie them firmly together. (Fig. 1.)

Fig. 1

Saddle grafting is when the sides of the scion are pared to the form of a wedge turned on its base, on which the scion is made to sit by means of a slit up the centre, pared down to fit the sides as closely as closely as possible. (Fig. 2.)

Fig. 2

INARCHING.

Is a plan similar to layering, wherein however the branch to be grafted is not separated from its parent stem until the process be completed, this mode is frequently pursued, and is in fact, the usual one resorted to in India.

BUDDING.

Is the introduction in the like manner of the bud, only, with a small portion of bark adhering to it, within the bark of the stock; this is done by making a slit in the bark of the latter, length ways, and crossing it with another cut at the top like a T; the bark is then gently raised and the scion inserted, so that the bud rests on the naked wood, and the upper lips of both stock and scion are brought into close and accurate junction.

All the preceding processes of grafting, &c. are best performed in the spring, when the sap begins to circulate freely from the accession of heat, whereby the operation is greatly facilitated; and in them great care must be taken to cut both the scion, (or graft,) and the stock, (or growing plant,) whereon it is to be placed, very clean and smooth, as well as to unite exactly with the inner bark of the stock, in order not to check the free course of the sap; this being done, it must be carefully and evenly wound round with soft *pat*, or plantain fibres, if small; or coir string, if large, to keep the two firmly together, over which should be placed a ball of well kneaded grafting clay, so as completely to exclude the air, and prevent the access of rain to the wound, as well as to check the sudden drying of the wood. This last is made from stiff yellow or blue clay, to which is added about a fourth part of fresh horse-dung (the French use cowdung)free from litter, and a portion of chopped hay, the whole being well mixed together, with the addition of a little water, and well beaten with a stick upon the floor, adding more water as the mass becomes dry. This process must be repeated several days, until the clay be quite ductile, and yet not so tough as to be apt to crack; it may occupy a week before being fit for use; observing to let it lay for not less than six hours after each beating. Some add ashes, drift sand, or even salt, to prevent cracking; but this is secured by the horse-dung, if properly incorporated. This clay it will be safest to leave on the graft for three months, although frequently the progress of the buds of the graft will show the scion has fully united long before that period; the ligatures should then be gradually removed to allow the parts by degrees, to become innured to the air.

Grafting is occasionally resorted to with herbaceous plants, but in its application to them, great care must be taken not to crush, or injure the scion.

Mechanical Operations.

It appears desirable before entering on the various processes more immediately affecting the culture and maturing of individual plants in the garden, to make a few remarks on the mechanical operations necessary to all vegetable growth: these may be divided into three classes,—Those affecting the soil below the surface;—Those acting merely on the surface;—Those on the plants themselves while growing above the surface. To these may be added such as are resorted to for increasing fruitfulness, as well as for accelerating, or retarding vegetation.

OPERATIONS AFFECTING THE SOIL BELOW THE SURFACE.

These are Ploughing, Digging, Excavating, Leveling, and Ridging.

Ploughing,—is generally resorted to in the first formation of a garden, for the purpose of breaking up the soil, and in some measure preparing it for succeeding operations; but it is not always necessary, and need seldom be repeated after the garden is once formed. A single plough, with a pair of bullocks, should give one good ploughing to a beegah of 14,400 square feet, in the course of a day; or say three ploughs to an acre. The common Bengalee plough is a miserably inefficient

contrivance opposed to every principle of usefulness, or it presents a flat surface to the opposing resistance of the earth, and has the form best suited to facilitate its way through the ground at the back, where such is useless; it can, therefore, only tear its way by main force, when it does at last penetrate, no assistance being given to the operation by the form of its share, if, indeed, the lump of iron attached to it can be so termed. Add to this, the yoke used to attach the bullocks for its draft, is clumsy and galling to the unfortunate animals that are condemned to draw this implement; and, no rule being attended to in fixing the angle of the bar by which the plough is attached to the yoke, the plough is rendered even more inefficient than it naturally is; for this angle is commonly so great, as to bring the part where it is attached to the yoke, considerably above the shoulder of the bullock, and hence, in depressing, to attach it to the yoke, the plough itself is raised on the share, or point, so as to make a mere scratch, that, combining with its primitive form, increases the weight, or labor of draft very considerably, at the same time that it lessens its power of penetration and makes it necessary to repeat the operation some six, nay, even sometimes, twelve or fourteen times before the land is sufficiently broken up to receive seed; any thing like stirring the subsoil, or making a furrow, is out of the question. The plough used in the Upper Provinces is a little more efficient, from its

wedge-like shape, but still very unequal to the task assigned to it.

These evident deficiencies led the attention of the brother of the author, and himself to endeavor at constructing some instrument that should obviate these evils, and at the same time be less ponderous than the English plough, which, they were convinced, was far too heavy for the cattle of the country in their present condition. In their efforts at this so essential a reform, they received no small encouragement from a recollection that in Anglo-Saxon times, their own country possessed no better instrument than the Bengalee plough, and they were thence, not less than from experience, persuaded that improvement was more likely to be successful by keeping as nearly as possible to the instrument already in use, and thus with progressive steps, leading the native to a new implement: with these objects in view, they adapted a light ploughshare to the same block of hard wood that forms the basis of the Indian *Nangul*, fashioning it however, to a form somewhat like that of the English plough in miniature; the left side being at a right angle with the base, and constructing the right side in an acute angle from the point, where the share was fitted until it attained the full breadth permitted by the size of the wood at the back. Its success equalled the best wishes that could be formed,—it was found to do as much, or rather more work in one ploughing as

was formerly effected by several repetitions, throwing in its progress a goodly furrow, that, in comparison with the result produced by the native instrument, would have delighted the European agriculturist: the additional cost of its construction being but a few annas, and the only objection yet made by natives, having been, that, "should the cattle become unmanageable, and break from the ploughman, the new plough might, in consequence of the greater sharpness of the share, cut their heels:" and a native, ever ready to find fault with what is new, must be hard driven indeed for an objection, when such is the utmost he can find, or imagine.

DIGGING.

Is performed in this country with the digging hoe, or *khodal*, which is a thin wedge of iron, having a lever or handle of wood attached to it at an angle, the end where the two parts join forming the fulcrum; of these the most remarkable forms are annexed (figures 3, 4, 5 and 6,) two of which belong to lower

Bengal, and the other two are found, more generally, towards the westward. In figure 3, it is clear that much power is lost by the fulcrum being in the centre, between the hand, or power, and the resistance, or earth to be dug; whilst in figure 4, from the angle of union being so acute, this evil is increased, the blade being brought so close to the hand as to obstruct the operations of the digger, and preclude the possibility of penetrating to any depth; to obviate which, as much as the instrument will allow, the hoe is not unfrequently delivered altogether from the hand, this must of course occasion great delay, and but slow progress can be expected from it; it may, however, be useful in shaping and cleaning the almost perpendicular banks of tanks, *pagars*, or mounds. The next instrument, figure 5, is in use in the province of Behar, and is, as may be observed, a far more powerful hoe, the length of the handle allowing of more force being given to the blow, by the increased impetus created by passing through a larger space, while the fulcrum, being nearer to the resistance, adds strength to the power used; its defect is, however, to be found in the great breadth of the blade, affording a wider field of direct resistance; this is improved upon, however, in the hoe, fig. 6, the blade of which inserts itself more gradually into the earth from its tapering wedge-like form, whilst additional power is also gained by a yet greater length of handle; this kind of hoe is

originally found in Ghazeepore, and the districts above. The handles of all these should be smooth, that the hand may readily slide along them, in raising them from the ground, and the blade should be strengthened by a greater thickness or ridge in the centre.

The *mattock*, fig. 7, called also the hoe-axe, and the grubbing axe, is an useful implement in loosening hard surfaces, and for grubbing up the roots of small trees or bushes. Another form of the hoe, having two prongs, fig. 8, known as the *hoe fork*, may be used in loosening the soil below the surface, digging up potatoes, or other roots, &c.

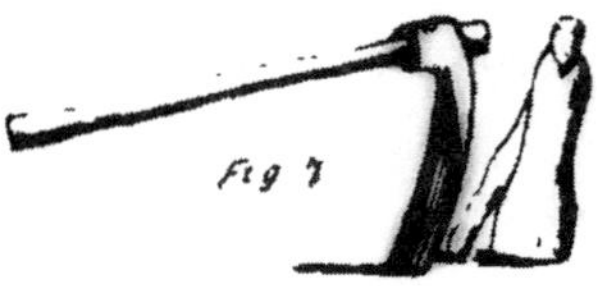

In digging a piece of ground, the separation between the dug and the undug portion, forms a trench or furrow, and in beginning, a furrow should first be opened at the end where the work is to commence, the earth taken out being carried to the part where it is to terminate, that it may serve to close the last furrow. Care must be taken to maintain an uniform depth throughout, reversing each spitful, or portion taken up at one cut with the hoe, so that what was on the surface may be buried; each spit should also be well pulverized, for on this depends much of the

fertilizing power of the soil, and where the object is to add manures, they should be spread uniformly on the surface, and then turned in regularly through all parts; weeds ought to be buried, whilst the roots of strong grasses, bricks, and other extraneous matter, should be carefully removed; the depth of pulverisation of the soil, in this operation, should never fall short of 9 inches, and the best weather for undertaking the work is after one of the showers, usually falling in February or March, or at the close of the annual rains in September or October, when the soil is sufficiently moist to admit the hoe with ease; the ground being at other periods, (except indeed in the rains, when it is over saturated,) generally too hard to admit of being broken up, save at the expense of great labor, and with the mattock, or the pickaxe, which instruments, strongly as they are generally made, are often broken by the flinty hardness of an Indian soil.

For the operation of digging, from ten to fifteen men will be requisite to the beegah, costing, at the usual rates in lower Bengal, from one rupee six annas to two rupees, and in the Upper Provinces from eight to twelve men at a cost of one rupee to one rupee eight annas; but if the soil be hard, as it usually is from the end of November to the end of February, this will be increased to as much as three to five rupees.

EXCAVATING.

Is the operation requisite for formation of ditches for draining land, or for surrounding particular spots with mounds or embankments, as a defence from trespass; or called for in the construction of tanks, to secure a supply of water, as well as frequently to afford the means of raising ground otherwise too low to be suitable for a garden. The cost of this depends in a great measure, on the distance that it is required to carry the earth dug out, and will vary, accordingly, from four hundred, to as high as a thousand cubic, or solid feet for the rupee; this last being the rate allowed in the construction of public embankments, where the earth is taken from close to the site of their formation.

TRENCHING.

Is a mode of pulverizing and mixing the soil to a considerable depth, and should always be the first operation in making a garden; it is true that the labor and expense of so doing is considerable, but it amply repays the undertaker, both by the stimulus it gives to the soil, and the lightness imparted to the earth for a depth sufficient to suit the deepest penetrating roots, all descriptions of which are aided by having the

means afforded them of extending their fibres in all directions, in search of the nourishment they require. According to the ordinary mode of trenching the surface soil would be turned to the bottom of the trench, and the subsoil brought to the top; but this, in many soils, would be to exchange a good turfy loam, or alluvion, for clay or sand, and, even in the best ground, would bring up earth that had not, perhaps for years, been exposed to the action of the air or sun, hence deficient in many of the properties necessary to fertilization, which it would require a long period of exposure to obtain; care must be taken, therefore, to keep the top soil to the top. The directions for doing this, as laid down by Cobbett, are the plainest and most clear that can be given, and have besides, been long successfully, pursued in this country: they are as follow—The "piece of ground ought to be marked into *strips* or *lifts*, each a rod wide, in the manner following.

Fig. 9.

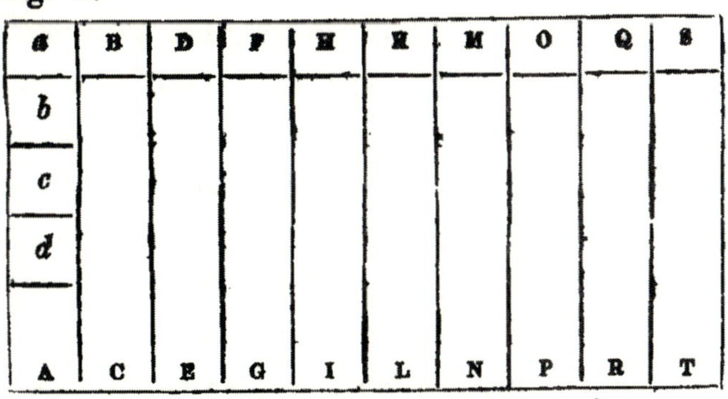

"This division into narrow strips takes place because

a and *b*, an empty trench at the end, and the trench next to it with the top earth taken off. You then proceed with the rest of this strip as you did with that of the other, until you come to B, when you turn in at D, and do just the same as you did at C. You then go on to E; when you get there, you turn in again at G, and thus you proceed till you come to S, when you will find yourself with the last trench completely empty, and with the next to the last wanting the top earth. These are both ready for you. You take the heap of bottom earth, which came out of *a* and put it into your empty trench; then you take the heap of top earth which was wheeled from *a* and *b*, and lay it on upon the two last trenches; and thus all the ground will have been completely moved to three feet nine inches deep; every part of it will have changed its place, and you will find it to stand a foot, or fifteen inches higher than the ground in the neighbourhood of it." The expense of this process will be about double that of ordinary digging, and it requires personal supervision or the native laborer will not execute it.

In India it will be well to leave a space of about a foot between each of these strips, for the purpose of drainage during the period of the heavy rains, from June to September, when it is desirable to keep the beds of the garden as dry as possible; these spaces also, afford facility of access to the plants on the beds, whether for weeding, gathering, or other purposes.

LEVELLING.

Fig 10

In gardening, this process, consists in so spreading abroad the soil as that it may be nearly level, which may be ascertained by the *Triangular level,* (fig. 10,) or at least form an even surface. In India, however, it is better to construct your beds, when these are necessary, so that the middle may be a little more elevated than the sides, forming a slight curve or slope, which may be made by the *Regulating level,* (fig. 11) which will enable the horticulturist to

Fig 11.

fix the the exact ratio of rise desired for each foot of breadth.

RIDGING.

Is required for some plants, and consists of forming the surface of the ground into a series of triangles, or close ranges of parallel elevations, (fig. 12).

Fig 12.

The best instrument for performing his operation is the

Spade (fig. 13), commonly used for digging in England, and too well known therefore to those of that country, to require description ; it makes a smoother cut into the earth, and offers means of flattening down, not to be found in the hoe, or *khódal.* Where potatoes are extensively cultivated, they are usually sown in drills, and as the plants spring up and advance in growth, the earth should be drawn up on each side of them so as to form a high ridge along what was originally the seed drill. Many other plants are benefited also by ridging in like manner.

OPERATIONS AFFECTING THE SURFACE OF THE SOIL.

These are surface Hoeing, Pulverising, Sifting, Raking, Scraping, Weeding, Sweeping, Rolling, Beating, and Wheeling.

Hoeing is best effected by the *American hoe*, fig. 14, the *Dutch hoe*, fig. 15, and the *Pronged hoe*, fig. 16.

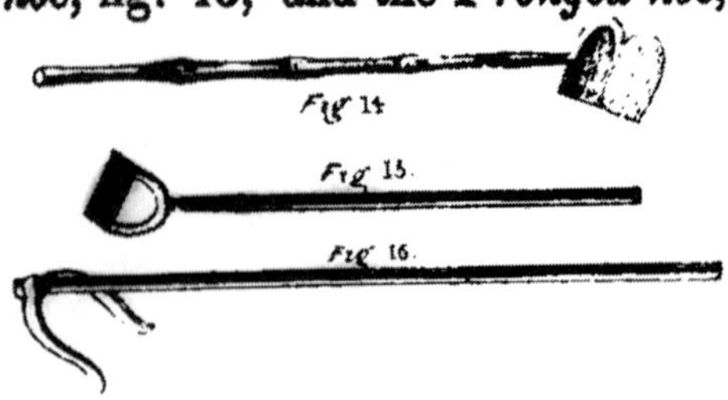

It is performed by dragging or thrusting the hoe along the soil, so as to cut the weeds at, or under the surface, and slightly to pulverise the soil. This is done for four purposes—1st. to loosen weeds so that they may die for want of nourishment, be raked off, and thrown into the hole for forming vegetable mould; which will be most efficiently done with the Dutch hoe an *useful* implement; it is extraordinary has not obtained more extensive adoption in India, since it is so very manageable, that wherever it has been used, it is rather liked by natives than otherwise; 2nd. to stir the soil, for which the long handled pronged hoe would be most useful, though hitherto hardly known as a garden implement in India; 3rd. to draw up the soil about the stems of plants; and, 4th. to form a sort of drill or gutter in which to sow seeds,—these two last requiring the American hoe. All of these operations will be best performed in dry weather.

Pulverising is requisite in this country, from the hardness of the soil, which forms itself into clods, requiring to be separately broken. The natives employ for this purpose a *Beater* or *mallet* of wood, or the root of bamboo, and it has been found a sufficiently effective instrument.

Sifting, and Screening are to separate the coarser from the finer particles of earth, &c. The materials require to be dry and well broken, and then to be thrown on the screen, or *ch'hutna* made of thinly split bamboo, in a square frame, about five feet by three, if required in large quantities, as for ground intended for bulbous, or other tender and succulent rooted plants; or of circular form, known as a sieve or *chulnee* having a rim about three inches in depth, the interstices between the split bamboo not exceeding a fourth of an inch; this is used where a fine mould is required for pots, or to sift lightly over small seeds.

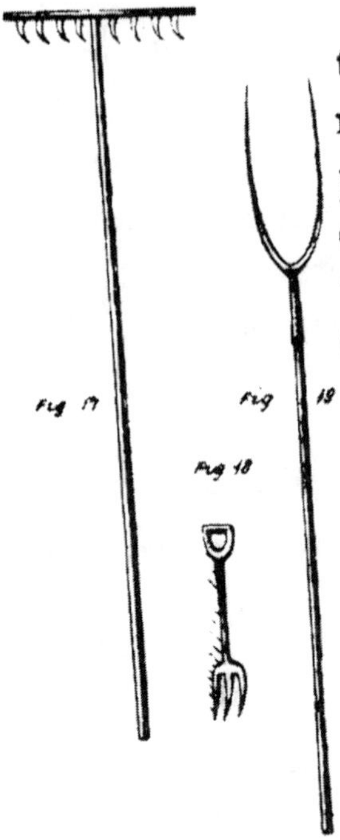

Raking, is performed by drawing through the surface soil the instrument called Rake, fig. 17, either to pulverise the soil, or to collect weeds, or such other extraneous matter as will not pass through the teeth of the instrument; this last may, however, be done in larger quantities by the Potato fork, fig. 18, or the Pitch fork, fig. 19. The teeth of the rake being nearly at right angles with the handle the lower the handle is held in performing the operation, the deeper will be the pulverisation; but the angle at which the handle of the rake is held depends on the object intended; if only to remove small weeds, it should be held higher, but the medium is forty-five degrees. All raking should be done in dry weather, and it will be found often necessary a day or two after sowing seeds, as the soil is apt to harden on the surface, or become what is called *chuppuree*, or caked, after watering, and too hard for the young seed to penetrate; the best time for this last operation, being whilst the soil is somewhat moist, but by no means wet.

Scraping is drawing a broad blunt hoe, or a *scraper* formed of a flat piece of wood, or iron, placed at right angles across a long handle, on hard surfaces, as grass plots, or the walks made of broken brick, or *khoa*, to remove the subsoil thrown up by worms, &c.

Weeding is best, and most expeditiously performed with the hoe, especially for the longer weeds, as thistles, &c. when the Dutch hoe is a most useful instrument: for the deep rooted short grass, however, the native weeder, either the *Neeranee*, (fig. 20,) or the *Khurpee*, (fig. 21,) are tolerable instruments, slow in operation, but suited to the habit natives have of squatting down to every employment.

Fig 20

Fig 21.

Sweeping is resorted to for collecting grass that has been cut, or leaves; for both which purposes the dewy mornings are best fitted, as the leaves or grass then adhere together; a good broom for this purpose may be made with the side branches lopped from bamboos.

Rolling—is little resorted to in India; such a thing

as a roller (fig. 22), being seldom found in a garden, although in England it would be difficult to meet with one of any extent, wanting this useful implement. It is difficult to keep walks or roads in order without it, whence it is not to be wondered at, that smooth and level paths are seldom to be found in our Indian gardens. It should be drawn over the surface of all walks at least once a week, and produces the best effect when the ground is dry on the surface, but well saturated with moisture below.

Fig 22

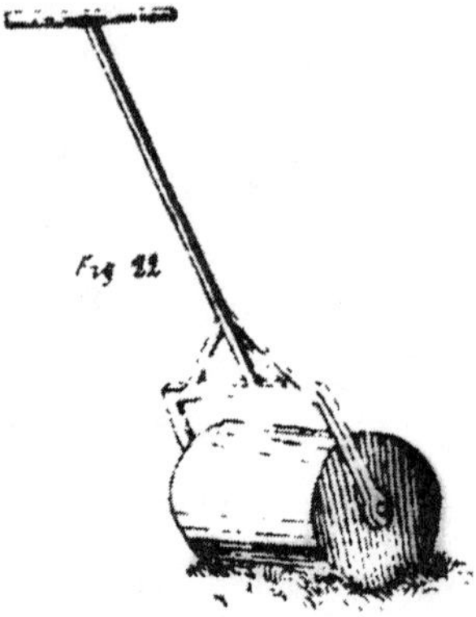

Beating—this is made, in this country, to supersede the last mentioned operation. It is performed sometimes, with a small block of wood used by the hand, but more effectually by a beetle or *Durmus*, (fig. 23); being a block of wood, of some weight, into the centre of which a bamboo handle is inserted. A rammer, however, formed like one of the moogdars natives of the Upper Provinces use as an article for exercise, but on a larger scale, has lately been employed in repairing roads, and is a far more useful instrument, of easier management, and, from being

Fig 23

in one piece, less liable to derangement by work; the handle of the durmus being, however, taken out quite as frequently by the labourer as an excuse for sitting down idle, when the master's eye is off, as by accident.

Beating is useful for turf, or brick walks, as also to make the soil under fruit, or around rose trees, compact and hard, so as to keep in the moisture, and check the growth of weeds in such situations; likewise in claying the bottoms and sides of tanks, to give them solidity, and prevent the escape of water.

Wheeling—for the carrying materials from one place to another, is little resorted to in this part of the world, where labor is so cheap that few entertain the idea of making a saving in that branch of expenditure: the vehicle most used for removal of weeds, conveyance of manure, &c. is a small basket carried on the head; it is, however, a recorded fact, that two men with a wheelbarrow (fig. 24,) will get through more work in a day, than three with baskets; in removing large quantities of earth, or manure, a

Fig 24

small Truck, on two wheels, has been found of great service; it may be made with a moveable back, so that the contents may be easily shot out where required.

OPERATIONS OF PLANTS WHEN ABOVE THE SURFACE OF THE EARTH.

These comprise the items of Thinning, Planting, Transplanting, Watering, Draining, Pruning, Clipping, Training, Blanching, Potting, and Shifting.

Thinning. This is necessary with all plants sown broad cast, where they are intended to remain, but especially with carrots, beet, &c. that form long tap roots; in doing it, care should be taken to pick out the smaller, or less healthy plants; and in no place to leave any so near as to incommode, or draw from each other's strength; it is a part of gardening generally neglected, and in which all native gardeners require instruction.

Planting, is of two description; first—as applied to seeds, or seed-like roots, such as potatoes, bulbs, &c.; it is most frequently done in drills, or separate holes made with the *Dibber*, (fig. 25,) into which the seed or bulb is dropped, and then trodden, or pressed down, so that every part shall be brought in close contact with the soil, and no interstices allowed for the accumulation of moisture, which is sure to occasion rot; this subject deserves the strictest attention, for to its neglect is attributable the great proportion of failures of seed, &c. that is found, when native gardeners alone have the management of a garden.

Fig 25.

The second kind of planting applies to plants already

originated, and consists in inserting them in the earth to the same depth, and in the same position as they previously occupied; care being taken to preserve the fibrous roots as much as possible from abrasion, distributing them evenly around the stem in contact with fine mould, and keeping the plant upright, or, if injured cutting them off altogether; as well as that the plant be not placed deeper in the soil than it was before removal; without this precaution—it will be apt to rot at the part where the soil formerly surrounded the stem, as has been explained, in a former part of this work when treating of the organic construction of plants. The soil that is to be placed in immediate contact with the root fibres should be well pulverized, and made completely to fill the interstices between each; shallow planting is also recommended, as it tends to drive the fibres downwards in their search for food; but care must be taken, by shading, that the sun does not dry the upper soil near the plants, as that would injure the roots, and destroy their powers of absorption. Abundant watering is generally desirable in planting, to meet the extra demand made by the mouths of the root fibres, as before desscribed: and the best time for the operation is either during, or immediately after, the rainy season, on account of the greater degree of moisture in the ground.

Transplanting; about the most important branch of horticulture, is the operation of removing plants from one situation to another; this is often done, with woody plants, to add to the number of fibrous roots, and thus to accommodate young subjects the better to a removal from the places where they have been propagated, to those they are destined permanently to fill; but, with vegetables, it is resorted to for the purpose of increasing the fibrous roots in relation to the larger and more woody ones, so as to add to the size and succulency of the leaves, fruit, or flowers. There are, in this operation, three things necessary to be attended to—1st. the preparation of the soil to which the plant is to be removed;—2nd. the removal of the plant;—and, 3rd. its insertion in the prepared soil.

1st. The preparation of the soil comprises the stirring, loosening, and mixing of the earth with such compost, or manure, as may be required, according to the character of the plant, and the nature of the soil to which it is to be removed.

2nd. The removal of the plant is to be effected by digging the earth around it, either with the digging hoe or garden trowel, (fig. 26,) or, if the soil be very hard, with a spud, (fig. 27,) and then drawing it out of the soil by hand, taking as much care as possible not to tear or severely injure the root fibres; the consequence of such injury to these is, that for a time they are rendered less able to support the stem then before; this evil, however, decreases in proportion to the season,

Fig 26

Fig 27

being far less important in cold weather, when the plant is in a torpid state, than at any other period: and during the rains the excessive moisture in the soil partially obviates this evil, by the profuse supply of nutriment it affords to keep up the perspiration of the leaves. Under the most careful removal of a plant however, some portion of the root will receive injury, and, when this occurs, all the larger wounds should be pruned by a clean smooth cut, for these, if left in a bruised, state, would lose their vitality, and decaying, become the seat of disease, eventually affecting the whole plant. But whilst care is directed to the roots, it is to be borne in mind that a consideration to the future welfare of the plant may require the abstraction, of large portions of the stronger branches, to compel the root to throw out, in the place of these old and inactive members, a series of young and active fibres; this process is not confined to the period of transplanting, but may be performed with advantage to many trees when the roots are laid open after the rains; an increase of spongelets occuring from the principle, before laid down of the elaboration of root fibres by the downward descent of organisable matter, the strength of which would have otherwise been exhausted in increasing the size of the old branch, the amputation of which directs its whole force to effect the granulatory process necessary to heal the wounds, and, immediately after that is completed, to the production of new spongelets—each eventually forming itself into fibres, and seeking food for the nutriment of its parent, which thus exchanges many mouths for the one taken away; in some cases the plant may be lifted with a ball of earth, containing all its roots, by means of the trowel, or of a transplanter (fig. 28,) formed of two semicircular pieces of iron, or more simply of a couple of tiles, or *kupruls*, thrust into the ground on each side of the root, and drawn up with it, so as to preserve the earth unbroken, around the root, until well fixed in the place to which the plant is removed. For some large plants or trees it may, sometimes, be necessary to cut the roots at a certain distance from the plant some time before its removal.

Fig 28.

Many writers have urged the top pruning of all plants when removed, but if we consider the laws which regulate the organization of plants in general, it will be self-evident that this practice is likely to be far more generally the source of injury than of benefit, for the renovatoin of the roots, depending so much on the healty action of the leaves and buds, the amputation of the branches, by checking this process, must seriously affect the tree. The chief thing to be guarded against, is exhaustion by too great perspiration, and this seldom occurs with careful planting.

3rd. Insertion of the plant in the place prepared for it, is performed by making an excavation, the size of the root, either with the dibber, trowel, or digging hoe, placing the plant in the hole to the same depth as it was previously to its removal, and then covering its roots with fine earth firmly pressed to it; the interstices being carefully filled by pressing the fingers well between the fibres, so as to leave no room for lodgments of water, or to give access to insects; if small plants be put in with the dibber, this may be done by inserting the instrument, at a couple of inches distant, in a slanting position, so as to pass partially under the roots, and pressing it by an upward movement of the hand towards the plant:—lastly a moderate supply of water should be added.

By many able gardeners the process of puddling, as it is termed, or deluging the roots with water so as to reduce the soil about them to the state of liquid mud, is advocated as the treatment to be adopted towards all plants: it may certainly be useful in securing a plentiful supply of moisture immediately to the roots of large plants, as well as in causing the earth to settle closely round their fibres; but with small plants, and with such as are not evergreens, it is never required, and may do injury, especially if they be sickly or have been kept for some time previously rather dry; as the weakened powers of the plant are not then able to dispose of the excess of moisture that puddling would introduce through the wounds, which must, even with the greatest care, have been made in the roots. Mr. Knight, in such cases, has had recourse to moistening the bark, whereby water is taken up by the cortical integument, and conveyed through the liber into the circulatory system, where it accompanies, and adds bulk to the sap in its usual progress, and thus gives vigor to the plant.

If the root be removed in a ball, it is well gently to break away the old earth on inserting it into the hole, so as not to leave it caked about the root, and this is the more necessary in diseased plants, especially if the disease appear to be in the root, in which case it would be safer not to leave a particle of the old earth about it. After filling in the hole, and smoothing the surface, a space of the full extent occupied by the roots should be covered with dung or litter, or as it called mulched, to prevent evaporation, and preserve the moisture around the roots.

Pricking out—is the transplanting seedlings at a short distance from each other, for the purpose of strengthening the young plants, and increasing the root fibres: and it is with vegetables, especially of the cabbage kind, a preliminary operation to transplanting.

Watering—is requisite in all stages of vegetation, alike for the purposes of furnishing nutriment, of keeping down insects, and of cleansing the leaves; care must be taken, however, not to wet these during the sunshine, whence the evening is best suited to this operation, whenever requisite, and every precaution is necessary, in this country, to prevent the lodgment of any water in the axils or joints of the leaves, or branches, or even on the leaves themselves with the more delicate plants; it may, indeed, be found best to order your native gardeners, as a general rule, not to wet the leaves at all, as you are sure not to be obeyed to the letter, and you would thus secure some degree of carefulness regarding it.

This operation is chiefly required in the dry and hot weather; but in the latter its effect must be very limited, and it must not be expected to be, by any means, so beneficial as the irrigation nature supplies, for the moisture forming in the atmosphere, by this last, reduces the temperature, whence also, by lessening the perspiration of the plants, it prepares them for benefiting, to the greatest extent, by the supply of moisture which is consequently, gradually absorbed into the system: whilst, on the other hand, artificial watering, having no such atmospheric influence, the air seizes the opportunity to snatch from the leaves, by perspiration, the supply afforded them so long as any lasts, by which means the roots are for a time over excited, until, by absorption, evaporation, filtration through the earth, &c. the water given is exhausted, and a re-action occurs that is very likely to prove injurious. This is another reason for preferring evening watering in the hot weather, as the absence of light and heat, during the ensuing night, enables the roots to absorb the moisture given gradually, and to better advantage. During weather that is dry but cold, a watering in the morning, or before noon, may be preferred, as the temperature is often less than is wholesome for the plant, under the natural cold of the night, especially when accompanied by heavy dews, as is commonly the case. The fittest time, therefore, at that period for the administering water to plants, will be the morning, because it affords a good supply of moisture to meet the increased demand made by the day's heat, as the influence of the sun, at that time of year, is proportionally greater than at any other: the variation of temperature being often above 30°, whilst at other periods it will scarcely exceed 7° or 8°. Watering the roots, although the preferable time is undoubtedly the evening, may be done at all hours; for this —a flat fanshaped spout is, good (fig. 29), if the plants be in rows, as it can be carried below the leaves to convey the water to the root only; a fine rose (*b*) may be used in watering seed beds, or the larger one (*c*)

Fig. 29.

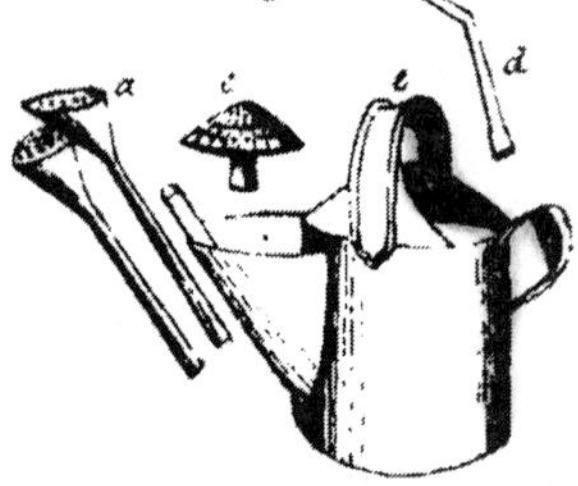

for the leaves of pineapples, trees, &c. and the spout (*d*) alone of the watering pot for giving water to the roots of trees, cauliflowers, &c.

For extensive irrigation, always to be preferred, so as to flood the large beds of cabbages, turnips, &c. the most effectual method is to have the garden divided into compartments, and intersected by drains diverging from one common centre (either a well, or a reservoir near the tank), to which water may be raised in a very simple manner, customary in Behar, and the Upper Provinces, as shewn in (fig. 30); *aa* being two

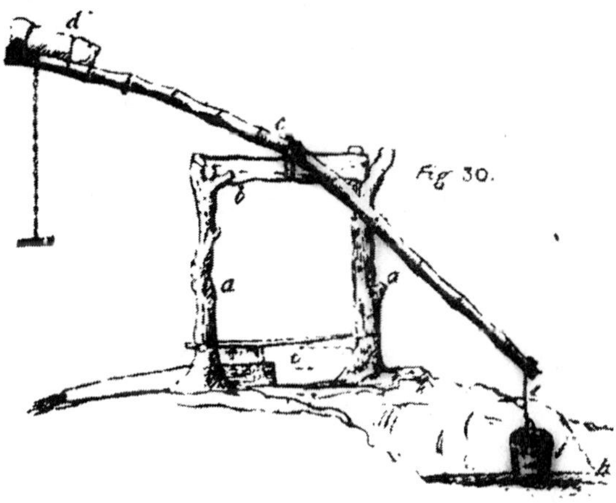

Fig 30.

posts, or supports affixed in the earth, on which rests a cross bar *b*, to this is fixed a bamboo, *c*, having a weight, *d*, at one end, and the cord, *e*, for support of the bucket, *f*, at the other extremity; with a rope under the weight that the laborer, at *g*, pulls down until the bucket is plunged into the water in the well, tank, or river, *h*, more frequently, however, the only rope is the one suspending the bucket itself, and the koolees pull this down, and allow the weight, which is made heavier for that purpose, on slackening their hold, to draw up the bucket by itself at *d*, the water being emptied into the reservoir, *i*, whence it is distributed, by drains, through the garden. Where the ground is extensive, a row of three or more of these machines may be employed to raise a proportionate supply of water.

Another method of extensive irrigation, resorted to chiefly in Bengal on the banks of rivers or streams, sometimes also to raise water from tanks is the *seoonee*, a basket tied together into a triangular form and supported at each corner with cords, which are hold by two men, and dipped into the water, being raised and emptied into a wooden drain or reservoir by a kind of jerk, (fig. 31,) *a* being the mat basket, and *b* the cords.

Fig 31.

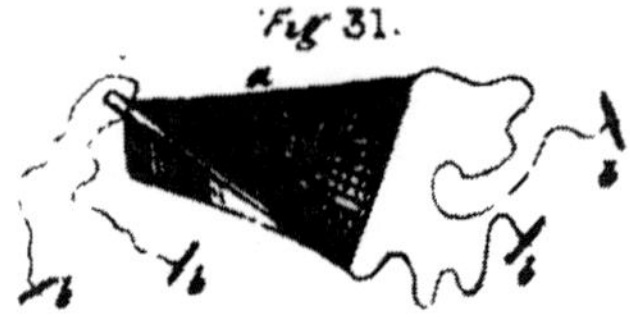

There is a method, somewhat similar in principle, however, to (fig. 30,) resorted to where cocoanut timber is plentiful, and the dip of water not very great as in (fig. 32,) wherein *a*, *a* are the posts supporting a moveable cross piece of bamboo, *b*, on which another rests cross ways *c*, having a weight *d*, at one end and a rope *e*, supporting the broad end of a hollowed cocoanut tree on which the koolee stands until it is filled with water, and then relieving it of his burden, the weight at the end draws it up and empties the water into the trough or drain at *g*.

The great benefit derivable from such extensive watering is indisputable, and is thus adverted to, by Mr. T. A. Knight, in a paper published in the transactions of the Horticultural Society of London (vol. i. of the second series)—"The quantity of water which may be given with advantage to plants of almost every kind, during warm and bright weather, is, I believe, very much greater, than any gardener, who has not seen the result, will be inclined to suppose possible; and it is greater than I myself could have believed, upon any other evidence than that of experience." He further explains that water, distributed by the watering pot, only wets the surface, and that, although, by so doing, it may afford a temporary relief; it ultimately, in most instances, does injury, since the roots are induced to throw out fibres, near the surface, in search of this transient food, and thus place themselves in a situation that exposes them to danger; whereas copious irrigation, sinking into the subsoil, leads the roots downwards to seek nourishment. The same method recommended by Mr. Knight in transplanting weakly trees (vide p. 97), may be resorted to as a means of giving water to such as are in a sickly state, and may frequently recover them when all other methods have failed of success.

Tilley's metallic garden engine is an useful implement, where the expense of obtaining it from England is not an object.* Some of its forms are ornamental, and may be used, even by a lady, for syringing the plants in a verandah, or in plant sheds.

Draining—is a not less necessary operation of gardening than watering, and demands at least equal attention, on account of the great danger that follows the allowing too great a quantity of water to collect about the roots of plants, in the subsoil. This operation is most called for in situations that are low, or where the soil is of a very tenacious nature: for by a due

* Vide "Mechanics' Magazine," vol. 27, p. 225.

attention to its usefulness, borders and orchards, that have been long unproductive and useless, may be rendered fruitful, and valuable. The garden, therefore, should always have a sufficiency of small drains, communicating with main drains leading into the tank, to secure the soil from a lodgment of water in any parts; thus rendering the operation for benefiting the garden in this respect, subservient also to the securing a good supply of water for irrigation, at the seasons when it is required. For any part of a garden or orchard that is very much lower than the rest, the only permanent remedy is to raise it by additional earth; this may be obtained by the excavation of tanks, and it will be found cheaper in the end to adopt this method at first than to waste time, patience, and money upon any speculative plans for draining land so situated.

Pruning, is the cutting off parts of a plant to benefit the remainder, either by promoting growth and bulk; by lessening bulk; by modifying forms; by promoting the formation of blossom buds; by enlarging the fruit; by adjusting the stem or branches; by the renewal of decayed portions of plants or trees; or by the removal of diseases. The instruments requisite are a sharp knife, (fig. 33,) a bill (fig. 34,)

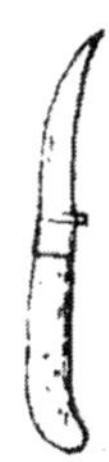

Fig 33

Fig 34

for lopping hard trees, a saw for the larger branches of fruit trees, and a sickle, or *Husseea* (fig. 35,) for the lesser ones.

Fig 35

The principle that should guide the pruner in this operations on a healthy plant, is, that the sap which would have been expended in support of the part removed, will be diverted into the parts remaining; and hence, if the leading bud of a branch be removed, the side ones, that would be otherwise dormant, are made to shoot out with more vigour; and if a growing branch be shortened, the lower buds, seldom otherwise productive, will push forth vigorous shoots; a branch, therefore, that crowds the tree must be cut off very close, for if any part, having a bud, or a knur, remain, it will only serve to produce many shoots in place of the one removed. If also, there be two unequally growing branches from the same stem, the stronger being shortened to check its growth, the other will gain an accession of strength. Bleeding, as it is called, is a flow of sap from a wound made in pruning; it is very injurious to trees, and can only be prevented by carefully avoiding to prune whilst the sap is flowing with vigor, reserving the operation for the cold season, when the tree is in a dormant state.

1*st.* Pruning, *to promote growth and bulk,* is seldom requisite in this country, where the rapidity of vegetation is already rendered too great by the heat: it can only be called for to infuse strength into the stronger branches by removal of the weaker side shoots. In pruning to increase growth, besides cutting off the weak shoots, the strong ones should be shortened, in order to produce three or four, instead of one; and, in general, bulk being the object, upright shoots are encouraged rather than lateral ones, except in trees that are trained, where shoots should be encouraged at various angles as required. In old trees, this object is promoted by the removal of the dead, or already scaling off, outer bark.

2d. PRUNING, *merely to lessen bulk, or create dwarfs*, is an unnatural process, which, if persisted in, renders a tree knotty and unsightly, and in stone fruit trees is apt to produce canker and gum; it is only necessary where trees are crooked, or too close to the walks, and then even the better plan is to remove them.

3rd. PRUNING *to modify the form of a tree.*—Where trees are planted for shade or shelter, as also in avenues, and sometimes in hedge rows, it is desirable that the lowest branches should be at some distance from the ground; in the first instance that room may be given to pass under them, and in the last that they may not harbour snakes, or other vermin. The shoots are to be cut off cleanly, near a bud, if it be intended only to shorten them; but if to be altogether removed, this should be done as near to the stem as possible, to assist the healing, and growing of the bark over the wound. In purning fruit trees, the chief object must also be to assist, or increase their bearing; where this is done on standards, or on such as are allowed to assume a natural form in an open space, no shoot of the young plant should be permitted to take the lead, but a number must be encouraged to radiate upwards from the graft, at as regular distances as possible; but, at the same time, scope should be given to the natural form of the tree, which has generally a tendency to a cone; the operations of the pruner being chiefly directed to thinning out the weak and crowded shoots, and preserving the balance of the tree, by taking care that an equal portion of branches be allowed on every side, and, while allowing the light to penetrate into the tree carefully preventing any interstices through it.

4th. PRUNING, *to promote the formation of blossom buds*, depends, in a great measure, on the description of the tree to be operated upon. The mango and the leechee, for instance, produce their blossoms from the extremities of the last year's shoots, and hence a sufficient proportion of these should be preserved when these trees are submitted to the pruning knife; whilst the peach requires a regular distribution of young sprays to be preserved, as it produces its fruit on the preceding year's wood; in the plum, the blossoms proceed from short leafy protuberances called spurs;

whence, in these last, the production of blossom buds is promoted by cutting out weak wood to strengthen what is left. The rose, and many other shrubs, have their blossoms on the wood of the current year, and pruning should, therefore, remove both new and old wood, if it have once yielded flowers.

5*th*. PRUNING *the blossoms, to enlarge the fruit*, is performed by diminishing or shortening the blossom, bearing branches, so as to add to their strength. And if all the blossoms be removed before full formation of fruits in any one year, the produce of the next will be both finer, and more abundant.

6*th*. PRUNING *for adjustment of the stem or branches*, is analogous to that intended to modify its form, applying chiefly to trees just transplanted, or to those that are very young; and in the former it may be properly done in the process of removal, whilst the plant is yet out of the earth.

7*th*. PRUNING, *to renew parts of old or decayed trees*, is chiefly of use when it is desired to preserve a fruit of superior flavor, the tree bearing which has become exhausted by age; and this is done by cutting down the stem to within a foot or two of the surface of the ground, or sometimes only to the summit of the stem.

8*th*. PRUNING, *for removal of disease*, may be done by cutting off whole branches, the entire head, single shoots, or merely the diseased portion of the wood or bark; but in doing this, care must be taken to cut away the whole of the part affected, and even a portion of the surrounding wood or bark that is sound, so as to be certain that all contamination is effectually taken away.

The best time for all pruning operations is the commencement of the cold weather, when the circulation of the sap is less rapid, and the leaves have began to fall off. Attention should be paid in all such operations, whether with the saw or bill hook, as required to remove large branches, or with the knife for smaller ones, that the instrument be sharp, so as to produce a clean, smooth section, and to leave the bark uninjured; and also that the section of the living plant should be so inclined as not to afford lodgment for water or overflowing sap, as well as so far turned downwards, or to the north, as to be inaccessible to the direct rays of the sun.

Clipping.—In connection with this subject is clipping, used for the excision of the small shoots, and for preserving the form of hedges, as also for pruning turf, border edgings, &c.; this is best done with Hedgeshears (fig. 36), in using which lines ought always to be fixed, to guide the course of the native gardener, as this is a new instrument, and he is generally little acquainted with its use.

Fig. 36.

Training—is conducting the shoots of trees or plants

over walls, espalier rails, trellises (or *meropes* as they are here called), &c. its objects are to mature and improve the quality of fruits, to afford facility to their growth, and maturity, to increase the quantity or size of the fruit, or to render them more ornamental and productive of flower buds. Their increased productiveness is also occasioned by placing the branches under some restraint, in training, so that the sap may be prevented from returning downwards, so rapidly as it flows upwards, and its nutriment, therefore, retained for the supply of the flowers or fruit; for it will be clear to the reader of the preceding pages, that a stem trained in an erect form will be more luxuriant in its growth, than in any other, and that it will, therefore, possess a greater disposition to produce leaves than flowers, so long as it continues in that position.

The most general modes of training woody stemed trees are the fan, (fig. 37,) the horizontal, (fig. 38); and the vertical, (fig. 39.) Of these, fan training is

Fig 37.

Fig 38.

Fig 39.

the most common, and particularly applicable to stone fruit trees; the summit of the stem not being allowed to exceed one or two feet from the ground, and the side shoots laid out in radii from the centre. Trees of a flexible nature, such as the vine, and other climbing plants allow of various kinds of training, (fig. 40, 41, 42, and 43,) peculiarly suitable to

Fig 40

Fig 41

Fig 42

Fig 43

themselves; particularly as vines bear the sweetest fruit at the greatest distance from the root.

Many plants, especially the hoya, &c. look best when trained round spiral frames; but as all kinds of training must be regulated by individual taste, it is unnecessary to describe more than the above principal modes, which form the basis of all the others.

Preparatory training—is the same in all modes, and is as follows:—at the end of the first season, after the graft or plant has been put into the ground, the side branches are fixed at an elevated angle, to encourage the throwing out lateral shoots, the stem being maintained in an erect position; the second season in this country will complete the growth necessary for training, when the side shoots must be shortened, and all superfluous branches removed, the required shoots being fixed in their proper positions by shreds, or rope; but if the latter, pieces of old leather should be placed over the branches, before they are tied, to preserve them from friction, and *Khoa* rope is the best, as being most durable.

Herbaceous training—is performed in various ways. Plants that twine of themselves, such as the convolvolus, &c., should be furnished with poles proportionate to their height, whilst those that are supplied with tendrils, as the pea, the passion flower, &c. require sticks with sprays (the small lateral branches of the bamboo answer well for these,) that the plant springing up through them may attach itself by its tendrils. Props or supports are necessary for upright, tall, slender growing plants, such as the dahlia; whilst creeping and trailing plants, as the melon, cucumber, &c. are trained on the ground, or on a low platform, in a star-shaped form, by means of pegs.

Blanching—is the art of whitening certain plants by the exclusion of light, and is performed in various ways, as the kind of plant directs; such are the following.

By earthing, as performed on asparagus, celery, &c.; the latter being an annual, by drawing up the earth in ridges, so as to press on, and lay close to the leaves as they grow; and in the former, being a perennial plant, by covering it over with manure, and loose earth and sand, through which the young stalks shoot up.

By tying the leaves together, as performed on lettuce; the plant being in its most leafy state, the heads of the leaves are gathered together, and tied round with plantain or other fibre, whereby the centre, or heart, becomes more solid and tender, and the inner leaves, being excluded from the light, are blanched.

By overlaying with tiles, or pieces of board, when nearly full grown, as sometimes performed on endive, and other salad; but the next mode is to be preferred:

By covering with blanching pots of a bell shape, or flower pots reversed: this operates most successfully on endive, &c.

Potting,—is resorted to chiefly on account of the facility it affords to the removal of plants from one spot to another; it may also be made subservient to securing a perfect drainage to plants, and defending their roots from any excess of moisture; besides this, it is convenient for the purpose of raising, and giving attention to delicate seedlings. But it must be borne in mind, that a plant so situated, is reduced to a very different condition from that which it naturally holds when in the ground, for the roots, unable to spread laterally, and being thrown back on themselves, their supply of food is necessarily very limited, they are also subjected to the influence of temperature, more than in their natural position, through the sides of the pot allowing its variations to be felt by the whole mass of the roots.

Shifting,—is resorted to, to obviate the disadvantages just detailed; plants in pots should be frequently removed to larger sized pots as the roots spread, but in doing this, it is not sufficient to take up the root in the ball of earth entire, with the fibres matted and hard pressed, and then put it into a larger pot, with a little loose earth, as will be done by the native mallee if left to himself; the ball must be broken, and the fibres carefully spread out with the hand, in their new position all decayed, or broken portions being removed with the knife.

One great advantage to be sought in all potted and shifted plants, is to secure perfect drainage; this is best obtained by filling a part of the bottom of the pot, before putting in the earth, with broken brick, crocks, pieces of stone, &c., and by keeping the earth in the centre, around the stem of the plant, raised above the edges of the pot, in form of a small hillock, covering it with broken brick, in small pieces, or, when procurable, pebbles.

When kept too long in pots, the main branches of

the root are apt to assume a spiral form, which they are likely to retain even when planted out in the garden, and from want of good spreading side shoots, having little hold on the soil, such plants are easily blown down; great care, therefore, is necessary in spreading the root wide abroad when taking the plant from one pot to another, or from a pot to the ground; and plants so grown, should be regularly shifted from the smallest sized pot that it will occupy when quite young, to the larger ones, in regular gradation, and not at once, from very small to large; the reason of this seems to be, that in large pots the roots are apt to be chilled and rotted by the retention of more water than is requisite for their well doing. It is to be observed also, that plants generally thrive best in small pots, most probably because the air passes more readily to the roots, through their porous sides, which are from their size, nearer to the point of requisition than in larger ones.

OPERATIONS FOR INCREASING FRUITFULNESS.

These are sometimes called for in India, as the rapid vegetation, induced by the heat, often prevents trees from blossoming, or makes them barren of fruit.

Laying open the roots.—Various means have been adopted to remedy the evils just noticed, and among the most successful is, after the annual pruning of the branches, to lay bare the roots, and keep them exposed to the action of the air and the dew until the buds begin to burst; a process that is suitable to almost every description of tree; some gardeners also prune the roots before filling in the earth around them, with the view of checking the growth of useless wood.

Ringing.—For the like purpose ringing is resorted to. This is the removal of a portion of bark from around the base of a tree or branch, whereby the quantity of blossom, or the size of the fruit, is greatly increased; because the downward course of the sap being thus intercepted, it returns again to the upper part of the branch, and increases the quantity of nutriment maintained in that particular part, causing the whole to be reserved for the support of the fruit.

This operation is best performed in the spring, when the sap begins to rise with vigor, and the bark separates freely from the wood; the easiest method of doing it, being with a double bladed penknife, both blades being open at the same time; the space between the two is generally sufficient to remove, as the extent of bark cut out should never exceed what a stone fruited tree can fill in one year, or a kernel fruited tree in two. But ringing should not be too often, or two thoughtlessly resorted to, for such a violation of nature, as may be expected, materially affects the health of the tree, and if too often repeated will eventually kill it.

The simplest method of increasing production is, as has been before related, by seeking the same effect as ringing, in the more natural method of allowing occasional seasons of rest in production of fruit, by removing the blossoms or embryo fruit, and thus accumulating an increased store of nutriment, for the ensuing season, uniformly throughout the tree.

Ringing may, however, be had recourse to, either to cause increased production, or to increase the size, and accelerate the ripening of the fruit. If for the latter purpose, it should not be done until the plants are in blossom, and its effects will be seen the same season; but if to increase production, the operation must be performed in the spring, and its effects will be made evident in the following year.

Renewal of soil, about the roots especially, of peaches or figs, will restore or increase fruitfulness, if conducted with reference to the state of the plants; thus, if the trees be weakly and unthriving, changing the soil about them for a rich, loamy, well manured earth; or, if too great luxuriance indicate that the existing soil be over rich, a poor limey soil, mixed with sand, must be applied.

Bending down the branches, by stagnating and checking the too free circulation of the sap, will conduce also to fruitfulness.

OPERATIONS FOR ACCELERATING OR RETARDING VEGETATION.

Acceleration is little called for in India; but the easiest mode of affecting it is by manures of a hot or stimulating nature, such as pigeon dung for cucumbers, blood for vines, &c. or by adding lime, rubbish, or sand, to stiff soils, to make them more porous, and give free access to moisture, which must be liberally given. Attention also to select, for such sowings as you wish to produce an early crop, seeds that have been the first to ripen in the previous year, will accelerate vegetation considerably, as will also the sowing them on a hot bed, which last has, moreover, a good effect on scarce seeds that may have been long kept.

Retarding, a less easy process, may be effected in the early part, or spring of the year, by forming beds in an east and west direction, with a considerable slope towards the north, and some shelter towards the south, on which salading, spinach, or turnips, may be sown with *less* fear of their shooting up into flower stems than if sown in beds of the ordinary description. Placing a shade either over, or on the south side of growing plants, allowing at the same time a free circulation of air, will have the effect of checking or keeping back their vegetative powers.

HOT BEDS.

At first view the very idea of a hot bed in India, appears startling, and as hardly to be imagined, save by the wildest of theorists; but in a tropical climate even, many seeds come to hand that either from the long, close confinement of a sea voyage, or from the natural causes of a hard shell, an oleaginous quality, or a variety of other causes demand the highest obtainable stimulus to make them germinate, or to acclimate them to the future excessive stimulus that the naturally heated atmosphere, and general high temperature of an Indian clime imposes on them in their subsequent career. This had long been the opinion of the author, but he would have hesitated, ere he put it forth to the public, had he not found support in that of one of the ablest and most distinguished botanists and horticulturists in India, Dr. Robert Wight of Madras; who thus accounts for the usefulness of hot beds, in an article published in the third volume of the *Transactions of the Agricultural and Horticultural Society of India*, remarking on an experiment on this point—" Plants raised from European seeds all retain, it would appear, a high degree of excitability. He (Mr. Speede) while sprouting them, applies a powerful stimulus (heat) by which part of this excitability is exhausted, and their constitutions changed from those of hardy northern, *excitable*, to tender tropical, *unexcitable* plants, thereby assimilating them to the climate, by not only fitting them to resist a high temperature, but absolutely rendering it necessary to their after existence,"—and I am satisfied that were hot beds more extensively used, not only should we not hear of so many failures of seed, but we might, even in the plains of Bengal, Coromandel, &c. succeed in raising seed from plants, thus acclimated, of most European vegetables and flowers.

The following is the mode of preparing a hot bed, which has been found most successful :—Collect the stable dung and litter in a conical heap on the spot selected for the site of the hot bed, until a sufficient quantity has been gathered. It should then be well and carefully shaken together into a long flattish heap, putting the short stuff on the top, watering at every six inches of height, and leaving it for two or three days. It must then be thoroughly turned, putting the outside litter to the centre, and the inside out, watering as before, and again leaving it for two or three days, and then this operation must be repeated, so that in the course of nine days it shall have fermented three several times. The site of the intended hot bed should then be marked out, and the earth taken out for a depth of about six inches, the bottom being carefully levelled and beaten down with a rammer; in this the bed may be proceeded with, by shaking in the stuff so sufficiently that each particular straw may be separated from its fellow, watering and beating, however, at every four or five inches of height until it reaches from three to four feet; on this must be immediately placed the frame, or, if you have not such a thing, mat walls may be substituted, with moveable mat coverings, or *jamps*; the bed must, however, be kept closely covered for about twelve hours, when the heat will be found to rise, and air may then be given. In about three days the bed will be in full heat, which may be ascertained by thrusting the finger down in the centre; when this begins to abate, six inches of fine, moderately moist mould may be put on, and as soon as it is ascertained that the heat has risen into this the seeds may be sown. The after treatment requires only that the bed have air regularly in the middle of the day, and that it be occasionally watered with water from a watering pot that has stood some time within the influence of the sun's rays, being only administered in the hottest part of the day.

Mr. Forsyth recommends the annual collection of leaves to form hot beds, which by occasional addition of fresh leaves may be made to keep up a succession of gentle heat for nearly two years, and then afford a good manure for borders, especially where fruit trees stand; better indeed, than dung, which he disapproves for trees generally.

Gardeners.

Useful as this class of men is, they are hardly ever considered worthy attention or instruction in India, where although most gentlemen, who have gardens, are ready enough to complain of that ignorance and stupidity, as they call it, which will not even enable them to recognize in the young plant the distinction between a *turnip*, and a cauliflower; yet all unite in an indifference to their improvement, if it costs ever so small a modicum of personal trouble. It is true we have not here those most useful schools for gardeners that are found at home, in the numerous nurseries and market gardens, but if every gentleman who possesses a garden were to spare a few minutes daily to instruct his gardener, and explain to him the reason of the operations he directs, much might yet be done for the advancement of horticulture, to especially if backed by increase of pay proportionate to, but not in excess of the man's advance in knowledge; for, after all, it is really too much to demand intelligence and information where it is not encouraged, or familiarity with a science from a man paid and treated as a common *koolee*, although there is often quite as much injury done to the science of horticulture by over-paying a blundering booby who is proud of murdering botanical names, and making himself unintelligible, as by this under remuneration.

The head gardener ought always to be able to read and write some one of the native languages, that he may be able to keep and exhibit to his master, from time to time, registers of the plants in the garden, the period when sown, or transplanted, the adjuncts used, and so forth; but a man can hardly be expected to acquire this knowledge for the paltry pittance generally now allowed of from three to five rupees; let that sum be trebled, nay, quintupled, to deserving, active men; and there may be a chance of securing a class of people, as gardeners, who will conduct the culture of their charge on correct principles, and take pains in obtaining, and a pride in securing success. But before all, let no proprietor of a garden be above expressing, or of practically shewing, the knowledge he himself possesses, and there will then be little or nothing to prevent our having as good gardeners in most parts of India as may be had any where else.

It is, indeed, a subject for gratulation to the real gardener to find, that the Horticultural Society have at last taken this matter up, by establishing a school for gardeners at their garden, under charge of their superintendent whose active diligence, and earnest endeavors to improve himself are the best security the Society can have for the success of the project, and if to this establishment they would obtain the assistance of some educated, and well-known horticulturist in giving occasional lectures after a time when the scholars have made themselves masters of the rudimental branches, together with the assignment of annual prizes to the most deserving, which might, perhaps, be done without much cost, beyond what is at present incurred, out of the residue of unclaimed premiums, at the several quarterly shows, there is no doubt of the institution becoming in this way, as it has in so many others, eminently useful, and affording that so much called for desideratum, a good supply of usefully practical, and intelligent of gardeners; proprietors of gardens however, bearing in mind that these must be well paid, and no longer treated as mere *koolees.*

LIST OF TOOLS REQUIRED IN THE GARDEN, ETC.

Plough,
Digging hoe,
Mattock,
Pickaxe,
Forked hoe,
Spade,
Potatoe fork,
Spud,
American weeding hoe,
Dutch, ditto,
Pronged, ditto,
Rake,
Native weeder, *nuranee*,
Ditto———, *koorpah*,
Pitch fork,
Scraper,
Garden trowel,
Transplanter,
Dibber,
Wheelbarrow,
Truck,
Roller of stone or iron,
Beetle,
Rammer,
Beater, or mallet,
Triangular level,
Regulating level,
Pins (iron) and line,
Pump,
Watering pots of sizes, with spouts, and roses of various forms,
Axe,
Bill hook,
Saw,
Sickle,
Pruning knife,
Grafting ditto,
Ringing ditto,
Chissel,
Mallet,
Gathering scissors,
Scythe,
Hedge shears,
Training rods,
Wire,
Screen,
Seive,
Broom,
Blanching pots,
Flower pots of sizes.

Destructive Animals, Insects, etc.

ANIMALS—*Janoour.*

It need hardly be said that the garden must be protected from the incursion of the larger of these by strong fences, but still there are some that such defences are no protection against.

The HARE, Lepus, *Khurgoosh* or *Susa,* does extensive injury to fruit plantations, where this creature abounds, by gnawing the bark of young trees: the part of the stem, therefore, that is within their reach should be smeared with cow-dung or tar, occasionally renewed; or protected with thorns.

The FOX, Canis Bengalensis, *Loomree, Looktee* or *salub,* will often obtain access to the garden if the fence be imperfect, or not sufficiently high, and if it be extensive will burrow before he is discovered, and thus cut up the garden seriously; beside, the fox of this country is believed to feed principally on roots.

The JACKAL, Canis aureus, *Geed'hur,* or *Seear,* finds entrance chiefly by drains, or ditches, if left without gratings, as well as over, and through fences if too low or damaged: he will do serious injury to pine apples or other fruits within reach, and must, therefore, be destroyed. The most common trap is an old chest with a drop door, similar in construction to the common rat trap.

The COMMON RAT, Mus decumanus, *Chooha*; the MUSK Rat, Mus zibethicus, *Chuchoondur*; and, the FIELD MOUSE, Mus sylvaticus, *Moosa*, by burrowing under shrubs, and destroying the roots, or eating the fleshy part of tuberous plants, as well as by grubbing up peas, beans, and other large seeds, do an infinity of mischief. Mr. Forsyth in his valuable "Treatise on Fruit Trees" cautions gardeners against the use of arsenic or corrosive sublimate in getting rid of these vermin, because "nux vomica will generally answer the end as well, without the danger;" —he recommends, as a bait for rat traps, a mixture of good flour, treacle, crumbs of bread, and few drops of oil of carraways; the traps are to be baited with this mixture, and set near the holes; "but, for two or three days, so as not to fall or strike on the rats going in, and let them have free liberty to go in and out at pleasure; this will make them fearless." The traps should not be cleaned after rats have been caught in them, for rats will generally enter boldly where they find others have gone before them. For mice the same authority recommends traps "made by stringing garden beans on a piece of fine packthread, as you would string beads, then driving in two small stakes at the breadth of a brick from each other, and setting up a brick, or stone, or a board with a weight on it, inclining to an angle of about forty-five degrees; then tie the string with the beans on it, round the brick and stakes, to support the brick in its inclining position, taking care to place all the beans on the underside of the brick. The mice in eating the beans will also cut the packthread, and so disengage the brick, or stone, which, falling on them, kills them." But, perhaps, the easiest mode of destroying them is to smoke them in their holes; this may be done by filling a native water jar, or kulsee, with dry straw or leaves, and turning the mouth down on the hole, closing every orifice perfectly; then perforating the upper or bottom side, and setting fire to the straw within, blowing occasionally through a hollow bamboo, at the perforation, to drive the smoke as much as possible into the hole.

To stop the holes in brick-work, or terracing, Mr. Forsyth recommends the following composition:—"Take a pint of common tar, half an ounce of pearl ashes, an ounce of oil of vitriol, and a good handful of common salt, mix them all well together in an old pan or pot. Take some pieces of paper and lay some of the above mixture very thick on them, then stop the holes well up with them, and build up the mouth of the holes with brick or stone, and mortar: if this be properly done, rats will no more approach these, while either smell or taste remains in the composition."

The WILD CAT, Felis catus, *Kutas*, is a troublesome animal, though more destructive to the poultry yard than the garden, it should therefore be destroyed whenever it appears.

The Wild Hog, Sus crofa, *Soo,ur* it need hardly be said, must be kept out of the garden, for an hour's visit from this destructive animal will destroy the hopes and labor of years.

The Squirrel, Sciurus, *Chukhoree, or Cheekhur*, is very destructive to fruit, and also to young plants, but these animals are only to be overcome by killing them individually, although perhaps a tiresome task.

BIRDS—*Chureea*.

Many species of birds are troublesome to the horticulturist, and among these the most annoying are the Parrot, Psittacus, *Tota* or *Tootee*, of which the long-tailed green kind is found in all parts of the country; and the Pea Fowl, Pavo, *Moour;* the former being a great enemy to ripening fruit, maize, &c. and the latter more particularly, to growing plants.

The Flying Fox, a species of Vespertilio, *Badoor*, is to be dreaded in the fruit garden, especially as he generally destroys more than he eats; lines are frequently cast from tree to tree, which entangle and make him an easy prey.

Many of the smaller birds of the Sparrow kind, Fringella domestica, *Chura* or *Churee;* and of the beautiful class of Seed-eaters, as well as the Crow, Corvus carone, *Kag*, *Kuooa*, attack fruit as it is ripening and do an infinity of mischief if not guarded against:

the best protection is to cover the trees with nets, or coarse bunting, which admit the free circulation of air, at the same time that they prevent access to the destroyers.

REPTILES—*Keera mukoora.*

The SNAKE, Serpens, *Samp*, *Chutee* ; although most persons destroy all for the sake of protection from a few of the venomous kind, there are many descriptions that are useful, by keeping down frogs and large insects, and for the sake of the good they do in this way they may be forgiven an occasional trespass on a pine-apple, or a cucumber.

The FROG, Rana, *Béng*, *Dadur*, if not allowed to multiply too extensively, is serviceable by destroying many insects ; but if too numerous, their anxiety to obtain these becomes so great, that they will even ascend trees, and in their eagerness eat the leaves along with their prey.

The LIZARD, Lacerta, *Ch,hupkulee*, *Ch,hupkee*, or *Bustooee*, is a harmless reptile, useful to the gardener by the enmity it bears to all flies, and moving insects : it is very curious to observe the varieties of this species apparently changing their hue, in accordance with the color of the plant to which they attach themselves, and one may often be found amongst the leaves of the pine apple, of that peculiar reddish tinge, that you would pass it as one of the young floral shoots.

INSECTS—*Keera*.

These are the worst enemies we have, and their species are so numerous that it is difficult to obtain a correct knowledge of their habits and economy, so as to oppose their devastations with any prospect of success. All insects in their larvic, or caterpillar state, feed most voraciously, and the gardener's eyes must be ever open to discover where they are at work; or in a short time every particle of vegetation within their reach will have disappeared. Of these a few of the most destructive may be worth noticing.

BUTTERFLY,—*Teetree. The Swallow-tailed Butterfly.* The Caterpillar *(Janj'ha,)* is green, having a black band at each division, relieved by small round reddish colored spots; it does little injury, confining its feeding to the carrot, or fennel leaves.

The Cabbage Butterfly, Pontia or Papilio brassicæ, *Buree sofĕd teetree*, of a greenish white. The caterpillar is of a greenish yellow, irregularly marked with black spots in the larger kind, and of a delicate green with small yellow rings on each side of its body, in the *Small white Butterfly*, Pontia or Papilio rapæ, *Chōtee sŏfĕd teetree*; these two cause great destruction among the beds, frequently getting into, and hiding themselves in the hearts of cabbages and cauliflowers.

Guinea fowls feed freely on the caterpillars of these two species, and they find another enemy in a species of fly (Ichneumon globatus, *Rasoo*), which depositing its eggs in the body of the caterpillar leaves its larva to feed on its inside.

The white Butterfly, Pontia napi, *Sofêd teetree,* with green veins, is also a great pest; the caterpillar is green, with orange stripes, and infests the turnip and the radish.

The caterpillar of the Papilio deiphobus, also infests many trees. Washing with a mixture of soap suds and urine is recommended as a good preservative from these insects.

MOTHS, *Putunga,* or *Purooana.* *The hawk Moth,* Sphinx occellata, *Burree purooana,* of which some species are found here, has a green caterpillar with pale colored, or white stripes: it feeds chiefly on the young and tender shoots of trees and shrubs, but some varieties are believed to live on the nectar of flowers, which they extract with their long tongues. A variety of the Sphinx exitiosa is also found here attacking the mango, and peach trees.

The genus *Phelæna,* the caterpillars of which are hairy, *b'hooeen,* are extremely destructive to lettuces, marjoram, parsley, geraniums, &c.

In some varieties the hairs have an effect on the skin, like cow-itch, if touched; among these are P. flaviolala, P. lepida, &c.

Phalæna paphia, is called *Jarroo* when it appears on the *Baeeur* or wild plum tree, and *Bughee* when found on other trees; in both positions, however, it produces the tussur silk; it is a most voracious destroyer of the foliage of any tree it approaches—of the same family is the Phaleena cynthia, *Arundeh,* which feeds on the Castor oil plant (palma christi) and produces the *Areea* silk, as it is called.

Plant louse, Aphis. *Ashbus,* (cor). Plant lice, or green flies, are most destructive insects; almost every plant is subject to their attacks, and they vary according to the description of vegetable they feed on; generally maintaining, however, the color of the plant, from which they are hardly distinguishable, and hence to be observed only, on minute examination; their fecundity is so enormous, that it has been calculated by Reaumur that 5,904,900,000 may be produced in five generations; and it is supposed that in one year there may be twenty generations. They fortunately find many enemies, all classes of birds feeding on them as well as many insects of the beetle kind and ants. Mr. Forsyth recommends lime water as a destroyer of this pest, which should be carefully syringed on the under part of the leaves, &c. One of the most formidable enemies of the Aphis is the larva of the lady-bird (Coccinella).

Plant-bug, Coccus. Plant bugs are almost as destructive as the preceding, and are concealed by their resemblance in form and colour to the leaf buds that form in the axils of the leaves; other again, as the Coccus persicorum, (frequently found on fruit trees,) assume the appearance of the scales that occur on the bark of the trees on which they feed. Another kind appear like little spots of white cotton, and attack many trees, but especially the vine, and those of the plum kind.

These insects should be scraped off wherever found, and the trees washed, as for the destruction of butterflies. One very destructive species of coccus, known commonly under the name of Aphis lanigera, may be destroyed by brushing the tree with brown impure pyroligneous acid, if it can be procured. The white bug, also of this species, is easily destroyed by syringing, under the leaves of the plant attacked, with lime water. The cochineal insect belongs to this class.

The WEEVIL, Curculio, *Putaree soonda*, or kun. Weevils, most of them very small, live upon seeds and vegetables, and commit vast devastation, especially in the former, by destroying the germ.

Curculio contractus, a species of which may be sometimes met with here, causes the club in cabbages, and another species, Culundra oryzee, may be found in rice. Smoking with wet straw, or tobacco, stupifies these insects, but no means of actually destroying them appears to have been yet discovered, except by handpicking when they fall off, in their stupefaction.

THE ASPARAGUS BEETLE, Crioceris punctata, *Lal Goobréla*, is in its larva condition very destructive;

is then of a slately green color; the best mode of getting rid of them is to destroy the beetle, which is of an orange and black color, but is extremely cunning, turning under the stalk of the plant as soon as approached, and when pursued dropping on the ground as if dead.

Dr. J. T. Pearson (vide Proceedings of the Horticultural Society, vol. vii.) has lately given a description of a turnip-fly inhabiting Doojeelung, in the Himalya mountains and their vicinity, where it makes great ravages among the young plants of the cabbage, cauliflower, turnip, radish, and other similiar vegetables. He classes it as the Haltica nigro-fusca; and describes the failure of various expedients for its destruction, amongst the rest dressing the land with lime, but as he does not mention in what form this was applied, it is possible that quicklime may not have been tried, and from its general success in destruction of insects it might be worth the experiment.

The LOCUST tride, Gryllus, *Tudee*, *Teeree*, or *Muluhk*. Grasshoppers and locusts of various sizes abound, and commit extensive depredations in the garden.

The *Locust*, Gryllus migratorius, *Tudee*, often visits parts of India, especially to the westward, in such flocks as to destroy every green thing, and to produce serious famine. There seems no remedy against them, and they continue their ravages until a storm destroys them.

The *Grasshopper*, Gryllus tettigonia, *P,hunga* or *tuda* is not so destructive as the last, though still a great enemy to vegetation.

The *Cricket*, Gryllus acheta, *J,heengur*, or *j,hulee* is the most innocent of this class.

The *Mole cricket*, Gryllus gryllotalpa, called *Mál pók* in Dacca and that neighbourhood, where a species of it abounds, is a most curious insect, bearing the common name of the "carpenter;" it lives entirely on vegetables, and commits its ravages mostly by night, when it issues from its hole, and cuts off the young plants at the crown dragging them to its burrow, which is often betrayed by the young leaves left sticking out;—frequent moving of the soil is the best check to the increase of this pest to the garden, and it should be dug up whenever it can be traced.

The *Frog-Hopper*, or *flea-locust*, Cicadia, does not appear to have any specific name among natives, although met with wherever there is vegetation; some, however, call it the *Bhang-ké-thók* from the larvæ of the ordinarily found species, covering itself with a quantity of frothy matter, which is at once unsightly and hurtful to the trees to which it attaches itself; this should be sought for every morning, and removed with the hand.

The Fly, Musca, *Mukhee or mugus*. Of flies, the small maggot, *Mukhee-ka-peelooa*, that is the larvæ of various species, are nearly all destructive to vegetable life and growth ; one kind attacking radishes, another the cauliflower, another the onion; this last is called the *Onion fly*, Anthomyia ceparum, and the larva finds its way between the layers of the bulb causing great destruction; no certain mode of getting rid of this insect is known, as most of the methods hitherto suggested will also destroy the onion itself.

The SPIDER, Aranea, *Mukree*, or *muchra*. Spiders of various kinds, abound in our gardens, especially those of the green and yellow descriptions; there are several kinds of the former, seeking their food on the pine-apple, the vine, the rose, &c.

The *Red Spider*, as it is called, is properly a *Mite*, Acarus, *Lal mukree;* it is one of the most destructive insects that attack vegetables: there are an immense number of species infesting different plants, but especially the melon, on which their effects are observed long before they themselves are visible, by the leaves curling and cracking in the middle; and when that is perceived, the leaves should be lightly watered from a fine rose.

The CENTIPEDE, Scolopendra, *Goojun*. Of this insect there are several varieties; some of them venomous, all injurious by eating into the roots; some kind of ringworms, as they are called, do the same, and curling themselves up in the holes they have made, remain concealed, extremely difficult to be discovered.

The Ant, Formica, *Choontee.* Ants of numerous kinds meet the view at every turn; of these the most destructive is the red ant that attacks almost every thing that come in its way, fruit, the roots of turnips, radishes, and so forth. The destruction of all these insects is only to be accomplished by patiently watching the progress, and habits of each, so as to learn the fittest time to destroy them. Lime is of effect with many species, and pounded turmeric is offensive to ants of most descriptions; but boiling water is their only real destroyer, and that should be poured into their holes until they are all killed, or quit the spot; with the small red ant this is most easily ascertained, as they bring out the dead insects, and place them in a heap near the holes, so long as any remain alive to perform that operation; whence it is easy to conclude that when no more dead are brought out, the nest is destroyed or the remnant of the colony have deserted it.

The White Ant, Termes, *Deemuk, deeook.* These are the most destructive and insidious enemies of the garden, and commit more devastation than can be well imagined; they abound in all parts of the plains of India; and most frequently the only intimation the gardener has of their presence, is the sudden death of a tree; when, on taking up the dry trunk, it will be found that these laborious insects have completely divided the crown. Frequent moving of the soil, attention to under drainage, and destroying their nests with boiling water, wherever discovered, are the only known remedies. It has, however, been lately discovered, that manuring the roots of trees with blood, will keep them away; and as this effect is supposed to arise from the ferruginous matter it contains, burying old iron, or giving a supply of oxide of iron to the roots, might be worth trying as a preventive; instances being known of its good effects, so far as good judgment may lead one to suppose.

The WORM, Vermes intestina, *Kurum*, *keer*, *or puloo* often destroys the roots of plants, and raises unsightly mounds of earth on walks, grass plots, &c. The leaves of the walnut tree strewed on the ground will, it is said, annoy them; and watering the earth with a decoction of the leaves will drive away or kill the worms.

The RED BEETLE, Scarabæus, *Gobreela*, of a small red, or rather orange kind, known as "the soldier," is a great enemy to all plants of the cucumber or melon family, eating the young shoots, and destroying all the fleshly part of the leaves; it must be removed by handpicking whenever is appears.

THE GARDEN.

A garden will consist of a combination of that part appropriated to culinary vegetables, or the kitchen garden; of the fruit garden; of the shrubbery, or garden for ornamental trees; and of the flower garden; united together in one spot of ground, but so divided into compartments that each portion may be kept distinct. Of the two last however we have nothing to do here, these being proper subjects for a separate work.* The garden should always be well drained, on which account a slight slope would be preferred if procurable, and the neighborhood of low swamps should be avoided, as they attract frogs, besides generally causing the subsoil to be too damp for the roots of plants; it should be well open to the east, that every spot may receive the benefit of the morning sun, and equally sheltered towards the north and west sides, to break the force of the winds from that quarter: the trees employed for this purpose being such as have bulk, with close and compact foliage, relieved, for the sake of ornament, by firs, or such like trees of light foliage.

But, above all things, a good supply of water is essential to be secured in the formation of a garden; this may be varied in form, so as to be made very

---

* The author has in progress, and shortly to be published a work on these subjects called, "The Indian Floriculturist."

ornamental, and to avoid the dull formality of the four-sided tanks generally used in India; and facility should be given, when constructing a garden, for conducting the water to every corner of it. It is to be remembered, that besides the supply of water obtained by digging tanks, the further advantage, from that operation, is secured in this country (so generally too flat by nature), of placing at disposal a supply of earth to form ornamental knolls, or at all events so to fill up any low parts as to secure a good and sufficient drainage to the whole.

The best fence is undoubtedly a wall, but if your ground be extensive, the cost of walling the whole, might be too much for your means. Next, therefore, to this a mound or *pugar* surmounted with the prickly pear, or woodey aloe; what is called the Nepal thorn, a species of prickly mimosa, if planted thick, and kept in form by frequent clipping, forms a compact and good hedge; and a light, but tolerably close hedge of rapid growth, may be found in the plant commonly known as the *Rungcheettreh*, but it requires support;—of course all hedges and mounds should, for security against trespass of cattle, &c., be accompanied by a tolerably deep ditch.

Interior fences should always be made to divide one part of the garden from another: as the flower garden from the kitchen, and that again from the fruit garden. For this purpose hedges of dwarf shrubs, such as Lawsonia inermis, Malpighia nitida, or Myrtus communis, kept closely clipped; or sweet-briar for a higher division may be usefully, as well as elegantly assorted to. A good rustic fence may be made from the branches of trees, or a pretty light division fence by split bamboos, placed in various forms, fixed together with nails and then painted green; in using either of these last, the parts that serve as posts, should be embedded in brick work, to protect them from white ants; or what is yet better, the portion that is buried may be treated after the manner recommended by Mr. Kyan, and brought to the notice of our Horticultural Society by Dr. Drummond. "The proportion of oxymuriate of mercury used by Dr. Drummond, as well as he recollects, was a pound to fifteen gallons of water, and the wood steeped in the solution for ten or twelve days." *Vide, Proceedings of the Horticultural Society, for June* 1840.

The best fence as a boundary one, is, perhaps, the Nagpore thorn, a variety of the *Gum Acacia*, Acacia Arabica, *Bubool* which may be sown at any time, except in the Upper Provinces, during the prevalence of the hot winds, when nothing can be expected to germinate, it will run up into a thick defensive hedge in six or eight months, but requires to be constantly looked after, or it becomes straggling. It is said that the *Prickly parkinsonia*, Parkinsonia aculeata, for which there appears no native name, if shortened two or three times during its growth, and not planted too close it answers well for

The Kitchen Garden.

In laying out ground for this purpose, care should be taken not to place it adjoining to the house as such an arrangement would be unsightly; at the same time, it should not be at such distance as shall put it beyond the reach of constant supervision, or easy access; above all, it must have the command of a plentiful supply of water, and be well fenced in, for it is always better to secure your garden from temptation, by preventing general access of servants, or strangers, than to rely on the punishment of individuals after you have been robbed, as a prevention from further loss. It need not be added, that its extent must entirely depend on the wants, or wishes of the owner, for which no rule can be given, at the same time bearing in recollection that the preferable evil is, to have a little too much ground, rather than allow yourself to be cramped for room, to over-work any part of it by the too frequent cropping of the same spot, or to run the chance of not having space sufficient to afford a due observation of the rotation of crops.

SEED, &c.

The component parts of all culinary vegetables are

starch, gluten, sugar, and fibre, and of these the most nutritive is the first; contained, in the largest proportion, in esculent roots of various kinds.

It is not easy to separate our vegetable productions into their several distinct classes, since so many of them approach each other nearly, and gradually,—each appearing to claim more than one variety. Most kinds are raised only from seed, of which the best undoubtedly comes from New South Wales; the next to this is procurable from France, after which the Cape of Good Hope offers well, but is seldom true to its professed kind, the voyage from England being too long to expect the seed to preserve its full vigor in the manner in which it is generally packed; unless, as is now often practised, it is sent by what is called the overland route, when it is known to have arrived in good order. American seed, especially of turnip and beet, as well as of the cucumber and gourd kind, and of the tomato, is commonly found very good; great attention is necessary to these particulars, as nothing is more disappointing, after you have taken every pains to secure a good supply of vegetables, than to find all your hopes frustrated by the seed made use of having been bad, either in quality, in kind, or variety of species.

THE CABBAGE TRIBE.

Brassica,—*KOBEE KE KISM.*

The leaves of some, and the unexpanded flowers of others of this class of vegetables, are eaten boiled, or made into a pickle, and it is too generally known to need a particular description.

WHITE CABBAGE, Brassica oleracea, *Sofēd kôbee.* In this, the object of culture is to produce close, firm, and compact heads, green externally, but within white, and mild in flavor; the young plants being also sometimes eaten as greens, before the head forms.

Early York, and *Early Battersea Cabbage*, Brassica capitata, *Chôtee bundee kôbee*, are the most delicate in flavor, and well worthy of more attention than has hitherto been paid to them in India, until lately, when prizes given by the Horticultural Society of Calcutta, having been properly limited to quality, not quantity, the cultivation of these has there increased accordingly. They may be sown during the rains, in pots, under shelter, say at the beginning of August, but little time is gained to the crop by commencing so early, as plants sown at this period will not anticipate those put in at the end of the month, or the beginning of September, by more than a few days. The sowings may be repeated till the end of October, at intervals of fourteen days, by which means a supply will be continued until the end of February; they will take about four or five days to come up, should be pricked out about a fortnight after, provided the rains have ceased, and finally transplanted, at a foot and a half distance, in the place where they are to become perfect, in about another month ; being fit to cut in three months from the time of sowing.

Sugar-loaf cabbage, Brassica capitata, *Bundee kôbee*, is a larger and less delicate kind, forming a very white heart, and may be sown at the same time as the last description; although it takes a longer period to come to perfection, being seldom fit to cut under four, or four months and a half; half of which time this cabbage should be in the spot for perfecting, planted at not less than two feet apart; a continuous supply may be kept up by sowing at intervals until as late as the middle of November, which will yield a late crop in the middle of March. When Europe or other good seed cannot be procured in the Upper Provinces, it is not unusual to propagate by slips planted during the rains in highly raised beds, or in pots, subsequently treating the plants in the same manner as seedlings.

Drumhead Cabbage, Brassica castata, *Buree bundee kôbee*. This, though the most usual cabbage of our bazars, is of a very coarse and strong flavor, and used in England chiefly as a field cabbage for feeding cattle. It may be found sometimes as much as eighteen inches in diameter within the outside leaves. The sowing of drumhead cabbage should take place at the same time as the before mentioned, but it requires between four and five months before it is fit to cut, and when transplanted must be put at fully three feet apart.

Savoy, Brassica bullata, *Sikoree kôbee, kurum kula,* is distinguished from the other close hearted cabbages by its wrinkled leaves. The globe, and the dwarf green savoy, are the best varieties for this country, as they soonest come to perfection, and do not so much feel the want of the degree of cold they are accustomed to in Europe, where it is a common belief that a hard frost is indispensable to the perfecting of their flavor. If sown at the same time as the other cabbages, and planted out at about two feet apart, they will be fit for the table in December and January; but they are apt to form a long stem, and become in consequence, reduced, in the size of the head, sometimes dwindling, to only three or four inches in diameter, if not taken care of, and plentifully supplied with moisture.

Red Cabbage, Brassica capitata, *Lal kôbee*, though used chiefly for pickling, is nevertheless a very nice vegetable stewed, the best sort being the red Dutch. If sown towards the end of September, and transplanted into good soil about a month afterwards, with two previous removals to strengthen and fill out the stem, it will give a good firm head about the middle of February.

Propagation—of all the above descriptions of cabbage, is the same, by seed sown annually, well scattered and not put in too thickly, and covered with a thin layer of fine earth, not above a quarter of an inch in depth. The quantity of seed for a bed of sixteen feet long by five broad, should be about 2½ ounces of the smaller kinds, and of the larger sorts 1½ ounces.

Soil, &c. The soil for seed should be light, and, except for the early sowings in August, not rich. They require an open situation; and when transplanted should have a rich, highly manured mould, rather clayey than sandy, being a very exhausting crop. In this operation, which may be finally done when the plants have several leaves of from two to four inches in breadth, care must be taken to keep each kind distinct, as also to press the earth well up to the root fibres by a sloping insertion of the dibber, as before described. The best way of planting out is to put them in small trenches, branching from the water drain at right angles, so that a large supply of moisture may be readily given at the roots as soon as they begin to form heart, when too much water can hardly be bestowed. At this time too, the earth should be drawn up about the stems to give support to the superior weight above, and preserve their erect position; when also all that fail, or shew a tendency to run up to flower, should be immediately extirpated. If some of the stems of the larger sorts be left on the ground, after the cabbage has been cut, and carefully trimmed from all side leaves, they will afford a supply of good sprouts from the leaf axils for several months, when other vegetables are hardly procurable.

BORECOLE, Brassica acephala, *P,hueltee kôbee, kurum kulla*; or Kale, as it is more commonly called, comprehends many varieties; all, however, distinguished by having a somewhat large open head of leaves more or less curled, as well as being exceedingly hardy, giving sprouts during the greater part of the year, and lasting several seasons. The object of the cultivator will be to keep up a large succession of fresh sprouts.

The *German*, or *Scotch kale* as it is called, and the *Purple kale*, are the best sorts; they may be sown at almost any period of the year; perhaps, the end of June is the best time; the young seed leaves appearing in seven or eight days, and in a fortnight after they may be pricked out, and then transplanted to the place they should occupy, in about a month; thus treated they will give the first crop about the end of September.

Propagation, Soil, &c.—The same mode of proceeding should be pursued as with the larger sorts of cabbage; the quantity of seed, however, being fully what is requisite in sowing the smaller description, but they may be also propagated by cuttings.

BRUSSELS SPROUTS, Brassica bullata, *Goonogoon kôbee*, are little known in India; they produce a long stem, often three feet, or more in height, the top resembling a savoy planted late in the season, and from the joints of the leaves, shoots sprout out, forming small close miniature cabbages, which constitute a delicious vegetable, at a time when others are going out; they are extremely prolific, renewing the supply of small shoots almost as fast as they are removed, and may, by judicious sowing and care in cutting, be made to continue their supply nearly to the commencement of the periodical rains, or even partly through them, if sufficiently well drained to prevent the accumulation of water about the stems.

Propagation, Soil, &c.—This plant is raised from seed, which should not be sown too thickly, but in the same quantity as for the smaller sorts of cabbage; after a shower of rain is the best time for so doing, and in the beginning of November they will shew their seed leaves in three or four days, be fit to prick out in about twenty or five and twenty, and ready for final transplanting in the beginning of January, in beds at about eighteen inches apart, as they do not spread much in width, and the side leaves soon drop off. They require the same description of culture as all others of the cabbage tribe, and a plentiful supply of moisture. The plants should be kept well earthed up, and the first crop will be fit for the table in the beginning of March.

Cauliflower, Brassica botrytis, *P'hool kóbee*, is the most delicate of the cabbage tribe, the eatable part being the young flower buds, forming when well grown, and from good seed, a close, firm, and white cluster. There are only two varieties, the early, having a head of only about four inches diameter, and the late, growing to a much large size.

Propagation.—Some people consider that an early crop may be secured in dry situations by sowing in February or March, and shifting the plants during the rains; the success, however, of such a proceeding is doubtful; and as the seed is generally scarce, from the great demand for it by all classes, it would be best not to run the risk of such an experiment, but be content with sowing the early seed in the beginning of August, in pots, or in the open ground under shelter, an ounce and a quater being sufficient for a bed of sixteen feet by five; some in the Upper Provinces during the end of June or July, or as the rains come in, setting out the plants at that period, but this is dangerous; however, generally speaking the whole of these operations are there a month earlier than in Bengal, where they will show their seed leaves generally in three or four days; may be pricked out in the early part of September, and transplanted about the middle of October, giving an early crop in November, or the beginning of December. To secure a succession, it has been recommended by one experienced in the Upper Provinces, to split the stems of a portion of the plants put out, to retard their forming heads.

The larger kind may be sown any time from the beginning of September to the end of October, and will show themselves in three or four days; they should be pricked out to a light soil when three inches high, and in about a month after, say from the beginning of November to the middle of December, they should be finally transplanted at three feet apart, into holes of six inches in depth; this is advisable, that the supply of water may be sufficiently and retentively given, and the roots never allowed to get dry.

As soon as the flower begins to form, these holes should be filled with water morning and evening; if instead of water, liquid manure be procurable for these waterings occasionally, so much the better, and at this time the larger leaves should be turned down over the heads to defend them from the sun and dew, and to preserve them white and close; about a month or six weeks from the time of their being transplanted will suffice to make them fit to cut.

Soil.—The soil for the seed bed should be light, but when transplanted the mould cannot well be too rich; strong stable manure should, therefore, be liberally supplied to the roots, and the situation chosen must be warm. Mr. Russel, however, found pounded bones to be the best manure, with which assistance he grew, at Berhampore, some of the best ever seen in India.

BROCCOLI, Brassica botrytis, *Chôtee p'hool kôbee,* has seldom succeeded India until lately, and the seed rarely reaches here sufficiently fresh for culture, except from New South Wales. The whole treatment and culture is the same as for the cauliflower, but some are of opinion that they need not be transplanted, and that it will suffice to let them remain where pricked out, only thinning away the week plants, to afford more room for the rest.

THE INSECTS affecting the Cabbage Tribe, are chiefly of the caterpillar kind, particularly those of the cabbage, and the white butterflies; guinea fowls, and turkeys are great destroyers of these, which must otherwise be picked off by hand. Mr. J. Busch, in the Transactions of the Horticultural Society of London, vol. iv. says—"If in the patch of ground where cabbages are to be planted some hemp seed be sown all round the edge, in the spring, the strong smell which that plant gives in vapour will prevent the butterfly from infesting the cabbages;" the experiment has not yet been tried in this country, but it is simple, and well worth testing.

The worm, the centipede, and the weevil sometimes attack their roots; and a small black species of plant-bug eats the leaves of weak cabbages; the best means of destroying these last are wood ashes, but if discovered before many plants are attacked, it would be better to pull up all those infected.

DISEASES. The principal is called the club, in the root; this is a large tubercle or swelling, caused by the larvæ of a kind of weevil, commonly called the grub; deep trenching, or the addition of new soil of a loamy kind, by burying the grub, checks this disease, and frequent transplanting palliates it, by promoting the growth of fibrous roots; the only actual cure, however, is carefully cutting out the diseased part.

LEGUMINOUS PLANTS.

Leguminosæ, *MASEENADAR.*

The fruit of which is eaten boiled, either enclosed in the pod, when tender; or, the seeds alone taken out, or shelled.

THE PEA, Pisum sativum, *Mutur*, is too well known, and esteemed to require description. The object of culture is to produce a full pod, and at the same time to preserve the skin of the seed tender, and the flavor sweet. When dry they contain about forty-six parts of fibre, the remainder of the half, or four parts, being nearly equally divided between sugar and gluten, whilst fifty parts are pure starch; but when green, the sugar exceeds the starch in quantity. There are two principal divisions or kinds; the dwarf, generally also the early, the tall, and the late pea.

Early Dwarf Pea. Pisum viridum, *Ugeetee chôta mutur*; of these the earliest is the early Warwick, which takes somewhat less than a month from the time of sowing to its being fit for the table; it may be put in the ground at the distance of half an inch. If sown in a sheltered and elevated spot in the garden, a very early crop may be planted as early as the middle of August, giving a supply for the middle of September; but this will only be worth trying when you have an abundant supply of seed. A sure early frame crop, growing 2¼ feet high, may, however, be sown about the middle of October, which will come in about the middle of November, whence it will be easy, by sowing every tenth day, after the middle of October, to keep up a regular supply.

The Early Frame, and the Early Washington pea, Pisum viridum, *Ugeetee mutur*, the latter from America, are very superior flavored peas, and take about six weeks to fit them for the table. These two sorts should be put in the ground in the proportion of three in an inch, and if they be sown at the same time as the last mentioned kind, they will form a good succession to it; they attain about three feet in height.

The Dwarf Prussian pea, Pisum viridum, *Chóta mutúr*, might, if sown also at the same time, at the rate of three in two inches, form a further succession, as it requires two months; it grows from three to four feet in height.

Knight's Dwarf pea, Pisum viridum, *Oowlaeeta mutur*, is a very superior pea for a late crop in India, growing some three feet high, and if put in the ground towards the middle of December, at a distance of two in an inch, will begin giving its crop in February, and continue throughout the greater part of March and even to the end of April, as it stands the heat of that period better than any other kind of pea yet tried here. It has a small, but full pod of sweet flavored peas, in appearance very like the indigenous variety, and is a most prolific bearer, one plant yielding as much as half a dozen of most other kinds.

Tall Marrow-fat pea, Pisum majus, *Bura mutur*, is a very fine growing plant, giving full pods, and a tender seed; it should be put in the ground an inch and a half apart, and often grows nine or ten feet in height; this requires from nine to ten weeks to yield a crop; and if required for the end of December, or as a Christmas Pea, for which it is generally sought, must therefore, be put in the ground about the middle of October; the best time, however, if quality be studied, is the end of that month, which will give a fine January crop. The sowing may be continued every fortnight till the middle of December, whereby a supply may be secured to as late a period as the middle of April, provided care be taken in watering.

Imperial blue pea, Pisum sativum, *Neel mutur*, takes a somewhat longer time in coming to perfection, but yields a very large sized and good flavored pea; if sown in the middle of November, at an inch and a half distance, it will give a good crop by the end of January; it grows some eight feet high in good ground.

Green marrow pea, Pisum sativum, *Gool mutur*; and *Green scymetre pea*, Pisum sativum, *Lumbar mutur*, the latter a delicious pea, may be sown, at an inch distant from each other, in the end of November, and will give a crop in the beginning of January; they are sweet and tender, not growing so high, however, as the other tall kinds.

The Native pae, Pisum arvense *Desee* or *kuraoo mutur* may be sown if desired, which is questionable for they are tough skinned, and deficient in flavor about the same time as the dwarf sorts.

Propagation—of peas is only practised by seed; and, as a general rule, there may be taken a pint of the smaller sorts as the proper quantity for a row of fifteen yards, whilst of the tall kinds the same quantity may be extended through twenty-six yards. For the early sorts, make the drills an inch and a half deep, and about three to four feet asunder; but in sowing the tall description of pea, the drills must be two inches deep, and from four to six feet apart if it be desired to obtain a full and rich crop. In the Upper Provinces the early varieties are but little known, and the time of sowing appears to be from September to November, or, if the early sorts are attempted to be cultivated, not beginning before the end of August, and not sowing later than February.

Soil, &c. The soil for peas ought to be moderately rich, manured with fresh, sandy loam, mixed with decayed vegetable matter, if for the larger sorts to some depth; but fresh unfermented dung is liable to hurt them. As the plants reach two to three inches in height, the earth should be drawn up to the stems, gradually earthing higher as they grow; there need be little fear of bringing the earth too high on the stems, as the more the ridge is raised the greater are the number of root fibres produced from the axils submersed, and the greater, in consequence, the amount of nutriment the plant will receive; if the sun be hot, it will be advisable to shade the peas, until they are from ten to twelve inches high. As they throw out tendrils, the peas should be sticked with well branched twigs; the loppings, or side branches of bamboos are very good for the purpose, selecting them of a height proportioned to the description of pea, and putting them in on the sunny side, that the action of the sun may incline the plants towards them. Topping the leading shoot, when the second or third set of blossoms appear, will accelerate the setting, and promote the filling of the pod.

The GARDEN BEAN, Vicia faba, *Bakla*, *been* (cor), contains similar proportions of starch, &c. to the pea, but a rather less quantity of sugar. It is an annual plant, rising from two, to four feet in height; the seeds being either boiled separately, or put into soup. There are two principal varieties,—the early, and the late; of these the Mazagon among the former, and the Windsor among the latter, are the best sorts.

Mazagon Bean, Vicia faba, *Chóta been*, is small, good flavored, and hardy; it should be sown in the middle of October, taking advantage, if possible, of a shower, and this bean will then yield a good crop towards the end of January; it is an abundant bearer.

Windsor Bean, Vicia faba, *Burra been*, is large, and when gathered young, sweet, and agreeable in flavor; but does not in India bear plentifully. *The Long pod*, is a large bean of very good mild flavor, and possesses the advantage of being a prolific bearer. The middle of November is the best time for sowing these, and they will then begin to blossom about the middle of January, and about the twentieth of February yield a good crop.

Propagation—is carried on by seed, of which a pint, of the smaller sorts, will be sufficient for a row of sixty feet, the like quantity of the larger kinds serving for eighty feet; the smaller being put in drills, two and a half feet apart, at a depth of two inches, and about three inches apart in the row. For the larger sorts, the rows may be three feet distant from each other, put in three inches deep, and four inches apart in the row, each root throwing up several stems; they should have the earth well trodden down before covering in. Some prefer soaking the seeds for about three hours before sowing them, but the use of this is very doubtful, excepting so far as it facilitates the rejection of bad seed.

Soil, &c. A stiff heavy clay is the best soil for beans, and as the plants spring up from two to four inches in height, the earth should be hoed up to the stems, taking care, however, that none fall into the centre of the plants to bury them, as that would occasion rot; the hoeing must be frequently repeated to some depth, for which the forked hoe is the best instrument, both for the purpose of removing weeds, and for well stirring the soil between the rows to promote the production of root fibres. As the plants come into full blossom, or just as the first flowers fade, the tops should be pinched off, to promote production of well filled pods.

KIDNEY, OR FRENCH BEAN, Phaseolus, *Fras been* (cor), *Bakla;* the unripe pods form a well known vegetable, and need little description, as few tables are without them; they also make a good pickle. The pods, as eaten, contain more sugar than starch in the young beans, and some sugar with a larger quantity of fibre in the pod; they are considered wholesome and nutritive. Of these there are two kinds, the dwarf, and the climbing, or tall.

Dwarf kidney bean, Phaseolus vulgaris, *Chóta Bakla* or *zun,* is esteemed generally the most delicate in flavor, the early white kind being the best; it takes about two months from the time of sowing before it yields fruit fit for the table, and in about three months more will ripen its seed. This bean may be sown any time from the beginning of August to the end of December, and although it is not usual in England to stick this kind of kidney bean, but it will be found better to do so in this country.

The Scarlet runner, Phaseolus multiflorus, *Lal bakla*, is a tall climber, the pod being of coarser flavor than the preceding; the seed always leaves its cotyledons below the surface of the earth, and it takes three and a half months from the time of sowing before it is fit to gather, requiring then another month to ripen the seed; it may be sown any time from the beginning of October to December: with careful draining this plant may be made a perennial, in which character its roots from tubers like the dahlia, and in this state may be taken up, and preserved from year to year.

The Yellow Canada bean. This is one of the dwarf varieties, the seed of which is brought from the Cape, and is of recent introduction, having no particular native name; it may be treated as the foregoing; the seed also forms a delicate article for the table, dried like the haricot in France.

The Lima bean, is rarely met with, but the seed forms an extremely delicate article for the table, and is highly esteemed in the West Indies, as well as by all who have had the good fortune to meet with it; it is a tall climber, and if sown in October, gives a crop in February.

Propagation—of these beans is entirely by seed, of which a pint is sufficient for a row of sixty feet, putting them in at two and a half inches asunder, letting the rows be full four feet apart, and the seed buried to a depth of three inches.

Soil, &c. The soil for all kinds should be light, and but moderately moist; they must be earthed up and sticked in the same manner as peas.

The LONG BEAN, Dolichos, *Seem*, or *loobeea*, for many years supposed to belong to the same class as the kidney bean, is peculiar to warm climates, and many species of it are to be found growing wild in India; there are also several varieties cultivated, of which the best are,

1. *Small White Bean*, Dolichos gladiatus, *Mukhun seem*, sown in May or June, and giving produce in February.

2. *Red Bean*, also a variety of Dolichos gladiatus, *Rungeh mukhun seem*, sown, and yielding produce at about the same periods.

3. *Large White Bean*, another variety of Dolichos gladiatus, *Burra mukhun seem*, is also to be cultivated at the same time.

4. *Pertab Sing's Bean*, Dolichos purpureus, *Purtab Sing ke seem*, is of very large size, and when cut up forms a tolerable representative of the kidney bean. Sown in the latter end of May, it gives produce towards the close of July.

5. *Small Fruited Bean*, Dolichos catjang, *Burbutee*, or *boora*, sown in June, it gives a crop in August.

6. *Black Seeded Bean*, Dolichos lablab, *Bun seem*, *jeea seem*, or *goordal seem*, may be sown in April or May, in sandy loam, and will produce in June or July.

7. *Hill*, or *Asparagus Bean*, Dolichos sinensis, *Lobeea*, or *puharee boora*. This kind produces a long, thin, roundish pod, which forms a tolerable vegetable when boiled; it may be found in many parts of the hills, and higher lands, andhas lately been brought to more particular notice by Mr. Piddington; *vide Proceedings of the Horticultural Society of Calcutta, for August*, 1840.

8. *Assam Bean, a kind of cowage*, Stizolobium altissimum, as is supposed, *Kulee seem*, *Assam keh keeooach*, is but recently introduced as an article of food, though it grows wild in great abundance in the Hills, especially on the eastern range, and their neighbourhood; it possesses the advantage of coming in season when other vegetables are scarce; the seeds only are eaten, boiled like garden beans, which they much resemble in the taste, they ought to be gathered young, or if left to attain a large size, the skins must be taken off before they are brought to table. This should be sown in the beginning of June, and will come up in a few days, becoming fit for gathering in the middle of September.

9. *Black Bean, or Pois Noir* of the Mauritius, appearing to belong to the genus Stizolobium, *Kalee seem*, is of yet more recent introduction chiefly by Dr. Wallich, who took much pains in procuring it from Bourbon, where it is a common article of food, and may be used in the same manner as the last kind, over which it possesses the advantage of the pod not being covered with the light prickles that coat the Assam bean; it is also valuable as a food for cattle.

10. *The Winged Pea*, Tetragonolobus edulis, *Pank kee mutur*, though belonging to a different tribe, may be included under the present head, from being used in the same manner; it may be sown in the month of May, and will yield its produce about August.

Propagation, Soil, &c.—These of the long bean tribe are all grown from seed, and require a tolerably rich soil, in which the plants grow to a very large size.

INSECTS. All the leguminous plants are liable to attacks from the plant louse, those on the pea being green, and such as attack the bean most commonly black; these can only be successfully opposed by taking off the shoots on which they are found, and destroying the insects by fire, or otherwise, at a distance from the place of growth. A beetle, or weevil frequently gets into the pods and deposits its egg in the seed when near ripening, and caterpillars will destroy the leaves being only overcome by close and frequent inspection, and removal whenever discovered.

ESCULENT ROOTS,

Esculentiæ—*ALOO KE KISM.*

The esculent rooted plants generally delight in a deeply dug, light, sandy, and well cultivated soil, the better kinds requiring tolerably dry subsoil, and moderate temperature.

POTATOE, Solanum tuberosum, *Ooulaeetee aloo*, this is the most useful, and the most generally known of this class of vegetables; when mealy one-thousand parts are found to contain two hundred of starch, forty of gluten, and twenty of sugar, the remaining seven hundred and forty being fibre. There are upwards of thirty varieties, few of which are known, or even thought of in India. They are generally procurable of sufficiently good quality in the bazar, at all times of the year, and hence in a small garden it is not generally thought worth while to attempt rearing them; unless, indeed, you desire small crops of very early new potatoes; or for the purpose of propagating any particular description. Very fine potatoes for seed may be procured from Hobart Town, and if loosely packed in barrels, shortly after they have been dug, without washing, will arrive in Calcutta in good order. A specimen of excellent white potatoes was some few years since sent to the Calcutta Horticultural Society, by Dr. J. T. Pearson, from Dôrjeelung (*vide Horticultural Society's Proceedings for August*, 1840) and there is little doubt that Calcutta, and other parts of India, may soon be supplied with seed from that source.

Much more attention should be bestowed on the selection of seed, than would be readily credited by the casual observer, for on this depends much of the future success of the crop ; the late Mr. Knight, in an article of great interest, printed in the *London Horticultural Society's Transactions*, vol. vii., says, "the fact that every variety of potatoe when it has been long propagated from parts of its tuberous roots, becomes less productive, is I believe unquestionable. * * * * The propagation of expended varieties, therefore, appears to me to be one of the causes why the crops of potatoes generally, have been found so much less than those which I have stated to have been produced here." The Futtehghur potatoe is considered the best of the Upper Provinces ; but they treat it exactly as at home, generally preferring the eyes, to every other mode of planting, although elsewhere the half, or the whole potatoe is found preferable.

Dr. Patrick Neill, in a recent work published in Edinburgh, brings to notice another circumstance with regard to the selection of seed that deserves to be generally made known, "an important fact in the cultivation of the potatoe, was observed about the year 1806 by the late Mr. Thomas Dickson of Edinburgh, viz. that the most healthy and productive plants were to be obtained, by employing as seed stock, unripe tubers, or even by planting only the wet, or least ripened ends of long shaped potatoes ; and he proposed this as a preventive of the well known disease called the *curl.*" This view has been comfirmed by Mr. Knight. Such considerations have hitherto been unthought of in this country, but they are of too great importance not to demand the attention of every cultivator, for without a regard to them productive crops cannot be expected, and the cry will still be, that such vegetables cannot be made to reach that perfection in India which they attain in Europe.

Propagation.—This may be done by seed, but it is a mode never resorted to, except with the view of obtaining new varieties; planting out sections of the tubers, containing each two or three eyes, is the most general method pursued, and was long considered the best, or only means of planting this root.

But with reference to the adoption of this system in India, Mr. J. W. Masters, in an article read at a meeting of the Horticultural Society in Calcutta, says, "So " far as my experience goes, a potatoe of a moderate " size, having three or four good eyes, is far better " than a part of a large one, and generally produces a " better crop." This is fully borne out, as a general rule, by experiments in England, where the late Mr. Knight suggested (*London Horticultural Transactions*, vol. vii.), that planting whole tubers at greater distances than had usually been adopted, would afford a larger proportionate produce. On this subject, too, another authority gives the following results of experiment—" we planted out sets of apparent excellence in some drills; and being hard run for seed, we used for some contiguous drills (of precisely similar soil, and with dung from the same heap) the refuse of our potatoes, not larger than walnuts. These have grown *luxuriantly* and without a single failure; while the cut seed failed altogether in numerous instances, and in no case pushed forth such vigorous stems as those which proceeded from the whole potatoes."—*Practical Husbandry by Mr. Martin Doyle.*

It is worthy of observation that the eyes near the top end have been found to produce a crop that comes to maturity much earlier than those from the root end of the potatoe, and this is deserving particular attention by those having small gardens, and hence planting this esculent for early production, rather than for quality; the proper time for planting is September and October. They should be put in drills about three feet distant, and from eight to twelve inches apart, being covered with earth from three to five inches in depth.

Soil, &c. The best is a light, fresh, unmixed loam, in which they will thrive without any manure, and in such land unimproved though it be, they will always possess the finest flavor. In a wet soil the potatoe gets sickly and watery, as well as infested with insects and worms, fresh unrotted manure gives a disagreeable flavor to the root, and those cultivated in soil tempered with old mellow dung, rotten leaves, or *vegetable* mould, are, on this account, most esteemed, although what is called littery soil will produce the earliest, and largest crop. After the plants have appeared, a deep hoeing with the pronged hoe, should be given, and when they reach about four inches in height, the earth around them should be brought up to strengthen their growth, and promote increase below, repeating the operation until the original set is at least fifteen inches below the top of the ridge, at the same time carefully eradicating all weeds; until the plants spread sufficiently to be able themselves to keep them down, and lastly, when they appear, pinching off the blossoms to increase the crop; an operation which, trifling as it may appear, Mr. Knight estimated would—"add an ounce in weight to the tubers of each plant, or above a ton of produce per acre." *Vide London Horticultural Society's Transactions*, vol. i.—The drying up of the stalks, or holm, as it is called, is a sign that the crop is fit to take up, and it should not be touched, save to dig a few new potatoes, before this sign appears; the digging is best done with the pronged digging hoe, which is less liable to injure the tubers than the flat kind. The holm makes a good manure.

Before quitting this subject, although perhaps not, strictly speaking, a part of horticulture, a few remarks may not be considered, misplaced on this root as an article of agricultural produce.

It is but a few years since this most useful esculent was only grown by a few, for the supply of European residents alone; its good qualities have, however, now become known to most natives, and there are, consequently, but few bazars in the country where the potatoe is not to be found; this is especially the case in Buhar and the Western provinces, where they may be met with as large, and as good flavoured as the ordinary run in Great Britain; and where they also form a common article of diet among the natives of all classes and castes. Nevertheless much remains to be done with respect to the culture of this article; no attention appears to have been yet paid to the character, or sort of what is cultivated, whether as regards quality or productiveness, nor do we find even that any inquiry has been made as to the most fitting soil to be found in India for its culture; we are told, it is true, and personal experience leads to the same conclusion, that Tirhoot, Arrah, and the neighbourhood of Hooglee yield, as is supposed, the largest proportion of potatoes, but as yet there does not appear to have been any attempt made at accounting for this greater production, nor do we find it any where accurately recorded, what the amount of produce has been from any given portion of land, and we are consequently ignorant of its value as a crop; the only account published that attempts such an estimate, appears in Mr. L. DaCosta's translation of the "*Deewan Pusund*;" by this, the ground requires seven or eight ploughings in its preparation, besides four or five harrowings; the seed required is three seers to the beegah; the subsequent culture being four hoeings, and twelve to fourteen times irrigating. It is to be remembered that this calculation applies only to the Upper Provinces, where the soil being more clayey requires more ploughing, and watering than in Bengal; a fair average account, therefore, will stand thus for one beegah:—

Rent one half, as other crops will occupy the lands during the remainder of the year,................	2	0
5 Ploughings,....	1	4
Harrowing,......	0	6
3 Men planting,..................	0	6
Cost of 3 seers of seed,............	0	9
Hoeing twice,....................	1	8
Watering 4 times, ...	1	8
Expense, ... Rs.	7	9

The produce of this, on the authority of the before mentioned work, would be from seven to ten maunds; in the latter case giving, at one rupee twelve annas per maund, about Rs. 17 : 8 : 0, the number of pounds being about eight hundred and twenty. But this is on such very doubtful authority, that it can hardly be taken as a datum for calculation—which has yet therefore, to be found. In the absence of such information we can only refer to results in England. Some fifty years ago 400 bushels were considered as an extraordinarily good return from an acre,—equalling about 21,400 pounds—this would, however, be 87 maunds per beegah. But the Encyclopædia of Agriculture, published in 1831, by Loudon, calculates the produce per acre at from five to eight tons, and adds that " the greatest produce is from the yam, which has been known to produce twelve tons, or 480 bushels, per acre"—the average of the former return being equal to 14,560 lbs., and the amount of the latter 26,880 lbs.

Mr. Robertson, of Kilkenny, in an article that appeared in the Gardener's Magazine of October 1838, states his improved culture to have raised the produce to 200 barrels of 20 stone each, or about 32,000 lbs. per acre, about 130 mauns from a beegah. Speaking of various experiments on the varieties of the potatoe, another writer, in the same periodical, (March 1836) states, that in the previous year he had obtained from the agricultural sort 572 bushels (38,324 lbs.); from the bread fruit potatoe 689 bushels (46,163 lbs.); and from the poor man's profit 636 bushels (42,612 lbs.), each per acre, or, on an average of sorts, about 172 mauns per beegah. This last kind is described as " a round purple and white potatoe, very good for the table," hardy and easy of culture, very similar, apparently, to the description ordinarily met with in India. Another author pronounces that "the produce of the potatoe varies so greatly, that it is difficult to say what may be regarded as a medium return. Generally speaking, the crops produced in England and Ireland are greater than those produced in Scotland. In Lancashire the produce is reckoned to be from 8 to 12 tons per acre; in Scotland a fair produce is held to be 8 tons per Scotch acre, which is equal to 62-5 tons per English acre," (14,336 pounds —Ms. 174 33-4 about Ms. 58-4 per beegah)—*David Low's Elements of Practical Agriculture.*

But the most extraordinary improvement on record appears in the experiments made by the late lamented Mr. T. A. Knight, published in the Transactions of the Horticultural Society of London; and these are the more deserving of attention, because they exhibit a regular progressive improvement: it is not, however, necessary here, to trace the early steps of improvements, the object being only to shew what may be done with this valuable root; and this notice is therefore confined to his paper, appearing in the *5th part of the 1st vol. second series, of the Transactions*; in this Mr. Knight says, that he "*found some difficulty in obtaining credit for the accuracy of his statement,*" that one acre had yielded 670 bushels of 80 lb. each, or 53,600 lbs. and he, therefore, invited several farmers and gardeners to witness the digging of his crop in 1832, when the internal plantation, after removing the outside rows, and end plants, yielded 964 bushels and 43 lbs. or 77,163 lbs. per acre; this appears, it must be confessed, scarcely credible, except on such undoubted authority, but being so proved, it may serve as a text for improvement wherever it is mentioned; forming a series of facts well deserving of being considered wherever the root itself may take its way, since they shew a progressive rise, the consequence of careful and assiduous attention to results; this, in all their various branches, amounting in the example last shewn to a rate of produce equal to 314 mans from the small space of one beegah. The average of the above quoted rates of produce would equal one hundred and forty-nine mans from the beegah, which at even eight annas per man would give a return of somewhat above Rs. 74: a sum that would certainly bear the expense of a much higher cultivation than has ever yet been bestowed, still securing to the grower a superior rate of profit to almost any article of Indian produce. It is much to be regretted, however, that there is no accurate detail of produce in the north western provinces.

INSECTS AND DISEASES. The red worm, and the grub are the most injurious insects, but these may be remedied by mixing a small portion of lime with the soil; but as an excess of this would injure the potatoe, a frequent change of soil, not cultivating the same spot with this vegetable two years in succession, is the only sure preventive. The *curl* is a disease common to potatoes, and is by some supposed to arise from the tubers, whence the sets have been taken, having been exhausted by over ripening; although others assert it to arise from a grub in the roots.

JERUSALEM ARTICHOKE, Helianthus tuberosus, *Khoor purst, khana la'ek,* is a species of sunflower, growing often to ten, or twelve feet in height; it bears on its roots large clusters of roundish tubers, something like potatoes, or perhaps in appearance more assimilating to ginger, which are sweet and pulpy, containing a large portion of sugar, whence they form a nourishing and wholesome food, and were formerly, before the introduction of the potatoe, which it surpasses in nutritive qualities, in very high esteem. If planted in rows from east to west, they will afford an useful shade to such plants as require it in the hot weather.

Propagation—is best performed by planting the tubers whole, but some prefer sets, or cuttings of the roots, in rows two feet apart, running north and south inserting them from four or five inches deep in the soil.

Soil, &c. They will thrive in almost any soil, prefering however a light, friable loam, but like most other vegetables are apt to degenerate if continued too long in the same ground; the best way, therefore, to secure continuance of good roots is, to take them up every cold season, replanting them in fresh soil; this is the more advisable, as they multiply so fast, that it is not easy to clear the ground of them when they have once established themselves in any spot; on this account also, it is necessary, in taking them up, to be very careful to clear out every particle of root, its off-sets, and out runners. The earth, if a large sized tuber be desired, should be kept clear of weeds, and occasionally brought up round the stems.

The TURNIP, Brassica rapa, *Shulgum*, needs no description, as the use of the root is familiar every where. It is a nourishing, and wholesome article of food, containing seven parts of starch, and one of gluten, with a large portion of nitrogen and water, out of the thousand. The tops, or young leaves, form a pleasant vegetable if boiled as greens. In estimation of sorts, the first place, both as respects tenderness and flavor, must be given to the *American flat winter turnip*, of which Cobbett observes most justly, it is "the finest turnip I ever tasted." This grows to above four inches in diameter, but is never more than from an inch and a half to two inches in thickness, with a fine tap root springing exactly from the centre. This kind should not be sown till the beginning of November, when it will be fit to pull early in January. It will be best if transplanted, rejecting all the week or sickly plants; as, indeed, is the case with turnips generally, in this country.

The early Dutch, the early stone, and *the globe,* Brassica rapa, *Sofêd shulgum,* are the next best sorts, and, if English seed be used, will be found to give the finest flavor if sown from the middle to the end of November; they require about two months and a half to be fit to pull.

The Botân is a good flavored turnip, of a yellow color, and if left to come to perfection in the spot where sown, it will be ready in five, or six weeks.

The Swedish Turnip, Brassica rutabaga, or campestris, *lal shulgum,* is coarse and strong flavored, often growing to a very large size, and should not have a place at the table, though affording fine wholesome food for cattle; and, in this respect, deserving more attention than it has hitherto received in India; whence, although not strictly a part of horticulture, a few remarks may be excused on a root that has become of such importance, to the farmer and the grazier; the more as it does not appear that any work has yet referred to it, as an article of fodder in India. It appears to delight in the description of soil most easily procurable in Bengal, and that is, a sandy loam; this, in field culture, should be liberally treated with manure, well rotted, to which bone dust may be added with good effect, and might be supplied in every village,—the whole being inserted in drills, on which the seed should be sown, so as to place it in direct contract with the manure; the young plants being subsequently thinned out to some eight or ten inches apart.

It appears that with careful culture, in Norfolk, this crop will yield fifteen tons per acre, according to the calculation in Mr. Loudon's "Encyclopædia of Agriculture;" but Mr. Martin Doyle, in a late work on Husbandry, shews forty-six tons, and frequently even sixty tons weight of fodder for cattle, to be the produce of an acre; the average of which estimates would be equal to some three hundred and sixty mâns from a beegah, and would, even at four annas the mân, yield a return of ninety rupees.

Propagation—is wholly by seed. If to be left where sown, a bed of four feet broad, by twenty-eight in length, will require half an ounce of seed, but, of course, it should be sown much closer should the intention be to transplant. If the ground be dry, the seed must be well trodden down, before covering with earth, and this may be lightly sifted over to a depth of about an inch and a half, or the seed may be raked in to a moderate depth. For an early crop the sowing may be made towards the end of August, or beginning of September, at which time the turnip will often begin to put forth the seed leaves within twenty-four hours; when so sown, this will yield a crop by the end of October; the sowings for late crops may be continued until January.

Soil, &c. The turnip requires a light, rich soil,

well broken by cultivation; if a large portion of sand predominate it is to be preferred; and should dung be requisite, it must not be fresh, or it will afford shelter and encouragement to the fly; a plentiful supply of moisture, however, must be afforded during the whole period of growth. As soon as the young leaves are about an inch broad, the turnips should be transplanted, and if such be intended, or if left to grow, they should be thinned out to about six, or eight inches distant from each other. As the roots increase in size, a few should be pulled, so as to thin the remainder out to some ten, or twelve inches apart, which should be the space allotted them in transplanting, whenever that course is pursued. A good supply of water must be daily given.

INSECTS, &c. The most injurious of these is a kind of beetle, commonly called the fly, which commences its attacks as soon as the seed leaves appear above ground: the best cure is to be found in scattering quick lime over the plants, renewing it should a shower of rain fall, before the rough leaves appear, after which it is out of all danger from this insect. At that period, however, it may be attacked by a weevil, the grub of which often makes all the leaves complete skeletons; as well as by a species of mole-cricket that burrows in the earth, and, cutting off these from the stalks, drags the leaves, to its hole. As soon as the leaves get large enough they are attacked by the green caterpillar; and when the root has formed, the turnip becomes the prey of the red ant, if kept too dry, which eating off the outer skin, gives admission to the water, causing the inside to rot, affording room to a new species of weevil to obtain admission, and deposit its grub.

The TURNIP-ROOTED CABBAGE, KOHL RABI, or KNOLE-KOLE, Brassica caulo rapa, *Ole Kole* (cor) or *Gool jur ka kula*, is perhaps not fitly named, as the bulb, or excrescence, whence the name is derived, is not on the root, but forms a sort of head to the stem. It is a good, well flavored vegetable when young, but becoming strong and disagreeable as it gets old. There is a yellow kind seldom met with in India, that forms its bulb partly in the earth, and is of superior flavor.

Propagation—is by seed, sown about the middle of September to November, or in the Upper Provinces from July, to the end of that month. Recent experiments have also shewn that slips from the previous year's plants will succeed well: especially if of a year or two standing, planted out in October, or in the Upper Provinces about September.

Soil, &c. The soil and treatment are in all respects the same as for the Cabbage.

The CARROT, Daucus hortensis, or carota, *Gajur*, is a wholesome and nourishing root, containing in a thousand parts, ninety-five parts sugar, three parts starch, and the remainder water and fibre; there are properly speaking, only two varieties; the early, and the late, these are however divided as follows:—

The white, Daucus hortensis, *sốfêd gajur*, is the earliest kind, and may be sown in the latter end of August, to yield a crop in the beginning of November; of this kind Patna seed, which answers well, is always procurable: it seldom exceeds six inches in extreme length, but will grow to a circumference of nine inches or more, and is of very good flavor.

The early horn, Daucus hortensis, *Chôtee gajur*, is the next in succession, and should be sown about the beginning of October, whence it takes three months to be fit to pull: Cape seed is generally preferred.

The long orange, Daucus hortensis, *Lumbee gajur*, is best if sown from the latter end of October, to the end of November, giving its crop in February, of full size. American seed yields the finest produce, often from twelve to fifteen inches in length, and above eight in circumference, found too, even in April, at Calcutta, of a weight, without the tops, of a pound and upwards each root; of this kind the *Altringham carrot* is in high repute, and is remarkable for a portion of the root always remaining above the ground.

Propagation—is by seed only, sown where they are to remain, as no long esculent roots should be transplanted, that operation occasioning the production of side shoots, that destroy the main root for the table.

This seed is difficult to sow, as the short hairs on the sides cause them to adhere together in lumps, whilst their lightness renders a calm day necessary for the operation; before scattering, therefore, it will be well to rub the seed between the hands with a portion of sand, or wood ashes. Some people in this country, and especially in the north western provinces prefer germinating the seed before sowing in the spot selected, by tying it up in a piece of cloth, and burying it a few days in a warm, but moist corner of the garden, but this is unnecessary. The seed ought to be very equally distributed, and trodden in before raking; about an ounce will be required for a bed of twenty-six feet long and five broad.

Soil, &c. The soil for carrots must be light and mellow, mixed with sand, and should be well dug and broken fine, to a depth of at least a foot and a half, so that no obstruction should intervene to divert the downward striking of the root from its straight course. When the young plants reach two or three inches in height, they should be carefully weeded, and thinned, to a distance of from three to five inches; and then again thinned out to six or eight inches apart, as soon as of sufficient size to draw as young carrots for soup, &c. Some of the longest and best roots of the early kinds may be planted out in December or January, in rows, at a distance of two feet, and the plants six inches apart, for seed; sticking the flower stalks as they

being roasted in the hot embers, after a partial boiling. The plant has tender stalks, climbing a great height, and the roots often grow to so large a size, as to weigh from ten, to twenty pounds each. The best kind, found in the plains, is the round yam, but this must yield to the superiority of those found in the hills, the best of which is small in size, and of yellow flesh. The most common is the spined yam, but it is hard, dry, and tasteless.

Propagation—is effected by planting out the smaller tubers, or part of the large ones, at a distance of two feet apart in April and May, coming to maturity in November and December.

Soil, &c. The earth for this root should be light and open, with a good mixture of vegetable mould, or decayed leaves, &c. It requires little, or no subsequent culture.

The SWEET POTATOE, Convolvolus batatas, *Pund aloo*, or *Shukur kund aloo*, is a plant of the convolvolus species; the root long, and from an inch to three inches in diameter, with a red outside skin, and the flesh, a transparent white; sweet, and tender when young, but getting stringy as it grows old. It is, however, a wholesome root, possessing much nourishment, containing a larger portion of water, and considerably more sugar in its composition than the yam; the leaves are used by natives as sag, or greens. The usual time for planting is April; which will then be fit to dig from

September to December. A second crop may be put in the ground in August or September.

Propagation—is by dividing the roots, or by planting out the smaller tubers, about three feet apart.

Soil, &c. The soil and cultivation is the same as for the potatoe.

The EGYPTIAN ARUM, Arum colocasia, *Kuchoo, Kuchooa*, or *Arooee;* this plant has a large thick oblong or round root, which, when raw, is hot and acrid, but becomes more palatable by cooking, though after all but a coarse article of food; several species of Arum are used in the same manner by natives, some of them having a slightly acid flavor.

Propagation—is performed by dividing the roots, which should be planted out from July to November.

Soil, &c. Most soils agree with it, but it chiefly delights in a sandy loam; producing from September to January.

Before closing the subject of esculent roots, it may be as well to mention that there are two plants of this class that have of late years come into use in Europe, which, from their character, and the soil they require, as well as the circumstances of others of the same genera being known to thrive in this country, are well deserving attention by such as are curious in horticulture. These are the Tuberous rooted Oxalis (O. crenata), producing tubers about the size of a walnut, of quality excellent, somewhat resembling a new potatoe, with the additional flavor of a nut; the young leaves, and shoots are a good addition to a salad, being a pleasant acid, and the stalks peeled, may be used in tarts like rhubarb. Another is, a new species of Indian cress (Tropæolum tuberosum), considered equal in quality to the Oxalis, and, when boiled, of very delicate flavor.

SPINACEOUS PLANTS—*SAG KE KISM*.

The excellence of this class of vegetables consists in the succulency of their leaves.

The SPINACH, Spinacia, *Isfanaj*, or *Isfanakh* of the true kind, according to horticulturists, is composed of very little sugar, with a great deal of water and pulpy fibre; the leaves being used either boiled, alone or with gravies, &c. The several varieties differ little in their actual quality, or flavor as partaking of a bitter principal, but the Spanish is to be preferred for India, as more easily cultivated, and affording a larger crop of leaves, as well as not being so subject as the other sorts to the attack of insects.

The Prickley Spinach, Spinacia spinosa, *Isfanakh*, should be the latest sown, say, for instance, the middle of October, and requires a month to yield a good crop, the leaves being then very juicy, and of a lighter, and brighter green than the other sorts, as well as of better flavor.

The Round Spinach, Spinacia glabra, *Isfanakh*, is

also very good; it may be sown from the beginning of September to the end of November, and takes about a month to be fit to gather; very good seed is obtainable from Patna.

The Spanish Spinach, Spinacia olearacea, *Pulung*, as it is called here, and by the seedsmen at the Cape; appears to be the same as what is termed in England the Flanders spinach, and of which the editor of the *Gardener's Magazine, January*, 1836, says, "The plant is as economical as it is superior in quality;" the seeds are round and smooth, and the leaves large, dark colored, and extremely succulent. It may be sown from the end of September, to the end of November, and takes somewhat less than a month to perfect its crop; it should have a good supply of water while growing, and will then rapidly renew its leaves as they are taken off for use.

The Green Nepal Spinach, appears to be the same as is known in England as *New Zealand Spinach*, Tetragonia expansa, *Nepal kè sâg*, where it is esteemed as an excellent substitute for the true spinach; and if well watered will continue giving large quantities of succulent leaves during even the driest weather; it may be sown early in April, when it will yield a good supply of leaves for the end of May; the sowings should be continued from time to time, until the end of August, which last will give its crop as late as the middle of October.

Propagation.—Seed is the usual method adopted:—sown broad cast, in the proportion of one ounce to a bed of fourteen feet long, by five broad, treading the seed well down, and covering it with earth about an inch deep.

Soil, &c. Almost any soil will do for this plant, but for the late growing crops as dry a spot as possible should be selected; when the young leaves are an inch broad, they should be cleared from weeds, and thinned, wherever crowded, to about three inches apart, giving them a subsequent thinning, to double that distance, as the leaves spread.

The White Beet, Beta cicla, or B. Bengalensis of *Rox*, *Paluk sâg*, has its leaves much larger than the red, very thick and succulent; these, boiled as spinach, form a good vegetable; in England it is also esteemed for the mid-ribs and stalks which are separated from the lamina of the leaves, being sometimes stewed and eaten as asparagus under the name of chard. *The Great White*, or *Swiss* variety is the best, and may be sown at any time between the beginning of August and the end of November; if the chard be desired for use, the watering should be profuse, to promote the succulency of the stalks.

The Green, or Sea Beet, Beta Maritima, *Paluk sâg*, is but a variety of the last, and bears the same character in every respect.

Propagation, Soil, &c.—These are the same as for

spinach, save that the plants must be kept at a distance of from ten to fourteen inches from each other.

The ORACHE, or, MOUNTAIN SPINACH, Atriplex hortensis, and rubra, *Buhtooa*, and the OVAL SPIKED AMARANTH, Amarantus gangeticus, *Subsee-sâg* and *Lal-sâg*, are commonly known here as red, and green *sâg*, the leaves possessing a slightly acid flavor; the green kinds are boiled as spinach, but the red, which are the most esteemed, are best dressed with butter and spicy seasoning; they may be sown at any time of the year, and will afford leaves fit to gather in a few days.

Propagation, Soil, &c.—No peculiarity of soil is required for these plants: they should, however, be kept moist, and a succession of sowings must be maintained to ensure a constant supply, except during the cold weather, when it may be allowable to give way to other vegetables of European origin.

The BLADDER SORREL, Rumex vesicarius, *Ooulaeeta chookeh*, is much used by the French and Dutch, but little by the English, who in this instance, as in many others where cooking is concerned, shew a want of taste, and deficiency of wisdom; it forms a very good sauce, or garnish, either dressed with butter, oil, &c. like the red orache, or *lâl sâg*, as it is here called. There is a species of this plant called *the Bladder dock*, Rumex vesicarius, and known among natives as *Chooka paluk*, or *chookeh*, that very much resembles the common sorrel in taste as well as in other qualities; it is believed to be indigenous, and is found in most gardens throughout India: although not always recognized, Europeans being generally better acquainted with R. Acetosa, the common field sorrel than with this variety.

Propagation—is effected either by seed or separating the roots in the beginning of November.

Soil, &c. The sorrel though growing wild in many parts of Europe in all its varieties, requires some care in India, and is best raised in a compost of sand, old dung, and garden mould in equal parts; it should be planted out at a distance of a foot asunder, and as the stalk runs up it must be cut down and the stool encouraged, by the addition of fresh mould, to throw out new shoots with large broad leaves, the common sorrel has never been known to succeed, although often tried. Other kinds of Rumex are cultivated as spinach generally by natives, but form a very inferior article for the table. The Bladder sorrel, grows well up the country, if kept constantly watered, and is worthy of more attention than is given to it if only as an *addendum* to curries.

The RED, WHITE, and SHINING MALABAR NIGHTSHADE, Basella rubra, *Póee ság;* B. alba, *Sóféd póee;* and B. lucida, *Póee,* are three varieties of an indigenous native vegetable of the climbing kind, growing to a very large size, and well known in most parts of the country; propagated either by slips, or by seed sown in September or October. It needs no peculiarity of soil, and affords an abundant supply of succulent leaves, and young shoots, which are the parts eaten, and much esteemed by natives.

The leaves of various plants of Urticaceæ, Tetragonia, and other tribes growing wild in this country, are gathered by the natives, and eaten under the general term of *sâg*, but they are little known to Europeans. Of the most common of these are the following:—

The Three stamened achyranthes, Achyranthes triandra, *Sanchee*, or *Sanchee sâg*.

The Bristly-leaved corchorus, Corchorus olitorius, *Meeta* and *khuta pät*.

The Creeping bind-weed, Convolvulus reptans, *Kulmee sâg*.

The Fenugreek, Trigonella fœnum-græcum, *Meet,hee juljulan*.

The Horse-radish tree leaf, Hyperanthera moringa, formerly Guilendina moringa, *Suhujna, or munjee*.

The Common dill, Anethum graveolens, *Sooee chooka* or *soou*.

The Knot grass, Polygonum aviculare, *Machoota sâg*.

The Ladies bed straw, Pharnoceum molluga, *Gooma sâg*.

The Meyera, Enhydra repens, *Hungtsha sâg*.

The Pumpkin leaf, Cucurbita pepo, *Shan-chee kumruhee sâg*.

The Radish leaf, Raphanus sativus, *Moolee sâg.*

The Round nettle, Urtica globulifera, *Lal looteea*, or *Lal loota kudum.*

The Snake gourd leaf, Trichosanthes anguina, *Chee-cheenga sâg.*

The Sow thistle, Sonchos orixensis, *Bun pulung.*

Besides many others; in fact, almost every green thing that is not absolutely poisonous, and comes in the way of a poor native, is termed a *sâg*, and turned to use, as an addition to his curry, or to his insipid mess of plain rice.

ALLIACEOUS PLANTS—*PEEAJ KEE KISM.*

The Onion tribes are universally known and esteemed for the stimulus and flavor they give to our food; but, though wholesome, they contain no nutriment, consisting chiefly of fibre, and possessing a very small portion only of starch.

The Onion, Allium, *Peeaj*, is familiar to all; and it is not easy to give an estimate of sorts for cultivation in this country, as the European varieties are extremely difficult to raise.

The Portugal onion, Allium cepa, *Burra peeaj*, is the largest sized, and the most mild in flavor; but the seed seldom reaches here in good order, and even when it germinates, it is hardly possible to secure a plant to reach its full size.

The Dutch blood-red onion, Allium cepa, *Gool peeaj,* is, of all the European kinds, the best suited to India; it may be sown in October or November.

The Bombay onion, Allium cepa, *Bumbuee peeaj,* is a white description, much esteemed, it should be sown towards the close of September, thinned out about six weeks after, to afford young onions for salad, and will be fit to transplant by the beginning of December.

The Patna onion, Allium cepa, *Putn'eh peeaj,* is a red kind, of good flavor; and may be sown at the same time with the preceding, but not planted out till January.

The Small red onion, Allium cepa, *Chôtee peeaj,* of native growth, may be sown at any time from the close of the rains to the end of February, the last named month being the period for putting in the most extensive crops, which may be planted out in March, and will be fit to gather in May or June.

Propagation—may be performed, either by seed, or by planting out the offsets; one ounce of seed being sufficient for a bed five feet broad by twenty in length, unless it be desired to draw a crop of young onions for salad from the ground, when two ounces of seed should be scattered on the same space.

Soil, &c. The best is a rich mellow ground, manured with very old dung, on a dry subsoil, unless required for pickling only, and then they should have a poor soil to keep them small; powdered bones, or

ASPARAGACEOUS PLANTS—*MARCHOOBA KEE KISM*.

Of this class, which comprehends nearly all the more delicate flavored vegetables, the young shoots or incipient blossoms are the eatable portions.

The ASPARAGUS, Asparagus officinalis, *Marchooba, nokdoon,* or *isfuraj*, is the chief of this class, and gives name to the whole, the young shoots being well known as a delicate article for the table; it is considered a wholesome article of food. The few varieties in Europe are the result of cultivation, but are little known in this country; the Battersea kind has been sent out here occasionally, and has proved pretty good. The American has however, turned out the best.

Propagation—is best performed from seed, but it is more tedious than the common mode of dividing the roots, generally resorted to in forming a bed, on account of the plants so put in becoming productive one, or more properly two seasons before seedlings, these last however, generally yielding the finest shoots for the table. The seed should be trodden down gently before raking in; it may be sown at any time that it is procurable fresh and healthy, though the end of September is, perhaps, the fittest period; the quantity requisite being a pint to a bed of 5 feet broad by 30 in length. The young plants must be kept cleanly weeded until pricked out, and again as they grow fit for transplanting.

Soil, &c. The soil for asparagus can hardly be too rich or too strongly manured with dung and litter; at the same time it should have so much of sand, as will make it sufficiently light to allow the young shoots to force their way easily through it, or they will be stunted and deformed,

The best plan, in forming a bed, is to trench the ground to a depth of two and a half feet, with a width of some five feet, placing a layer of brick or *konkur* below all, and then putting sand mixed with plenty of good dung upon this formation at the bottom of the trench, for a depth of a foot and a half; over that should be deposited about six inches of dung alone, and above that again the like depth of rich light mould; bearing in mind that above all things a wet subsoil is to be avoided, as it would rot the shoots. When you have filled up the trench over these layers of dung, &c. with a strong, rich, loamy, or sandy soil, make small trenches at a foot apart, and six inches deep, and put in the young plants from the growing bed, or the divided roots, as it may be, at about nine inches apart in the row, covering well in and lightly with the earth taken out of the trench. For the first one or two years the plants must be allowed to run up to stalk, only clearing the bed from weeds, and occasionally stirring the surface; but in the second year if from divided roots, and the third if seedlings, when the plants have runs to seed and begin to dry, cut them down close, and loosen the earth all over the bed with the pronged hoe, dressing the whole with a fresh layer of sand, vegetable mould, and well rotted dung. The bed should then be well watered every day, making a ridge of earth all round to prevent the water from running off, and when the young shoots appear, cut only the largest, leaving the others to run up to seed, as too large a crop must not be exacted, or the crowns* will be weakened for future supply. From this period, with care, a bed will continue to furnish a good supply for ten or twelve years. The supply of water during the time that the stools are giving their crop can hardly be too plentiful, it is, therefore, well to have the asparagus bed near the tank, or at all events on the side of the main stream from the pumps, so that it may be flooded once a day during the hot, and dry weather. If an early crop be desired, one of the beds, after the plants have been cut down and dressed, should be guarded with a ridge all round, and flooded, allowing the water to remain on for two or three days. Every year, about the month of June, the stalks that have run to seed, beginning to decay, should be cut down close, the weeds must then be cleared

---

* The clusters or heads of the roots whence the young shoots are grown up, sometimes called also stools.

off, a good dressing of strong manure should then be given, and the whole well dug with the pronged hoe.

The SEA KALE, Crambe maritima, having no native name, is a hardy, but highly esteemed vegetable; the young shoots, and stalks of the unfolded leaves being the parts used. It is mentioned here more as an article deserving of attention, than as one of actual cultivation, as it is believed few if any instances have occurred of its having been yet successfully cultivated. Within the personal knowledge of the author of this little work, several experiments have been made in sowing the seed, most of which failed altogether, none even germinating; four attempts, however, so far succeeded as to prove the practicability of adding this delicious vegetable to our Indian stock of garden productions; the plants in these instances having, after thriving well to from four, to twelve leaves, been destroyed partly by insects, and partly by having the dressing of ashes, or sand put on to the bed too soon.

Propagation—must at first be from seed, and gardeners agree that it is generally best so to raise this vegetable. The fittest time for sowing is believed to be about the middle of November; the quantity of seed being, if sown to transplant, in the proportion of two ounces to a bed of seven feet long by five in breadth, but if sown to remain, the same quantity will serve for a plot five feet broad and thirty in length, sown in drills two feet apart; the seeds must be put in at a depth of two inches, and require about a month before the plant shews itself above ground. It may also be propagated by offsets, but seed is preferable.

Soil, &c. For the seed bed, a good compost of well rotted dung, sand, and vegetable mould in equal parts; perhaps, even a larger portion of sand would be preferable for beds where the plants are to remain. For which a spot must be selected, having a dry bottom, and it must be trenched in the same way as for asparagus, mixing a rather larger portion of sand with the compost with which the trenches are filled, and in this the plants are to be inserted at a distance of two feet each way. No crop ought to be taken for the first two years; but in the third, when the plants are beginning to shoot, the beds should have a covering thrown over them of about an inch of pure sand, or sand and ashes. and a blanching pot should be put over each plant, pressed down closely to exclude all light and air; stable litter must then be put closely all round the pots, and even raised a little above them, taking care, however, that the temperature within the pot shall not exceed 90° of Fahrenheit, in a short time the shoots may be well blanched, and ready for cutting. The proper pot for sea kale is made with a moveable lid to facilitate the examination of the plants and gathering the shoots without disturbing the litter.

The ARTICHOKE, Cynara Scolyma, *Kungur*, or *artuchuk* (cor.) is cultivated for its flower heads, which in an immature state, freed from the leaves, bristles, and seed-down, are a favourite vegetable; the conical is the best flavored variety here.

Propagation—by seed is the best mode of extending this plant, sown in the beginning of August, or in the upper provinces in June and July, under shelter, either in a small bed, or what is preferable, in pots; but it may be done by slipping off the young shoots or suckers, and planting them out after the close of the rains, say in September, into sheltered beds of rich earth.

Soil, &c. The soil best suited to the artichoke is a rich mould, with a small admixture of sand, and the best way to form your bed for these plants is to select a spot, in the month of June or July, and cover it, to the depth of from four to six inches, with a mixture of decayed vegetable matter, and well rotted cow dung, in the proportion of three parts of the former to one of the latter, letting this be well dug in, and the ground allowed to remain untouched, except to keep it clear of weeds. As soon as the seed leaves fall off, the young plants should be pricked out into a sheltered bed, at a distance of four inches apart; and at six inches distance when they reach the height of about three or four inches. About the end of November or beginning of December, mark out the spot you have retained for your bed into squares of about two feet on each side, and two feet apart; take out the earth to a depth of about one foot, and fill the hole with a mixture of sand, vegetable mould, and rotted cow dung, in equal portions; then transplant the artichokes into these squares; putting four in each, at a distance of one foot from the centre, fixing the root firmly, and giving water every day until it begins to shew new leaves, and then continuing a more moderate supply of moisture until the blossom shoots appear, when the earth must be brought up, leaving a sort of channel round each group, and the watering increased to the roots, to enlarge the size of the main heads; all the lateral ones should be taken off in a very young state, to increase the strength of the principal stems; some cut off the ends of the large leaves for the same purpose. Mr. Gordon, a well known grower of this vegetable in England, found that running a bit of lath, or rather splinter, through the stem, at right angles, about four inches from the head, and keeping the wound open, greatly increased the size of the head, operating in the same manner as ringing on trees.—*Vide* "*Gardener's Magazine, January,* 1835." As soon as they have done giving fruit, the plants should be taken up, and the shoots and slips put out in a sheltered bed to form the next year's supply of plants.

ACETACIOUS PLANTS—*KAHOE KEB KISM*

are generally eaten raw, and are rather articles of condiment and luxury, than of food.

The LETTUCE, Lactuca, *Kahoo* or *kuma*, is a cool and wholesome salad, containing a little sugar, and a large portion of water and fibre, together with a bitter milky juice of a slightly soporific nature. The varieties are numerous, but these are little sought for, or attended to in India.

The Cos Lettuce, Lactuca sativa, *Bura kahoo* or *k'hus* from which latter, the Arabic name, it would appear that the English one was derived, proving the variety to be of Eastern origin; it is upright, of an oblong shape, and when full grown tender, and of delicate flavor. It should not be sown before the middle of November, and may then be continued at intervals to the middle of December; if sown later it is apt to run to seed, without forming heart. The plants from Patna seed will require only six weeks to be fit to cut, but cannot be depended on as true to their kind, whilst those raised from English seed, will require from eight to ten weeks.

The Cabbage Lettuce, Lactuca palmata, and crispa, *Bunda kahoo*, are the proper descriptions for early and late sowings, and these may be commenced in the middle of August, or even earlier; but in this case they must be cut when small, and not full grown, or they will run to leaf, and to seed in a straggling, unhealthy manner. Sown in July, very good lettuces may be had in September, and continued every ten days until the end of December; they take from six weeks to two months to be fit to cut. An up country correspondent says,—"You may have salad (lettuce) almost the whole year, in the month of January mark half a dozen of the finest lettuces for seed, when the seed begins to ripen, gather it every day, and collect the different kinds separately in phials, after drying in the sun." It would be better, however, only to seek in each season one variety, as that will be the only means of keeping true to each kind, since when several varieties are within any short distance of each other the bees and other insects will transfer the pollen, so as to hybridize to the degeneration of the produce, and hence it is that what is known as Patna seed can now be so little relied upon for the truth of its crop."

"Sow once a fortnight in the following manner; prepare some rich mould in a small bed, and make a trench all round six inches deep, water the bed and sprinkle the seeds upon it thinly, and sift some dryish mould over them, and cover the bed with a mat laid on sticks till the plants come up: if the bed wants water, fill the trench but do not pour water over the bed as the earth will cake *(ch'hupree)*, and prevent the seeds from growing. When the plants come up remove the mats, except in very hot weather, at which time they must be put on in the middle of the day, plant them at 6 to 8 inches apart in a fine soil, and shelter them from rain or heat."

The Brown Lettuce, Lactuca sativa, *Kala Kahoo*, is vapid, coarse, and indifferent both in flavor and appearance.

Propagation—is performed only by seed, the early crops being sown in sheltered beds, or pots under cover; a quarter of an ounce being sufficient for a bed of eight feet long and five broad; the seed must be lightly raked in, and then the earth gently pressed down to make it more difficult for the ants to abstract; for if not carefully watched, they will take the whole away in a few hours after the seed is sown; on which account it is advisable to strew the ground thickly with pounded turmeric, at the time of sowing.

Soil, &c. A rich mellow soil is requisite for lettuces, and they are better if transplanted when about three inches in height, into rows ten inches apart, and from ten to fifteen inches distant in the rows. Such as it is desired to forward quickly for the table should be tied up to whiten the hearts, but for the main crop this is not necessary, except with the Cos lettuce.

The Endive, Cichorium endivium, *Kasnee*, or *kuroo* is a pleasant salad, but requiring to be blanched to remove the bitter taste; it has the same properties as the lettuce. The white curled, is the best kind in this country, and as its seed ripens well, a portion should always be preserved for early sowings, which may commence in the middle of August, and be continued till January. Endive requires about ten weeks before it is cut It is one of those vegetables which the encouragement given by the exhibitions of the Horticultural Society have best succeeded in improving, and from the period of its being in season may be considered an acquisition.

Propagation—is by seed, an ounce being a fit quantity for a bed fifteen feet in length by five broad. The seed should be thinly scattered, and well raked in.

Soil, &c. A rich mellow earth gives the finest heads, the plants being early thinned in the seed bed, and transplanted when they attain a height of about four inches, into rows about eighteen inches asunder, and about twelve inches apart. In planting, the tap root must be shortened, and the long leaves trimmed; the plants must have a good supply of water while growing, and when the heart becomes full, they should be blanched, by covering with a blanching pot, a flower pot reversed, or by tying up the leaves by the tops, during which but little water should be given, and that close on the roots without touching the leaves: and it is to be borne in mind that this operation must not be performed on too many plants at once, but in regular succession, with so many only as are required for daily consumption, as when once blanched the endive soon rots, from the confinement, and want of air.

The CELERY, Apium graveolens, *Ujooa'en khorasanee, or kurufus*, is used as a salad when blanched, the tops, and unblanched plants adding a fine flavor to soups, stews, &c. When blanched it contains a little starch and sugar, and much fibre. There are four varieties, all deserving of cultivation.

1. *The Red solid,* Apium graveolens, *Lal ujooa'en,* is a fine hardy description, but rather apt to be strong. It should not be sown before the middle of November, when, if the seed be English, it will take about ten days to germinate, and will be fit for the table at the end of March, or the beginning of April.

2. *The White solid,* Apium graveolens, *Sôfêd ujooa'en,* is an early sort, and may be sown in August, in a sheltered spot; by so doing it may be made to give a crop in December.

3. *The Italian,* Apium graveolens, *Chôta ujooa'en,* is a tender, well flavored variety, but does not reach so large a size as the two former kinds. The middle of October is a good time to sow, and you will by so doing have the plants fit for the table in January: but in the upper provinces the latter end of March, or the beginning of April is considered the best time for sowing; even then, however, some have found January or February suited for this operation, and English seed put in, in November, will generally give a crop from February to April.

4. *The Turnip-rooted,* or *Celeriac,* is little known in India.

Propagation.—All sorts are raised from seed, a

Propagation—is performed by seed only, which may be put in at any time of the year, taking care, however, that it is sheltered during the heavy rains; it germinates rapidly, requiring only a few hours in the hot weather. One ounce should be sown on a bed of three feet by five, in small drills, and rather thinly scattered on a light well pulverized mould, covered very thinly by sifting the earth over it from a small sieve.

The WATER-CRESS, Nasturtium officinale, *Deeoo-kandur*, *suzal*, or *panee ka halum*, is a favorite salad, especially as eaten with bread and butter at breakfast.

Propagation—is performed either by seed or dividing the roots or offsets, put out in large pots or gumblas, and kept nearly covered with water in a sheltered situation. The water must be frequently changed, and the plants renewed every year, or they will acquire a disagreeable earthy flavor. Where the water-cress is desired to be grown more extensively, a bed may be formed in a shady situation, of a moderate slope, so that the water may run off gradually—and at the most elevated part one or more jars should be placed with small holes at the bottom so as to allow the water to escape slowly; care must be taken that the jars are regularly filled once a day, and that weeds are not suffered to intrude among the plants.

The PURSLANE, Portulaca Quadrifida, and oleracea, *Choolee nooneea*, or *kurfeh*, have round full stems and fleshy leaves, very slightly acid in flavor; esteemed cooling, by some. It is used as an ingredient in salads, but is a poor tasteless thing. There are two varieties differing only in the mode of growth, the one producing an upright stem, and the other having its branches prostrate.

Propagation, Soil, &c.—The Purslane is raised by seed sown in almost any kind of soil, and at almost any period; though it thrives best if sown in July, when its crop will be fit to take from September to January.

CUCURBITACEOUS PLANTS.—*KHEERA KEE KISM.*

This class of vegetables are all of a cooling nature and generally much esteemed by all classes.

The CUCUMBER, Cucumis, *K'heera,* is used green, sliced as a salad, or pickled when young. There are very many varieties; those best known and esteemed in India, are the following:—

1. *The Long green,* Cucumis sativus, *Lumba k'heera* growing about ten inches in length. American seed is preferred; it is best if sown at the end of April, when it will fruit freely in July.

2. *The Nepal,* Cucumis sativus, *Naépala k'heera,* is a fine delicate flavored cucumber, of a white color, and large size. It may be sown at any time between the beginning of June and the beginning of August, yielding its fruit from August to November.

3. *The Cape Dwarf*, Cucumis sativus, *Chóta k'heera*, is a good little cucumber that may be advantageously sown from March to October.

Propagation—is by seed, sown at a sufficient distance to give the plants room to run, putting several seeds in each hole however, and afterwards thinning out such as are weakly.

Soil, &c. The soil should be rich and light, well manured with stable dung;—when the plants acquire the fourth leaf, they should be thinned to two plants in each hole, and these stopped by pinching off the leading shoots;—as the runners spread, they should be so trained as to be kept pretty clear from each other, and if the soil be low or wet, or the rains heavy, it is well also to raise them on a trellise, or *muchan*.

The Gourd, Cucurbita lagenaria, *Toomra*, and *tudoo;* of these there are very numerous varieties in India, the fruit being used in many native dishes as well as in European cookery, and the tender shoots boiled by natives as a kind of greens. The fruit is considered cooling, but has not much flavor. The most approved and generally grown kinds are the *Pumpkin*, cucurbita pepo, *kumruha*, rather sweetish in flavor; and the *Bottle gourd*, cucurbita lagenaria, *kudoo*, watery and almost tasteless.

The Most useful cucumber, Cucumis utilissimus (Roxburgh), *Kukree*, will, from its appearance as brought to market, be more generally classed as a gourd than a cucumber, especially as it has more the flavor and use of the former: the fruit is oval, smooth, and variegated with shades of yellow and green, keeping a long time if hung up in the shade, and by the natives is held in high esteem. The seed is sown from April to the end of the year, and grows to the extent of about four feet as a trailer; yielding fruit from June, or July to January.

Propagation.—They are all propagated by seed, and some of them run to a very large size, covering a small native hut in a very short time. The soil and cultivation is the same as for the cucumber.

The SQUASH, or VEGETABLE MARROW, Cucurbita melopepo, or rather it is believed ovifera, *Sufura koomra* is a very delicate vegetable of the gourd kind; and has, several varieties not, however as yet, distinguished by natives; the chief of which are—

1. *The Crook-necked,* when about six inches long is well flavored, but it soon gets hard and stringy. Seed sown in January will give fruit in April.

2. *The Early long-warted,* is more delicate than the foregoing, and if sown in October will give its fruit in December. The sowings may be repeated every fortnight until the end of January, and again in April until June.

3. *The early Scollop,* is the best flavored of any of the squash kind. It may be sown advantageously from the middle of October to the end of January, and

will give fruit in perfection and abundance from the middle of December to the middle of April.

Propagation—is only by seed, and it is best not to transplant them, but let them remain where sown, in little cricles about six feet apart, drawing out the weakly plants. The best seed is from America.

Soil, &c. The soil should be a rich loam, and they must be trained on upright sticks, or a small trellis, to insure the setting of the fruit. It will be well to fertilize the female blossoms by approaching the anthers of the male flower, when well charged with pollen, to the stigma of the female blossom.

INSECTS. The greatest enemies to the above named cucurbitaceous plants, are the ants, which pierce and destroy the young fruit, and the red beetle, called the soldier, attacking the leaves, and blossoms.

The DIOECOUS SNAKE GOURD, Trichosanthes dioica, *Puloonl*, is a small creeping plant of the gourd kind, yielding a fruit about the size of an egg, much used in curries.

The COMMON SNAKE GOURD, Trichosanthes anguina, *Chuchoonga*, or *jeenga* produces a fruit about a foot long, used by natives in curries, and pleasant flavored enough, but apt to be woody.

Propagation—of these two last is by seed sown from January to March, to yield fruit from March to September, or they may be increased by parting the roots.

Soil, &c. The plants require a great deal of room, but almost any soil is equally productive.

The LUFFA, many angled, Luffa acutangula, or fœtida, *Turaee, jeenga* is another indigenous plant, that affords a nice vegetable from May to the end of September, or even sometimes, later.

There are varieties of this vegetable besides the one just mentioned but none of them so much esteemed in that capacity though useful in medicine. They come in season from July to October; the chief is the *Clubbed*, Luffa clavata, *Bunturaee*, this is eaten in an unripe state in curries.

Propagation, Soil, &c.—is by seed only, sown from April to the end of June, and giving produce from May to October; any soil suits them, but they should have a trellis, or sticks for support, and to prevent the fruit from being injured by laying on the ground during the rains.

The BITTER GOURD, Momordica, *Kurêla*, has several varieties, distinguished among natives by distinct names, most of them are only found in a wild state, but the three following are cultivated, and are used in curries, to which they give a bitter flavor, that is very agreable, though not generally liked at first:—

1. *The Hairy bitter gourd*, Momordica charantia, *Kurêla*, yielding a small sized fruit used in an unripe state.

2. *The Egyptian bitter gourd*, Momordica luffa, or Luffa petandra, *G'heea tooree, puroola keendee*, having a middling sized fruit but unless very young inclined to be stringy.

3. *The Spiked bitter gourd*, Momordica muricata, *Bura kurêla*, or *aoocheea*, has a somewhat smaller fruit than the last, and is more cultivated, from being held in higher esteem.

Propagation, &c.—is by seed sown from April to the end of the year, in almost any soil. They grow to the extent of about four feet as climbers, although naturally belonging to the class of trailing plants, and yield fruit from June, or July, to January.

PLANTS, THE FRUIT OF WHICH IS USED AS A VEGETABLE.

These are most of them of a delicate nature, and chiefly of use in pickles.

The TOMATO, or LOVE APPLE, Solanum lycopersicum, or stramonifolium, *Goot bégun*, or *oowlaeeté bégun*, has a slight sub acid flavor, esteemed in soups and sauces, as well as in a green state as pickle.

The Large Red, is the best flavored, but is long in coming to perfection; the best time for sowing is the middle of October, when its fruit will be ripe about the end of January.

The Small round or *cherry*, is inferior in taste as well as size to the foregoing; its color either pale red or yellow, but it is very prolific. It may be sown either in September or October, and will give its fruit early in December.

Propagation—is performed by sowing the seed in pots, or in a small bed, where they should remain only until they reach about two inches in height. The best seed is from America. With a little care and attention in keeping the roots well earthed up, and the plants carefully sticked, they may be made to last, and give fruit all the year round.

Soil, &c. A moderately rich soil is desirable, into which they should be pricked out when from two to three inches high, at a distance of four inches, and removed when from six to eight inches in growth, to the bed where they are to fruit, standing in rows two feet asunder; the plants being eighteen inches distant from each other in the rows. They must have sticks to support them, especially if planted out late so as to be exposed to the rains.

The GARDEN EGG, OR BRINJAL, Solanum Melongena, *Bégun, b'hangun.* There are an immense variety of this plant, most of which are held in esteem, but they all require the same treatment. The chief sorts are the *Ordinary purple, the Large purple,* the *Tapering purple,* the *Bombay white,* (attaining a very large size,) the *Ordinary white,* and the *Small white.*

Propagation—is by seed, which may be sown at any period, though the best time for the large sorts, is in April or May.

Soil, &c. No particular soil is required, provided it be not too heavy, or too hard. The plants should be put in at two feet apart, and kept well weeded.

The MAIZE, or INDIAN CORN, Zea mays, *Bhuta* or *boota*, is chiefly cultivated for its ears, or cobs; which are eaten green, after being roasted over the fire, and form thus an agreable vegetable. There are several varieties, of which the white kind, grown in the hills, is the largest, and superior to the American, which has been by many supposed the finest, but not quite equal to some recently brought from Sydney; the white sort from Juanpore is also very fine, giving from 6 to 700 grains; but the small yellow kind, yielding from 4 to 500 grains, common in Bengal, is perhaps as delicate flavored as any, and the seed always procurable.

The produce of this article in England is considered good if yielding from 2 to 300 grains on each cob, and in the Gardener's Magazine for 1834, mention is made of one that gave 350 grains, as of an extraordinarily large amount.

It is an useful and wholesome grain, that deserves far more attention than has been bestowed on it in India, and coming in as a crop, when the garden is unoccupied, is well worth sowing, as it serves to keep down weeds, and its stalks yield, by burning, a large portion of ashes to manure the soil against the return of the sowing season for vegetables. In the West Indies its good qualities are duly appreciated, and this grain is almost the only food given to every kind of stock; horses fed on it thrive well; cattle and pigs are easily fattened with no other food, and all sorts of poultry become white, firm, and fat in a short time on Indian corn, whilst here its virtues are little known, and it is seldom used or turned to any good account, or even thought of by Europeans, save in its green state, roasted as an occasional vegetable. In the year 1840, and for several subsequent years near Calcutta, it has been known to yield fifteen mauns of grain, separated from the ear, from a beegah of ground.

Propagation, Soil, &c.—It is produced from seed sown in the latter end of May, which takes about two months to be fit to gather; many people, however, sow an early crop, but this generally turns out poor and indifferent, unless taken great care of; for of late years maize has been exhibited in the May vegetable show of the Horticultural Society, as firm as could be grown at any other season.

The Nasturtium, or Indian Cress, Tropæolum majus, and minus, having no native name, the seeds are used pickled, like capers, possessing an agreable pungency: or the leaves and flowers may be used in salads, or as garnish. There are a double, and a dark colored variety, but these belong more properly to the flower garden, and the plant is difficult to bring into any sufficient extent of seed growing.

Propagation, Soil, &c.—It is cultivated by seeds only, which, if sown in the middle of October, will give seeds fit to gather in March; unless the weather become too hot by that time. To secure a fine crop, however, the best way is to sow in pots, under shelter, during the rains, and put out the plants into the open ground as soon as these cease.

The CHILI, GUINEA, OR INDIAN PEPPER, Capsicum, *Murucha*, or *murcha*, needs no description to any one in this country, where it is so universally used as a condiment. The varieties are far too numerous to mention here, a few only, therefore, are noted of those most deserving the attention of Europeans.

The Large pepper, Capsicum grossum, *Bura gach murucha*, is the best for pickling, and grows to a great size; it must be gathered before it becomes red, for this purpose. The seed should be sown in August, in pots under shelter, and the fruit will be fit to pull in November.

2. *The Nepal pepper*, Capsicum sinense, *Nupala murucha*, is a good sort for use green, as a condiment, or when ripe for putting in pickles. It should be sown about the same time as the preceding.

3. *The Black round pepper*, Capsicum bicolor, *Kala murucha*, gives a good flavor to pickles, and is therefore worthy of cultivation.

4. *The Long red pepper*, Capsicum frutescens, *Lunka murucha*, is the best for drying when ripe, as a condiment; it should be sown in September.

5. *The bird pepper*, Capsicum baccatum, *D'han murucha*, is small, but very hot, and best suited for making cayenne pepper, for hot vinegar, &c. It may be sown in pots in July.

6. *The cherry pepper*, Capsicum cerasiformum, *Gool murucha*, is as biting even as the last mentioned, and is described by some authors as the species from which the Cayenne pepper of merchandize is made. This pepper serves all the other uses of this condiment, and may be sown at the same time as the last mentioned.

Propagation—is effected by seed, sown in pots, a quarter of an inch deep, and afterwards transplanted.

Soil, &c. A light, well manured soil is the best for all kinds, in which the plants should be pricked out at about four inches apart, when they attain a growth of three inches; and afterwards put out into a bed of rich light earth, when they attain six inches in height; giving them a good supply of water, and keeping them clear from weeds.

The Okro, Hibiscus esculentus, *D'hunroos, ramturuee*, or *b'heendee*, the fruit of which, in a green state, affords a very mucilaginous vegetable, much liked by some people: it is indigenous.

Propagation.—The seeds may be sown at any time

sheltered bed, from the early part of September to the end of October, by dividing the roots.

Soil, &c. When of sufficient size, the plants should be put out at eight or ten inches apart, in a poor sandy soil; they require a good share of moisture to make them flower freely.

The INDIAN WORMWOOD, Artemisia Indica, *Afsunteen, doona*, or *mustaroo*, grown chiefly for its seeds; its leaves are also useful to poultry.

Propagation Soil, &c.—Any soil suits this plant, and it may be grown either from seed, cuttings, or by division of the roots.

The COMMON BALM, Melissa officinalis, *Badrunj-booee,eh*, or *budrunk*, affords, by infusion, a grateful drink in fevers, and every garden should therefore have a few plants of it.

Propagation, Soil, &c.—It grows freely in any good garden soil, and is readily increased by dividing the roots, or by slips planted out at the close of the rains.

The LEMON GRASS, Andropogon schænanthus, *Gund bél, ug'hun gas*, like the foregoing, yields, on infusion, a refreshing drink in fevers, and should therefore be cultivated.

Propagation, Soil, &c.—It requires no particular soil, and is easily multiplied by dividing the roots.

The COMMON ROSEMARY, Rosmarinus officinalis, *Buburee'eh*, is used in infusion, and the flowers in distillation of perfumed water.

Propagation.—The finest plants are raised from seeds, but it is more generally propagated by slips.

Soil, &c. The plants should be twelve inches apart, and they like an open, free, limey soil, especially the rubbish of old buildings.

The LAVENDAR, Lavendula spica, *Nurd,* or *nardeen,* is an aromatic plant well known to Europeans, but cultivated in India only with great difficulty.

Propagation.—The most usual mode in Europe is by slips and cuttings, but it is extremely difficult to make these strike in India. The seed should be sown in the middle of November, and will find assistance either by being sown on a hot bed under glass; or, if in pots, from having a wet blanket placed over the pot, and exposed to the evaporation of the sun, as otherwise much of the seed usually fails, and even with this aid it will require a fortnight, or more, to germinate; on account of the hard shell of the seed.

Soil, &c. When the seed-leaves fall off, the plants should be put out separately into small sized pots, freely watered, and kept under shelter until they reach the height of about six inches, when they are fit to be put into the open ground; but this should only be done between the end of September and the beginning of February, as they must have sufficient time to become well rooted before the hot weather sets in; or, they will be unable to bear it.

remain, selecting as dry a foundation as possible; reconstruct the bed thereon, keeping it still with a sloping ridge in the centre, treading down the dung as you proceed, and mixing the litter well with it. When this has remained a sufficient time for the heat to become moderate, cover the sloping bank about two inches thick with fine sifted mould, leaving the ridge in the middle open for the steam to evaporate as it rises; but when this ceases the top also may be covered with mould. Then divide the spawn into small lumps, planting them six or eight inches asunder in rows at about the like distance, inserting them close down to the surface of the dung. The bed should be afterwards very lightly watered from a fine rose, with water about the temperature of new milk; cold water at all times inevitably destroying not only the growing crop, but the whole of the spawn likewise, and thus renders the bed of no further use.

In gathering the mushrooms, care must be taken gently to twist the head removed, so as not to disturb the young plants that will be found clustering at its foot, and at the same time not to leave any portion of the stem of the one gathered, as that would rot, and seriously injure all around it. It will be necessary to make new beds every eight or ten months.

The TRUFFLE, Tuber cibarium, *Kum*, or *kuma*, is too celebrated in the annals of gastronomy to need description; it may be used to greatest perfection stewed in various ways alone, or with other succedance. This fungus is found under the ground in parts where the soil is light, and dry, but it is difficult to discover, and is but little known in India. In Europe dogs are trained to hunt for the truffle, and it is curious to observe the perfection they attain in pursuing their search.

The Fruit Garden.

It has been but too often subject of remark in India that so little attention is paid to the preparation of the ground, and a full enquiry into the nature and qualities of its subsoil, in the first formation of a garden, so as to have a soil either natural or artificial, sufficiently well fitted for the plants it is to receive and nourish, and to remedy the defects of the latter whenever these are of a nature likely to affect their health or produce. But if this previous preparation be called for in other parts of a well ordered garden, how much more is it needed in the FRUIT GARDEN which forms the next subject of consideration. This, like the Kitchen Garden, should be well trenched, and attention must be paid that the subsoil, be not of a corroding quality, and that it be free from white ants, rats or other destructive vermin: a thorough drainage must also be carefully attended to, that the water may not lodge on any part, either above, or below the superstructure of soil; this may be easily secured to the former by so constructing the fruit borders, that they may have a gradual slope towards the tank, or the principal drains leading to it, and the depth of good mould should be fully three feet; a rich mellow loamy soil being preferred. The worst scite for a fruit garden is where the upper soil exhibits a stiff heavy clay, and in preparing such a soil for an orchard, a good admixture of lime rubbish from old buildings, together with a good portion of pure sand should be added ; but, if the soil be weak and cold, sand, and decayed vegetable matter, plentifully bestowed, will be found of service, or a layer of old, well rotted dung laid in at the bottom of the trenches.

Drainage of the subsoil is a subject of most serious consideration, especially as it is one but little known, or thought of in India, where however, the variety of its structure, the inundation and heavy falls of rain, and the prevalence of matter calculated seriously to affect the roots, especially of plants disposed to penetrate deeply for nourishment, renders such enquiries of more importance than elsewhere. In Great Britain this subject has received much attention, especially in agriculture, for there it is generally admitted, that upon it depends much of the trouble and hazard of planting the surface ; but in a work of this kind it is hardly possible to enter much on the details attending this most important part of forming an orchard, and we must be satisfied with noticing the three principal conditions of the subsoil in a cursory, and concise manner ; these are a clayey foundation with retention of all moisture falling from above whereby the surface becomes constantly soaked, chilling and retarding the vegetative powers of the plants inserted in it, until the roots eventually rot and the trees are destroyed. Strong subsoil if not horizontal, but bearing a slope towards any point where a drain may be run, is only injurious where the surface soil is thin, but may by care be made very productive, although always attended with the objection of harboring worms which collect in, and injure the roots. A light subsoil possesses the advantage of readily disposing of any superfluous moisture, and much assists the benefits derivable from manures, of preventing their becoming speedily exhausted; it may generally be considered the best adapted therefore, for a fruit garden requiring little attention to draining, any evil that may attend their being so absorbent being easily overcome by forming an artificial substratum of konkur, or broken brick, closely beaten down to prevent too rapid a departure of the moisture necessary for healthy growth; whereas the first, clayey substratum requires deep and expensive drainage and if for that reason alone should, if possible be avoided, although it is unfortunately a very prevalent condition of land in India particularly in Bengal.

In commencing, therefore, the formation of a Fruit Garden, after these points have met our consideration it will be well to trench the entire ground to the whole depth, or nearly so of the surface soil, manuring it well, but moderately; for it is to be remembered that as the trees extend in growth there does not exist that facility of frequently renewing, or improving the soil that is found in the constant succession, and change of crops, with alternations of fallowing that is afforded in the Kitchen Garden, and that a tree once planted is not so easily altered in its condition, and assisted, by improvement of soil, &c. in its growth, or power of production as a cabbage or a lettuce.

A good supply of water is indispensable, for distribution of which, drains should pass from the tank to all parts, and branches must be brought to each tree, so that in the blossoming, and fruit setting season, trenches may be carried round every tree at a distance of from three to six feet from the stem, according to the stretch, or expansion of the branches that the sponglets of the roots may have a plentiful supply of moisture daily, especially when in blossom, or when fruiting has commenced.

It will be found a good plan in burning weeds, &c. to select the period when the trees are in blossom for that operation, and to do it to the windward of the fruit garden, so that all the smoke may be sent among the trees, as it will be found a good destroyer of insects, a protection against blight, and an occasional potatoe, or other crop between the rows of trees is generally useful to their growth if only by the careful digging they afford, and the suppression of weeds.

Trees should not be too much crowded ; as is so universally the case in native orchards, whose owners still adhere to the long exploded, and mistaken notion of the greater the number of trees, the greater the crop, of a good kind of fruit, the tree producing which has ceased to bear, or to equal its former production; this operation should be performed towards the close of the cold weather, when the sap begins to resume its active circulation, but as it is in direct violation of theco urse of nature, it must be effected gradually, removing a part only of the main branches in the first year, leaving the rest to preserve the circulation of the sap, until new shoots are produced, and become capable of keeping up this function, when the remainder of the old wood may be cut away; observing, that in doing this, as well as in all cases where wounds are made, the composition recommended by Mr. Forsyth should be applied.

INSECTS. As a preservative against insects on trees generally, having already referred to these destroyers more particularly as affecting all vegetable matter, that is well worthy of trial in this country, the following wash is recommended by Mr. Forsyth to be applied every year in the spring, especially to the bark, being at once well calculated to afford nourishment to the tree, and to keep the bark fine, clean, and healthy:— "Mix fresh cow-dung with urine, and soap-suds, and with this mixture wash over the stems and branches;" if the washing be repeated at the beginning, and close

---

save one leading shoot, removed the year after, when the new wood produced some of the finest flavored fruit ever tasted, and fully equal to its original character.

of the rains, it will destroy the eggs of insects that may at the former period remain on them, and at the latter give vigor to the bark after the exhaustion produced by the excess of moisture; at the same time that it will generally be of great service to the future health and productiveness of the trees.

SINKING OF THE SOIL. One more observation is necessary before closing these general remarks on the Fruit Garden. It is a well known fact, that in the progress of even one year, and certainly after a few years, the subsoil of the fruit garden, unless repeatedly trenched and added to, will sink, thus bringing a tree, planted, in the usual mode, with the surface around it levelled, to have the collar or neck buried some 5 or 6 inches deep in the soil, thereby deranging the healthiness of the tree, and bringing on premature decay. To obviate such a serious evil the best course in planting is to take care that the earth, well mixed with manure, should be raised in the form of a flattened cone, having a hollow basin at the top, whereon the young tree should be planted, and, after covering in, well mulched with small pebbles, or broken bricks.

In a country where the fruits of Europe are but little known, and not every-where attainable, they should, perhaps, form a separate class; but as such an arrangement can be but seldom called in requisition by the horticulturist, who cultivates either for his amusement, or for profitable return in India, when they so seldom come under his care, and when they are as yet only considered as rare exotics, whereof the true culture to suit the climate is yet unknown, or at the least in its infancy, it would lead to enlarging on so fruitful a topic, of separate interest only as yet to the enthusiast, and far beyond what is intended in the present work, it has been considered a preferable form to introduce the most prominent of them in their proper class under the general description.

STONE FRUIT—*DANEH*, OR, *GUT'HLEE KÉ PHUL.*

The Peach, Amygdalus persica, *Aroo, shuftaloo, peech phul* (*cor.*) is the most generally esteemed of this class, and has become naturalized to all parts of India. The criterion of a good peach is, that the flesh be firm, the skin thin, of a bright red color on the side next to the sun, the stone small, the pulp plentiful, of a yellowish color, and the juice abundant. The best variety is the round peach *B,humee*, having a small stone, seldom met with in Bengal, but common in the West, and North-west of India. The China flat peach is a good sort; but the most common kind is the China long peach, of a hardy habit, and an abundant bearer. The few varieties yet found in India, shew the little attention hitherto paid to horticulture; for Mr. Forsyth in his work on fruit trees, enumerates not less than eighty-six kinds; whilst the catalogue of Mr. George Lindley contains sixty; and those of the London Horticultural Society, two hundred and twenty-four; though Dr. Patrick Neill mentions only one hundred and eighty-three varieties of this fruit.

Propagation.—New varieties may always be raised from the stone, although only with much labor and perseverance, for, until the tree produce fruit, it is impossible even to conjecture, whether the produce will be a new kind, a repetition of an old sort, or a degenerate failure; but to perpetuate those that are already approved, budding or grafting is resorted to, for which the plum is recommended as a good stock, and in England the almond has been found valuable, particularly, for the finer sorts; in this country, however, the seedlings peach is commonly used for this purpose; and these, people in the Upper Provinces generally sow in February, or March about an inch deep, and a cubit apart; but they have a fancy there for looking to such seedlings, if from good varieties, as their stock, which is, to say the least, a great risk and likely to introduce a spurious and degenerate fruit, in supercession of the good kinds they have hitherto had to boast of in that part of the country. So far as regards stocks, however, seedlings are useful, and it has been generally found advisable to select such as have been raised from the stones of the best flavored peaches, those being preferred which are a full year old with a portion of firm wood. It does not appear that the same objection is to be taken to seedling peach-trees as applies to most other fruits raised from seed, viz. that they are much longer in attaining maturity than grafts or layers, as Mr. Knight found that seedlings would produce fruit in three, or four years.

Soil, &c. A light, mellow, loamy soil is the best, of a depth of a foot and a half, to two feet, with a tolerably dry bottom, too much manure causing the tree to run to wood, and therefore to be avoided. If the soil be clayey, it will be advisable to take out a part, and mix with it sand, or old lime rubbish, with a portion of leaf mould. One of the great evils that cultivation has to contend with, in the growth of the peach in Bengal, is the wet subsoil that pervades the whole province; this may, however, be obviated by digging down to the wet stratum, and then throwing in broken brick, and lime rubbish on the bottom, beating it down with a rammer, and watering it until it forms a solid and tolerably smooth surface, into which the roots cannot penetrate, thus preserving them from contact with the wet soil; over this the mound should be raised, as described in a former page,* to receive the young plant. In choosing

* Page 255.

young plants for the garden, preference should be given to such as have clean, and strong single stems, or, if only double stemmed plants are procurable, one should be cut off so as to leave a good healthy leader.

Culture. After a graft has been planted out for a season, the buds that are within a foot, or eighteen inches of the ground should be all rubbed off, and in January the leading shoot should be cut down in a sloping direction to six buds; as the new shoots extend themselves, they should be trained laterally, so as to form an espalier in the fan, or horizontal manner; for though usually allowed to become standard trees in this country, experiments have shown, that training benefits the fruit in quality, affords it greater protection against storms, and opens it to the sun, to say nothing of the greater facility of access afforded by that mode to all parts of the tree; the espalier may be about eight or ten feet high, by eighteen or twenty in extent when full grown. In the two following seasons the leading shoots should be again shortened, leaving one central, and a succession, or a regular course of side shoots, according to the form of training adopted; after this the tree may be considered formed, and the endeavor must afterwards be to preserve the form unaltered as much as possible. None of the leading shoots should be shortened, nor any that are well situated, or full of blossom buds, unless they grow so long as to become weakened, greatly exceed the bounds of the training, or appear unhealthy; and the trees should be frequently looked over to remove superfluous wood buds by rubbing off, or cutting out such shoots and buds as are crowded; but care should be taken not to shorten any branches that are intended to bear fruit in the season next ensuing, though if they grow too long they may be bent back to check their progress. The punch-bowl fashion, as it is called, is a good plan of pruning; taking out the centre wood and thereby forming a space for the air to circulate, and the sun to penetrate, but it is not so good as the espalier, though less trouble. When the rains set in it will be well to cover the mound around the stem with tiles, to prevent the water penetrating to the the roots; and at the close of the rains the earth should be opened to expose the roots, at not less than two or three feet around the stem; at the same time all the root fibres that shew mildew, or are otherwise injured, must be carefully pruned off with a sharp knife, washing the trunk, &c. with the mixture recommended by Mr. Forsyth; as the sap ceases to circulate rapidly, and the leaves fall off, a thorough pruning should be made, removing all wood that has borne fruit, or otherwise become useless, or crowded, and shortening all shoots not intended to bear in the next year to four eyes each, preserving an equal distribution of the bearing shoots As soon as a few blossoms appear, the roots may be covered in with good strong loam, avoiding all fresh dung or rich manure, as calculated to promote too great a production of wood, repeating also the wash on the trunk, &c. If there be any disposition to frost in the cold weather, mats should be put over the trees to protect the blossoms at night. Some are, however, content with digging to the depth, of two or three feet round the roots at the fruiting time, and after all is gathered filling in with loam mixed with well rotted manure or vegetable mould; giving a top dressing of a stronger kind in January. The Revd. Mr. Proby states the following as a good compost for this tree:—Two parts Cowdung, two parts oil-cake, one part wood-ashes, and one part lime, the two last being reduced when the soil is light.

As the fruit sets, they should be thinned regularly, care being taken not to leave two peaches any where on the same spur; and as the blossoms are passing to fruit, water must be plentifully supplied to the roots, and continued until the fruit changes color; this is best supplied by a trench round the tree, at a distance of three to six feet, to be filled with water every day. Some people ring the trees to increase the production of fruit, but, with a tree bearing so readily as the peach, this process is hardly necessary. The fruit ripens in April and May.

Insects, Diseases, &c. The red spider, and a species of plant louse, that attacks the leaves and raises tubercles on them, are among the enemies of the peach;

soap or tobacco smoke, or syringing under the leaves with lime water are considered the best destroyers of these insects. The red ant, and a large species of lizard attack the fruit when set; but the greatest enemy to this tree is the white ant, which insidiously destroys the root, as already mentioned under the subject of insects. The mildew, caused, as is supposed by minute fungi, is among the diseases of the peach; this may be destroyed by dusting with sulphur, but the only sure remedy is renewal of the soil, and abundance of air. Gum is another disease very weakening to the tree; and must be treated as shewn in the opening of the subject of the Fruit Garden.*

The APRICOT, Prunus Armeniaca, *Zurd aloo*, is very rare in India, and even when produced has been generally found inferior to the fruit obtained in Europe, although a white kind is occasionally found in Upper India of good size, and tolerable flavor; the general management and culture are the same as required for the peach.

The ALMOND, Amygdalus communis, *Badam-u-farsee, looz*, is unknown in lower India, though obtainable in the Upper Provinces.

The TERMINALIA, Terminalia catappa, *Badam-u-hundee*, is used very frequently as a substitute for the almond. The germ is beautifully rolled, and eaten as

---

* Page 253.

a fruit has much the flavor of a green almond, or filbert; the tree is common to all parts of the country affording a fine shade, and when young, grows in a series of vertical branches, having at a distance the appearance of a dumb-waiter, and, when grown to full size, is an abundant bearer. It may be raised from seed, requiring no particular cultivation, although an ornamental tree in all stages of its growth.

The PLUM, Prunus domestica, *Alooch'eh aloo*, and the DAMASCENE, or DAMSON, Prunus insititia, *Alooee Bukhara*, are both rare, but may be met with occasionally, the latter being indigenous in the hills; it is, therefore evident, that they only require to receive attention to be as common as the peach; like which they should be cultivated, except that they do not require so much train; some good varieties are to be found in the Western provinces.

The NATIVE PLUM, JUGUBE, Ziziphus jujuba, *Baeer;* a small species grows wild, but a larger sort, *Narkoolee Baeer*, is esteemed by some people, as having somewhat the flavor of an apple.

Propagation—of the large kind is performed by grafting on the stock of the wild tree. Both yield fruit in January, and February.

The CHERRY, Prunus cerasus, *Shah aloo, shahdaneh,* or *keeras*, is found only very far to the north-west, and in Affghanistan, but it is to be hoped that it will soon spread over all parts of India; the black cherry, and a variety similar to the May-duke, are common in those parts, whence the seeds have been sent to various quarters, the success of which has yet to be proved, their not appearing any good reason why it should not be grown successfully in all parts of the country.

The Java Plum, Eugenia jambolana (or Calyptranthes jambolana of Linnæus), *Jamoon, kala jam*; the berry is of a sub-acid, astringent taste, black, about the size of a large cherry, and containing a single stone.

Propagation—is generally by seeds or suckers, but it is found wild as well as cultivated, flowering in the beginning of the hot season, and ripening its fruit in July and August.

The Indian Olive, Olea dioica, of Roxburgh, *Ata jam*, is a fruit in little estimation, of a dark color, growing on a tolerably large tree, indigenous to the eastern part of Bengal, the fruit ripening in July. No particular cultivation is requisite, or indeed is ever bestowed on it, though it thrives best in a peaty loam.

The Native, or saw-Leaved Olive, Elæocarpus serratus, *Julpaee*, grows on a small tree, never exceeding twenty feet in height, the fruit having the size and appearance of a large Olive, which is eaten fresh or preserved dried, also by natives pickled, and in curries.

Propagation, &c.—Any garden soil will suit this tree, which is easily produced from cuttings.

The MANGO, Mangifera indica, *Am*, or *amb*, is a highly esteemed and well known fruit, growing on a large spreading tree. The varieties are very numerous, the best being the Bombay, the Small scarlet, and the Malda; latterly also, attention has been paid to the introduction of a double bearing species of good flavor, giving an early and a late crop every year.

Propagation—may be effected by seed, but this is a slow process, and necessarily uncertain, as no dependance can be placed on the quality of the fruit. The best way, therefore, is to graft from an approved tree, on a stock raised from seed, of which every garden should always possess a good supply, ready to receive grafts. It is, perhaps, deserving of notice, that Dr. Macfadyen in his "Flora of Jamaica" points out that, in that island, "in order to obtain a good variety the only plan is to employ the seed of the desired sort;" a method so fraught with doubt, that its continuance is much to be wondered at. The reason, however, that this author gives against grafting is, that the bark abounds with so much resinous gum, that all scions fail: either some mismanagement has occasioned such repeated loss, or the species that we have here must differ greatly, since failures very seldom ioccur in grafting mangoes; the subject deserves nquiry.

Soil, &c. A fair garden soil of any kind will suit this tree.

In selecting trees for planting, such should be chosen as have strong, straight, and clean stems. Shallow planting is the best with a solid subsoil either natural, or artificial, to encourage lateral rooting, and the young trees must be carefully sticked, to prevent their being shaken by the wind.

Soil, &c. A clayey, soft soil, with some admixture of chalk, on a dry subsoil, is necessary for the good culture of the apple, and this should be well drained, or the lodgment of wet will produce canker.

Culture. The period for bearing may be forwarded in seedlings, by attention to their culture, making them grow vigorously when young. Fresh manure is, however, to be avoided, but a liberal supply of vegetable mould and well-rotted turf should be given to the bed on which they are raised, as well as to the spot where they are put out; this must be well worked, and sheltered from the sun and wind, and in the early prunings care should be taken to remove the interior shoots, and prevent the tree from becoming crowded. When the trees, whether seedlings or others, are planted out to remain, the ground must be kept clear from weeds, and the roots should be moderately watered from time to time. The trees might be successfully trained on espaliers, as facilitating the frequent examination of the trees to destroy insects, and to cut out canker wherever it may appear; dwarf trees are however, generally considered the most abundant bearers. Too much pruning is injurious, and only dead wood, weak, sickly, or worn out shoots, as well as such as in cumber or cross each other should be removed; but in this operation, (which should be a little later than for stone fruit trees,) it must be borne in mind that the mode of bearing is on small lateral spurs, on strong short shoots, from an inch to two inches in length, springing from healthy branches of two, or more years' growth, the same spurs producing fruit for several successive seasons. All blossoms appearing at improper periods should be removed, as they do not yield fruit, and only tend to weaken the tree; the true blossoms generally appear in October or November, the fruit ripening in April. The tree to prove a good bearer, and to yield fine flavored fruit requires to be about ten years of age before it is allowed to produce.

The PEAR, Pyrus communis, *Amrood*, or *nashputee*, has, it is believed, only once* been known to bear fruit in lower Bengal, but, that one experiment having been successful, augurs well for future attempts, and holds out sufficient encouragement, to those who are interested, to pursue the cultivation of this delicious fruit; to this may be added, that the pear has been successfully grown in the North-western Provinces, in Cashmere, &c. The cultivation is the same as for the

---

* In Mr. C. Steer's garden at Kishnugur.

apple, but it does not require to be so old before allowing it yield to a crop, seedlings as usual take longer to reach the period of bearing; Mr. Knight says from 12 to 18 years, in England; how long it would require in India having never been tried, is doubtful.

This fruit is generally considered a native of England, where the list of those varieties cultivated, as published in the London Horticultural Society's Catalogue, amounts to 622. Mr. Forsyth describes ninety-three sorts, besides enumerating sixty kinds without any particular description, and Professor Van Mons, at Brussels, is said to have "upwards of 800 approved sorts of new pears raised from seed by himself" and Mr. Duquesne, of Mons, in the course of fifteen, or sixteen years, had selected from probably 8000 new seedling plants. "*See Loudon's Encyclopedia of Gardening.*"

The QUINCE, Cydonia vulgaris, or rather it is supposed: Chinensis, *Bêh*, is only found in Upper India, where there are three varieties. But little is known of its culture as adapted to this climate; a moist soil is preferred by it, which would indicate its suitableness to Bengal, and although in other respects resembling the apple and pear, it is easily raised by layers, or cuttings, the young plants being shaded until they acquire strength. Dr. Roxburgh says that the wild pear, Pyrus tomentosa "is the Quince tree of Hindoostan, and, most likely that which furnishes the

Quince seed brought from Muscat to Bengal for sale, where they are much used for medical purposes, under the name of "*Bêhee ke beej.*"

The Rose apple, Eugenia jambos, *Jam*, or *gulab jam*, bears a whitish yellow fruit, of but little flavor, sweetish, and rose-scented, whence its name.

Propagation—may be performed either by seed, slips, cuttings, or suckers.

Soil, &c. It will thrive in any moist soil, and requires no culture beyond pruning off the lower shoots, and occasionally digging around the roots. It produces fruit in March and April.

The Loquat, Eriobotrya japonica, *Lókat*, is a highly esteemed juicy fruit, with a tough, woolly outside skin, of yellow color when ripe; the flowers rise in spires from the extremities of the branches, on which the fruit afterwards forms in bunches.

Propagation.—It may be raised from seeds, but the preferable mode is by layers, or suckers.

Soil, &c. A rich, but rather moist soil is preferable for this tree.

Culture. When the layer has been planted out for a season, the lower branches should be pruned off to promote the formation of an even, well-formed head, to which it has naturally a disposition, and the tree should not be allowed to bear fruit until it be fully five years old; on attaining that age, when the blossoms open, a small trench should be dug round the stem, at the distance of about three feet, or more, according to the lateral spread of the branches, to be daily filled with water until the fruit begins to ripen, in February and March little further is required. It is well, however, at the beginning of the cold weather to apply fresh manure to the roots, decayed vegetable matter and cow-dung being the best suited to the loquat.

It is well worthy of remark by the horticulturist, that the chief cause of this excellent fruit being too often undervalued here, is, that the native gardeners commonly gather it before fully ripe; an observation that holding good also with a great number of the fruits of this country, should be carefully attended to, by those who take an interest in their gardens. This fruit has, however, a tendency to ripen too fast if left unremoved but this may be obviated, and the size of the produce improved by tyeing the bunches in bags of cloth, or in well-drilled tin boxes.

The MALAY APPLE, Eugenia alba, or Malaccensis, *Jumrool,* is an indigenous fruit of white color, pear-shaped, having a highly polished surface, but possessing little or no flavor; the tree grows almost wild, and needs no particular cultivation. There is a pink fruited variety, looking pretty enough in the desert at a large table, as an ornament, amongst other fruits.

The LEECHEE, Nephelium litchi, Dimocarpus Litchi Scytalia Litchi of Roxburgh, called also Euphoria Litchi by Jussieu, (*vide London Horticultural Society's*

Transactions, vol. II, 28, 1*st series), Leechee*, a highly esteemed fruit, originally brought from China, but long since fully naturalized in India; where it grows, and ripens to great perfection, bearing the next place to the mango in general estimation; the outside is a stiff, rough, reddish in skin, and the pulp is rich, sweet, and firm.

Propagation.—is best performed by layers, or Chinese grafting, the plant readily throwing out root fibres, under either system.

Soil, &c. A rich mould, not too dry, is the best suited to the leechee.

Culture. After the young plant is put into the fruit garden, it must be carefully watched for the purpose of training the stem, and removing the lower shoots and suckers, as this tree when young grows very rapidly being also much disposed to become crooked, straggling, and ill-shaped. In the sixth year it may be allowed to bear a moderate, but only a moderate portion of fruit, but till it attain that age, the blossoms should be entirely removed as soon as they appear, and even then at least three fourths should be taken off and not permitted to set. When bearing, the roots should be occasionally moderately watered; the fruit ripening in March and April.

The LONGAN, Nephelium longan, Dimocarpus longan, Scytalia longan of Roxburgh, called Euphoria longan, by Jussieu, *Ashphul*, is in form somewhat similar to the leechee, but smaller and more round, being at the same time very inferior in flavor; some people however like it. It requires little culture, and fruits in June, and July.

The CHINESE WAMPEE, Cookia punctata, *Ooampee*, or *ooampéch*, is a rough, brown-skinned fruit, having, a strong flavor of turpentine, tempered with a slight degree of acid, very grateful to the palate, especially of the invalid; it fruits plentifully, without requiring any attention to cultivation, and in almost any soil, ripening in May, June, and July.

The MONGOSTEEN, Garcinia Mongostana, *Kurundra*, is a rich flavored, most highly esteemed fruit, the pulp being juicy, and of a red color; it is very rare in India, though indigenous in Singapore, Penang, &c.

Propagation—is sometimes performed by seed which, however, requires to be put in the earth almost immediately after it is abstracted from the fruit, and has but seldom even germinated here; but cuttings or layers are to be preferred, as some trees produce only male blossoms.

Soil, &c. A rich vegetable mould, on a dry rocky bottom, is the natural soil of this tree, which deserves introduction, into this part of our Indian territory.

The CUSTARD APPLE, Annona, is a general name for a class of soft pulped fruit of agreeable flavor, the chief varieties of which are—

1. *The Sweet sop*, called here the *Custard apple*,

Annona squamosa, *Ata*, or *shureefeh*, the outside skin is thick, and divided into many reticulated compartments, the pulp sweet, luscious, and filled with small black, long-shaped seeds.

2. *The Custard apple*, called here the *Bullock's Heart*, or *netted custard apple*, Annona reticulata, *Nóna ata*, is coarse flavored, and grows almost wild in a soil impregnated with salt, but requires a wet subsoil; it is seldom found out of Bengal.

3. *The Sour sop*, Annona muricata, having as yet no native name, is very rare in India, but is mentioned here as well deserving of culture, and has lately been exhibited frequently at the Fruit shows of the Horticultural Society.

Propagation—of all may be effected either from seeds, cuttings, or layers.

Soil, &c. Any ordinary garden soil suits these trees, but they should be kept moist, especially the custard apple.

Culture. Little is required beyond attention to the shape of the tree, to form a well balanced head, and to keep the roots clean from weeds. The fruit of the Sweet sop ripens from June to October, whilst that of the Custard apple is procurable at almost all seasons.

The Sapota, Achras sapota, a native of China, having no native name, beyond a corruption of its own, is a fruit of rich smell and taste, the pulp being of a deep yellow color, but not much known in India, centre. They are abundant bearers and begin to give fruit in the third year after they are sown.

The POMEGRANITE, Punica granatum, *Anar*, is by some much admired, particularly the large red-seeded kind, grown in upper India. The fruit has on the outside a hard woody rind, very astringent, and covering a mass of seeds surrounded by a juicy sub-acid pulp, the root being useful for medicinal purposes, as is also the rind of the fruit.

Propagation—is effected by cuttings, suckers, or layers, the last being the best mode.

Soil, &c. It requires a rich, but at the same time a rather sandy soil.

Culture. The pomegranite needs much pruning, the centre shoots being kept thinned out, or it will soon get crowded, with a quantity of useless wood.

The CARAMBOLA, Averrhoa carambola, *Kumrung'eh*, is a small five-celled, angular fruit; of which there are two kinds, one producing a sweet, and the other an acid fruit of rather pleasant flavor, something like an insipid apple.

Propogation, &c.—is performed by cuttings in sandy loam, and it may be easily grown in any common garden mould. The tree grows to the height of about twenty or thirty feet, and possesses the peculiarity of producing its pretty pink blossoms from the trunk and main branches. The fruit ripens from December to

February, and again a smaller crop is obtained at the close of the rains. Another variety of this fruit is produced by a small shrub called Averrhoa bilimbi, *Bulumboo*, but its fruit is smaller, and more tasteless.

The PIERARDIA, Pierardia sapida, *Lutkeo*, indigenous to Tipperah, and other parts to the Estward, is claimed by the Chinese as a native fruit in their country, under the name of Lutqua; this is a shrub not more than ten feet high, and the fruit is a round berry, about the size of a gooseberry, smooth and yellow skinned, and the pulp of an agreeable sub-acid flavor. It was named and described by Roxburgh, and may be worth cultivating, for improvement in its character, when the garden is of sufficient size to afford spare room.

The CURANDA, JASMINE FLOWERED CARISSA, Carissa carandas, *Kuroondee* or *kurumcha*, is a large thorny shrub, yielding in July and August, and from thence to the end of September, as it approaches to the North-west, a long-shaped, dark-colored berry, of a pleasant sub-acid flavor, when ripe. When not quite mature, the fruit makes a very delicious jelly, and is pleasant for tarts.

Propagation, &c.—is effected by cuttings planted in sandy loam, requiring but little after-culture. The shrub forms a good fence, almost impenetrable on account of its long spines.

The PANEOLA PLUM, MANY SPINED FLACOURTIA,

The catalogue of the London Horticultural Society contains seventy-five varieties, and of these Mr. Forsyth describes seventeen as worth cultivating; these are the 1 Brown chesnut colored Ischia, 2 Black Ischia, 3 Green Ischia, 4 Small brown Ischia, 5 Yellow Ischia, 6 Small white early, 7 Black Genoa, 8 Large white Genoa, 9 Malta, 10 Murrey or brown Naples, 11 Long brown Naples, 12 Madonna, 13 Brunswick or Hanover, 14 Common blue or purple, 15 Gentile, and 16 Brown, and 17 Black small Italian, this last being capable of culture in pots, producing small round and very delicious fruit, of which this author says—"I have gathered from one plant in a twenty-four pot, two dozen of figs at one gathering."

Propagation—may be effected in any way, but that most generally approved is by layers and suckers, which root in less than a month, in the rains.

Soil, &c. This tree thrives in all soils that have no too wet a sub-soil, but they produce the greatest quantity of good fruit in a strong loam, the tree requires also a free open air.

Culture. The moist climate of Bengal, causes the fig to throw out shoots so rapidly as to prevent its maturing its fruit; this must be checked by drainage and pruning; this last, however, should not be done in autumn, the best time being the beginning of March, or in January higher up, at which time also it is well to manure; some experiments have, however, shown

November and December to be good months in that quarter for this operation, preserving always the double eyes as one is almost sure to be a fruit bearing one; branches that have run up naked should then be taken out as close to the bottom as poossible, and about a month afterwards the ends of the branches must be stopped to make them throw out side shoots for the next year's bearing. If, in pruning, the shoots bleed profusely, a little of Mr. Forsyth's composition, before described, had better be put on the ends to heal them; and the fruit should be thinned to not less than six inches apart on the bearing shoots; when the fruit begins to swell, which it will do in the month of April or May, the neighbouring leaf shoots should be topped and each fruit should be protected by a small tin box made either in bars, or pierced with holes, to give free access to the air, this will cause it to grow to a larger size, and prevent its ripening prematurely.

In the cold weather, the superabundant side shoots should be removed, and the roots opened and supplied with fresh well rotted vegetable manure; the trees produce fruit in the second year.

The fig tree thrives well if trained in espalier fashion which admits, too, of its being kept in better order.

The PLANTAIN TREE, Musa, is too well known to need a description, but there are several varieties, the larger kind, Musa paradisiaca, *Mouz*, or *kéla*, requiring to be dressed as a vegetable to become palatable.

The sort eaten as fruit being more properly called the Banana, Musa sapientum, *Kéla*, of which the variety known as the *Cheen'ch chumpa'h*, is the most esteemed; a large kind from Malacca, and one of middling size from Chittagong, and Dacca are worthy of attention.

Propagation—is by suckers, of which the tree gives an abundant supply.

Soil, &c. Any soil moderately rich will suit the plaintain.

Culture. No particular care is required, but it is advisable to keep the ground near the roots tolerably free from weeds, and occasionally to earth the stems up with soil from the bottom of a tank; old stems should also be removed as soon as the spine of fruit is cut off.

The Pine Apple, Bromelia ananas, *Anunas*, is, when properly cultivated, one of the finest fruits of the garden, but from neglect, has fallen to be so deteriorated in India as to be hardly desirable, as a fruit, especially gathered, as it generally is, in an unripe state, and kept until ripe, when of course by fermentation it becomes most unwholesome, especially to those who are subject to disordered bowels, or predisposed to Cholera. The varieties in the gardens of the London Horticultural Society amounted to 95: Dr. Neill mentions 56 sorts; of these he enumerates the *Queen pine*, as an useful, quick fruiting kind, seldom exceeding 3 lbs. in weight; *The Black Antigua*, averaging 5 lbs.; *The Black Jamaica*, having oblong fruit, about 4 lbs., an excellent kind; *The White Providence,* a pale yellow kind common in India, and averaging in England from 7 to 12 lbs.; as good varieties.

Propagation—is performed by planting the tops or offsets, which speedily take root; they fruit in the third year, or sometimes sooner in the country.

Soil, &c. No soil can be too rich, and no manure too strong for the pine apple; an admixture of salt and lime is said to improve their flavor, but the fruit should be well ripe before it is cut, and not allowed to remain for any length of time after separation from the stock.

Culture. The plants should be put out in rows two feet asunder, the rows about four feet distant from each other, and the earth well drawn up to the stems; in the third year they will begin to produce fruit, and as soon as the blossoms appear, which will be in February, giving previous indication by a peculiar red tinge of the young leaves in the centre of the plant; the roots must be laid open, and all sides hoots and suckers carefully removed to plant out for a fresh supply of plants, if desired; a basket of rotted cow-dung should then be put to each plant, and above that, the like quantity of *fresh strong* stable dung, with litter covering the whole; this will form a ridge about the stem, over which a thin layer of earth should be placed; a trench should then be dug on each side of the plants, which must be every day filled with water, a moderate quantity being also thrown from a fine rosed watering pot, once a week, over the leaves and fruit. The fruit will ripen to most perfection in April, May and June, and by pursuing the method here recommended, pines may be obtained of as large size, and what is more, as highly flavored as the finest procurable, with the utmost care, in any part of the world.* The stem producing the fruit should be removed immediately that the fruit is cut, a new shoot being encouraged, and no offsets should be allowed to remain round the base of the fruit, whilst it is growing, as they would draw off the nourishment, and deteriorate the flavor.

The fruit ripens, in this country, in the same month (June) as in the ordinary cases in England, as a prelude to which, Dr. Neill gives the following as the preparatory rate of the temperature fittest for ripening :—

	During night.	During day.
March, ...	60° to 70°	70° to 80°
April, ...	70 to 75	80 to 85
May, ...	75 to 80	90 to 100
June, ...	80 to 85	100 to 120

* In my brother's garden, in the years 1839 and 1840, pines were grown weighing from 6 to 7½ lbs. each, exclusive of the top; and of a flavor, and fragrance that I have never known to be surpassed in the best cared for pineries of Great Britain, at the same time certainly unequalled by any thing of the kind ever met with by him in India during a residence of nearly twenty years, nor by myself since I have been here now almost the same period.

being the temperatures actually maintained in the pineries of the Royal Gardens at Kensington in 1825. This is mentioned as an encouragement to better cultivation in this country, since the natural temperature is here nearly the same, especially during the last two or three ripening months, shewing in this year—

	Mean of minimum Temperature.	Mean of the maximum Temperature exposed to the sun.
May,....	79.1	.... 121.8
June,....	81.3	.... 120.0

and leading to the conclusion, that as good pine apples might, with care, be grown in the open air in India, as in the pineries of England.

Insects, &c. The spider is the most troublesome, and should be removed whenever observed; snakes, and lizards also attack the fruit whilst ripening, and must, therefore, be closely looked after and destroyed, as they approach the pinery; the last has the property of assuming a singular likeness, as well in appearance as in color, to the long red tinged, pointed leaves that grow next to the fruit.

BACCIFEROUS FRUITS—*DANEH KEE P'HUL.*

These are numerous fruits and highly esteemed, comprising the most delicate portions of the desert.

The Grape Vine, Vitis vinifera, *Tak* or *ungoor*, ranks the first among this class of fruits; it is a hardy plant, reaching a very great age, and containing numerous varieties. The London Horticultural Society's catalogue contains 182 varieties; of these Dr. Neill describes twenty, and Mr. Forsyth fifty-five, besides enumerating twenty-eight more, of which those known here are—

1. The *White muscadine*, *Sŏfēd ungoor*, *nahur*, most commonly cultivated, producing middling sized bunches of small round fruit, rather crowded unless thinned out, the flavor sugary and rich, and the plant an abundant bearer, requiring comparatively little attention.

2. The *Black muscadine*, *hubshee ungoor*, is less common than the white, and the fruit rather sm ller, but in all other respects, except color, resembling that variety.

3. The *Cashmere*, *Kushmeer'eh*, or *oolaeetee ungoor*, or as it is called in England, *the White Portugal.* The bunches are large and loose, and the fruit also large and long shaped, hard skinned, and sweet, slightly mixed with acid; this grape keeps a long time after ripening, and is commonly packed in cotton in small boxes that are sent to all parts of India.

4. The *Malaga*, *Sŏfed oolaeetee ungoor*, has been lately attempted to be introduced by seed from America; the bunches are large, as is also the fruit, besides being firm and deliciously flavored; it is generally considered, indeed, one of the finest and richest grapes extant, and deserving particular attention.

5. The *Constantia, Kala ungoor*, originally from the Cape, is of a black and purple variety, though there is also a white kind, but not so deserving of cultivation as the dark; the bunches, as well as the fruit, are of medium size, the latter of a rich flavor; the plants are somewhat delicate, and the leaves of very large size.

6. *The Muscatel, Muskutel kè ungoor*, has been introduced from the Cape; the bunches are of medium size, the berry large, round, and transparent, very luscious, and saccharine; it is but a moderate bearer.

Propagation.—The vine is raised by seeds, layers, cuttings, or grafting: the first mode is pursued if it be wished to obtain an esteemed variety where cuttings are not procurable; but if adopted with the intention of producing new varieties, the blossoms should be impregnated by the pollen of some other sort; not more than six or eight seeds should be sown in a small sized pot, as, if put in too thick, the plants draw and become weak; too much water can hardly be given them in this country, and they will generally be a long time before the plants come up, though they afterwards, if well watered, grow very rapidly. When about six inches high, the plants ought to be put out separately into middling sized pots, filled with rich vegetable mould and supported by rods; and again, when they reach a foot and a half in height, they must be transferred to the largest sized pots. Layers produce strong showy plants the first year, but cuttings are to be preferred for affording plants with well formed tops, proportioned to their roots; these should be taken from well ripened wood of a year old, having short joints.

The Gardener's Magazine for September 1831, contains an article recommending the raising vines from "Spur eyes," whieh are thus described by Mr. R. Crawshay:—"suppose a vine, on the single shoot system of one year's growth, from the bottom to the top of the rafter breaks every eye on the same, and fruits, or not; I remove in the winter pruning of the year, every year one of these shoots, to the last bud that had a leaf at its side; this small remaining bit of wood I call a spur, which has two minute buds, sometimes quite invisible to the naked eye, one on each side;" these buds are what are called spur eyes, or spawn eyes, and should be planted an inch and a half deep in a well prepared soil of leaf mould, horse dung, &c. which, fermenting, attains a very sensible heat, and promotes the bursting of the eye, and when the shoot has appeared, continues to yield that degree of nourishment, which keeps it continually growing whilst forming its root."

Soil, &c. The vine thrives in any soil, having a dry bottom; in that which is rich and deep it will grow luxuriantly, and produce an abundance of large sized fruit; but in shallow, dry, or chalky soil, the produce is of better flavor, though rather less in quantity. Manure should not be put to the roots of a young plant too fresh, but should have good time to get mellowed before being applied; but when old, the vine is old, blood, offal, horn, bone dust, leather, are all of benefit; or fresh fish, and oil cake applied at a distance from the roots, are good.

Culture. In planting out the vine, it should be placed so as to be protected from the easterly or other strong wind; and where a hard bottom is not otherwise obtainable, it will be well to make a sub-soil of stones, bricks, broken pots, shells, bones, &c. with a small portion of time, such trash being much desired by the young fibres and lower shoots of the roots; the best time for planting out being during the rains; and in this operation it is advisable to reduce the young plant to not more than two feet in length, rubbing off all but three buds. In the beginning of the second year, select the strongest of the three shoots that the buds reserved will have produced, and cut off the other two, rubbing off at the same time, any superfluous shoots or buds that may have appeared; in September cut down the vine to two buds again. Any blossoms that appear in the third year must be removed; the tree being again cut down, at the close of the rains, to three or four buds. Should any blossoms shew themselves in the following March (the fourth year), they should be pinched off, and the tops of the shoots, as they reach any length, must be taken off, or bent down to check their growth. As the girt of the stem will, at the close of the rains, have attained fully three inches, preparations may be made for the tree bearing in the following season, and to this end the two shoots that are to remain must be cut down to seven buds on each, and if the bark of the stem be decayed it should be rubbed of clean; bending down the shoots retained, securing them in a horizontal position, and cutting out all the buds that by this means are placed underneath; —as the shoots from those that are uppermost appear, let them be trained, as directed for climbing plants; and if more fruit appear than is equivalent to the scale shewn below, let it be cut off before the berries set. When the fruit is gathered (the fifth year), or at the close of the rains, cut the two shoots nearest the stem on each side, to as many buds as may be necessary to give the required quantity of fruit for the next year; remembering to leave none but round wood and such as have good plump eyes, as flat, lanky shoots seldom bear fruit, or if they do, it is small and poor; all others cut to one bud only, pulling off the loose bark from the stem (the sixth year.) Bearing shoots are always of the production of the previous year, and such as have already borne fruit should be cut out.

In December, or January train the two shoots reserved for fruiting carefully, and, also as they appear, train those issuing from the other reserved buds, and henceforth pursue this system of training two shoots for the succeeding year, and fruiting from two shoots alternately. At this period, too, the root should be laid bare, washed, and all decayed or unhealthy fibres pruned out, allowing the roots to remain open until the leaf buds swell, when they should be filled in with good vegetable mould and a supply of well rotted manure or fish, dug in at a distance of two feet from the stem of the tree, which process must be repeated every year; as soon as the fruit sets, a liberal supply of water should be daily given to the root of the vine, and continued until the berry attains nearly its full size, leaving off, however, whilst the fruit ripens.

The following scale for bearing fruit on vines, being clear, and well adapted to their culture in this country, is extracted from a recently published work as an useful guide.

" Scale of the greatest quantity of grapes which any vine can perfectly mature, in proportion to the circumference of its stem, measured above the ground.

cir.	*lbs.*	*cir.*	*lbs.*
3 inches	5	7 inches	45
3½	10	7½	50
4	15	8	55
4½	20	8½	60
5	25	9	65
5½	30	9½	70
6	35	10	75
6½	40	10½	80

"It will be seen, that if $2\frac{1}{2}$ inches be deducted from "the circumference of the stem of any vine, the capa- "bility will be equal to the maturation of ten pounds "of grapes for every remaining inch of girt. The "proportionate quantity for fractional parts of an inch "may be easily calculated.

"No vine in taken cognizance of until its stem mea- "sures three inches in girt, as, under that size, vines "ought never to be suffered to ripen any fruit.

"The manner in which it is intended that this scale "should be applied, is to measure the stem of a vine "at the autumnal pruning, and to retain no more good "well-ripened fruit buds, than is supposed necessary "to produce the given weight of fruit that corresponds "to its girt; and I consider every bud, rejecting the "two bottom ones on each shoot, as equal to the pro- "duction of half a pound weight of fruit."—*A practical Treatise on the Cultivation of the Grape Vine, by Clement Hoare.*

In Portugal, where the grape is so extensively grown, the vines are pruned in January, lopping off every shoot of the past year, except one, and of this only about a foot and a half is left, which they double down, and keep in that position by a bit of thread. The surface of the ground being then dug.

When in bloom the superfluous bunches, or such as would overburden or weaken the tree, are lopped off.

The GREWIA, Grewia asiatica, also G. sapida, *P,halsa*, a small dark colored berry, growing on a shrub about ten feet high, and yielding fruit in July and August. The plant requires no particular culture, and is easily propagated by cuttings planted in sandy loam.

The MILNEA, Milnea edulis of Roxburgh, *Gumee*, is only inserted here from a presumed possibility that it might be improved by cultivation; the tree grows wild in Sylhet, and the Garrows, and in August and September yields an oval berry of rather more than one inch in diameter, the pulp of which is of rather pleasant flavor, having something the character of the Litchee.

The MULBERRY, Morus Indica, *Toot*, of India, is here a poor vapid fruit, of extremely easy culture; but it is most desirable that attention should be paid to the introduction of better varieties.

Propagation—is performed by cuttings, which strike easily in moist ground.

Soil, &c. Any tolerably moist soil will answer for the mulberry of India, but the better sorts delight in rich sandy loam, well manured.

The RASPBERRY, Rubus pauciflours *anchoo*, of good flavor and size, is abundant in the hills, but will seldom succeed in the plains, the heavy rains abstracting all taste from the fruit. There are two varieties most common, the small crimson fruited, of very rich flavor, and the large red.

Propagation—is performed by planting out the young sucker shoots, which rise plentifully from the root; new varieties are obtainable from seed.

Soil, &c. Although the flavor of the fruit suffers from superabundant moisture, yet this shrub requires a moist soil, which should be a rich loam, well manured with vegetable mould, rather sandy, and on a dry stony bottom.

The Strawberry, Fragaria vesca, or Indica, and grandiflora, *Kuhuj*, or *asasunoo*, is universally esteemed as one of the most delicious of fruits, and of it there are numerous varieties; the second edition of the Catalogue of the London Horticultural Society, enumerating one hundred and twelve, which are every year extending. The pine and hautboy are to be preferred; the small scarlet is, however, the most commonly found.

Propagation.—The plant rapidly multiplies itself by numerous runners and suckers, each of which, if planted out, will produce fruit the same year; seed produces new varieties.

Soil, &c. They thrive best in a light soil, well treated with strong manure, such as fresh stable manure, or what is preferable, pig-dung.

Culture. Strawberries should be replanted every year. As soon as the rains subside, raised beds, on a dry, well drained sub-soil should be prepared, and strongly manured, pig's dung is the best; in this the young plants are to be put out in clumps of five each, at about eight inches between each plant, four plants being placed diamond fashion, and the fifth in the centre; these clumps being about a foot distant from each other; they should be watered every third day, but not with well water if other can be procured, and, when the blossoms appear, it will be desirable to afford a moderate supply morning and evening, taking care that no water lodge in the joints of the stools or axils of the leaves; the fruit ripens in February or March; a month or more after which the extending shoots and suckers appear.

The WINTER CHERRY, called here the Country gooseberry, Physalis Peruviana, *Tupareea*, is a fruit found in most parts of India, of pleasant sub-acid taste, growing on a small straggling plant, about two feet in height, yielding produce in the cold season; it should be put in a distant corner of the garden, as it is an ugly looking plant, that, once established, soon runs into a complete jungle, very difficult to eradicate.

CURRANTS, Ribes rubrum, and album, *Ooulacetee zubeeb;* and GOOSEBERRIES, Ribes grossularia, and R. uva crispa, *Kureea*, have not yet been successfully cultivated in India, and will therefore afford amusing experiment to the speculative horticulturist. The attempts made hitherto by the curious to introduce these fruits, although they have failed, yet afford encouragement. The author has seen the plants brought from England, but they have been killed, in his opinion, by over carefulness, being kept constantly covered with mats during the rains to protect them from an excess of moisture; but this covering, confining the vapor that is naturally produced from the action of a hot sun on the moist ground, formed an unnatural and unwholesome atmosphere around the plants, that produce mildew, and, finally, rot, destroying them after they had been about six months in the ground; at the same rime their continuance for so many months, comprising the whole of the hot weaher, augured well for future attempts made with *less care*.

Another attempt occurred within the author's practice with seed imported from Hobart Town, which arriving in May was immediately sown in pots under shelter, and daily watered; these did not germinate until the beginning of November, when they came up abundantly, and continued to thrive until the following May, when the gardener, to take care of the plants, and keep them out of the sun, put them, in his master's absence, on a jomney, into a dark godown, where the want of light and air destroyed them, being then about eight inches high, and well covered with leaves and young shoots.

The EARTH NUT, Arachis hypogæa, *Cheena badam* or *moong p'hulee*, is the produce of a small plant, which has the peculiar property of thrusting its germ into the earth to ripen and sow itself. When cultivated it should be in a sandy soil, by offsets; the fruit ripening about May or June.

The NUT, Corylus avellana, *Jooz*, or *gurdooee*, the tree being called *buhhkul'eh*, is little known in India, but it is of easy culture, and deserving attention by those who are permanent residents in the country. The nut grows plentifully in the hills about Simla.

The WALNUT, Juglans regia, *Akhrôt*, and the CHESNUT, Castanea Indica, *Buloot badamgootee*, or *nékaree*, both abound in the hills, attaining great perfection in the the neighbourhood of Dôrjulung and Simla; but the long time they require to attain that degree of maturity that is necessary for the production of fruit, makes them of little interest to the mere sojourner like most of the European residents in India, who appear to be the only individuals here who take real interest in the country. The Walnut may be raised from seed, and a very healthy seedling of three years old might lately have been seen in a garden at Burhampore. The Chesnut commonly found, is of small size but well flavored; some from Dorjelung were presented by Colonel Lloyd to the Calcutta Horticultural Society in January, 1840, bearing this character, and offering promise of what might be done by cultivation to effect improvement.

CUCURBITACEOUS FRUIT.

The MELON needs no description, in a country where it grows so commonly as India.

The *Sweet melon.* There are several varieties of the *Sweet melon,* Cucumis melo, *Kuchree,* cultivated here, the most remarkable being the *Common musk melon, Khurbooz'eh, p,hootee;* the *Nutmeg melon,* the *Sweet melon of Ispahan, Shumam;* the *Cabul melon,* the *Large Istumbol melon,* and *the Bokhara melon.*

The *Water melon,* Cucurbita citrulla, *Turbuz,* or *sufunjeh,* is a very refreshing fruit, of which the best is the *Large round water melon* (that from American seed being the best), the *Pink Cabul water melon,* and the *Persian water melon.*

Propagation—is by seed sown where the plants are to fruit, for though many people transplant them, the plants are never so healthy, or the vines so strong, as when they remain where sown; seed should not be too new, as if less than two years old, it is apt to run too much to vine, and to produce only male flowers. The seed must be put in from the beginning of February to the middle of April.

Soil, &c. The soil can hardly be too sandy, but it should be thickly manured with compost of two parts old well rotted cow-dung, one part stable manure, and one part sand, dug into the soil to a depth of not more than six inches; a layer of about two inches of sand being put over the bed. Some of the finest melons ever seen have been grown on sand, which had been left by the inundation, in which holes were dug down to the soil wherein the seeds were planted, the vines being trained on the sand, whereby fields of some hundreds of beegahs were made productive after having been considered lost to the cultivator. Before sowing the seed, the beds should be moistened, and the seeds put in holes not less than six (eight is better) feet apart, at a depth of an inch and a half.

Culture. When the seed leaves fall off, or wither, the plants must be thinned so as not to leave more than four plants in each hole, at the same time the leading shoots must be pinched off to encourage the lateral shoots. As those advance, they should be pinned down at intervals with small wooden pegs to prevent their interference with each other, or being blown about by the wind, and the earth must be brought up about the stems. Such shoots as produce only male blossoms must be cut out. When the fruit blossoms open, it is advisable to assist the setting of the fruit by impregnation with the male blossoms. As the fruit increases to the size of an egg, each should have a tile or potsherd placed under it as a protection from any dampness in the earth, or late sown melon plants had better be raised on a low muchan, to prevent their being injured by the rain; during the whole time of their growth the plants should be watered daily; the fruit ripens from the middle of April to the middle of June.

INSECTS. The melon is subject to the ravages of a red bettle, commonly called the *soldier*, that destroys the leaves and young shoots; these should be carefully removed by the hand and destroyed, no other method having yet proved effectual.

NATIVE HARD SHELLED FRUITS, ETC.

The COCOANUT, Cocus nucifera, *Nueeral*, is but little esteemed by Europeans, and then only in an unripe state for the sake of its refreshing liquor; the shell being then soft, and the kernel but just forming in a pulpy state has rather an agreeable flavor, and is less unwholesome than when it hardens.

Propagation, &c.—is performed by seed, which thrives best in a moist soil near water, and hence, most probably, its not thriving out of Bengal, although that is by some said to proceed from its preferring the vicinity of the sea shore. It grows to the height of 50 to 60 feet, having all its leaves at the top of the stem.

The BORASSUS, Borassus flabelliformis, *Tal*, or *taree*, is a species of palm yielding a fruit about the size of a child's head, within which are several kernels having a tough skin that, being removed, discovers a pulpy matter very insipid, but liked by some people for its coolness; this tree also yields the taree or *toddy* as it is called, so much drank by natives, and serving as yeast in the making of bread; this is procured by making a triangular incision, the apex downwards, within the outer layers of leaves, at the base of a young shoot, and affixing thereto an earthen pot to receive the juice which runs out freely, and is pleasant enough while fresh, but it soon ferments.

Propagation, &c.—is effected by seed. The tree prefers a dry soil, and is found in great abundance in Buhar and the Western Provinces, growing to about thirty feet in height.

The ELEPHANT, OR WOOD APPLE, Feronia elephantum, *Kutb'hél*, is a hard shelled fruit, containing a pulp that has a strong terebinthine odour, seldom liked at first, but generally considered wholesome.

Propagation, Soil, &c.—the usual mode of producing this tree is by cuttings, which strike freely. It grows to a large size, and reaches the height of about 40 feet, preferring a sandy loam, rather rich than otherwise. The tree is handsome in appearance.

The BENGAL QUINCE Aegle marmelos* (Cratæva marmelos of *Linnæus*) *Bél*, or *sreep,hul*, growing on a moderate sized tree; the fruit is nutritious and fragrant, its cells, twelve in number, containing a tenacious transparent gluten, considered very wholesome, and esteemed an useful laxative, and very good roasted, as a cure for Dysentery.

Dr. Roxburgh appears to think the *Sreep,hul* of Bengal a distinct variety from the *Bél* of the coast

---

* "Corrupted from the Marmeleira of the Portuguese, given to it because this people seem to have prepared a marmalade from its fruit."—*Hamilton*.

of Coromanded, the former is evidently, however, the one mentioned by Sir W. Jones, in the *Asiatic Researches (vol.* ii. *page* 349), as having a claim to religious reverence among the Hindoos, chaplets of its flowers being offered to Jowarra by them.

It requires little, or no cultivation, though it prefers a rich loam: the shrub grows from six to sixteen feet in height.

The Tamarind, Tamarindus Indica, *Imlee*, is a well known, large, and handsome tree, its leguminous fruit, when ripe, having a strong but agreeable acid flavor, and either fresh, dried, or preserved, making a pleasant sherbet. The fruit ripens from December to February, but it is seldom cultivated, though few gardens are without a tree of spontaneous growth, and none ought to want it, being strongly recommended alike by its usefulness as its beauty.

The Indian Sorrel, as it is falsely called, or Indian Hibiscus is Hibiscus subdariffa, *Mésta*, of which the capsules are of a crimson, rather succulent, substance, that makes a good tart, a jelly, or a cheese similar to damson cheese, the fruit becoming ripe towards the end of November.

Propagation—is effected by seed, thriving in any good garden soil.

Kalendar.

JANUARY.

Kitchen Garden.—Sow Snake gourd; Country radish; Small red onion; and Orache; or *lal säg*. Plant out Brussels sprouts, and Patna onions; reset Jerusalem artichoke; plant out Red celery in trenches, and in the Upper Provinces sow the White Italian kind; as also country Cauliflowers and French beans; sow Crook-necked squash, and *Puloоul*; plant out Small-leaved green sage. Water must be freely given to all vegetables during this month: at the same time a few lettuces for seed should be thought of.

Fruit Garden.—Cut down the leading shoot of old Peach trees, and trim other young plants; also open out, train, and prune espalier and standard Peaches; and as the blossoms appear, dig a trench, for watering, round the roots. Manure Mango trees, if not done last month. Prune Apple and Pear trees, if in the garden; dig a trench for water round Loquat and Leechee trees as the blossoms appear. Sow Orange pips for stocks. Trim Shaddocks. Trim and break off straggling and superfluous branches of Fig trees, planting some cuttings. Thin out decayed shoots, and leaves, and suckers of Pine-apples; putting the last into a nursery. Train and manure Vines, and plant cuttings, if not done last month.

FEBRUARY.

Kitchen Garden.—Sow Snake gourd; Small red onion, for the main crop; Orache, or red and green *säg*; *Puloоul*; Gourds and Cucumber. Plant out Red celery in trenches, if not done last month. Water all vegetables freely.

Fruit Garden.—As the blossom of the Mango appears, make trenches round the trees for watering. As the blossoms appear, earth up and manure fruiting Pine-apples, digging trenches on each side to be filled daily with water. Sow early Melons, and Water-melons.

MARCH.

Kitchen Garden.—Plant out Small red onion; and Turmeric; sow Orache or red and green *säg;* Cape dwarf Cucumber; *Pulooul; Brinjal;* and Gourds, of various kinds. In some parts of the Upper Provinces the cauliflower is sown under shade, but its success is more than doubtful. Water cannot be given too plentifully to such plants, as remain. Dig well for fallowing such parts of the garden as are out of use.

Fruit Garden.—Thin out Pomegranates, Biar,&c.; as also the fruit on Peach trees. Manure, and thin out Plantains. Water the leaves of Pine-apples once a week, and look over them to remove all side-shoots from the fruit stems, and suckers from the roots, as they appear. Pinch off blossoms from young, immature Vines. Continue sowing Melons, and train those sown last month.

APRIL.

Kitchen Garden.—Sow Jerusalem artichoke; Skirret; and Country radish; Orache, or red and green *säg;* Long green, Cape dwarf, and most-useful Cucumbers; also early Scollop squash; and *Turaee;* sow, and plant out *Brinjal;* Bird pepper; Okro; Gourds; and Bitter Gourd. Plant Yams, Sweet Potatoes, Ginger, and Turmeric. Give water freely, and distribute manure wherever the ground is out of use.

FRUIT GARDEN.—Thin out the fruit on Mango trees; put on tin cases to Figs for ripening, and thin out superfluous fruit; cover Loquats to preserve them; plant out young Plantains; look over Pine-apples to keep them earthed up, and watered, and to remove shoots and suckers; sow late Melons and Water-melons; train Melon vines.

MAY.

KITCHEN GARDEN.—Sow Small white bean; Red bean; Small fruited bean; Pertab Sing's bean; Winged pea; Skirret; Country radish; Orache, or red and green *säg;* Cape dwarf cucumber; Early scollop squash; *Turaee;* Indian corn; and Okro. Plant out Ginger; Turmeric; and Mango ginger; Yams; and *Brinjals.* Close in the ground manured as soon as possible after the first shower of rain.

FRUIT GARDEN.—Raise mounds, and put river weeds round the stems of Peach trees to protect the roots from the rain and heat; graft Peaches as soon as the fruit is off; sow Peach stones, Apricot stones, &c. for stocks; graft Apples and Pears; sow Pomegranate seeds; graft Oranges; thin the fruit on Shaddock trees; case the fruit of Figs, if not done as before directed; make plantations of Pine-apples, and tie up fruiting Pine apples below the fruit, if the weakness of the stem require it; sow the seeds of Grapes; train Melon vines.

JUNE.

KITCHEN GARDEN.—Sow Borecole, or kale; Small white bean; Red Bean; Large white bean; Small fruited bean; Brazilian pea; Assam bean; Black bean; Orache, or red and

MARCH.

Vegetables. Sugar loaf cabbage, Brussels sprouts; Knight's and Marrowfat pea; Lima bean, Scarlet runner, *Mukunseem*, Brazilian pea; Potatoe; Knole kole; Early horn carrot, Large orange carrot; Long blood beet; Salsify; White beet; Sorrel, Orache or red and green *säg*; Leek; Asparagus; Endive; Red celery; Long-warted and Scollop squash; Pulwul; Snake gourd; Large tomato; Long red pepper; and Okro.

Fruit. Rose apple, Loquat, Leechee, Bullock's heart, Strawberry, Water-melon, Terminalia or Country almond, Malay apple, Tamarind, and Apple where it can be found to fruit.

APRIL.

Vegetables. Lima bean, Mukunseem; Potatoe; Sugar loaf, and Early York cabbage; Early horn carrot; Small white turnip; Long blood beet; Salsify; Sweet potatoe; White beet; Orache or red and green *säg*; Leek; Asparagus; Artichoke; Red celery; Dwarf cucumber; Crook-necked, and Scollop squash; Pulwul; Large tomato; Okro; Gourd; and Snake gourd.

Fruit. Peach, Apricot, Apple, Pear, Rose apple, Leechee, Bullock's heart, Melon, Water-melon, Banana, Corinda, Terminalia or Country almond, and Green mango for tarts, &c.

MAY.

Vegetables. Potatoe; Salsify; Sweet potatoe; Large and Small red onion; Orache, or red and green *säg*, Beet spinach; Leek; Garlic; Asparagus; Artichoke; Dwarf cucumber; *Pulool*; *Turaee*; Large tomato; Gourd; and Cabbage sprouts.

Fruit. Peach, Mango, Rose-apple, Leechee, Wampee Jack fruit, Fig, Pine apple, Grape, Melon, Water melon

Jumrool, Pomegranate, Custard apple, Papeeah, Terminalia, Banana, Earth-nut, and *Aloobokhara* wherever in ripens.

JUNE.

VEGETABLES. Potatoe; Country radish; Black-seeded Small white, Red, and Large white bean; Sweet potatoe; Small red onion; Red and green *säg*; Asparagus; Artichoke; Dwarf cucumber; Long-warted squash; *Turaee;* Large tomato; *Brinjal;* Gourd, and Snake gourd.

FRUIT. Longan, Wampee, Sweet-sop, Fig, Pine-apple, Grape, Melon, Mango, a few Peaches, Guava, Papeeah, Shaddock, Paneola plum, Banana, and Earthnut;—with some late strawberries at Meerut, and elsewhere.

JULY.

VEGETABLES. Pertab sing's and Black-seeded bean; Country radish; Red and Green *säg;* Asparagus; Long green Dwarf and Most useful cucumber; Long-warted squash; *Turaee; Brinjal;* Indian corn; Okro; Tomato; and Snake gourd.

FRUIT. Grapes in the Upper Provinces, Wampee, Bullock's heart, Sweet-sop, Fig, Pine-apple, Shaddock, Guava, *Cumrunga,* Çorinda, Papeeah, Java plum, Paneola plum, Grewia, and Banana.

AUGUST.

VEGETABLES. Assam bean, Winged pea, Small-fruited bean; Red and green *säg;* Asparagus; Nepal Dwarf and Most useful cucumber; Long-warted squash; *Turaee; Brinjal;* Indian corn; Okro; and Snake gourd.

FRUIT. Shaddock, Sweet-sop, Bullock's heart, Alligator or avocado pear, a few Pine apples but indifferent, Banana, Guava, Java plum, Paneola plum, and Grewia.

SEPTEMBER.

VEGETABLES. Borecole or kale; a few very early Peas; Assam and Black bean; Yam; Green Nepal spinach; Small cabbage lettuce; Dwarf, Nepal and Most useful cucumber; *Brinjal;* Indian corn; and Bitter gourd.

FRUIT. Sweet-sop, Guava, Shaddock, Paneola plum, and Banana.

OCTOBER.

VEGETABLES. Turnips of kinds; Early Peas; Skirret; Scarlet radish; Yam; Sweet potatoe; Round and Spanish spinach; Cabbage lettuce; Small endive; Nepal Dwarf and Most useful cucumber; Bitter gourd.

FRUIT. Sweet-sop, Pomegranate, Guava and Banana.

NOVEMBER.

VEGETABLES. Early York, and Early Battersea cabbage; Early cauliflower; Early pea, for regular succession; Dwarf French bean; Early new potatoe; Botan turnip; Knole kole; White carrot; Skirret; Scarlet and Turnip radish; Yam; Sweet potatoe; Round, prickly, and Spanish spinach; White beet; Young onion; Cabbage lettuce; Endive; Nepal and Dwarf cucumber; Large capsicum; Nepal pepper; Okro; Arum or *kuchoo;* and Bitter gourd.

FRUIT. Orange, Shaddock but scarce, Papeeah, Banana, Indian sorrel, with Sweet-sop but scarce.

DECEMBER.

VEGETABLES. Early York and Battersea cabbage, Savoy; Cauliflower; Early pea; Dwarf French bean; Potatoe; Early dwarf turnip; Knole kole; White carrot; Dwarf red beet; Scarlet turnip, and Spanish radish; Yam; Sweet potatoe; Round spinach; White beet; Cos and Cabbage lettuce; Endive; White solid celery; Scollop squash; Small tomato; Black round pepper; Okro; *Brinjal;* Arum or *kuchoo;* and Bitter gourd.

FRUIT. Orange, Tipparee, Plantain, Banana, Hog plum, Averrhoa, and Tamarind.

Glossary.

Abbreviated.—One organ shorter than the other.

Abortive.—Barren, as of flowers producing no fruit.

Absorption.—The process by which vegetables obtain nourishment from the soil, &c.

Acerose.—Needle-shaped, as the leaves of the fir tribe.

Acetic Acid—A vegetable acid found in the sap of many trees.

Acini.—The granulations of berries.

Acclimation.—The act of accustoming plants to a climate differing from their natural one.

Acotyledonous.—Having no lobes to the seed.

Aerial roots.—Roots issuing from the stem at some height, from the soil, and descending to afford the plant additional support to that ordinarily afforded.

Æstivation.—The folding of the various parts of a flower before its expansion.

Affinity.—The relation by which plants are referred to the same tribe, &c. from having similar structure.

Aggregate flower.—One composed of a number of minute florets.

Air-cells.—Openings occuring in the interior of plants.

Albumen.—The organ forming the bulk, or farina of many seeds.

Alburnum.—The outer layer of the woody part of the stem of plants.

Algæ.—Plants of the flag kind, or having leaf and branch united.

Alpine.—Plants indigenous to mountains.

Annual.—Plants that spring up, and mature their seed in the course of a single year.

Anther.—The small bag at the extremity of each filament in the flower, containing the fine powder, called pollen, causing fructification.

Aquatics.—Plants growing in water.

Armature.—The defences of plants, as thorns, spines, stings, &c.

Aroma.—The odour of plants.

Assimilation.—The process of incorporating the nutritive part of vegetable food into the substance of the plant.

Axilla.—The angle formed by the leaf stalk with the stem, or branch.

Bark.—The external covering of the stem.

Barren flowers.—Such as produce anthers but not pistils.

Berry.—A soft pulpy sack, or fruit, containing seeds.

Biennials.—Plants occupying the space of two years to grow, and perfect their seeds, also applying to a duration of that period.

Blanching.—The process of rendering certain plants crisp, and tender, by exclusion of light.

Bleeding.—The exusion of sap caused by incision, or accidental wound.

Bloom.—A fine soft glaucous powder found on the leaves, and fruit of many species of plants.

Bracte.—A leaf situate on the flower stalk, so near the flower as to be sometimes mistaken for its calyx.

Buds.—The small conical substances issuing from the axilla, or the extremity of the branches, containing the rudiments of branches, leaves, or flowers.

Calyx.—The exterior covering of the flower, or the flower cup.

Cambium.—The descending sap.

Canker.—A disease chiefly affecting the branches, and young shoots of fruit trees, corroding their substance.

Capsule.—A dry kind of pericarp, or seed-vessel separating into valves.

Carina, or Keel.—The lower petal of flowers, like the pea.

Caryopsis.—A species of pericarp, or seed vessel, one-celled and adhering to the seed, as in wheat.

Caudex.—The stem, or trunk.

Cellular tissue.—The pulp constituting the chief part of herbaceous plants, and a great part of the more woody; abounding likewise in seed lobes.

Chromule.—The substance from which a leaf or flower derives its color.

Claw.—The narrow base, or lower portion of the petal.

Clôstres.—The tubes conducting the cambium.

Clove.—The young bulb growing in the axilla of the scales of an old one.

Compound flowers.—Such as contain several florets on a common receptacle with anthers connected.

Contortion.—The irregular rolling up of a leaf caused by the puncture of insects.

Cormus.—The disk remaining after all the scales are removed from a bulb, from whence the fibres spring.

Corolla.—The interior envelope of a flower, consisting of one, or more petals.

Cotyledons.—The seed lobes which contain the first nourishment of the plant, forming, what are familiarly called, the seed leaves.

Cryptogamus plants.—Those whose organs of fructification are not visible to the naked eye.

Culm.—The stalk, or stem of grasses.

Decomposite organs.—Compound organs whose component parts are themselves compound. The root, trunk, and branches are of this class, because they consist of bark, wood, and pith.

Dehiscent.—Fruits that open of their own accord to discharge their seeds.

Detached calyx.—A calyx that includes the ovary, without adhering to it.

Dicotyledonous plants.—Such as have two cotyledons.

Diœcious plants.—Having their male, or stameniferous parts on one flower, and the female, or pistiliferous part on another.

Digestion.—The process by which the nutritive fluids taken up by the root are elaborated through the plant.

Diplŏe.—The pulp laying between the upper, and under net-work of leaves.

Disk.—The central portion of such flowers as have the florets of the outer ray differing from those of the centre.

Dissepiments.—Partitions of the cells of a compound fruit, or ovary.

Double flowers.—Having some of their parts multiplied to the exclusion of others, generally by a conversion of the stamens into petals.

Drupe.—A fruit having a soft, and pulpy exterior enclosing a nut, or stone.

Ducts.—The vessels conveying the various juices of the plant.

Duramen.—The several circles of wood in the trunk of a plant, forming the heart-wood.

Elaboration.—The process by which the food of plants is prepared for assimilation.

Embracing leaf.—One the base of which surrounds the stem, or branch whereon it grows.

Embryo.—The germ or rudiment of the plant existing in the seed; comprising the radicle, or root part formed for striking downwards, and the plumule or sprout, that takes an upward course, and eventually becomes the plant.

Endocarp.—The shell immediately investing the seed of stone fruit.

Endogenous.—Plants whose growth is effected from the centre, as in the palm.

Endosmose.—Is applied to the impulse by which moisture of the soil enters the extremities of the roots.

Epicarp.—The outside skin of stone fruit.

Epidermis.—The outer coat, covering the surface of a plant.

Epigynous.—Stamens originating in the ovary, or pistil.

Epipetalous.—Stamens originating in the petals.

Ergot.—A disease attacking cereal grasses; apparently a prolongation of the grain, but really a parasitical and poisonous fungus.

Etiolation.—A morbid affection that renders plants pale and sickly.

Exogenous.—Plants whose growth is caused by additions to the circumference.

Face.—That side of a seed which is parrallel with the axis of a compound fruit, or the line of union in a simple one.

Fascicle.—The mode of flowering under which the flower stems form a compact bundle.

Fecula.—See starch.

Fecundation.—The act of fertilizing the embryo seed by conveyance of the pollen to it through the pistil.

Fertile flowers.—In plants that have the stamens and pistils on separate individuals—are such as bear the pistil and ovary, because they only produce seeds.

Filament.—That portion of the stamen, which generally supports the anther.

Floral leaves.—See Bracteæ.

Florets.—The individual flowers, or divisions composing a compound flower.

Flower.—A general term for that part of the plant which comprises the calyx, corolla, stamens, and pistil; distinguished generally for its tints and fragrance.

Flux of juices.—Tnis occurs when the sap ascends too copiously and forms a fissure, whence it flows out, to the great injury of the plant.

Foliation.—The mode in which incipient leaves are folded up within the leaf bud.

Folioles.—The leflets of compound flowers.

Foxtail root.—A woody root is so called, when finding its way into water it puts forth a number of fine filaments from an elongated axis.

Frond.—An incorporation of the leaf, leafstalk, and branch, forming apparently but one organ.

Frondescence.—The leafing of plants is so called by Linnæus.

Fruit.—The ovary, after all the other parts of the flower have withered and fallen.

Frutex, or Shrub.—A woody plant that sends out its branches from the surface of the soil without a main stem.

Funniculus.—The thread attaching the ovulum to the placenta.

Fungns.—The tribe of mushrooms.

Galls—Excrescences caused by the puncture of an insect of the genus Cynips.

Gamosepalous.—That union of the sepals which causes the calyx to appear a single expansion.

Gangrene.—A kind of rot affecting leaves, and young shoots, from too wet, or too rich a culture; also sometimes caused by excess of heat or cold.

Gems.—Buds.

Genera.—A Botanical classification—or family of plants having the same form, or structure.

Germ.— The embryo is sometimes so called.

Germination.—The process of bringing into action the vitality of a seed, whereby the embryo becomes developed, and rises to a plant.

Glands.—Smoll organs on the surface of the leaf, and petiole, supposed to be those of secretion.

Glans.—A one-celled fruit seated in a cupule, as the acorn, chesnut, &c.

Glume.—The chaffy calyx of the grasses.

Gluten.—The residuum of flower.

Grafting.—The artificial application of a shoot from one tree, set, or fitted on another.

Habit.—The outward, and perceptible appearance of a plant, as shewing it to belong to a particular tribe or family.

Head.—A group of flowers on the extremity of a stem, or branch.

Heart-wood.—The central layers of the stem of dicotyledonous plants. See *Duramen.*

Helmet.—The upper side of lipped plants much arched.

Herbs.—Annuals, and plants of soft texture.

Hermaphordite.—A flower uniting the two sexes, or producing stamens and pistils in one individual.

Hilum.—The mark on the surface of a seed where it has been united on the seed vessel.

Hybrids.—The production of plants springing from sexual union of two individuals of distinct species—the same as mules among animals.

Hygroscopicity.—The property by which vegetable tissue tends to absorb moisture.

Hypogynous.—When the stamens originate in the receptacle.

Imperfect plants.—Such as want any one or other of the conspicuous parts, or organs common to vegetables.

Impregnation.—The same as fecundation.

Indefinite inflorescence.—When the principal axis ends as it extends in a leaf bud.

Inferior calix.—A flower cup including the ovary, but not adhering to it.

Inflorescence.—The mode of flowering, or aggregation of flowers distributed over a plant.

Inhilation.—The act of introduction of gases into a plant.

Insolation.—The exposure of plants to the light of the sun.

Intercellular passages.—The spaces between the cells of plants.

Internal structure.—That part of the vegetable fabric which is discoverable only by dissection.

Internode.—The space between knot and knot, or between the joints of stems.

Intervenium.—The pulp lying between two, or more veins of a leaf.

Integuments.—The envelopes of the organs of plants.

Introsusception.—The act of taking either fluids, or gases into the system of plants.

Involucrum.—A species of floral leaf peculiar to umbelliferous plants.

Irrigation.—Watering

Irritability.—The excitement produced by excess of light, heat, or other stimuli.

Kernel.—The seed contained within the shell of stone fruit.

Knots.—Excrescence caused generally by an obstruction in the channel of the plant's juice.

Labiatæ.—Plants with lipped flowers.

Latex.—The vital fluid of plants.

Panicle.—An assemblage of flowers on one stem subdivided into lesser stems, and forming a spike or spire.

Papilionaceons flowers.—Such as have winged flowers, the pea, &c.

Parasites.—Plants vegetating neither in earth nor water, but attaching themselves to other plants, the bark of which their root-fibres penetrate.

Paries.—The divisions of any containing organ, as of the ovary.

Partitions.—The divisions between the cells of the seed vessel.

Pedicles.—The ramifications of the main flower stem.

Peduncle.—The stem that supports the flower, or flowers, but not leaves.

Pellicle.—Any thin skin.

Perfect plants.—Such as have all the parts, and organs common to plants in general.

Perianth.—A cup-like envelope having the same use as a calyx, or corolla.

Pericarp.—The outer case of the ripened ovary. It is considered to have three parts; the epicarp, or outer integument of the fruit; the endocarp, called also putamen, closely surrounding the seed; and the sarcocarp, or pulp that lies between these two first.

Petals.—The divisions of the corolla are so called, forming in the aggregate what is called the flower.

Petiole.—The foot stalk that supports the leaf.

Phytography.—That department of Botany which describes the entire plant.

Phytology.—That branch of science which treats of the phenomena of vegetable life.

Pistil.—A column-shaped organ, occupying generally the centre of the plant, and surrounded by the stamens; it is divided into the ovary or seed vessel, a fine tube called the style, and the stigma, at the extremity, for receiving the pollen from the stamens.

Pith.—A soft spongy substance, occupying the centre of the stem, root, and branches of Dicotyledonous plants.

Placenta.—That portion of the seed vessel in which the seeds originate, occupying one angle of each cell.

Plant, or Vegetable.—"A living and organized body, insentient, "and incapable of locomotion; but originating in a seed "which springs up into a plant, again producing seed."

Plantlet.—That part of the embryo invested by the cotyledons, and being the future plant in miniature.

Plumule, or Plumelet.—A minute feather-like part of the embryo at the summit of the infant plant.

Pollen.—The fine powder contained in the anther, and supposed to be the active means of fecundating the seed.

Polygamous plants.—Those producing male, female, and hermaphrodite flowers indifferently.

Pomum.—A fleshy pericarp, or fruit enclosing a capsule, generally divided into distinct cells, as the apple.

Pores.—Openings in the membrane of the cellular tissue.

Prickles.—Stiff, sharp-pointed substances issuing from the bark of some plants.

Primine.—The outside coat of the seed in its early stage.

Proliferous flower.—One that protrudes other flowers from its own disk.

Pubescence.—The hair, hooks, scales, or down that covers some plants.

Pulp.—The soft succulent portion of the cellular tissue of frutis.

Pubinus.—The small protuberance on the stem, or branch which a fallen leaf leaves.

Putamen.—The shell of a nut, or stone of fruit.

Pyrena.—The cell of such stones, or nuts as are divided.

Radicle.—The part of the embryo that descends into the earth, and becomes the root.

Raceme.—An assemblage of flowers, each on its own stalk, proceeding from one common stem—a cluster.

Ramenta.—Small scattered scales appearing on the stems of vegetables, giving them a rough appearance.

Rays.—Divergent rays appear on the transverse section of the stem of woody plants. The outer petals of compound flowers are so called.

Receptacle.—The base whereon the several parts of fructification rest.

Regma.—Pericarp consisting of three or more cells that burst with a degree of elasticity from the axis into two valves.

Productive organs.—Such as have their functions specifically operating for the propagation of the species.

Ringent corolla.—A corolla is so called in labiate flowers that have the two lips separated from each other by a wide and regular orifice.

Root.—The part of the plant which attaches itself to the soil on which it feeds.

Runners.—Young shoots issuing from the collar of the root, creeping along the surface of the soil, and producing new roots at their extremity.

Sap.—The ascending fluid that furnishes aliment to all vegetables.

Sarcocarp.—The fleshy pulp lyeing between the outer skin and the shell, of stone fruit.

Scales.—The floral leaves when they have a scaly appearance.

Scape.—The flower stalk when it issues directly from the root, and is the only stem of the plant, as in most bulbous plants.

Seed.—That part of the mature plant which contains the rudiments of a new individual whence the species may be propagated.

Sepals.—The divisions of the calyx.

Shrub.—A perennial plant is so called ift he branches proceed direct from the head of the root without an intervening trunk.

Siliqua.—A dry elongated seed vessel, having two valves with opposite seams to which the seeds are attached.

Slips.—Shoots detached from a branch, and placed in the soil to vegetate for production of new plants.

Spathe.—The floral leaf, or sheathe that encloses the unexpanded flowers of the lily, and some other similar plants.

Spike.—That form of flowering which consists of an assemblage of flowers, rising in close succession, on one common flower stalk.

Spindle-shaped Root.—One that tapers down for some depth in the soil, gradually lessening towards the end.

Spines.—Sharp hard points formed frequently on leaves, or on the divisions of the calyx.

Spiral vessels.—Small corkscrew-formed tubes, interspersed occasionally with the other tubes of plants, supposed by some to be organs of insolation.

Spongiolæ.—The pulpy succulent ends of the root fibres, absorbing moisture, and performing the functions of mouths to the plant.

Stamens.—Slender fabrics, consisting of filament and anther, and forming the male part of every flower, to the perfect formation of whose fruit they are indispensable.

Standard.—The upper petal of a papilionaceous flower.

Stem.—The main channel of the ascending sap, and descending juices of every plant.

Stigma.—The summit of the style.

Stings.—Awl-shaped projections on the cuticle of the leaf, or stem, projecting a venomous fluid when lightly pressed.

Stipules.—Small leaves appearing at the base of the leaf stalk of some plants.

Stomata.—The pores, or minute openings, in the cuticle of the leaves of most plants.

Straw.—The culm, or trunk of grasses.

Style.—The filament, or tube of the pistil connecting the ovary with the stigma.

Sucker.—A supernumerary stem sent out by the root, and which if separated forms a new plant.

Superfœtation.—Occurs when an ovary, impregnated by the pollen of two distinct species, produces seeds some of one kind, and some of another.

Suture.—The edges where two valves unite.

Tail, or Cauda.—The feather-like appendage surmounting some seeds.

Tendril.—A spiral thread issuing from the stem, branch, petiole and even sometimes, the leaves of plants, by which they attach themselves to other substances for support, or assistance in climbing.

Tepals.—The divisions, or parts of a perianth.

Testa.—Applied by some to the outer coat of the seed.

Thalamus.—The receptacle of the flower.

Thorn.—An indurated spike orginating in the wood, and serving to arm a plant.

Thyrse.—A mode of inflorescence, having an assemblage of flowers, on a primary flower-stalk, having lower ones branching out in a horizontal direction, and the upper gradually becoming shorter, and more erect.

Trunk.—That part of a plant which ascends direct from the root perpendicularly, giving support to the branches.

Umbel.—A mode of flowering when a number of flower stalks diverge from a common centre, having flowers at their summits.

Umbilical cord.—The thread by which some seeds are attached to the placenta.

Valves.—The distinct pieces into which the seed vessel divides, when the seed is ripe.

Vascular organs.—The longitudinal fibres, or tubes for conveying the nutriment, and juices through the plant.

Veins.—The branches of the petiole disposed through the leaf.

Vernation.—The leafing of plants is so called.

Warts.—Small roundish tubercles, occuring on various parts of some plants.

Wax.—The upper surface of some leaves is found to hear a varnish, having all the properties of wax.

Wings.—The side petals of papilionaceous flowers.

Winged leaf.—A compound leaf, having leaflets on opposite sides of the petiole.

Wood.—The firm compact substance forming the body of the trunk.

ERRATA.

Page 7 line 6 for "pot" read "spot."
" " " 17 for "an" read "on."
" 26 " 24 for "druning" read "pruning."
" 37 " 10 for "expect" read "except."
" 41 " 8 for "*argillous*" read "*argillaceous.*"
" 45 " 21 for "with" read "to the."
" 54 " 8 omit "from"
" 61 " 18 after "oxalic" supply the word "acid."
" " " 26 for "there" read "they."
" 70 " last omit "as closely."
" 74 " 2 for "or" read "as."
" " " 20 for "Scartch," read Scratch; and for "that" read "this."
" 123 " 17 omit "to."
" 125 " 10 omit "of."
" 127 " 14 for "*salub*" read "*sa lub.*"
" 136 " 1 for "is then" read "it is then," and for "slately" read "slate."
" " " 20 for "tride" read "tribe."
" 137 " 20 for "*Bhoug*" read "*B'hang.*"
" " " 27 ditto ditto ditto.
" 138 " 22 for "*Goojun*" read "*Goojur.*"
" 140 " 20 for "fleshly" read "fleshy."
" 141 " 24 for "part" read "parts."
" 155 " 1 for "kind" read "kinds."
" " " last for "succeeded India" read "succeeded in India."
" 160 " 10 for "pae" read "pea."
" 164 " 5 omit "but."
" 176 " 11 for "62-5" read "6-2-5."
" 178 " 15 for "it surpasses" read "surpasses it."
" 180 " last for "contract" read "contact."
" 182 " 8 after "transplanted" omit "and."
" 188 " 2 for "colar" read "color."
" 190 " 16 for "fleshly" read "fleshy."
" 191 " 20 for "go" read "grow."
" " " last for "degenerates" read "degenerate."
" 209 " 22 after "covering" read "them."
" 210 " 1 for "runs" read "run."
" 219 " 22 for "then" read "there."
" 222 " 10 for "*Suzal*" read "*Suzab.*"
" 228 " 2 for "petandra" read "pentandura."
" 242 " 9 for "or" read "to."
" 250 " 6 after "each" read "tree."
" 254 " 17 for "matter" read "matter)."
" 263 " 16 for "train" read "training."
" " " 18 for "JUGUBE" read "JUJUBE."
" 265 " 25 for "ioccur" read "occur."
" 275 " 6 after "reddish" omit "in."
" 288 " 9 after "Gentile" omit "and."
" " " 18 for "no" read "not."
" 92 " 1 for "OF PLANTS" read "ON PLANTS."
" 108 " 3 for "purning" read "pruning."
" 297 " 2 for "when old, the vine is old" read "when the vine is old."
" 297 " 11 for "nine" read line."
" 298 " 6 for "of" read "off."
" 300 " 7 for "in" read "is."
" 333 " 15 for "*Neetary*" read "*Nectary.*"

د د ...... *d*

ذ ذ ...... *z*

ر ر ...... *r*

ز ز ...... z

ژ ژ ...... *zh*

سـ س ...... *s*

شـ ش ...... *sh*

صـ ـصـ ـص ص ...... *ss*

ضـ ـضـ ـض ض ...... zz

ط ط ...... t

ظ ظ ...... *zz*

عـ ـعـ ـع ع ...... a (broad and guttural)

غـ ـغـ ـغ غ ...... g (guttural)

فـ ـفـ ـف ف ...... *f*

قـ ـقـ ـق ق ...... k

کـ ـکـ ـک ک ...... *k*

گـ ـگـ ـگ گ ...... *g* (hard)

لـ ـلـ ـل ل ...... *l*

مـ ـمـ ـم م ...... *m*

نـ ـنـ ـن ن ...... *n*, m

و و ...... *oo*, *ó*

هـ ـهـ ـه ه ة ...... *h*

يـ ـيـ ي ...... *ee*, *é*

لا لا ...... *la*

VOCABULARY

OF

TREES, PLANTS, ETC.

COMPILED FROM THE MOST APPROVED SOURCES.

VOCABULARY

OF

TREES, PLANTS, ETC.

COMPILED FROM THE MOST APPROVED SOURCES.

In recording the botanical names, Loudon's Encyclopædia of Plants has been taken as the standard, and all those not otherwise marked, are therefore, on that authority. In the modern changes, Professor Lindley has been assumed as the most approved source, and such exceptions to these two as are derived from other authorities will be fouud noted accordingly. In some few instances, Roxburgh's Flora Indica has been the sole authority for native names, and these are respectively marked with the letter R.

The following is the system adopted in representing the powers of the Persian letters throughout this Vocabulary:—

Letters.	*Powers.*
ا ا	a (broad), i, *u*,
ب ب ﺑ ﺒ	b
پ پ ﭘ ﭙ	p
ت ت ﺗ ﺘ	t
ث ث ﺛ ﺜ	*s*
ج ج ﺟ ﺠ	j
چ چ ﭼ ﭽ	ch
ح ح ﺣ ﺤ	*h*
خ خ ﺧ ﺨ	kh
د د	d
ذ ذ	z
ر ر	r
ز ز	*z*
ژ ژ	zh
س ﺳ	s
ش ﺷ	sh
ص ص ﺻ ﺼ	ss
ض ض ﺿ ﻀ	*zz*
ط ط	*t*
ظ ظ	zz

ﻉ ﻊ ﻌ ﻋ ...... *a* (broad and guttural)

ﻍ ﻎ ﻐ ﻏ ...... *g* (guttural)

ﻑ ﻒ ﻔ ﻓ ...... f

ﻕ ﻖ ﻘ ﻗ ...... *k*

ﻙ ﻚ ﻜ ﻛ ...... k

ﮒ ﮓ ﮕ ﮔ ...... g (hard)

ﻝ ﻞ ﻠ ﻟ l

ﻡ ﻢ ﻤ ﻣ ...... m

ﻥ ﻦ ﻨ ﻧ ...... n, *m*

ﻮ ﻭ ...... oo, ô

ﻪ ﮦ ﻬ ﻫ ﮪ ...... h

ﻱ ﻴ ﻳ ...... ee, é

ﻼ ﻻ ...... la

MARKS DENOTING THE HABITS OF THE SEVERAL PLANTS FINDING PLACE IN THE VOCABULARY.

A. Aquatic,
B. Bulbous rooted,
C. Climber,
Cr. Creeper,
F. Fusiform rooted,
G. Grass,
H. Herbaceous plants,
P. Palm-tree,
Pa. Parasite,
S. Shrub,
T. Tree,
Tr. Trailer,
Tu. Tuberous rooted,
Tw. Twiner,
US. Under shrubs.

ABBREVIATIONS OF AUTHORITIES NAMED.

Burm.	Burmann, a Dutch editor.
Chois.	Choisy, a Swiss botanist.
Cole.	Henry Colebrooke.
DC.	De Candolle, a French botanist, founder of the Natural system.
Dr. Ro	Dr. Royle.
Dr. Wall.	Dr. N. Wallich.
Flem.	Fleming.
Gært.	Gærtner, a German carpologist.
Herb.	The Herbarium.
Jac.	Jacquin, an Austrian botanist.
Juss.	Jussieu, a French systematic botanist.
Kö.	König, a German naturalist.
Lam.	Lamarck, a French botanist.
Lém.	Lémery.
Lin.	Linnæus. The Swedish founder of the Linnæan system.
Lour.	Loureiro, a Portuguese traveller.
N.	Nees v. Esenbeck, a German botanist.
Pro. Lind.	Professor Lindley.
Retz.	Retzius, a German botanist.
Ros.	Roscoe, an English do.
Rot.	Rottboll, a Danish do.
Rott.	Rottler.
Rox.	Roxburgh.
Schr.	Schreber, a German do.
Va.	Vahl, a Danish do.
Will.	Willdenow, a German do.

USEFUL TERMS.

Acid, امل amul, ترش turush, چوک chook.

Acrid, چرپرا churpura.

Agriculture, زراعت *zuraut*, سیر seer, کنبت kum-but, کهیتي kheetee.

Air, باو baoo.

Alligator, کمهیر kumheer, کنبهیر kumbheer, ناکا naka.

Alone, یکیلا ékeela.

Alum, پهٹکري p'hutkuree.

Always, همیشه huméshel.

Ant, an, چمتي chumtee, چونتي choontee.

Ant, large black, پیلک peeluk, چونتا choonta, چیونتا cheeoonta, مکهورا muk'hoora.

Antelope, see Deer.

Ant hill, a white, دیارا deeara, راخ rakh.

Aquatic, آبي abee.

Arable, جتاي jutaee.

Arbour, an, چفته chufteh, مندوا mundooa.

Ashes, چهاي ch'haee, خاک khak, راکه rakh.

Autumn, خریف khureef, خزان khuzan.

Avenue, an, روس roos, روش roosh.

Axe, پهرسا p'hursa, تبر tubur, تبل tubul, کراري ku-raree, کلهاري kul'haree.

Bark, rind, skin, shell, بکل or بکلا bukul or bukla, چهال ch'hal, چهلکا ch'hulka, قشر kushur.

Barren, ابکیشي abkéshee, اوسرا *u*oosra, راندا randa.

Bason, round a tree to hold water, تهالا t'hala.

Basket, توکرا tôkra.

Bat, a, چمچرخ chumchurukh, چمگدري chumgud-ree, چمگیدر chumgeedur, موشک mooshuk.

Bed of flowers, &c. تخته tukhteh, خیابان kheeaban, کیاري keearee.

Beegah, a land measure of 14,400 square feet, بیگها beeg'ha.

Behind or in front of, آگا aga, آگي agé.

Behind, پیچهو peech'hoo, پیچهي peech'hee.

Below, زیر *z*eer.

Berry, a, حب *h*ub, حبه *h*ubeh.

Bent, جهبوا j'hubooa.

Bird, پکهیرو puk'heeroo, چریا chureea.

Bitter, تیتا teeta.

Bittern, a, چمربگلي chumrubgulee.

Black, کالا kala.

Blanket, کملي kumlee.

Blossom, a, منجر munjur.

Blossom, to, پهولنا p'hoolna, شگفتن shuguftun.

Blowing, of a flower, دمیدگي dumeedugee.

Bog, a, see Quagmire.

Border, a, مري muree.

Bough, a, شاخ shakh, فرع fura.

Boundary, سرحد sur*h*ud.

Branch, young, see Spray.

Branch, a broken, تندي tundee, توندي tondee.

Branch, a large, تهال t'hal, تهالا t'hala, تهالي t'halee, تهني tuhnee, دالي dalee, دهالي d'halee, دينا deéna, ساکهه sak'heh.

Break, to, توردينا tôrdéna.

Break, to, down, توردالنا tôrdalna.

Break, to, off or gather, تورلينا tôrléna.

Breeze, a gentle, نسيم nuseem.

Broken, پهوتا p'hoota.

Brook, a, جو joo, جوي jooee.

Bruise, a, چوت chôt.

Bud, a, توسي toosee, غنچه *g*uncheh, کلي kulee, زهر *z*uhur.

Burst, to, پهورنا phoorna.

Bush, see Underwood.

Bustard, a, چرز churuz.

Butterfly, تيتري teetree.

Canvas, تات tat.

Dove, turtle, پندک punduk, تلیهه tuleeheh, توترو tootroo, فاختة fakhteh.

Drain, a, نالي nalee.

Drain, to, الچهنا ulch'huna.

Dry, سوکها sook'ha, شبنم shubnum.

Duck, et id genus omne, هانس hans بدق buduk.

Dung, چرکین churkeen, کهاد khad ; of the cow, گوبر gôbur.

Dust, دهول d'hool.

Ear of corn, or spike of flowers, خوشه khoosheh, سبل subul.

Earth, بهولت b'hoolut, بهوین b'hooeen, تراب turab, ماتي matee, متي mutee.

—— potter's چکني متي chucknee mutee.

Early, as applied to fruit, &c. پیش رس peesh 'rus.

Early morning, سویري suooéree.

Earthquake, an, زلزله zulzuleh.

East, پورب poorub.

Egg, اندا anda.

End, انتها intuha.

Empty, خالي khalee.

Eradicating, استیصال isteessal.

Estate, an, or farm چک chuk.

Estate, a large, زمينداري zumeendaree.

Even, or alongside, برابر burabur.

Evening, سانجه sanj'h.

Every, هر hur.

Exact, تهيک t'heek.

Exotic, پرديسي purdésee.

Falcon, پندوري pundooree.

Falcon, royal, شهباز shu'hbaz.

Fallow, پتت putut, پتيت puteet.

Farm, or rented land, اجاره ajareh.

Fence, temporary, of thorns, خار بندي kharbundee.

Fertile, اپجاو apjaoo.

Fibre, a, رگ rug, ريشه reesheh.

Fill, to, بهرانا b'hurana.

Firm, ثابت sabut.

Fire-fly, جگنو jugnoo, کرمک kurmuk.

Flail, a, سانت sant.

Fish, مچهي much'hee.

Flower, پهلکا p'hulka, پهلواري p'hulooaree, شکوفه shukoofeh, پشپ pushp, پهول p'hool, سمن sumun, سنبل sumbul, ورد oourud.

Flower pot, a, چگير chugeer.

Fly, a, مکهي muk'hee, مگس mugus.

Force or strength, زور zoor.

Forest, اتوي atooee, جنگل jungul, جنگله jungleh, (see also Desert) کانن kanun.

Foggy, دهوندهرا d'hoond'hra.

Fox, a, ثعلب *sa*lub, روباه roobaeh, سمسم sumsum, لوکتي looktee, لومري loomree.

Fragrance, آمود amood, خشبوي khooshbooee, سباس subas, سگند sugund, مشموم mushmoom, نکهت nuk'hut.

Frog, دادر dadur, بينگ béng.

Fruit, پهر p'hur, پهل p'hul, ثمر sumur, ميوه meeooah.

Fruitful, سپهل sup'hul, مثمر mu*s*mur.

Full, complete, پورا poora.

Furrow, a, ريگهاري reeg'haree.

Garden, a, روضه roozeh.

Garden, enclosed, باري baree, باغ ba*g*, حديقه *h*u-deekeh, شاخسار shakhsar.

Garden, small باغيچه ba*g*eecheh.

Garden, flower, بوستان boostan.

Gardener, a, مالي malee.

Gate, پوري pooree, پهاتک p'hatuk, دوار dooar.

Germinate, to, جمنا jumna.

Germinating, رو roo.

Gnat, پشه pusheh.

Graft, see Scion.

Grain, a, or seed, دانه daneh.

Grant, a, royal, التمغا iltum*g*a.

Grass, گهاس g'has.

Grasshopper, پهنگا p'hunga, تدا tuda.

Grove, a, اپبن apubun, آرام aram.

Ground, rising, دهيها d'heeha, ديها deeha.

Glutinous, چمسا chumsa.

Gum, صمغ ssum*g*, گوند goond, ثمر *s*umur.

Hail, اول aool, اولا aoola.

Half blown, ادکهلا adk'hula.

Half ripe, ادهپکه ad'hpukeh, ادهکچا ad'hkucha.

Hare, a چوگرا choogura, خرگوش khurgôsh, سبرت suburt, سسا susa, لمها lum'ha.

Hard, سخت sukht.

Harrow, to, or plough in seed, بداهنا buda'hna.

Harrow, a, بزن buzun, سراون suraooun, ميي mee'ee or موي möee, هينگا hénga.

Harvest, خرمن khurmun.

Hawk, ترمتي turmutee, تونوا toonooa, جره jureh, چرغ chur*g*.

Heap, a, پنج punj, دهگار d'hugar

Heat, تابش tabush, تپ tup, تپن tupun.

Herbage, سبزه subzeh.

Hillock, تل tul.

Hired, or contract labor, تهيکا t'heeka.

Hoe, a, کودال kôdal, کودالي kôdalee.

Hoopoe, (the bird,) هدهد hud hud.

Hornet, a, زنبور *zumboor*, زنبوره *zumbooreh*

Hurricane, a, چواي chooaee.

Husbandman, a, جوتار jôtar.

Hyena, کفتار kuftar, بهالوک والا b'halook ôala.

Inundation, آهلا ahla, آهلو ahloo.

Irrigation, پتار putaoo.

Irrigate, to, سيچنا seechna, شيره sheereh.

Jackal, a, جنبو jumboo, سيار seear, سيال seeal, چقال chukal, گيدهار geed'har.

Joining, a, جور joor.

Juice, رس rus.

—— milky, دود dood, لبن lubun.

Juiceless, ارس arus.

Kernel, a, گتهلي gut'hlee, مغز mu*gz*.

Kid, حلوان *h*ulooan.

Kite, a, چيل cheel, چيلهه cheel'heh, زغن *zugun*.

Knife, a, چهري ch'huree.

Kottah, a measure of land equal to 720 square feet, كتها kut'ha.

Labor, or fatigue, دوادو dooadoo.

Lake, a, جلا jula, جهيل j'heel.

Land, زمين zumeen.

Landholder, a, زميندار zumeendar.

Lark, a, چكاوك chukaoouk.

Lattice work, جعفري jafree.

Leaf, پات pat, پتا putta, دل dul. ورق oouruk.

Leech, a, زلو zuloo.

Level, چورس chôrus.

Light, روشن rôshun.

Lightning, برق burk, دامن damun, دامني damunee, كوندها koond'ha.

Lime, چونا choona.

Little, a, تهورا t'hôra.

Lizard, بستوي bustooee, تكتكي tuktukee, چلپاسه chulpaseh, چهپكلي ch'hupkulee, چهپكي ch'hupkee, سرت surut, گرگٹ gurgut.

Lizard, a, red-tailed, بمني bumunee.

Locust, a, تدي tudee, ري teeree, ملخ mulukh.

Manure, سار sar.

Marsh, a, تراي turaee, جهابر j'habur.

Marshy ground, شوره shooreh.

Mat, a, چتاي chutaee.

Mattock, بيلک beeluk, پهاورا p'haoora, موتكي moot-kee.

Meadow, a, چراگاه churagaeh, چران churan, راغ rag.

Mildew, هردا hurda.

Mire, گچپچ guchpuch, کهت k'hut.

Misty, دهندهلا d'hund'hula.

Mix, to, ملانا mulana.

Moist, تر tur, رطب rutub.

Month, a, ماس mas.

Moon, the, چند chund.

Morning, the, فجر fujr.

Mortar, a, wooden اکهلي uk'hlee.

Mound, a, تپري tupree, پگار pugar.

Mountain, a, پربت purbut, پهار puhar, جبل jubul, گر gur, نگ nug.

Mouse, a, چوهي choohee, موسا moosa.

Mud, چيک cheek.

Mungoose, or weasel, (Pinera Ichneumon,) بيجي beejee, سمور sumoor, منگوس mungoos, راسو rasoo, نيول neeool.

Musquito, مچهر much'hur.

Net, a, جال jal.

Night, رات rat, راتر ratur, شب shub

Nursery, or seed plot, بہنور buhnoor, بیار beear.

Open, to, کھولنا k'hôlna.

Order, an, حکم hukum.

Ox, an, گورو gooroo.

Pace, a, قدم *k*udum.

Paddy-bird, بگلا bugla.

Pan, earthen, کنده kundeh.

Panther, a, یوز eeoo*z*.

Parrot, a, توتا toota, توتي tootee, سوا sooa.

Parterre, or bed, چمن chumun.

Partridge, a, تیتر teetur, دراج duraj.

Pasture, see Meadow.

Path, a, جادج jaduj.

Peacock, a, مور moour.

Peg, a, کھونتي k'hoontee.

Petal, a, پکھري puk'hree, پنکھري punk'hree, ورد oourud.

Pigeon, a, کبوتر kubootur.

Pith, هیر heer.

Plant, a, بقله bu*k*leh.

Plant, to, رونپنا roo*m*pna.

Throw, to, away, پهینک دینا p'hénkdéna.

Thrush, a, ننانوي nunanooee.

Thunder, چرا chura, چکتا chukta.

Tie, to, بندهنا bund'hna.

Toad, a, بهیکه b'heek'h.

Tomtit, پیدري peedree.

Tortoise, a, تانبیل ta*m*beel.

Tough, چمرا chumra.

Trample, to, روندنا roondna.

Tree, a, بتپ butup, پیر peer, تر turu, ترو turoo, ترور turoour, درخت durukht, درم durum, روکه rook'h, گاچ gach, جهار j'har.

Trees, a collection of, اشجار ashjar.

Trunk of a tree, تیرا teera, جروت juroout, ساق sa*k*, سلي sulee, نره nureh.

Turf, چار char.

Twine, ستلي sutlee.

Twist, a, or coil, پیچ peech, or péch, تاب tab.

Valley, a, دره dureh, نیچان nuchan.

Vegetables, esculent, ترکاري turkaree, سبزي subzee.

Vegetated, دمیده dumeedeh.

Vegetating, روي rooee.

Vegetation, رویدگي rooeedugee, نبات nubat.

Verdant, رطب ru*t*ub, سبز subz, شاداب shadab, هرا hura, هرب hurub, هريلا hureela.

Village, پوروا poorooa, گام gam, گانو ganoo.

Vineyard, a, آبسل absal.

Viper, a, تيرمار teermar.

Vulture, a, رنگت rungut.

Underwood, جهار j'har, جهاري j'haree, جهانکر j'hankur.

Unripe, خام kham.

Wages, طلب *t*ulub, اجوره ajooreh.

Warm, اشن *u*shun, گرم gurum.

Wasp, برلا burla, هدا huda.

Waste land, پرتي purtee.

Watchman, a, چوکيدار chookeedar.

Water, آب or آپ ab, or ap, پنيا puneea, جل jul.

Waterbag, a, پکهال puk'hal, چهادان ch'hadan, مشک mushuk.

Watering, a, چهرکاو ch'hurkaoo.

Water-lifter, a basket for lifting the water when not to a great height, دهينکي d'heenkee.

Waterpot, کلسي kulsee. تهليا t'huleea.

Weak, see Thin.

Weasel, see Mongoose.

Weed, a, چکهرن chuk'hurun.

Weed, to, نیرانا neerana.

Withered, چندرانا chundrana.

Weeder, a, کهرپي k'hurpee, نیراني neeranee.

Well, a, چه ch'uh, چهبچه ch'hubucheh, کند kund, بیر beer کور kôur.

West, مغرب mu*g*rub, پچم puchum.

Weevil, a, پتاري putaree, سوندا soonda, کن kun.

Weighing, or measuring, تول تال tool tal.

White ant, دیوک dee'ook.

Wide, چورا chooura.

Widgeon, a, سرخاب surkhab.

Wind, باد bad.

Wind, hot, جهانولي j'hanôlee.

Windfall, a, چوا chooa.

Winnow, to, پینچنا pénchna, چهنکنا ch'hunkna, دهریانا d'hureeana.

Winter, زمستان *z*umustan.

With, ساته sat'h.

Wood, timber, عود *a*ooud.

Wolf, هندار hundar.

Worm, guinea, نهاروا nu'harooa.

Worm, palmer, بهندلي b'hundlee.

Worm, a, پلو puloo, پلوا pulooa, جیوري jeeooree, خراطین khurateen, کرم kurum, کیر keer.

Year, a, سال sal.

Yellow, زردرنگ zurdrung.

Young, see Tender.

Yoke, a, جوه jooeh.

Young, or new, نو nuoo, نوا nuooa.

NAMES OF PLANTS.

Abelia, three flowered, كمكي kumkee. Abelia triflora, *Dr. Wall.* (C)

Abies khutrors, see Smith's pine.

Abrus precatorius, see Wild Jamaica liquorice.

Acacia catechu, see Medicinal catechu tree.

Acacia, gum, ببول bubool, ببوري bubôree, مغيلان mu*g*eelan, كيكر keekur, كلي كيكر kulee keekur, ام غيلان am*g*eelan. Acacia Arabica, or Mimosa Arabica, *Lam.* (T,) Common all over India, and well known for the fragrance of its flowers, and its hard wood, used for ploughs, &c.

Acacia, soft, لاكي lakee. Acacia mollis, (S)

Acalypha, Indian, كوپي koopee, سويت بسنت sooeet busunt. Acalypha Indica. (H.) The bruised root is cathartic, and is prescribed by native practitioners in consumption; the leaves being also given to children as a vermifuge.

Acanthus, holly leaved, هركوچ كانٹا hurkooch kanta, R. هركت hurkut. Acanthus ilicifolius, (US)

Achillea ptarmica, see Sneezewort.

Achyranthes, alternate leaved, گنگاتیه gunga-tee'eh, Achyranthes alternifolia. (US)

Achyranthes aquatica, see water centroostachys.

Achyranthes, climbing, نوریا nooreea. Achyranthes scandens, *Rox.* (US)

Achyranthes, rough, چرچرا churchura, آگارا agara, اگاری agurée, حلیم *h*uleem, محوط mu*h*oot. Achyranthes aspera, (US) A troublesome weed in the rainy and cold seasons; but used by natives in bowel complaints as an astringent.

Achyranthes, three stamened, سانچی sanchee, شالونچه shalooncheh, R. Achyranthes triandra, *Rox.* (Cr)

Achyranthes, woolly, چایا chaeea. Achyranthes lanata, *Rox.* (US)

Aconitum ferox, see Wild wolf's bane.

Acorus calamus, see Sweet flag.

Adamsonia digitata, see Ætheopian sour gourd.

Adantum, see Woolly brake.

Adder's tongue, winding, بهوت راج b'hoot raj. Ophioglossum flexuosum, (H)

Adelia, chesnut-like. بول کوکری bôl kookree. Adelia castinacarpa, *Rox.* (T)

Adenanthera, yellow flowered, رکت چندن rukt chundun. Adenanthera pavonina, (S)

Adhatoda vasica, see Malabar nut.

Aegiceras, greater, هلسي hulsee. Aegiceras majus, *Pro. Lind.* (T.)

Aegle mamelos, see Bengal quince.

Aerides guttalum, see Air plant.

Aeschynomene, hemp, دهنچي d'hunchee. Aeschynomene cannabina *Kö.* (H)

Aeschynomene, large flowered, see Agati.

Aeschynomene, marshy, شولا shôla, بهند b'heend. Aeschynomene paludosa, *Rox.* (A) The stem is one mass of pith, which is used for various purposes, such as floats for fishing nets, artificial flowers, and other ornaments used at native weddings, &c. &c.

Aeschynomene, sesban. جيت jeet. Aeschynomene sesban, *Rox.* (S)

Agallochum, see Aloes wood.

Agaric, اغاريقون agareekoon. Boletus Igniarius,

Rox. (Pa) Is used as a styptic, being a fungus growing on the Indian oak.

Agathotes chirayta, see Chirayta.

Agati, large flowered, اگتي agutee. اگست agustu. Agati grandiflora, Coronilla grandiflora, *Will.* Aeschynomene grandiflora, *Linn.* (T) The legume is eaten by natives in some parts, and the bark is a tonic bitter.

Agave. cantula, ولايتي اناناس oolaeetee *u*nanas. Agave Cantula, *Rox.* (S)

Ageratum, water, برا كيشتي bura keeshutee. Ageratum aquaticum, *Rox.* (H)

Aglaia polystachine, باندور پالا bandoor pala. Aglaia polystachya, *Dr. Wall.* (T)

Agrostis diandra, see Diandrous bent grass.

Agrostis linearis, see Doop grass, and Thread-like bent grass.

Air plant, spotted, بياردہ beearudeh, مور moor, كسپون akuspoon. Aerides guttalum, *Rox.* (Pa)

Ajugadisticha, see Opposite leaved bugle.

Alangium, six-petalled, اكراكانتا akrakunta, اكول akool. Alangium hexapetalum, *Rox.* (T)

Aleurites, three lobed, درخت اخروت durukht-u akhroot. Aleurites triloba, (T)

Alhagi mamorum, see Prickly stemmed manna plant.

Allium ascalonicum, see Shallot.

Allium cepa, see Common onion.

Allium porrum, see Leek.

Allium sativum, see Garlic.

Allium tuberosum, see Indian chive.

Almond, Indian, بادام هندي badam-u-hundee, Terminalia Catappa, (T) The kernel is eaten fresh, and has something the flavor of an English filbert.

Almond, Persian, بادام فارسي badam-u-farsee, لوز looz, لوزان loozan. Amygdalus communis, (T) Growing only in the Upper Provinces.

Aloe, common, گهيكوار g'heekuooar, ايلو *u*eelooa صبر ssubur, مصنبر mussumbur. Aloe vulgaris or, perfoliata, *Linn.* (US). This yields the Barbadoes aloes, and is easily cultivated here.

Aloe, spike flowered, ايلوا *u*eelooa, درخت عود durukht *a*ood, چهتا كنوار ch'huta-kunooar. Aloe spicata, (H). A native of Socotra easily cultivated here, but the most common is A. vulgaris, or perfoliata, *Linn.* the Barbadoes aloes.

Aloes wood, or agila wood اگر agur قلمبک

*k*ulumbuk, عودهندي *a*ood hundee, عودقاقاي *a*ood-*k*a*k*aee. Aquilaria Agallocha, *Rox.* (T) Found in the forests of Sylhet, and producing a fragrant resin, which there is little doubt is the Calambac, or Agallochum of the ancients; it is regarded as a cordial by natives, and has been used in Europe for gout and rheumatism.

Alpinia cardomum, see True cardomum.

Alpinia, Cingalese, تارا tara, تارکا taruka. Alpinia Allughas. (H)

Alpinia, loose flowered, see the greater Galangal.

Alpinia nodding, پوناگ چمپا poonag chumpa. Alpinia nutans. (H)

Althæa frutex, گرهل gurhul. Hibiscus syriacus. (S)

Althea officinalis, see common marsh mallow.

Althæa rosea, see Hollyhock.

Amaranth, black, بانسپتا bansputa. Amarantus atropurpureus. (H)

Amaranth, eatable, مرسا mursa, ماتکي بهاجي matkee b'hajee, چندي ساگ chundee sag. Amarantus oleraceus, (H) Grown as a pot herb, or *säg.*

Argyreia nervosa, see Vein leaved silver weed.

Aristolochia Indica, see Indian birth-wort.

Aristolochia longa, see Long-rooted birth-wort.

Aristolochia saccata, see Pouched birth-wort.

Arnotta, heart-leaved, لٹکن lutkun. Bixa orellana. (T) Yielding the dye called arnotta, which is however very fugitive, and chiefly used in Great Britain to color butter and cheese.

Arrowroot, East Indian, کوآکا نشستہ kooaka nushast'eh, تکھر tuk'hur. Curcuma angustifolia. (H) This is the Travancore arrowroot, but is seldom of good color, which has caused a prejudice against the Indian article even when of the true kind: the starch from this is also much weaker than that of the true plant.

Arrowroot, true, ارورروت *uroo* root, (cor) جیت الو jeet aloo. Maranta arundinacea. (H) This has been imported, and found to thrive well in Bengal; the first plants were introduced by the late Mr. Leycester, and a few were more recently brought out by the Earl of Auckland.

Artemisia Austriaca, or paniculata, see in dian Southern wood.

Artemisia, elegant, ابطنا abu*t*na R. Artemisia elegans, *Rox.* (H)

Artemisia Indica, see Indian wormwood.

Artemisia vulgaris, see Mug wort.

Artichoke, garden, حرشف *h*urshuf, کنگر kungur, ارتچک artuchuk (cor), Cynara Scolymus. (H)

Artichoke, Jerusalem, خورپرست خانالایک k'hoor purust khanalaék, Helianthus tuberosus. (Tu)

Artocarpus integrifolia, see Jack tree.

Artocarpus lakoocha, see Bengal bread fruit.

Arum, arched, بیس کچو bees kuchoo, بیربکي beer-bukee. Arum fomicatum, *Rox.* (Tu)

Arum, bell-shaped, آلو aloo, اول *u*ool, سورن *s*oo-run, Arum campanulatum. (Tu)

Arum, Egyptian, اروي aroee, گهویان g'hooeean, کچو kuchoo, کچالو kuchaloo. Arum colocasia. (Tu) The tuber is eaten.

Arum nymphæi folium, see Waterlily-leaved caladium.

Arundo Bengalensis, see Bangal reed.

Arundo Karka, see Karka reed.

Asarabacca, common, اسارون *u*saroon. Asarum Europæum. (H). The roots are purgative, emetic, and diuretic; but the plant is by no means common, and chiefly found in the Dukhun. London would derive its name from α, a primitive, and σειρα a bandage, but it is more probably obtained from its Syrian name "usaroon."

Asarum, see Asarabacca.

Asclepias asthmatica, see Emetic swallow wort.

Asclepias echinata, see Prickly swallow wort.

Asclepias geminata, see Double swallow wort.

Asclepias gigantea, see Curled flowered calotropis.

Asclepias odorotissima, see West coast creeper.

Asclepias pseudosarsa, see Indian sarsaparilla.

Asclepias rosea, see Esculent oxystelma.

Asclepias tunicata, see Coated swallow wort.

Asclepias volubilis, see Green flowered hoya.

Ash, floribund, لاک کري lak kuree, وشيج oosheej. Fraxinus floribunda, *Dr. Wall.* (T)

Asparagus, branching, سادابوري sada booree, R, ستمولي sutmoolee, (R) Asparagus racemosa. (H)

Asparagus, common, يراميع eerameea, ناکدون nak doon, رگيه margee'eh, اسفراج isfuraj, مارچوبا marchooba, هليون huleeoon. Asparagus officinalis. (H)

Asparagus, linear-leaved, سفيد موسلي sufćd mooslee, Asparagus sarmentosus. (Tw)

Asphodel, club-seeded, بروق burook, خنشي khun shee. Asphodelus clavatus. (H)

Assafœtida plant, درخت هنگ durukht-u-hung. كاشم kashum, درخت انگوزه durukht angoozeh, انجدان anjudan, سكبينج sukb'henuj. Ferula asafœtida *Pro. Lind.* (H) The fœtid alliaceous gum resin obtained from the four years' old roots is the Assafœtida of the druggists. This is the most genuine plant, but Dr. Royle mentions others as producing the article found in the Bazars in this country as from F. persica, and F. hooshee. It is much used by natives.

Astragalus, see Milk vetch.

Atiplex hortensis, see Garden orache.

Atropa belladona, see Deadly night shade.

Avena sativa, see Common oat.

Averrhoa acida, see Long leaved cicca.

Averrhoa bilimbi, see Bilimbi tree.

Averrhoa carambola, see Carambola tree.

Avicennia, downy leaved, بوعلي سينا booalee seena, بوعلي booalee, بينا beena, R. Avicennia tomentosa. (T) The bark is used at Rio Janeiro for tanning.

Balm, common, مكه سبزه muk'eh subz'eh, بقله الفرستم bu*k*l'eh ulfurustum, بادرنج بويه badrunj booee'eh بادرنک badrunk. Melissa officinalis, (Cr.) was brought to India from Arabia, and is only used as a tea, or diluent in fevers.

Balm of Gilead tree, درخت روغن بلسان durukht-u-roo*g*un bulsan, درخت اقويل اسمون رومي durukht a*k*ooél asmoon roomee, بلسان bulsan. Protium giliadense, *Pro. Lind.* Amyris gileadensis, *Rox.* (T) The resinous gum, called also *Balm of Mecca,* is reckoned, by all eastern people, a perfect panacea.

Balsam, گل مهندي gul mu'hndee, دوپاني doopatee, R Impatiens balsamina. (H)

Bamboo, common, بانس bans, بنبو bu*m*boo, قصب *k*ussub. Bambusa arundinacea, (P) A valuable medicine, according to the Hindoos, called طباشير *t*ubasheer, of a siliceous nature found by Turner to concise of *silica* with lime and vegetable matter indestructable by fire, unaffected by acid, and with alkalies making glass on fusion, is found in the female plant. Roxburgh mentions several varieties of bamboo. The seed is also eaten boiled in milk or broth. The young shoots making a good pickle, and when full grown too well known for its multifarious uses to need notice.

Banana, كيلا kéla, موچا mocha, موز moouz. Musa sapientum, (T) in India commonly called the Plaintain, which see; this includes however the best varieties used as fruit, such as the *chee-neh chumpah*, &c.

Banyan, see Indian fig.

Barleria, long leaved, تال مکهانا tal muk'hkana, گوک شورا gook shoora, گوکهرو gook'huroo. Barleria longifolia, or Ruellia longifolia *Rox*. (H)

Barleria, thorny, كانٹا جاتي kanta jatee. R. Barleria prionites. (US)

Barley, native, جو juoo, شعير shaeer سالت sult, کشک kushuk, يو eeoo, جبه jub'eh, R. Hordeum hexastichon, (G) Is mentioned by *Rox*. as the species cultivated in India, but this bears a greater affinity to H zeocriton.

Barringtonia, angular, ابج abju. Barringtonia acutangula, *Rox*. (T) highly ornamental tree of about 40 feet in height.

Bead tree, common, see Margosa tree.

Bean, aconite leaved kidney, موت môut, Phaseolus acconitifolius (Tw.) A small pulse much in use.

Bean, Assam, كالي سيم kalee seem. Stizolobium altissimum. (C)

Bean, dwarf kidney, باقلا ba*k*la, زن zun, نحبوع nu*h*booa, دسمري dusmuree, دجر dujur, حنبل hu*m*bul. Phaseolus vulgaris. (C)

Bean, garden, باقلا ba*k*la, بقلت bu*k*lut. Vicia faba. (H)

Bean, pointed kidney, بن بربتي bun burbutee. Phaseolus rostratus. *Dr. Wall.* (Tw.)

Bean, hairy podded kidney, or Black gram, اورد كالي kalee aoorud, ماش mash, Phaseolus Max, (Tr.)

Bean, huzar, كهرسنبل k'hursunbul. Dolichos cultratus *Thun*, (Tw.) Eaten entire when young, but when full only the seeds.

Bean, rayed kidney, هري مونگ huree moong. Phaseolus radiatus, (Tw.) Much used on the Madras side in *Mulligatawnee*, and curries.

Bean, small fruited, or Green gram, ارود arood, مونگ moong. Phaseolus mungo, (Tr.) A good pulse.

Bean, three lobed kidney, کلاي kulaee. Phaseolus trilobus. (Tr.) Used as food for cattle, having a great effect in fattening, but very coarse.

Bean, Tranquebar, لوبي کي پهلي loobee kee p'hulee. Dolicos Tranquebaricus, (Tw.) Not much unlike the French bean in appearance and quality.

Beet, Bengal, پالک paluk. Beta Bengalensis, *Rox.* (H) One of the greens, or sägs of the natives.

Beet, common, چُهندا chuchunda, سلک sulk, چقندر chu*k*undur, پازو pazhoo, غرمج *g*urmuj. Beta vulgaris. (H)

Bellis perennis, see Daisy.

Benzoin tree, بان ban, لوبان looban, لبان luban, عود لوباني *a*ood loobanee, عود *a*ooud. Styrax benzoin. (S) The resin is a stimulant particularly affecting the lungs.

Berberry, holly leaved, انبربارس ambur barus,

موبرج moobruj. Berberis ilicifolia, B: Asiatica of *Rox.* (S) Native of Nepal.

Berberry, Nepal, چیترا cheetra, انبرباري ambur baree, الرغيس a, argees. Berberis aristata. (T) The extract of the root (رصوت russôt,) is used in Indian medicine, especially in ophthalmia, which Dr. Royle supposes to be the λυκιον of Dioscorides.

Bergera, Kœnig's, کریپاک kureepak, برسنگا bursunga, R. Bergera Kœnigii, *Rox.* (T) The Hindoos consider the roots as stimulant, and the leaf as stomachic.

Bergia, ammanioidic, دولهچري dool'eh churce, R. Bergia ammanioides. (A)

Betel nut-tree, سپاري suparee, سپياري supeearee, فوفل fooful, کرامکا kuramuka, گواکه gooak'eh. Areca catechu. (P)

Betelnut, slender, رام گوا ramgooa, R. Areca gracilis, *Rox.* (P)

Betle pepper, پان pan, تانبول tanbool, برگ تامبول burg tambool, ناگبیل nagbél. Piper betle. (Tr.)

Betula accuminata, see Tapering birch.

Betula bhojpatra, see Indian birch.

Bignonia Indica, see Indian trumpet flower.

Bignonia suaveolens, see Tree trumpet flower.

Bilimbi tree, بلم بو bulum boo. Averrhoa bilimbi, (S) A syrup is made from the juice of the fruit, and a conserve from the flowers, both esteemed in fevers and bilious complaints. The fruit also makes a good pickle.

Bindweed, creeping, كلمي ساگ kulmee säg, Convolvolus repens, or reptans, (Cr.) The leaves are used as greens, the root being said, by some authors, to be purgative.

Bindweed, goat's foot, چهاگل خوري ch'hagul khooree, R. دوپاتي لتا dôpatee luta, R. Convolvolus pescapræ, *Will.* (Cr.) Growing on sands, which it serves to bind.

Bindweed, involucrated, جرد كلمي jurud kulmee, Convolvolus bicolor. (Tw.)

Birch, Indian, اتوسا atoosa, بهوجپتر b'hôjputur, غوش *g*oosh, غوشه *g*oosh'eh. Betula bhojpatra, *Dr. Wall.* (T)

Birch, tapering, وتيس ootees, بهوج b'hooj. Betula accuminata, *Dr. Wall.* (T)

Birthwort, Indian, اسري ويل isree oouee1, اسارمل

Bread fruit, Bengal, برهل bur'hul, لکوچا lukoocha. Artocarpus lakoocha, *Rox.* (T) The fruit is eaten by natives in curries.

Brinjal, see Egg plant.

Bromelia ananus, see Pine-apple.

Broom, Portugal, رتم rutum, علقي al*k*ee. Genista Lusitanica. (S)

Bryony, air living, راكس گده rakus gud'eh, لونا loofa, ازنل نيل azunul feel. Bryonia epigæa, (Tw.) The root is used in making a liniment for chronic rheumatism. It was once supposed to be the famous Colombo root.

Bryony, bristly, ناشرا fashura, اگمکي agumukee. Bryonia scabrella. (C)

Bryony, globe fruited, موس مسه moos mus'eh. Bryonia scabra, (Tw.) The tender shoots, and leaves after being roasted, are aperient.

Bryony, great flowered, بنب bu*m*b, كندوري kudooree. Bryonia grandis, Momordica monodelpha of *Rox.* (Tw.) The fruit is used in an unripe state as a garden stuff, it is slightly acid, but insipid when ripe.

Buchanania, broad leaved, پيار peear, پيال peeal.

Buchanania latifolia, (T) The timber is useful, and the fruit is sometimes eaten by natives as a substitute for almonds.

Buckbean, Indian, کمودني kumoodunee, براچولاي bura choolaee. Menyanthes Indica, *Will.* (A)

Buckbean, tufted, چولي choolee. Menyanthes cristata, *Rox.* (A)

Buddlea, Indian, نيمدا neemda. Buddlea neemda. (S)

Bugle, opposite leaved, گوبرا goobra, R. Ajuga disticha, *Rox.* (H)

Buglos, common, لسان الثور lusan-ul-soor, شنجار shunjar, ديمهاج deem'haj, گاوزبان kaoozuban. Anchusa officinalis. (H)

Bullock's heart, لونا اتا lôna ata. Annona reticulata, (T) see also Custard apple.

Bullrush, اسل asul, استوم astoom, بردي burdee, دخ dukh, ديس dees, لوخ lookh, نمج numuj, سوم soom, همار humar, بجرا bujra. Penicillaria spicata, Panicum spicatum of *Rox.* (G)

Burrage, see Thick leaved lavender.

Butea, downy branched, پراس puras, دهاكها d'hak'ha, پلاس pulas. Butea frondosa, (T) On this tree the lac insects are often found; the seeds are used by natives medicinally, and the gum gives a yellow dye. The juice of the flowers diluted with alum water, and clarified, yields an extract brighter than gamboge changing to a reddish orange with an alkali.

Buxus sempervirens, see Box tree.

Cabbage, a, کرم کلا kurum kula, کلا kula, کرنب kurnub, کلم kulum, کوبي kôbee, کرم کا ساگ kurum ka sag. Brassica oleracea. (H)

Cabbage tree, see oleander-leaved Cacalia.

Cacalia, oleander-leaved, or Cabbage-tree. لسان الثور lusan *u*lsoor, گوزبان goozuban. Cacalia kleinia. (US)

Cacalia, sow-thistle leaved, سفيد گوبهي sufécl goob'hee. Cacalia sonchifolia. (H)

Cactus, Indian, ناگ فنا nag funa, جپل سيند jupul seend. Cactus Indicus, *Rox*. (US) The inferior kind of cochineal insect feeds well on this plant.

Cæsalpinia sappan, see narrow-leaved brasiletto.

Cæsalpinia bonducella, see Small oval leaved guilandina.

Cajepute tree, کاياپوتي kaeeapootee, کاپوپوته kaee-oopoot eh. Melaleuca Cajuputi, PROF. LIND. M. Lencadedron as was formerly supposed. (T) Yields the essential oil so useful in rheumatism, &c.

Caladium, water-lily leaved, اسوي asooee, اروي arooee, سرکچو sur kuchoo. Caladium nymphæi-folium. Arum nymphæi-folium, *Rox*. (H) This plant appears to have been mistaken by some for C. esculentum ; all parts are eaten by natives.

Calambac, see Aloes wood.

Calamus draco, see Dragon's blood plant.

Calamus rotang, see Cane.

Calamus viminalis, or zulacca, see Java rattan.

Calla, poisonous, بيش کچو beesh kuchoo, Calla virosa, *Rox*. (H)

Callicarpe, hoary, مترہ mutureh, R. مترنجه mu-trunjeh, R. Callicarpa incana, *Rox*. (S)

Callicarpe, lance shaped, کوامورا kooamoora. Callicarpa lanceolaria, *Rox* (S)

Callicarpe, large leaved, بسترا bustura. Callicarpa macrophylla, (S)

Callitris quadrivalois, see Sandarach tree.

Calophyllum, sweet scented, سلطاني چمپا sul*ta*nee chumpa, R. سرپن surpun. Calophyllum inophyllum, (T) The seeds yield an oil; and a resin is obtained from the root, supposed to be the same as the Tacamahca of the Isle of Bourbon. Hindoos offer the flower to Sheva and Vishnoo, it being very fragrant.

Calotropis, curled flowered, ارك aruk, عشر *a*shur, آک ak, اكندا akunda, مدار mudar. Calotropis gigantea, Asclepias gigantea, *Linn.* (H) The juice, root, and bark are used in elephantiasis, leprosy, and convulsions, and the first is a common cure for ringworm.

Caltrops, downy, گوکهرو gook'huroo. Tribulus lanuginosus, *Will.* (H)

Caltrops, small, or Turkey blossom of Jamaica, گوگرو googuroo, گهوگرو g'hooguroo, خسک khusuk, بستيتاج رومي busteetaj roomee, سودمسترا soodumstura. Tribulus terrestris. (H) The leaves and root are said, by native practitioners, to have a diuretic property.

Caltrops, water, see Water caltrops.

Calyptranthes, clove leaved, چھوٹا جام ch'hota jam, جامون jamoon, Calyptranthes caryophyllifolia. (T) The fruit resembles a sloe in taste, but is white.

Calyptranthes jambolana, see Java plum.

Camilla viridis, and bohea, see Tea tree.

Camphor, tree درخت كافور durukht-u-kafoor, کپور kupoor. Laurus camphora, Dryobalanops aromatica *Gœrt*, D. camphora of *Colebrooke*, Shorea camphorifera, *Rox.* or Camphora officinarum, (S. T.)

Cane, or rattan, بيت bét, بيد béd. Calamus rotang, *Will.* (C) It is a very troublesome jungle in lower Bengal, and to the Eastward.

Canna Indica, see Common Indian shot.

Cannabis sativa, see True hemp.

Canscora, decussated, دنكوني dunkoonee, (R) Canscora, Prof. Lind. or Pladera decussata, *Rox.* (H)

Canthium, narrow leaved, كوتهملي kôt'eh mulee. Canthium angustifolium, *Rox.* (S)

Canthium, small flowered, كارا kara, كاري karee. Cupia tetrandra, Capthium parriflorum, *Rox.*

Webera tetrandra of *Will.* and *Schr.* (S) The fruit is eaten by the poor, a decoction of the leaves or roots is used in flux, and the latter is anthelmintic. The bark and young shoots also are used in dysentery.

Caper, common, كبر kubur, آصف assuf, كريل kureel. Capparis spinosa, (US) Does not grow in India, but appears well known. Roxburgh enumerates several species, particularly C. aphylla, but none with similar character to this.

Caper, Indian, اردندا ardunda, caperis horrida, *Linn.* (S)

Caper, prickly, كريل kureel, كبر kubur, آصف assuf, Capparis accuminata, *Rox.* (S)

Caper tree, three leaved, برن burun. Capparis trifoliata, *Rox.* (S)

Capsicum, or red pepper, مرچا murcha, or murucha, مرچاي murchaee. Capsicum frutescens. (H)

Capsicum baccatum, see Bird pepper.

Capsicum frutescens, see Cayenne, or Chili-pepper.

Capsicum grossum, see Kaffree chili pepper.

Carambola tree, كمركه kumruk'h كمرنگه kumrun

g'eh. Averrhoa carambola. (T) Yielding a fruit of angular shape.

Caranda, jasmine flowered, بري كروندي buree kuroondee, كرمچا kurumcha. Carissa, carandas. (T) The fruit is of pleasant taste like a damson, and makes a good jelly.

Caray thorny, see Small flowered canthium.

Cardomum, large, قاقلهكبار *kak*ul'eh kubar, هيلكلان heel kulan, بري الاچي buree *u*lachee. Amomum grana paradisi, (H) The seeds are aromatic, stimulant, and cordial.

Cardomum, Morung, مورنگالاچي môrung *u*lachee. Amomum aromaticum. *Rox.* (H)

Cardomum, true, الاچي ilachee, شوشمير shooshmeer, ابل abul, قاقله صغار *kak*ul'eh ssugar, قاپالاغا *k*apal a*g*a, هيلبوا heelbooa. Elettaria cardomum, PROF. LIND. Amomum repens, *Smith*, Alpinia cardamum *Ros.* and *Rox.* (H) The cardamum of commerce, carminative and stomachic.

Carey's tree, پيلو peeloo. Careya arborea. (T)

Carica papaya, see Papaw tree.

Carissa carandas, see Jasmine flowered caranda.

Carissa, spiny, چوتي كروندي chootee kuroondee,

and that only to a small extent, it is rather to be expected that, this being indigenous to a colder climate, some other varieties might be more successful, it being occasionally found in parts of Persia and Arabia.

Clubrush, articulated, پتپتي چيچكا putputee chéchka, R. Scirpus articulatus, *Linn.* (G)

Clubrush, barbed seeded, كسوري kusooree. Scirpus kysoor, *Rox.* (Tu)

Clubrush, erect, مورموري moormooree, R. Scirpus schœnoïdes, *Kön.* (G)

Clubrush, glomerate, برانربشي bura nurbushee. R. Scirpus glomeratus, *Linn.* (G)

Clubrush, tall, برا جواني bura juooanee, R. Scirpus tetragonus, *Rox.* (G)

Clubrush, tufted, گوري gooree. Scirpus squarrosus. *Linn.* (G)

Clubrush, two spiked, كسوري ملنگه kusooree mulung'eh, R. Scirpus bispicatus, *Kön.* (G)

Cnestis monodelphores سوكوا توتا sookooa tôta. Cnestis monodelpha, (S)

Cocculus cordifolius, see Heart-leaved moonseed.

Cock's-comb, common, تاج خروس taj-u-khuroos

جت jut, جتا juta, لال مرغا lal mur*g*a. Celosia cristata. (H)

Cock's-comb, silvery spiked, سيت مرغا sooét mur*g*a. Celosia argentea. (H)

Cocoanut tree, نارجيل narjeel, ناريل nareeul, نارجيلي narjeelee, نارجبل narjubul. Cocos nucifera. (P) The cabbage, as it is called, is the uppermost tender shoots, and known as the ناريل كا كروت nareel ka kroot.

Coffee, four stamened, چيلماري cheelmaree. Coffea tetrandra, *Rox.* (S)

Coffee tree, true, بوند boond, بن bun, كوا kuooa, قهوه *k*u'hoo'eh. Coffea Arabica. (T) Roxburgh mentions a wild variety, which he calls Coffea Bengalensis; since found commonly in the Rajmuhal range of hills by Mr. Pontet, and others. The coffee of commerce grows well in almost all parts of India, and its stimulating effects are too well known, it being truly to the student "the cup that cheers but not inebriates."

Coix lachryma, see Job's tears grass.

Colchicum autumnale, see Meadow saffron.

Columnea, balsamic, كرپور kurpoor, R. Columnea balsamica, *Rox.* (Cr)

Combretum, round leaved, كولتا kooluta. Combretum rotundifolium. (C)

Commelina, Bengal, كانشيرا kanshèra, R. كانوراقا kanooraka, R. Commelina Bengalensis, (Tr)

Commelina, common جوتا كنشيرا joota kunsheera. R. (Tr) Commelina communis.

Commelina, naked flowered, كاندولي kandoolee, R. Commelina nudiflora, *Linn.* (Tr)

Commelina, scape flowering, كورلي koorulee, R. Commelina scapiflora, *Rox.* (H)

Commelina, willow leaved, لانكلي lankulee, R. پاني كانشير panee kansheera, R. Commelina salicifolia. *Rox.* (Tr)

Commiphora Madagascarensis, see Camphoric amyris.

Conium maculatum, see Common hemlock.

Convolvolus batatas, see Sweet potatoe.

Convolvolus bicolor, see Involucrated bindweed.

Convolvolus, creeping, كلمي kulmee. Convolvolus reptans. (Tr) The leaves form one of the numerous greens, or *sag*, eaten by natives.

Convolvolus nil, see Purgative pharbitis.

Convolvolus paniculatus, see Panicled batatas.

Convolvolus pescapræ, see Goat's foot bindweed.

Convolvolus repens, or reptans, see Creeping bindweed.

Convolvolus scammonia, see Scammony plant.

Convolvolus turpethum, see Square-stalked ipomea.

Conyza anthelmintica, see Saw-wort.

Conyza lacera, see Torn fleabane.

Cookia punctata, see Chinese wampee tree.

Coral tree, Indian, ماندار mandar, R. Erythrina Indica. (T)

Coral tree, oval leaved, هریاکیکر huréakeekur. Erythrina ovalifera, *Rox*. (T)

Corchorus, bristly leaved, نرچا nurcha, پات pat. Corchorus olitorius. (H) The leaves used as greens, or *säg*.

Corchorus, heart leaved, نرچا nurcha. Corchorus capsularis. (H)

Cordia, broad leaved, برالسورا bura lusoora. Cordia latifolia, *Rox*. (T) This tree most probably produces the larger kind of Sebesten plumbs, described by Mr. H. Colebrooke, and which are not known in our Materia Medica, though used by natives.

Cordia, sloping, گوندني goondnee, لاسورا lasoora, Cordia obliqua *Will.* (T) The fruit is pleasant tasted, but glutinous.

Cordia, smooth leaved, بہوآر buhooar, لبيرا lubeera, لبخ lubukh, لسورا lusoora. Cordia myxa. (T) The fruit is the Sebesten of the European Materia Medica, and the bark is said, by Dr. Royle, to be a mild tonic.

Cordia, taper leaved, رامته ramuteh. Cordia acuminata, *Dr. Wall.* (T)

Coriander, common, كشنيز kushneez, نمشک numshuk, شنيز shuneez. Coriandrum sativum. (H) The seed is دهنيا d'huneea, and used as a culinary spice, as also to chew.

Coriaria, Nepal, بہوجنسي b'hoojunsee. Cariaria Nepalensis, *Dr. Wall.* (S)

Corinda, jasmine flowered, كروندا kuroonda. Carissa carandas, (T) yielding a pleasant subacid fruit.

Corinthian grapes, درخت زبيب durukht-u-zubeeb, بدسي زبيب budusee zubeeb. Vitis vinifera, *var:* Black Corinth, or Zante. (C) Produces the "dried currants" of commerce.

Cork tree, اغار a*g*ar, درخت منطر durukht-u-mun*t*ur. Quercus suber. (T)

Coronella, large flowered, هكتي hukutee. Coronilla grandiflora (S) An infusion of the leaves is given in cases of catarrh in some parts. See also Agati.

Cornel, or dogwood tree, غيزوران *g*eezooran, قرانيا *k*uraneea, سرخک surkhuk, زغال zu*g*al. Cornus mascula. (T) The fruit was formerly eaten, but is now in disuse.

Corylus avellana, see Filbert, and Hazelnut.

Corypha Taliera, see Talier's palm.

Costus, Arabian, قسط *k*us*t*, قشطم *k*ush*t*um, قيو *k*eeoo. Costus Arabicus. (H) An infusion of the root is considered, by native practitioners, as a stomachic and tonic, and is given in typhus fever.

Costus, beautiful, كت kut, كيو keeoo, قسط *k*us*t*. Costus speciosus. (H) Roxburgh says the dried root of this kind does not at all resemble the C. arabicus formerly used in medicine, but natives prepare a kind of preserve from it, that is considered wholesome.

Cotton tree, كپاس kupas, قطن *k*u*t*un, قارپاسي *k*arpasee, زعبل *za*bul. Gossypium herbaceum, (T) comprehends several varieties according to the place of growth and soil. The produce, or cotton of commerce is روي rooee.

Cotton tree, silky, صيمل sseemul, حتياں کا گوند huteean ka goond. Criodendron fructuosum, or Bombax pentandrum. *Lin.* (T) The wood is light, and of little value, and the produce is only used for stuffing pillows, beds, &c. A solution of the gum is given by native practitioners, with spices, in bowel complaints, and the seeds in some parts afford an article of food.

Cotyledon laciniata, see Cut-leaved navelwort.

Cowitch, or Cowage, see also Itching mucuna كيواچ keeooach, کانچکویل کي بينغ kanchkooeel-kee-beeng, كيوانچ keeooanch, كتول kutool, كوانچه koo-anch'eh کانچکوري kanchkoree. Stizolobium pruriens, since called Mucnna pruriens, *D. C. apud*, PROF. LIND. Dolichos pruriens, of *Linn.* (Tw) The bean is eaten by native. The hairs are a mechanical anthelmintic, and a strong infusion of the root is given by native doctors in cholera.

Cowitch or Cowage, Assam, commonly called

Assam bean, اصام كه كيواچ Assam k'eh keeôach, كالي سيم kalee seem. Stizolobium altissimum, chucuna altissima DC. *apud* Prof. Lind. (Tw.) Found in most parts of the Himalaya range, especially towards the Eastern portion of it, the seeds forming a vegetable very similar in flavor to the Windsor bean, and coming in at the close of the rains, when other table vegetables are scarce.

Cratæva marmelos, see Bengal quince.

Cratæva, religious, بيل bél. Cratæva religiosa *Va.* (S) The leaves are venerated by the worshippers of Sheva, as the *Toolsee* by those of Vishnoo, and being bitter and aromatic are used as a stomachic; the root also being supposed to have alterative properties.

Cratæva tapia, see Smooth garlic pear.

Cress, Chinese, هليم huleem, هرف huruf. Arabis Chinensis, *Rott.* (H) A stomachic and stimulant, but producing abortion if imprudently taken.

Cress, common, هالم halum, ونده oond'eh, رشاد rushad, چنسر chunsur, تره تيزك tur'eh tézuk. Lepidium sativum. (H)

Crinum Asiaticum, or toxicarium, see Poison bulb.

Crinum Cingalese, see Cingalese amaryllis.

Crocus, see Saffron plant.

Crocus sativus, see Saffron plant.

Crotalaria juncea, see Indian hemp.

Crotalaria, laburnum leaved, منا muna, R. Crotalaria laburnifolia. (H)

Crotalaria, silky, پیولي peeoolee, R. جهنجهن j'hunj'hun, R. Crotalaria sericea. (H)

Croton, plaited leaved, سنبالي sunbalee, خودي وكرا khoodeeokra. Croton plicatum, *Will.* (H)

Croton, purging, جمال گوتا jumal goota, باتو batoo, دند dund. Croton tiglium. C. jamalgota, *Hamilton* in *Linn. Trans.* (S) The nuts have strong purgative powers, and were formerly taken to England under the name of "Molucca grains;" they are said to cure the bites of venomous animals, and the venereal.

Crow's beak, see Winged clitoria.

Cubebs, کبابه kubab'eh, کباب چیني kubab cheenee. Piper cubeba, *Linn.* (C) The ripe fruit is the cubebs of the shops, but Dr. Blume considers that the fruit of this species is not sent to Europe; the cubebs of commerce being chiefly furnished by P. caninum, *Rumph.* P. cubeba of *Rox.* of which the fruit is smaller, and less pungent.

Cucumber, acute angled, or stinking luffa, ترای turaee, بن ترای bunturaee, جهینگا j'heenga, لواف loo*u*f, تری turee, توری tooree. Cucumis acutangulus, Luffa acutangula, *Rox.* and L. fœtida (Tr) A good native vegetable, either in curries, or plain boiled. Abundant in the rains. In Bengal, at least it cannot claim its last name.

Cucumber, bitter, اندراین *u*ndraeen, حنظل *h*unzzul, اندراوند indraoond, اندراوان indraooan, مخال mukhal, مره mur'eh, صاب ssab, کیستو keestoo, علقم al*k*um. Cucumis colocynthis, (Tr) The fruit contains the bitter resin known in medicine as colocynth or coloquintida, and although considered poisonous alone, in combination with other substances it is a commonly used cathartic. The oil is used in Southern India for lamps.

Cucumber, common, خیار k'heear, کهیرا k'heera, ابخور abkhoor, ککری kunkuree, وارنک ooarunk,

speciosa, D. indica, *Linn.* (T) The fleshy leaflets of the calyx have an agreeable acid taste, and are used by natives as a fruit.

Dillenia, rough, چلتا chulta. Dillenia scabrella, *Dr. Wall.* (T)

Dimocarpus litchi, see Leechee.

Dimocarpus longan, see Longan.

Dioscorea aculeata, see Prickly stemmed yam.

Dioscorea alata, see Winged stalked yam.

Dioscorea fasciculata, see Fasciculated yam.

Diospyrus ebenaster, see Indian ebony tree.

Diospyrus ebenum, see Smooth date plum.

Diospyrus embryopteris, see Date plum.

Diospyrus melanoxylon, see Ebony tree.

Dipterocarpus. terebinthina, درخت گرجن durukht-u-gurjun. Dipterocarpus turbinatus Prof. Lind. (T) Yielding wood oil.

Dock, bladder, چوکا پالک chooka paluk. Rumex vesicarius, (F)

Dock, sharp, جول پالک jool paluk. Rumex acutus, (F)

Dodder, bent back, آکاس پون akas pooun, درند durund, افتمون uftumoon. Cascuta reflexa (Pa)

Dodder, round headed, الكسي algusee. Cuscuta capitata, *Rox.* (Pa)

Dog's bane, سگانگور sugangoor. Apocynum, (H) It is doubtful, however, whether any of this genus are to be found here; this native name more probably applies therefore, to Ichnocarpus frutescens of PROF. LIND. the A. frutescens of *Linn.* sometimes used as a substitute for sarsaparilla, or possibly to Pæderia fœtida, the A. fœtidum of *Burm.* the root of which serves the Hindoos as an emetic.

Dog's tooth violet, جنگلي کاندا junglee kanda. Erythronium Indicum, (B)

Dolichos, bean shaped, متكي mutkee. Dolichos fabæformis. *Lin.* (C) It is much esteemed as a vegetable.

Dolichos, black seeded, بن سيم bun seem, لال سيم lal seem, جيا سيم jeea seem, گوردال سيم goordal seem, بلر bulur, R. Dolichos lablab. (C) Much used by natives, and often their chief food on a march or long journey.

Dolichos, Chinese, روانس rooans, لوبيا loobeea, لوبها loob'ha, پهاري بورا pu'haree boora. Dolichos

Sinensis. (C) Produces what is called the Asparagus bean.

Dolichos cultratus, see Huzar bean.

Dolichos, Pertab Sing's پرتاب سنگ کہسیم Pertabsing k'eh seem. Dolichos purpureus. (C) A good substitute, when cut up fine, for French bean before that vegetable is procurable.

Dolichos pruriens, see Cowitch.

Dolichos, sabre podded, مکھن سیم muk'hun seem, چوتي سيم chôtee seem, ابلم ablum. Dolichos gladiatus, (C)

Dolichos, small fruited, بورا boora, بربتي burbutee, فوک fook, لوبي loobee. Dolichos cutjang (C) Considered a good substitute for French bean.

Dolichos Tranquebaricus, see Tranquebar bean.

Dolichos, two flowered, کرتهي kurt'hee, کلتهي kult'hee, فول fool. Dolichos biflorus. *Will.* (Tw.)

Doodia, hare's foot. گولک چاکلي gooluk chakulee, R. Doodia Lagopodiodes, *Rox.* (H)

Doodia, painted, سنکار جتا sunkar juta, R. Doodia picta, *Rox.* (A)

Dorema, ammoniac, اشق ashu*k*. Dorema ammonicum (H) The stem and fruit yield gum ammoniac, used as an expectorant, and discutient.

Dracocephalum Royleanum, see Indian dragon's head.

Dracontium polyphyllum, see Purple stalked dragon plant.

Dragon's blood plant, دم الاخوين dum alakhooeen, ايدع رومي aeed*a* roomee, خون سياوشان khoon seeaooshan. Calamus Draco. (H) The resin is erroneously considered astringent by native practitioners.

Dragon's, head, Indian, بالنگو balungoo, Dracocephalum Royleanum, *Dr. Ro.* (H)

Dragon plant, purple stalked, جنگلي کندي junglee kundee, کانه کندي kanun'eh kundee, نوشت nooousht, اينا نوشت aeena nooousht, ارنبين arnubeen, رعلول r*a*lool. Dracontium polyphyllum. (H) *Lindley* says the species is not found in India, but *Ainslie* and *Loudon* both name it as an Indian plant. The root is said to be antispasmodic, and a valuable remedy in asthma; it is used by natives in homorrhoids.

Dryobalanops aromatica, or camphora, see Camphor tree.

Eagle wood, see **Aloes** wood.

Earth-nut, American, or Manilla gram, مونگ پهلي moong p'hulee, لايتي مونگ, ooulaeetee moong, چينا بادام cheena badam. Arachis hypogœa, (H) Generally roasted before eating it.

Ebony, see Smooth date plum.

Ebony tree, تيندو téndoo, ساج saj, اردج arduj. Diospyrus melanoxylon, PROF. LIND. (T) The wood is valuable, and the bark, mixed with pepper, is given for dysentery by native doctors.

Ebony tree, Indian, ابنوس *u*bnnoos. Diospyrus ebenaster, *Dr. Ro.* (T)

Echinops echinatus, see Prickly globe thistle.

Echites antidysenterica, see Medicinal Oleander.

Echites, clove leaved, مالتي ma-lutee. Echites carryophyllata, (Tw.)

Echites, long-leaved, هركي hurkee, R. Echites macrophylla, *Rox.* (Tw.)

Echites, shrubby, سيام لتا seeam-u-luta. Echites frutescens, *Rox.* (Tw.)

Echites, two-stemmed, هاپرمالي hapurmalee, R. Echites dichomata. *Rox.* (Tẃ.)

Eclipta, trailing, بهرنگراج b'hrungraj, بونگرا boon

gra, خشوریا khushooreea, بهنگرا b'hungra. Eclipta prostrata, (Tr) Used by native practitioners as an application to reduce elephantiasis.

Egg-plant, common, بن بهانٹا bun b'hantá, بهانٹا b'hanta, بیگن bégun, بادنجان badunjan, بهانگن b'hangun. Solanum melongena. (H) There is one variety that attains an enormous size, but the most esteemed is a white kind of moderate dimensions.

Egg-plant, cylindrical, کولي بیگن koolee bégun. Solanum longum, *Rox*. (H)

Ehretia, box leaved, پاله pal'eh. Ehretia buxifolia *Will*. (S) The succulent root, in decoction, is considered a purifier; and Mahomedans esteem it an antidote to vegetable poison.

Ehretia, umbelled, کنکا kunuka. Ehretia umbellulata *Dr. Wall.* (T) Dr. Wallich says he is, from not having seen the fruit, unable to decide the true genus of this tree, which is either an Ehretia or a Beurreria.

Elæcarpus serratus, see Saw leaved olive.

Elæocarpus lance-leaved, سفید پاي sufèd paee. æocarpus lanc e ofoli us, *Rox*. (T)

Elagnus conferta, see Close oleaster.

Elate, prickly leaved, سدولي sudoolee. Elate sylvestris. (T) The fruit is of sweetish taste and used by poor people to chew like the areca nut.

Elder, common, اقتي u*k*tee, خمان khuman. Sambucus nigra, (T)

Elecampane, راسن rasun, قنس *k*unus, النيون alneeoon, جناح juna*h*. Inula helenium. (H)

Elephant, or wood, apple, كيت keet, كويت kooét, كاويت kaooét, كيتبيل kétbél, كتهبيل kut'h bél, بهين‌كوبت b'heen koobutu. Feronia elephantum. (T) The young leaves have a perfume like anise, and are considered by native practitioners as stomachic and carminative: the fruit also has a strong odour.

Elettaria cardomum, see True cardomum.

Eleusine, Egyptian, مكرا جالي mukra jalee, R. Eleusine Egyptica, *Rox.* (G)

Eleusine, Indian, مال انكري mal ankuree, R. Eleusine Indica (G)

Eleusine, thick spiked مروا murooa, معاد maad. Eleusine coracana, Cynosurus coracanus *Lin.* (G)

The grain is of cooling nature much eaten by the common people especially on the Coromandel coast, and Japan. The Mahrattas make a fermented liquor from it called بوجه bôj'eh.

Eleusine, upright, راگي ragee, منروي munrooee, مرکا murka; Eleusine stricata, *Rox.* (G) A very prolific grain.

Elm, ناغ nag, سيخدار seekhdar, نارون naroon. Ulnus lancifolia, virgata, and integrifolia. (T) Are all mentioned by *Roxburgh* as inhabitants of the East, and the Telinga name of the last species is *Nalee.*

Embelia, currant fruited, باي برنگ baee burung, بابيرنگ babérung, R. Embelia ribes, PRO. LIND. (C) The berries have a slight pungency, and are used to adulterate black pepper.

Emblica officinalis, see Shrubby myrabolan.

Embryopteris glutinifera, see Date plum.

Endive, common, کاسني kasnee, کرو kuroo هندبا hundba. Cichorium endiva. (H)

Engelhardtia, Roxburgh's, بولس bôlus, R. سيلاپوما seelapôma. Engelhardtia Roxburghiana, *Dr. Wall.* (T)

Enhydra repens, see Creeping meyera.

Epidendron, پرگاچه purgach'h, باندا banda. Epidendrum, or perhaps cymbidium, two genera of parasites.

Epipactis, babiana-leaved, چتیا شوقر chuteea shookur, R. Epipactis babianafolia, *Rox.* (H)

Eranthemum, nervose, کالاجاتي kala jatee, گولشام goolusham. Eranthemum pulchellum. (US)

Eriodendron anfractuosum, see Silky cotton tree.

Eria, panicled, نواکوتي nôakôté. Eria paniculata. (Pa)

Erica, see Heath.

Eriobotrya japonica, see Common loquat.

Ervum hirsutum, see Hairy tare.

Ervum lens, see Lentil.

Erythrina Indica, see Indian coral tree.

Erythrina ovalifera, see Oval-leaved coral tree.

Erythronium Indicum, see Indian squill, and Dog's tooth violet.

Eugenia, bractiate, هجلي مينهدي hujlee mén'hdee. Eugenia bracteata. *Rox.* (S)

Eurya Chinensis, see Saw-leaved teruströmia.

Eugenia Jambolana, see Java plum.

Eugenia jambos, see Common rose apple.

Eugenia Malaccensis, see Malay apple.

Eugenia paniola, see Watery rose apple.

Eugenia pimenta, see Pimenta tree.

Eupatorium, spreading, ايايناه aeeuapunah. Eupatorium repandum. (H)

Ephorbia, see Spurge.

Euphoria litchi, see Leechee.

Eurya Chinensis see Saw leaved ternstromia.

Euryale, prickly, مکهانا muk'hana. Euryale ferox. (A)

Exacum, four celled, کوچري koochuree. Exacum tetragonum, *Rox.* (H)

Fæniculum panmorium, see Sweet fennel.

Fagara, ash leaved, بدرنگا budrunga. Fagara piperita, (S)

Fagaria, see Strawberry.

Fennel, Eastern giant, فيشوق féshook, هنگ hung. Ferula orientalis, F. ammonifera, *Lém.* (H) Yielding a gum resin similar to amoniacum, occasionally prescribed by the Hakeems.

practitioners; it is the λιβανος of Dioscorides.

Fraxinus floribunda, see Floribund ash.

Fringe tree, axil flowering, چنالتا chunaluta. Chionanthus axillaris. (S)

Fumaria, see Fumitory.

Fumitory, common, شاهتره shahtur'eh, بقلة الملک buḱl'eht ulmuluk, پتپپره putpupr'eh. Fumaria officinalis. (H) Native practitioners consider it diuretic, and it is slightly aperient, but its use in cutaneous diseases, and obstructions of the liver, has been discontinued by Europeans.

Fumitory, small flowered, شاهترج sha'h turuj. Fumaria parviflora, (H) Used with black pepper in ague, Dr. Royle considers the Indian plant, F. Vaillantii. It is the καπνος of the Greeks.

Furze, dwarf, رتم rutum. Ulex nanus, (S)

Galanga, narrow leaved, کنجان بورا kunjan boora. Kæmpferia angustifolia. (H) The root is used as a cattle medicine.

Galanga, round rooted, بهون چنپا b'hoon chumpa, بهواچنپا b'hooua chumpa. Kæmpfeia rotunda. (H) This has been erroneously supposed to yield the Zedoaries of the druggists, see Broad-leaved turmeric, and Zedoary; the flowers are very fragrant.

Galanga, sessile, چندرا مولکا chundra mooluka. Kæmpferia galanga, Alpinia sessilis *Kö.* (H) The roots have an agreeable odour, and warm aromatic flavor, slightly bitter, and are used medicinally by the native practitioners.

Galangal, the greater, خولنجان khoolunjan, خسرو دارو khusroo daroo, کلیجن kuleejun. Alpinia Galangala. (H) The roots are the *Galanga major* of the druggists, and much used by native practitioners for cure of dyspepsia; they are pungent, acrid, and aromatic.

Galbanum, common, قنه *k*un'eh, نارفیل narfeel. Galbanum officinale, (S) The gum has the properties of assafœtida, but is less powerful; the drug is called بیرزد beerzud, and بریجه bureej'eh. *Lindley* in his Flora Medica says, "It would appear that the opinion of this drug being furnished by Bubon Galbanum, *Lin.* or Ferula ferulago is unfounded."

Galedupa, Indian, کرنج kurunj, کرنجوا kurun-

Ginger, narrow leaved, ادرک adruk, زنجبيل zunjubeel Zinziber officinale. (H) Medicinally useful in many cases; there are several species of this genus, which are indigenous to the hills.

Ginger, wild, بن آدا bun ada. Zinziber casumunar. (H) Once used in medicine, but now out of repute.

Glasswort, Indian, جودوپالنگ jôdoo palung. Salicornia Indica, *Va.* (Tr) Soda may be made from this plant.

Globe-amaranth, annual, گل مخمل gul muk'h-mul. Gomphrena globosa. (H)

Gloriosa, superb, کاریاري kareearee, R. يشوي لانگلا eeshooee langula, R. Gloriosa superba. (B)

Glycine abrus, see Wild Jamaica liquorice.

Glycine tomentosa, see Madras horse gram.

Glycyrrhiza echinata, see Prickly liquorice.

Glycyrrhiza hirsuta, see Hairy liquorice.

Gmelina, tree, گمار gumar, جوگاني چوکر jooganee chuookur, R. Gmelina arborea. *Rox.* (T) Yielding good timber.

Gomphrena globosa, see Globe amaranth.

Gooseberry, country, see Winter cherry.

Gooseberry, smooth, كريا kureea. Ribes uva crispa. (S) Found only far to the North-west.

Goosefoot, white, بتهوا but'hooa, كلفي kulfee. Chenopodium album. (H) It forms one of the numerous greens, or *sägs* of natives.

Gosypium, herbaceum, see Cotton tree.

Gourd, Egyptian bitter, گهياتوري g'heea tooree, دوندول doondool, R. تراي turaee, پرولاكيندي puroola keendee. Momordica luffa, Luffa Pentandra *Rox*. (Tr) Used as a vegetable in curries.

Gourd, hairy bitter, كريلا kureela, or kuréla. Momordica charantia, (Tw.) There are two varieties, the long and the short, the former is the best.

Gourd, mixed bitter, كنكرول kunkrool, سوم soom. Momordica mixta, *Rox*. (Tr)

Gourd, single-styled bitter, بنب bu*m*b. Momordica monodelphia, *Rox*. (C)

Gourd, spiked bitter, براكريلا bura kuréla چيا *u*oocheea. Momordica muricata, (Tr.) Much esteemed for giving a pleasent bitter flavor to curries.

Gourd, bottle, تومرا toomra, تومري toomree, كدو kudoo, گهيا g'heea, هرياكدو hureea kudoo, قرع

kura, لوکا looka, یقطین ué*k*teen. Cucurbita lagenaria. (T) Used, as its name implies, by pilgrims and hill people, to carry water, when scooped out; it is then called تونبا too*m*ba, and hence the pipe used by snake charmers تونبي too*m*bee.

Gourd, common snake, چچوندا chuchoonda, چچونگا chuchoonga. Trichosanthes anguina. (Tr.) Used in curries, &c.

Gourd, dioceous snake, پرور puroour, پلول puloouL. Trichosanthes dioica, *Rox.* (Tr.) A common vegetable used in curries.

Gourd, palmated snake, مخال mukhal. Trichosanthes palmata, *Rox.* (C) The fruit is considered poisonous, but, pounded with warm cocoanut oil, is used for sores, in the ears, and in cases of ozœna.

Gram, black, or hairy podded, see Hairy podded kidney bean.

Gram, common, see Chick pea.

Gram, green, see Small fruited bean.

Gram, Madras horse, کلتي kultee, Glycine tomentosa, (C) It is used by the lower classes as food.

Grass, bearded apluda, گوروما gooroona, R. Apluda aristata, *Linn.* (G)

Grass, diandrous bent, بيناجوني béna jönee, R. Agrostis diandra, *Rox.* (G)

Grass, thread-like bent, جنيوا juneeooa, دوب doob. Agrostis linearis, *Rox.* (G)

Grass, cyperus, كسيرو kuseeroo. Cyperus tuberosus, *Linn.* (G)

Grass, bulbous-rooted cyperus, چهوتا گوتهوبي ch'hoota gôt'hoobee, R. Cyperus dubius, (Tu)

Grass, compressed cyperus, چونچا chooncha, R. Cyperus compressus, *Linn.* (G)

Grass, irregular cyperus, بهوا bu'hooa. Cyperus difformis, *Linn.* (G)

Grass, naked cyperus, گولا ميتهي goola mét'hee, R. Cyperus nudus, and seminudus, *Rox.* (G)

Grass, one-headed cyperus, گوتهوبي goot'hoobee, R. Cyperus monocephalus, *Rox.* (G)

Grass, pangorea cyperus, چماتي پاتي chumatee patee. R. Cyperus Pangorei, *Linn.* (G)

Grass, round stemmed cyperus, موتها moot'ha- Cyperus rotundus, *Linn.* (G)

Grass, running cyperus, پاني ملنگه panee mu, lung'eh, R. Cyperus distans, *Linn.* (G)

Hooded-milfoil, fasciculated, جانجي janjee, R. Utricularia fasciculata, *Rox.* (A)

Hooded-milfoil, two flowered, چهوتا جانجي ch'hôta janjee, R. Utricularia biflora, *Rox.* (A)

Hordeum hexastichon, or zeocriton, see Native barley.

Horse raddish tree, سهجنا suhujna, نيلكنته neel-kunt'h, منگي mungee, مونگي moongee. Hyperanthera moringa. Guilandina moringa, *Linn.* (T) The inner bark of the root, scraped, is used as a substitute for the real horse raddish, which it much resembles in flavor, the leaves are used as spinage.

Hound's tongue, spreading, لسان العصافير lusan-ul-*a*ssafeer. Cynoglossum diffusum, *Rox.* (H)

Hoya, green flowered, نكچنكي nukchuknee, تيت كنگا teet kunga. Hoya viridiflora, PRO. LIND. Asclepias volubilis, *Linn.* (Tw.) The root and tender stalks promote expectoration. The leaves peeled, and dipped in oil are esteemed by natives as a cure for boils.

Hyacinth, oriental, سنبل su*m*bul, ابرود abrood. Hyacinthus orientalis. (B)

Hydrilla, see Alternated valisneria.

Hydrocotyle Asiatica, see Thick leaved penny-wort.

Hymenodictyon, tall, کالابچناک kala buchnak. Hymenodictyon excelsum, PROF. LIND. Cinchona excelsa. *Rox.* (T) The inner layers of bark possess the bitterness and astringency of Peruvian bark.

Hyoscyamus niger, see Common henbane.

Hyperanthera moringa, see Horse-radish-tree.

Hyssop, common, زوفاي يابس *zoofaee* eeabus, ازوفا *uzoofa.* Hyssopus officinalis. (US)

Ichnocarpus, shrubby, سالسا salsa. Ichnocarpus frutescens. (S) See also Dog's bane.

Ilex dipyrena, see Holly.

Illecebrum Javanicum, see knot-grass.

Illicium anisatum, see Star anise.

Impatiens balsamina, see Balsam.

Indian corn, see Maize.

Indian madder, two-flowered, شاہترہ sha'htur'eh. کهیت پاپرا khét papura. Oldenlandia biflora, *Linn.* Antirrhinum humile, *Brum.* (H)

Ixora, waving, پالک جوهي paluk joo'hee. **Ixora undulata**, *Rox.* (S)

Jack tree, کتهل kut'hul, پهنس p'hunus. Artocarpus integrifolius. (T) The fruit has a strong odor, but is liked by some people.

Janipha manihot, see Cassava tree.

Jasmine, Arabian, بيل bél, زنبق *z*unbu*k*, موتيا mooteea, موگرا moogra, ياسمن eeasmun, غرنف *g*urnuf. Jasminum Sumbac, or Zambuc, Magorium sambac, *Linn.* (S) Of this there are several varieties, of which three are enumerated by Roxburgh.

Jasmine, auriculated, جتهي jut*h*ee, جوي jooee. Jasminum auriculatum. (C)

Jasmine, Cape, گندهراج gundu'hraj. Gardenia Florida. (S)

Jasmine, Catalonian, or Spanish, سجالاط sujala*t*, جاتي jatee, جاهي ja'hee, چنبلي chu*m*bulee, سمن sumun, کند kund, مالتي malutee. Jasminum grandiflorum. (C)

Jasmine, downy, قونده *k*oond'eh, قوندم *k*oondum. Jasminum pubescens, *Linn.* (S)

Jasmine, laurel-leaved, سمسق sumsu*k*. Jasminum laurifolia. (C)

Jasmine, narrow-leaved, بان ملي کا ban mulee ka. Jasminum angustifolium. (C) The root ground fine, and mixed with the root of Acorus calamus is considered useful as an external application to ringworm.

Jasmine, various-leaved, گوجه gooj'eh, R, جوانا juooana, R. Jasminum heterophyllum. *Rox.* (T) Described by *Dr. Wallich.*

Jasmine, woody, براکونده bura koond'eh, نوامالکا nooua muluka. Jasminum arborescens, *Rox.* (T)

Jatropha curcas, see Angular-leaved physic nut.

Jatropha glauca, see Glaucous-leaved physic-nut.

Jatropha manihot, see Cassava tree.

Java plum, جامون jamoon, کالاجام kala jam. R. Calyptranthes jambolana, now Eugenia jambolana, Prof. Lind. (T) The fruit is eaten, of a sub acid quality, but of very astringent quality.

Jonesia اسوک asook, اشوک ashook. Jonesia asoca, *Rox.* (T) A beautiful blossomed tree.

Juglans regia, see Walnut.

Jujube, بایر baeer, بیري beeree, چیلان cheelan, درختي عناب durukhtee anab, نازک بدن nazuk, budun, كول kool, R. Zizyphus jujuba. (S) The fruit is commonly eaten as the "native plum." The bark is used as a remedy for diarrhœa.

Jujube, or lote tree, زفيزف zufeezuf, سنج sunj, همسود humsood. Zizyphus lotus. (S)

Jujube, white, زفزوف zufzoof. Zizyphus nitida, *Rox.* (S)

Juniper, Chinese, اردج arduj, ارس arus, ابهال ab'hal, اورن aoourun, عرعر *arar*, ابهول ab'hool. Juniperus Chinensis. (S) *Dr. Royle* mentions J. communis as bearing the name of ابهول ab'hool, but considers it probable to be rather our plant, as being found in the hills whence the berries are brought.

Jussiæa, creeping, كنچنا kunchuna. Jussiæa repens, *Will.* (A)

Justicia, adhotoda, see Malabar nut.

Justicia, colored, بتارنگ buteearung, R. Justicia tinctoria, *Rox.* (S)

Justicia, curved-flowered, بهاگبت b'hagbut. Justicia curviflora, *Dr. Wall.* (S)

Justicia, double-calyxed, ناسابهاگا nasab'haga, R. Justicia bicalyculata, *Linn.* (H)

Justicia, long spiked, ودوجاتي oodoo jatee. Justicia ecbolium, Rhinacanthus ecbolius, *Pro. Lin.* (US) Said to be diuretic.

Justicia, many-seeded, چهوٹا مچیتا ch'hota muchéta, R. Justicia polysperma, *Rox.* (Cr)

Justicia, panicled, کریات kreeat, وزر oozur, مہاتیتا muha teeta, کالپناتھ kalupnat*h*. Justicia paniculata, now Andrographis paniculata, *Dr. Wall.* (US) Prized as a stomachic in cholera, dysentery, and intermittent fever; it forms the basis of what the French call *Drogue amère*; it is said also to be an antidote to poisons.

Justicia, spotted, بیجا beeja. Justicia guttata, *Dr. Wall.* (S)

Justicia, upright, کستولہ kustooleh, R. Justicia verticillata, *Rox.* (US)

Justicia, white flowering, پالک جوهي paluk joohee, کبوتر کي چهار kubootur kee ch'har, جوهي پانا joo'hee pana. Justicia nasuta, Rhinacanthus communis, *Pro. Lin.* (US) The fresh root bruised, is good for ringworms, and boiled in milk is considered aphrodisical, and an antidote to poisons.

Justicia, willow-leaved, ارس arus, کالي شمبالي kalee shumbalee, باکس bakus. Justicia gundarussa. (US) The leaves preserve clothes from insects.

Kæmpferia angustifolia, see Narrow-leaved galangale.

Kæmpferia rotunda, see Round rooted galangale.

Kale, or borecole, قمريب *k*umreeb, كرم كلا kurum kula, پهلتي كوبي p'hultee kôbee. Brassica acephala. (H)

Kayea, floribund, كرم جوا kurum jooa. Kayea floribunda, *Dr. Wall.* (T)

Knot-grass, Java, كهل k'hul, Illecebrum Javanicum, *Pro. Lin.* (H) The downy white flowers are used to stuff pillows under belief that their odor induces sleep, and allays headache; whilst the root is considered diuretic.

Knot-grass, sessile, پونه گتي poon'eh guttee. Illecebrum sessile, *Pro. Lin.* (H) Used as a spinage, but the botanical name is doubtful.

Kydia, calycine, چوپالتيا choopalteea. R. Kydia calycina, *Pro. Lin.* (T) An infusion of the bark is sudorific.

Kyllinga, one headed, سوت گوتهوبي soout gôt-hoobee, R. نربشي nurbushee, R. Kyllinga monocephala. (G)

Kyllinga, tufted, براگوتهوبي bura gôt'hoobee, R. Kyllinga umbellata. *Linn.* (G)

Lactuca sativa, see Lettuce.

Ladies' bed straw, گوما gooma, گوم goom. Pharnoceum molluga. (US)

Lagerstræmia, oblong-leaved, جارل jarul. Lagerstræmia reginæ, or Flos regina. *Retz.* (T) Loudon notes this only as an ornamental shrub growing 12 feet high; but it is commonly found here as a timber tree.

Lathyrus aphaca, see Yellow vetchling.

Lathyrus sativus, see Chickling vetch.

Laurus camphora, see Camphor tree.

Laurus cassia, see Cassia tree.

Laurus cinnamomum, see Cinnamon tree.

Laurus sassafras, see Sassafras tree.

Lavendar, spiked, نرد nurd, ناردين nardeen, Lavendula spika. (H)

Lavendar, thick-leaved, نرد nurd, ناردين nardeen سيتاكي پنجيري seetakee punjeeree, والله ooaluk'eh. Lavendula carnosa. (H) The fresh juice of the leaves mixed with pounded sugar-candy is prescribed by native practitioners in cynanche. *Dr. Wallich* has named this Anisochilus, and *Roxburgh* apparently places it as Plectranthus strobiliferus.

Lawsonia inermis, see Henna plant.

Leadwort, Cingalese, چترمول chuturmool, چتا chuta, چیترا cheetra, چیتا cheeta. Plumbago zeylanica. (US) A slice of the root serves to produce a blister.

Leadwort, rose colored. لال چیتہ lal cheet'eh, لال چتا lal chuta. Plumbago Rosea. (US) The bruised root is used as an external application in rheumatic affections.

Ledebouria hyocinthoïdes, see Indian squill.

Leea curled, بن چلتا bun chulta, R. Leea crispa. (S)

Leea, hairy, کاکجانگھا kakujang'ha, R. Leea hirta, *Herb; Banks.* (S)

Leea, long-leaved, دھول شمودرا d'hool shumoodra. Leea macrophylla. (S)

Leea, staphyl, کوکورجھوا kookoorj'hooa. Leea staphylen, *Rox.* (S)

Leechee, لیچی leechee, کوی پورا kôee poora.

Nephelium litchi, *Pro. Linn.* Dimocarpus litchi, *Lour,* Scytalia lichi, *Rox.* classed as Euphoria litchi, *Juss.* (T) This fruit is originally from China.

Leek, گندنا gunduna, زعلوک *za*look, کرات kurat, رکل rukul, طیطان *teet*an, کندانه kundan'eh, کراث kura*s*. Allium porrum. (B)

Leersia, bearded, جنگلي دال junglee dal. Leersia aristata, *Rox.* (G)

Lentil, مصوري mussooree, مسور musoor, عدس *a*dus. Ervum lens. (C) It a valuable pulse, much prized, it is very prolific, and even the straw is nourishing, especially to young cattle.

Lemon, see Lime.

Leontodon taraxacum, see Dandelion.

Lepidium sativum, see Common cress.

Lettsomia argenta, see White silver weed.

Lettsomia nervosa, see Vein-leaved silver weed.

Lettuce, garden, خس khus, کاهو kahóo, کما kuma. Lactuca sativa. (H) It would appear that we derive our English name for a variety of this vegetable, the *cos lettuce,* from the Arabic *khus.*

abundantly to the north of the Ganges, and especially in the ruins of Gour.

Liquorice, wild Jamaica, کونچ koonch, کونجا goonja, بتواس butooas, گنج gunj, گھنگچي g'hunguchee, گومچي goomchee. Abrus precatorius, Glycine Abrus, *Lin.* (C) The root is often sold in the bazars of Bengal for the true liquorice: its small seeds are used as weights, and termed رتي rutee.

Liriodendron grandiflora, see Large flowered tulip tree.

Lolium tenue, see Slender darnel.

Looking plass plant, lesser, شوندري shoondree, R. Heritiera minor, *Rox.* (T)

Longan, لونگان lôngan, اش پهل ash p'hul. Nephelium longan, *Pro. Lin.* Dimocarpus longan. *Lour.* classed as Euphoria longan, *Juss.* Scytalia longan, *Rox.* (T) A Chinese fruit of little flavor.

Loquat, common, لوقات lò*kat*, (a corruption, there being no really native name) Eriobotrya Japonica. (T) Yielding a justly esteemed fruit of Chinese origin.

Loranthus, round, چهوتاماندا ch'hota manda.

Loranthus globosus, (gen. apud *Pro. Lin.*) *Rox.* (Pa)

Loranthus, two-colored, براماندا bura manda. Loranthus bicolor, *Rox.* (gen. apud *Pro. Lin.*) (Pa)

Lotus, see Water-lily.

Lovage, اجواين ajooaén, اموس amoos, نانخواه nankhooa'eh. Ligusticum Ajowan, *Rox.* (H) Famous for its aromatic seeds; supposed to be rather from Sison amomum.

Lovage, spreading, جنگلي اجواين junglee ajooaéen, R. Ligusticum diffusum, *Rox.* (H)

Love apple, see Tomato.

Luffa acutangula, or fœtida, see Acute-angled cucumber.

Luffa, bindal, بندعل b▪nd*a*l. Luffa bindaal, *Rox.* (C) Believed in India to be a powerful drastic, useful in dropsy.

Luffa, bitter, کرولا kuroola. Luffa amara, (Tr) The fruit is violently cathartic and emetic, as also the ripe seeds. The juice of the unripe fruit roasted is considered by natives as good for headache.

Luffa, clubbed, بنترائي bunturaee. Luffa clavata, (Tr) Eaten in curries.

Luffa pentandra, see Egyptian bitter gourd.

Lupine, Egyptian, or Turkish, ترمس turmus. Lupinus thermis. (H)

Lycopodium clavatum, see Common moss.

Lycopodium imbricatum, see Club-moss.

Maba, box leaved, ايرم بلي aeerum bulee. Maba buxifolia, Ferreola buxifolia, *Rox.* (S) The fruit tolerably well tasted, and the wood is hard and durable.

Mad apple, دورلا doorla, solanum insanum. (H) It is a small inferior sort of *brinjal.*

Madder of Bengal, مجيته mujeet'h, منجيهته munjee'ht'eh, فوه foo'h; روناس roonas. Rubia cordifolia, R. munjista of *Rox.* (Tr) The root and stalks affording a red dye, and known in commerce as "munjeet." It is indigenous to Nepal, and native practitioners prescribe an infusion of it as a deobstruent.

Madder, two-flowered Indian, پت پاپره putpapra. Oldenlandia biflora. (H)

Mæsua, fragrant, ناكيسر nakeesur. Mæsua ferrea, (T) The blossoms are dried and used in medicine, as well as noted for their fragrance; and the arrows of *Rama*, the god of love, are said to be tipped with them.

Magnolia, the noble, سيتي seetee. Magnolia insignis, *Dr. Wall.* (T)

Mahogany tree, febrifuge, see Red wood tree.

Maize, بهتا b'huta, بوتا boota, جوارا jooara, مكي جاري mukee jaree, كوكري kookree. Zea mays. (G)

Malabar-nightshade, white and red, پوي pöee, پويا pooeea, بيل كي بچلي beel ké buchlee. Basella alba, and rubra. (Tr)

Malabar nut, اروس aroos, باكر bakur, باسوكه basook'eh, باكس bakus, R. Justicia adhatoda, Adhatoda vasica, *Pro. Lin.* (T) Possessing antispasmodic qualities.

Malay apple, جامرول jamrool. Eugenia Malaccensis, E. alba *Rox.* (T) The fruit is juicy, but insipid.

Mallow, common marsh, انجل anjul. Althæa officinalis. (H)

Mallow, round-leaved, پنيرك puneeruk, خباز khudaz, ملكك mulkuk. Malva rotundifolia. (H) obtained by tapping this tree, considered a good stomachic by Hindoo doctors. The tree is consecrated to Mariama.

Marica, marsh, چكاتي پاتي chukatee patee. Marica paludosa. (A)

Marjoram, common, مرزنجوش murzunjoosh, عنقز *anhuz*, ويش aooeesh. Origanum vulgare. (H)

Marjoram, sweet, مرزنجوش murzunjoosh, مروا murooa, صعتر ss*a*tur. Origanum majorana. (H) The Hindoos offer it to Vishnoo and Sheeva.

Marsilea quadrifolia, see Four-leaved pepperwort.

Marvel of Peru, گل عباس gul *a*bas, كرشنا كيلي krushna kélee. Mirabilis Jalapa. (F) Native doctors consider the root gently aperient.

Marygold, African, گيندا geenda, گيند gend. Tagetes erecta. (H)

Marygold, French, گل جعفري gul uj*a*free. Tagetes patula. (H)

Marygold, joint flowering fig, غاسول *g*asool. Mesembryanthemum geniculiflorum. (H) Yielding soda.

Mast tree, ديبدار deebdar, ديودارو deeoodaroo, اسوگ asoog. Uvaria longifolia, *Will.* (T)

Mastich tree, مسطاقي mus*ta*k*ee, ارله ara'h, علک بغدادي *a*luk bu*g*dadee, کنه kun'eh. Pistacia lentiscus. (T) The resin is considered by native doctors as corroborant and balsamic, and is used to strengthen and preserve the teeth.

Mathiola incana, see Gilly flower.

Meadow grass, داب dab, کوشا koosha. Poa synosuroides, *Linn.* and *Kö* (G) Having a religious character among natives.

Meadow saffron, سورنجان soorunjan. Colchicum autumnale. (B) It is a well known drug, acting sometimes as a sudorific; sometimes emetic and purgative; and in large doses, is a narcotic acrid poison.

Melaleuca cajuputi, see Cajepute tree.

Melanorrhœa, useful, خيو kheeoo. Melanorrhœa usitata, *Dr. Wall.* (T) Yielding the varnish of Martaban.

Melia azedaruchta, see Margosa tree.

Melia sempervirens, see Ever-green bead tree.

Melilot, upright, اكليل الملک ikuleel al-muluk, شاخک shakhuk, شنجار shunjar, مونلون moofloon. Melilotus erecta, Trifolium indicum, *Wil/.* (H)

Melissa officinalis, see Common balm.

Mulberry, Indian, توت toot. Morus Indica. (S) Grown as food for silk worms: the fruit being, though very indifferent in flavor, prolific, cooling and aperient, but apt to produce diurrhea if eaten too freely.

Mullein, common, بوصير boosseer, ازان الدب *uzan uldub*. Verbascum thapsus. (H) Indian doctors consider it a cure for hemeroïds.

Murray's tree, ash-leaved, بيلزار beel*z*ar. Murrayia exotica. (S)

Musa sapientum, see Banana.

Musænda, white-leaved, ببينا bubeena. Musænda frondosa. (S)

Mushroom, بينگ کا چهاتا béng ka ch'hata, قدرتي *k*udrutee, چترمار chuturmar, دهرتي کا پهول d'hurtee ka p'hool, کما kuma, ديو deeoou, سماروغ sumaroo*g*, ککرمتا kukurmuta, سانپ کي توپي sa*m*p ké tòpee, کوتي کي چهتري kootee ké ch'hutree. Psalliota campestris, (a fungus.)

Mustard, Bengal, سرسون sursôn. Sinapis dichotoma, *Rox*. (S)

Mustard, grey, سويت راي sooét raee, R. Sinapis glauca, *Rox*. (H)

Mustard, large white, رايا raeea. Sinapis trilocularis, *Rox.* (H)

Mustard, small-seeded, راي raee, خردال khurdal, سرشف surshuf. Sinapis ramosa, *Rox.* (H)

Mustard, spreading, كيل راي keel raee, R. كندري kundree. Sinapis patens, *Rox.* (H)

Myristica, moschata, see Nutmeg tree.

Myrobalan, belleric, بهيرا buheera, بلا bula, بليلج buleeluj, بليله buleel'eh. Terminalia belerica, *Rox.* Myrobalanus bellerica of *Gært.* (T) Ainslie reckons the fruit astringent, tonic, and attenuant; the kernels are considered intoxicating.

Myrobalan, chebulic, هرا hura, هليله كلان huleel'eh kulan, هرلا hurla, هلدا hulda, هليلج كاربلي huleeluj karbulee, هلده huld'eh. Terminalia chebula (T) The fruit is very astringent; with alum it gives a durable yellow, and with ferruginous mud a black dye; native doctors recommend it as a purgative.

Myrobalan, shrubby, آملا amla, سک suk, انولا anoola, املج umluj, امله aml'eh, املکا *u*maluka. اولا aoola. Emblica officinalis, *Gært*, Phyllanthus emblica, *Linn.* Myrobolana emblica of the *Materia Medica.* (S) The fruit is acid and astringent, but when dry a mild purgative, and the flowers are considered cooling and aperient.

Myrobalan plum, آمله aml'eh, هلدا hulda. Prunus cerasifera. (T)

Myrsine, half-serrated, بلسي bulsee, كلكاتها kuluka t'ha. (*Newaree.*) Myrsine semiserrata, *Dr. Wall.* (T) The ripe fruit is eaten, and the wood is esteemed for tool-handles, &c.

Myrsine, small headed, سياده seead'eh, بهوي بلو b'hooee buloo, (*Newaree.*) Myrsine capitellata, *Dr. Wall.* (T)

Myrtle, آس as, مورد moord, هدس hudus, اولايتي مندي oolaeutee mundee. Myrtus communis. (S)

Myrtle, dwarf, سنسق sunsu*k*. Myrtus dumosa. (S)

Myrtus pimenta, see Pimenta tree.

Nama, Cingalese, لانگليا languleea, R. Nama Zeylanica, *Pro. Lin.* (H)

Narcissus, polyanthus, نرجس nurjus, هرهفت hur'huft, نسرين nusreen, موژان moozhan, زرين قدع zureen *k*uda. Narcissus tazetta. (B)

Narcissus, pseudo narcissus, see Daffodil.

Nardostachys jatamansi, see Spikenard.

Nasturtium, officinale, Water cress.

Natchumy, see Eleusine.

Nauclea, four stamened, شویت کدم shooét-kudum. Nauclea tetrandra, *Rox*. (T)

Nauclea, heart-shaped-leaved کیلي کدم kélee kudum, R. Nauclea cordifolia, *Will*. (T)

Nauclea, shady, کدم kudum, کدمب kudumb. Nauclea cadamba, *Rox*. (T)

Navelwort, cut-leaved, زخم حیات zukhum heeat, حیمساگر *h*émsagur, حمدت الرباح *h*umudut alruba*h*. Cotyledon laciniata, *Will*. (H) The Mahomedan practitioners use the bruised leaves to foul ulcers.

Nectarine, شفتالو shuftaloo, فرسق fursu*k*, موندلا ارو moondla aroo. Amygdalus nectarina. (T)

Nelumbium speciosum, see Indian sacred bean.

Nephelium. danurine, دانورا danoora. Nephelium danurum, *Pro. Lin.* Scytalia danura, *Rox*. (T)

Nephelium litchi, see Leechee.

Nephelium longan, see Longan.

Nerium adoratum, see Sweet-scented oleander.

Okro, musk, کالاکستوري kala kustooree. Hibiscus abelmoschus. (S) The seeds have a strong musk flavor, and are used in Arabia to mix with coffee to give it flavor.

Oldenlandia biflora, see Two-flowered Indian madder.

Oldenlandia, chrystalline, پنکه punk'eh, R. Oldenlandia chrystallina, *Rox.* (H)

Oldenlandia, winged, گندهابادلي gund'ha badulee, R. Oldenlandia alata, *Pro. Lin.* (H)

Oleander, common, کرنوير kurnooeer, کنير kuneer. Nerium oleander. (S) A decoction of its leaves, or bark, makes an arid wash useful to destroy itch and cutaneous vermin; and its flowers are sacred to Sheeva and Vishnoo.

Oleander, medicinal, اندرجو indurjoo, کرايچا kuraeecha, درخت لسان العصافير durukht-ul-san-*ul*-*ass*afeer. Nerium antidysentericum, *Linn.* See *Ainslie*, who says "it is the Echites antidysenterica, *Rox.* and has given it the "English name of Tellicherry bark," but it does not appear in the Flora Indica. It should more properly be Wrightia antidysenterica, *Pro. Lin.* (S) The bark called "Cenessi" is common, and good for its astringent and febrifugal qualities, especially useful in dysentery. Decoction of the seed *(indurjoo)* is used in fever, gout, and worm cases.

Oleander, netted, کارنتا karunta, R. Nerium reticulatum, *Rox.* (Tw)

Oleander, sweet-scented, کربي kurubee, R. کرپد kurpud, خرزهره khurz'hur'eh. Nerium odoratum. (S) The flowers are called دردمگرا dood mugra, and the bark of the root, and the leaves, externally applied, are by native doctors, considered repellants; the root taken internally being poisonous.

Oleaster, close, گوارا gooara, R. Elagnus conferta, *Pro. Lin.* (S) The fruit is eaten.

Olive, Indian, اتاجام atajam. Olea dioica, *Rox.* (T) The fruit is eaten, but little esteemed.

Olive, saw-leaved, جلپاي julpaee. Elæocarpus serratus. (T) The fruit is chiefly used in curries, or pickles.

Olive tree, زيتون *zeetoon.* Olea Europæa. (T) Not grown in India, but often found in the northern parts of Persia.

Onion, common, براپیاج bura peeaj, بصل bussul, براپیاز burapeeaz, کاندا kanda. Allium cepa. (B)

Ononis spinosa, see Common rest-harrow.

Onosma, branching, گاوزبان gaôzuban. Onosma bracteatum. (H)

Ophioglossum flexuosum, see Adder's tongue.

Ophioxylon, red flowered, چوتاچاند chôtachand, چاندرا chandra. Ophioxylon serpentinum. (US) The root is used on the Malabar coast as a remedy in cases of bites by snakes, or of scorpion stings. It is also made use of by Telinga physicians as a febrifuge.

Opoponax chirorum, see Rough parsnip.

Orache, garden, سرمق surmu*k*, بهتوا bu'htooa, قطف *k*u*t*uf. Atriplex hortensis. (US)

Orange, نارنگي narungee, نارنج naruj, رنگترا rungtura, سنگتره sungtur'eh, کوملا koo*m*la, کولا koola. Citrus aurantium. (T)

Orchis mascula, see Salep.

Origanum marjorana, see Sweet marjoram.

Origanum vulgare, see Common marjoram.

Ormocarpum sennoïdes, see Senna-leaved hedysarum.

Ornitrophe serrata, see Saw-leaved schnidelia.

Oryza sativa, see Rice.

Osier, common, قندرق *k*unduru*k*. **Salix viminalis. (S)**

Oxalis, procumbent, انبوتي u*m*bootee, امرول amrool, امبشتا ambushta. Oxalis corniculata. (B) The leaves and flowers are cooling.

Oxalis, sensitive, لكهچنا lak'h chuna. Oxalis sensitiva, *Will.* (B)

Oxystelma, esculent, دودهلتا dood'h luta, دودهي dood'hee, R. Oxystelma esculentum, Periploca esculenta, *Linn.* Asclepias rosea, *Rox.* (Tw) A decoction is used is ulcerous affections of the throat and mouth.

Pæderia, fetid, گندالي gundalee, R. Pæderia fœtida. (C) See also dog's bane.

Palm, fan-leaved, or Palmyra, تار tar, تال tal, بلتار bultar, گين گول geen gool. Borassus flabelliformis. (P) The juice is commonly known as "toddy," the tough stringy fibres are made into a coarse cordage, and the leaves are used for a variety of purposes, as well as for writing on. The juice is boiled down to a coarse muscavado sugar, but it cannot be made, by any process yet discovered, to lose an acidity and predisposition to dissolve, or cake.

Palm, Talier's, تارا tara, درخت خرما durukht khurma, نخل nukhul. Corypha Taliera, *Rox.* (P)

Palm, toddy, see Date tree.

Palma, Christi, see Castor oil tree.

Palyporus, soft, غاريقون *g*aree*k*oon. Polyporus fomentarious (Fungus). Styptic and cathartic, used also for *Amadon.*

Panax, fragrant, گوتي سونا gootee soona, R. Panax fragrans, *Rox.* (T)

Pancratium, three flowered, سادا کنول sada kunool. Pancratium triflorum, *Rox.* (B)

Pandanus fœtidus, see Fœtid screw pine.

Pandanus odoratissimus, see Green spined screw pine.

Paneola plum, see Many-spined flacourtia.

Panicum ciliare, see Prickly panic grass.

Panicum colonum, see Purple panic grass.

Panicum dactylon, see Doop grass.

Panicum frumentaceum, see Wheat-like panic, or millet grass.

Panicum hirsutum, see Hairy panic grass.

Panicum holcoïdes, see Mountain panic grass.

Panicum interruptum, see Broken panic grass.

Panicum Italicum, see Italian panic grass and Italian millet.

Panicum miliaceum, see Bengal millet.

Panicum setigerum, see Bristly panic grass.

Panicum spicatum, see Spiked millet, also Bull rush.

Panicum stagnicum, see Stagnant panic grass.

Panicum verticillatum, or semiverticlatum, see Upright panic grass.

Pansy, خيرو kheeroo, خياري kheearee, رتن پروس rutun puroos. Viola tricolor. (H)

Papaver, see Poppy.

Papaw tree, پپیا pupeea, پوپايه poopaee'eh, عنبه هندي *am*b'eh hundee. Carica papaya. (T)

Papyrus, ancient, بردي burdee, فافير fafeer Papyrus antiquorum. (A)

Pareira-brava-root, six stamened, بيد روكهرا béd-rook'hura. Cissampelos hexandra, *Rox.* (Tw) This differs slightly from the genuine Pareira brava-root, although it possesses most of its properties.

Parietaria Indica, see Indian pellitory.

Paris, many-leaved, بيما beema. Paris polyphylla, *Dr. Wall.* (H)

Parsley, اجمود ajmood, كروز kurooz, كرفس kurufus, راندني randnee, انيسون aneesôn, اجوان خراساني ajooan khôrasanee. Apium involucratum, and A. petroselinum. (H)

Parsnip, or parsnep, garden, جزر juzur, اسطفين istufeen. Pastinaca sativa. (F)

Parsnip, or parsnep, rough, جاوشير jaoosheer, كاوشير kaoo sheer. Pastinaca opopanox, Opopanax chirorum, *D. C.* (T) The root gives a resin called opoponax, similar in effect to assafœtida, and considered as a discutient by Arabian physicians.

Paspalum, circular, كوده kodeh. Paspalum kora, *Linn.* (G) Cattle are found of this grass.

Paspalum kora, see Kora millet.

Paspalum, scrobiculatum, see Punctured millet.

Paspalum, wheat like, كودرو kooduroo, كودو koodoo. Paspalum frumentaceum, *Linn.* (G) The grain tastes something like rice, but there is a variety that is very unwholesome, producing vertigo.

Passion flower, laurel-leaved, جهومكا j'hoomka. Passiflora laurifolia. (Tw)

Pastinaca, see Parsnip.

Pea, common, بتاني butanee, کابلي kabulee, کرسنه kursun'eh, متر mutur, کشنه kushn'eh. Pisum sativum. (C)

Pea, field, کراو kuraoo, دهوروا d'hoorooa. Pisum arvense, (C)

Pea, pigeon, or hill-dhal, توار tooar, شاخسار shakhsar, ارهر arhur, شاخول shakhool, کشاخل kushakhul, بري تور buree toour. Cytisus cajan. (H) A very valuable pulse.

Pea, winged, پانک کي متر pank kee mutur. Tetragonolobus edulis. (C)

Peach, آرو aroo, شفتالو shuftaloo, خوخ khookh. Amygdalus persica. (T)

Peach, clingstone, کاردي kardee. Amygdalus persica, *var*. (T)

Peach, freestone, کلو kuloo. Amygdalus persica, *var*. T.

Peach, sweet common, بهمي b'humee. Amygdalus persica soligna. *Dr. Royle*. (T)

Pear, common, امرود amrood کمثري kumsuree, ناشپتي nashputee. Pyrus communis. (T) Not commonly found in India, though it has been grown and ripened by Mr. C. Steer at Kishnagur, and by others in the Upper Provinces.

Pear, wild, اخگور akhgoor. Pyrus tomentosa, *Rox.* (T) Supposed to be the tree that yields the spurious quince seed, sold commonly in the bazars as Beehee-ké beech.

Pedalum, prickly fruited, براگوکهرو bura gook'huroo, براگهوکرو bura g'hookuroo. Pedalium murex. (H) The leaves have the property of giving out mucilage in milk or water, and are used by sellers of milk to give a rich appearance to their adultered mixture; the seeds afford a meal useful for poultices, or when mucilaginous drinks are prescribed.

Peganum harmala, see Syrian rue.

Pellitory of Spain, عاقرقرحا *aa*k*ur*k*ur*h*a. Anthemis pyrethrum. (H) The pungent root is useful in toothache, or rheumatic affections of the face.

Pellitory, Indian, بلنجاسف bulunjasuf, عاقرقرحا *a*,a*k*ur*k*ur*h*a. Parietaria Indica. (H)

Penæa, heart-leaved, انزروت *unz*uroot, کنجده kunjud'eh. Penæa mucronata. (S) A gum resin exuding from this shrub, called Sarcocolla, is supposed by the Arabians to have the virtue of uniting wounds.

Penicillaria spicata, see Bull-rush.

Pennyroyal, بودنک boodunk, پودنه poodun'eh. Mentha pulegium. (H) Like other mints it is aromatic, and is chiefly used in hysterical attacks, obstructed menstruation, and hooping cough: though the vulgar use it for many other complaints.

Pennywort, thick-leaved, طلکرا *t*ulkura, R. Hydrocotyle Asiatica. (Tr.)

Pentapetes, scarlet flowered, دوپہریا dô p'hureea. Pentapetes Phœnicia. (H)

Pentaptera, arjun, ارجون *u*rjoon, R. Pentaptera arjuna, *Rox.* (T) A timber tree.

Pentaptera, hairy, عنس *a*ns, پیاسال peeasal, R. Pentaptera tomentosa, *D. C.* Terminalia tomentosa, *Pro. Lin.* (T) A large timber tree, the bark being an astringent febrifuge.

Pepper, betle, see Betle pepper.

Pepper, bird, دھانمرچ d'han muruch. Capsicum baccatum, (US)

Pepper, black كالي مرچي kalee murchee, فلفل اسود fulful usooud, فلفل سياه fulful seea'h, لاده lad'eh چوبا chooeea. Piper nigrum, (Tr.)

Pepper, cayenne or chili, لال مرچي lal murchee, گاچ مرچ gach muruch. Capsicum frutescens. (H)

Pepper, chaba, چاب chab, چوي chooee. Piper chaba. *W. Hunter* in Asiat. Res. (Tr) Cultivated in Bengal chiefly for its root, which is used in medicine; its fruit resembles closely the long pepper.

Pepper, kaffree chilli, كفري مرچ kufree muruch. Capsicum grossum. (US)

Pepper, long, پيپل peepul, پيپلي peeplee, دارفلفل dar fulful, طابي *t*abee. Piper longum. (S) It yields in Bengal on an average, about four maunds (80 lbs. each) to the beega (⅓d. of an acre) of fruit annually for three years, and the root is then useful in medicine.

Pepper-mint نعنع n*a*n*a*. Mentha piperita. (H)

Pepper-wort, four-leaved, چپاتي chupatee. Marsilea quadrifolia, *Pro. Lin.* (H) Growing in ditches and swampy places, its leaves are used by the poor native as a spinage, its properties are unknown.

Pergularia, lesser, لبان لتا luban luta. Pergularia minor. (C.)

Periploca esculenta, see Esculent oxystelma.

Periploca Indica, see Indian sarsaparilla.

Periploca secamone, see Alpine secamony.

Periwinkle, Madagascar, گل فرنگ gul-u-furung. Vinca rosea. (US) The pink and white varieties are common in India.

Persicaria, downy, سویت پانی مرچ sooét panee muruch. Polygonum lanatum, *Rox.* (A) It appears a variety of P. Hydropiper, or water pepper.

Persicaria, flaccid, پانی مرچ panee muruch. Polygonum flaccidum, *Rox.* (A)

Pharbitis, purgative, نیل کلمی neelkulmee. Pharbitis nil, *Chois.* Convolvulus nil, *Linn.* Ipomæa cœrulea, *Rox.* (Tw.) The seeds are sold by natives under the name کالا دانه *kala dan'eh*, and are an effectual cathartic when roasted like coffee, and administered in doses of 30 to 40 grains.

Pharnaceum, five-styled, دوسرا ساگ doosura sag. R. Pharnaceum pentagynum, *Rox.* (H)

Pharnaceum molluga, see Ladies' bed-straw.

Phaseolus aconitifolius, see Aconite-leaved kidney bean.

Phaseolus max, see Hairy-podded kidney bean.

Phaseolus mungo, see Small-fruited bean, or Green-gram.

Phaseolus radiatus, or black-gram, see Ringed kidney bean.

Phaseolus rostratus, see Pointed kidney bean.

Phaseolus trilobus, see Three-lobed kidney bean.

Phaseolus vulgaris, see Dwarf kidney bean.

Phellandrum stoloniferum, see Creeping rooted water hemlock.

Phillyrea, hardy, بهوين مورا bhooeen moora. Phillyrea robusta. (S)

Phlomis, Cingalese, هال کهوسا hal k'hoosa, R. گهمرا g'humra, هلکسا hulkusa. Phlomis Zeylanica, *Will.* (H)

Phlomis, eatable, or Indian, تنبي tumbee, گومرا

goomra. Phlomis esculenta, *Pro. Lin.* P. Indica, *Linn.* (H) Used as a spinage, but very acrid. It is said the juice of the bruised leaves drawn up the nose is a cure for the bite of snakes, but this is very doubtful as it has little aromatic flavor or scent. The Malays squeeze it into the eyes to make them bold and intrepid in war.

Phœnix dactylifera, see Common date palm.

Phœnix sylvestris, see Wild date tree.

Phrynium, double stemmed, وله ooul'eh, موكتپاطي mooktupa*t*ee, پاطيپتي pa*t*eeputee. Phrynium dichotomum, *Rox.* (H) This is the plant whence are made the *cold mats* called سيتل‌پاطي seetulpa*t*ee.

Phrynium, overlapped, پيتلي‌پاتا peetulee pata. Phrynium imbricatum, *Rox.* (Tu.)

Phyllanthus, cheramel, هرپهروري hurp'hurooree. Phyllanthus cheramela, *Rox.* (S)

Phyllanthus emblica, see Shrubby myrabolan.

Phyllanthus, Indian annual, بهين‌اونله bu'heen aoonl'eh, ارجتا arjuta, سداهزرمني suda huzur munee. Phyllanthus niruri. (H) The fresh root has been successfully used in jaundice. The root, leaves, and young shoots are by native practitioners esteemed as deobstruent, diuretic, and healing; and the leaves a good stomachic.

Phyllanthus longifolius, see Long-leaved cicca.

Phyllanthus, many flowered, کالا محمد kala mu*h*mud, پنجولی punjoolee, R. Phyllanthus multiflorus, *Will.* (S)

Physic nut, angular-leaved, بگرینڈی bugreendee, جنگلی ارنڈی junglee arundee. Jatropha curcas. (S) The oil is used as a remedy for eruption and rheumatism.

Physic nut, glaucous-leaved, عبب *a*bub, نقمبا nu*k*umba. Jatropha glauca. (H) A stimulating oil is extracted from the seeds, used in rheumatic and paralytic affections.

Physalis peruviana, or angulata, see Peruvian winter cherry.

Physalis somnifera, or flexuosa, see Clustered winter cherry.

Pierardia, palatable, لتکو lutkoo. Pierardia sapida, *Rox.* (T) The fruit is of acid flavor, but very inferior.

Pimenta tree, پلپل pulpul. Pimenta vulgaris,

now Eugenia pimenta, *Pro. Lin.* Myrtus pimenta, *Linn.* (T) The dried fruit is the Allspice of commerce.

Pimpinella anisa, see Common anise.

Pine-apple, اناناس anunas. Bromelia anañas. (H) Some are of opinion that this fruit is conducive to cholera, which is not improbable in the ordinary way of eating it, after it has been cut many hours, often days; as the profuse juice soon ferments, and cannot but then be injurious, but eaten when quite ripe and *fresh* cut, it has none of these bad qualities, and is a delicious and grateful fruit. The fibre of the leaf is very fine and strong, like flax.

Pine, dammer, درخت رال durukht-u-ral, دهوناگاچ d'hoona gach, علک aluk. Chloroxylon dupada, *Buchanan.* (T)

Pine, Devdar, دیودار deeôdar, دیواورد deeoou-aoourd. Pinus deodara, *Rox.* (T)

Pine, long-leaved, خور choor, صنوبر ssunoobur, سرل پیر surul peer, نوج nooj. Pinus longifolia. (T) The wood is called سرل surul.

Pine, Smith's, رگا raga, راتیانج rateeanuj. Pinus

Smithianus, *Dr. Wall.* Abies khutrow, *Dr. Ro.* (T)

Pink, China, قرنفل *k*urunful. Dianthus Chinensis. (H)

Piper betle, see Betle pepper.

Piper chaba, see Chaba pepper.

Piper cubeba, see Cubebs.

Piper longum, see Long pepper.

Piper nigrum, see Black pepper.

Pisonia, prickly, باگهاچاره bag'ha char'eh, R. Pisonia aculeata. (T)

Pistachia-nut tree, پسته pust'eh, فوستاق foosta*k*, درخت‌جلوز durukht-u-jooloo*z*. Pistacia officinarum. (T) This is very rare in India, and only found in the western and central parts, where it may have been introduced from Arabia.

Pistacia terebintha, see Turpentine tree.

Pistia, the floating, انترگنگا *u*nturgunga, توکا پانا tooka pana. Pistia stratiotes, *Pro. Lin.* (H) A decoction is considered demulcent by Hindoo doctors, and the leaves are used as a poultice for piles.

Pistacia lentiscus, see Mastich tree.

Pisum, see Pea.

Pladera decussata, see Decussated canscora.

Plantain, see Banana.

Plantain, common, موز moouz, کیلا kéla. Musa paradisiaca. (T) Differing from the Banana in having the fruit much larger and the skin tough. The fruit roasted or boiled when not quite ripe is frequently used instead of bread, or in curries, &c; the leaves make good mats, and when tender are used as a cool drawing for parts where there have been blisters. The skins being in some parts also used in dyeing leather black.

Plantain, Nepal, گومپوکیلا goompoo kéla. Musa Nepalensis, *Dr. Wall.* (T)

Plane tree, oriental, چنار chunar, ارس arus دلب dulub, سپیداه supeeda'eh. Plantanus orientalis. (T)

Plantago ispaghula, see Plantain flea-wort.

Plantane, see Fleawort.

Plectranthus, aromatic, پتھرچور put'hur choor. Plectranthus aromaticus. (Cr)

Plumbago rosea, see Rose colored lead-wort.

Plumbago zeylanica, see Cingalese lead-wort.

Plum, common, الو aloo, الوچه alooch'eh. Prunus domesticus. (T)

Plum, hog, امرا amra, امبرا ambura, جنگلي ام junglee am. Spondias mangifera. (T) The fruit is eaten, but is harsh flavored. The trunk yields an insipid gum like Gum Arabic. The root is considered an enmanagogue; the bark is held useful in dysentry, and decoction of the wood in gonorrhea.

Plum, Java, see Java plum.

Plum, native, see Jujube tree.

Plumieria, acuminated, گلاچين gulacheen. Plumieria acuminata. (T)

Poa cynosuroïdes, see Meadow grass.

Poa unioloïdes, see Smooth meadow grass.

Podocarpus, broad-leaved, سوپلونگ sôplông. Podocarpus latifolia, *Dr. Wall.* (T)

Poinciana pulcherrima, see Barbadoes flower-fence.

Poison bulb, سکهدرسن suk'hdursun, Crinum asiaticum, or toxicarium. (B) The bulbs are a powerful emetic.

Poison nut, کچلا kuchla, خنانق الكلب khunanukulkelb, جاوزالقي jaooz alkee, زهرزمين zu'hurzumeen, اذاراقي azarakee. Strychnos nux vomica. (T) The seeds are highly poisonous; but are effectively employed medicinally in paralysis, dyspepsia, dysentery, affection of the nervous system, &c. Dr. O'Shaughnessy has shewn the identity of this bark with what is called the *False angustura*, and also that brucea may be procured from it in abundance. The natives but too often use the seeds to increase the intoxicating quality of their distilled spirit.

Polyanthes tuberosa, see Common tuberose.

Polygala arvensis, see Wild milk-wort.

Polygonum lanatum, see Downy persicaria.

Polypodiaceæ, see Ferns.

Pomegranate, انار anar, دارم darum, رمان ruman, نار nar, تاغ tag. Punica granatum. (T) The best are found to the North Westward. The root is a vermifuge of the most powerful and certain efficacy.

Pongamia, smooth-leaved, کرنج kurunj, کرنجوا kurunjooa. Pongamia glabra, Galedupa Indica, *Lam.* Dalbergia arborea, *Will.* Robinia mitis, *Linn.* (T)

Pongatium, Cingalese, جيل مريچ jeel mureech, R. Pongatium zeylanicum, *Pro. Lin.* Sphenoclea Zeylanica, *Will.* (A)

Pontederia, sheathed, نوکا nooka, R. لوکا looka Pontederia vaginalis, *Will.* (A)

Pontederia, spreading, کاچري kachuree. Pontederia dilatata. (A)

Poplar, black, حور رومي *h*oour roomee. Populus nigra. (T)

Poplar, common, جنار junar, حور *h*oour, چنار chunar, تاغ ta*g*. Populus Græca. (T)

Poplar, white, سپيدار supeedar, پره pur'eh, شاشدان shashdan, غرب *g*urb, دردار, durdar. Populus alba. (T)

Poppy, prickly, see Prickly poppy.

Poppy, white خشخاش khush khash, کوکنار kooknar, پوست poost, هيشر heeshur. Papaver somniferum. (H) The juice of the wounded capsules being known as opium, افيم afeem.

Portilaca quadrufida, see Creeping purslane.

Posogueria dumetorum, see Emetic-nut.

Posogueria, marshy, پيرالو peraloo. Posogueria uliginosa, *Rox.* (T)

Potatoe, آلو aloo. Solanum tuberosum. (Tu) The term, *aloo*, is applied to nearly all tuberous rooted esculents.

Potatoe, wild, شونديكي shoondeekee. Solanum pubescens, *Linn.* (Tu) It is eaten fried, but is rather bitter.

Pothos, armed, كانتاكچو kanta kuchoo, R. Pothos lasia, *Rox.* (H)

Pothos, officinal, } see Useful scindapsus.
Pothos, officinalis, }

Pothos, peeplee, پيپلي peeplee, R. Pothos peepla, *Rox.* (Pa.)

Premna, entire-leaved, بهوت بهيروي b'hoot b'heeroouee. Premna integrifolia, *Pro. Lin.* P. serratifolia, *Will.* (S) The root is cordial, and stomachic in decoction.

Premna, herbaceous بهوي جام b'hooee jam, R. Premna herbacea, *Rox.* (S)

Premna, thorny, گونهوري goon'huree, R. Premna spinosa, *Rox.* (T)

Prickly poppy, see Mexican argemone.

Primrose, Stuart's, ماسونيتها masooneetu'ha, Primula Stuartii, *Dr. Wall.* (H)

Primrose, toothed, نيتها neetu'ha, (Nepalese.) Primula denticulata, *Sir J. E. Smith.* (H)

Prince's feather, کلگا kulga. Amarantus hypochondriacus. (H)

Protium giliadense, see Balm of gilead tree.

Prunus Arminiacus, see Apricot.

Prunus cerasifera, see Myrabolan plum.

Prunus cerasus, see Common cherry.

Prunus domesticus, see Common plum.

Prunus institutia, see Damson.

Prunus padus, see Bird, or wild cherry.

Prunus spinosa, see Sloe.

Psalliata campestris, see Mushroom.

Psoralia, hazel-leaved, بارچان baoochan, واوچي ooaôchee, هاقوچ ha*k*ooch. Psoralia corylifolia. (H) The seeds are prescribed by native practitioners in inveterate cutaneous diseases.

Psychotria, herbaceous, كودي منكوني koodee munkoonee, R. Psychotria herbacea. (US)

Psydium pomiferum, see Red guava.

Psydium pyriferum, see White guava.

Ptarmica vulgaris, see Sneezewort.

Pteris lumilata, see Woolly brake.

Pterocarpus, emarginate-leaved, پیت‌سال pét sal. Pterocarpus marsupium. (T) Roxburgh supposes this tree to produce *gum kino*, a well known astringent; but the real gum is rather obtained from P. erinaceus.

Pterocarpus senitalanus, see Red saunders wood.

Pterospermum, various-leaved, موچاکوندا moocha koonda, R. Pterospermum suberifolium. (T)

Pumpkin, common, or red, کدیمه kudeem'eh, کمرها kumru'ha, کوندها koond'ha, میتهی‌کدو meet'hee kudoo, سیتاپهل seetap'hul. Cucurbita pepo. (Tr)

Punica granatum, see Pomegranite.

Purslane, creeping, چولي choolee, چولاي choolaee, بقلة‌المبارک bu*k*lut'eh alumbaruk, وپدیکه oopudeek'eh. Portalaca quadrifida. (H) An infusion of the leaves is considered a diuretic and bruised, they are used as an external application for erysipelas.

Purslane, small, خرفه khurf'eh, کاندلي kandlee, لونا loona, لونیا looneea, نونیا nooneea, گهول g'hool, بقلة‌الحمقا bu*k*lut'h *ulhumka*. Portulaca oleracea. (H) One of the numerous greens, or sägs, of natives.

Pyrus communis, see Pear.

Pyrus malus, see Apple.

Quercus ballota, see Barbary oak.

Quercus fenestrata, see Open oak.

Quercus ilex, see Holm tree.

Quercus lanceœfolia, see Lance-leaved oak.

Quercus robur, see Sessile fruited oak.

Quercus spicata, see Pointed oak.

Quercus suber, see Cork tree.

Quillwort, Coromandel, گهي g'hee, Isoctes. Coromandeliana. (A) It grows in low moist grounds, and is eaten by the common people.

Quince, Bengal, بلب bulb, بيل bél, سريپهل sree-p'hul. Ægle marmelos, Cratæva marmelos, *Linn.* (T) Corrupted from the marmeleira of the Portuguese, given to it because these people seem to have prepared a marmalade from its fruit. The aperient and detersive quality of the fruit, and its efficacy in removing costiveness is well known; the unripe fruit roasted has also great effect in cases of dysentery.

Quince, China, سفرجل sufurjul, بيہ béh. Cydonia chinensis. (T)

Radish, common, ترب turub, فجل fujul, مولي moolee. Raphanus sativus. (T)

Ramoon tree, سيورا seeoora, نکچلني nukchulnee. Trophis aspera. (T)

Randia dumetorum, see Emetic-nut.

Randia, racemose, پيتنگا peetunga. Randia racemosa. *Rox.* (T)

Randia, upright, سويت برنا sooét buruna. Randia stricta, *Rox.* (S)

Raspberry, scant-flowered, انچو anchoo. Rubus pauciflorus. (US) Found in the Nepal, and the Himalaya range.

Rattan, بيت bét, بيد béd. Calamus rotang, *Rox.* or rudentum. (C) It furnishes the ratan canes, &c.

Rattan, Java, بيت bét, بطا bu*t*a. Calamus viminalis, or zalacca. (H) The fruit is eaten, and consists of two or three sweet kernels.

Red-wood tree, روهنا roo'hoona. Soymida febrifuga, *Pro. Lin.* Swietenia febrifuga. *Will.* (T) The bark is a remedy for the jungle fever, and in cases of gangrene. The wood, hard and durable, is used for posts, &c.

Reed, Bengal, گابانل gaba-nul, R. Arundo Bengalensis, *Linn.* (G)

Reed, karka, نرکت nurkut, برو buroo, نر nur, نال nal, ناي naee, قصب *k*ussub. Arundo karka, *Linn.* (G) What are called Durma mats are made of the stalks split open. Pens for Writing the Persian, and other Eastern characters are made of the dressed reed.

Rest, harrow, common, کيروج keerooj. Ononis spinosa (H)

Rhizophera, see Mangrove.

Rhubarb, medicinal, درخت راوند durukht-u-raoound, ريوند reeoond, دلب dulub, دلو duloo, راسنا rasuna. Rheum palmatum. (F) Producing the rhubarb of commerce; *Dr. Wallich* has also made us acquainted with another useful plant of this family, R. emodi, which has been found very efficacious as a purgative, with tonic and astringent properties also, and less disagreeable to take.

Rhododendron, aromatic, طاليسفر *t*aleesfur, معفر mafur Rhododendron lepidotum, *Dr. Ro.* (S) The leaves are highly fragrant, and of a stimulant nature.

Rhus coriaria, see Elm-leaved sumach.

Ribes uva crispa, see Smooth gooseberry.

Rice, ارز aruz, دهان d'han, برنج burunj. Oryza sativa. (G) There are an immense number of varieties known to natives.

Ricinus communis, see Castor oil tree.

Rivina paniculata, see Persian salvadora.

Robinia, white-blossomed, بتاس butas. Robinia candida. (T)

Rock rose, Cretan, لادن ladun. Cistus Creticus. (S) The resinous gum Ladanum is produced from this, it is stimulant.

Rondeletia, colored, تولا لوده toola lod'h, R. Rondeletia tinctoria, *Rox*. (T)

Roscoea, five-stamened, كنگيا kungeea, R. Roscoea pentandra, *Rox*. (C)

Rose, a, گل gul, گلاب gulab, گلبن gulbun, ورد, oourud. Rosa. (S) The generic name of all kinds.

Rose, Bussorah, گل سوري gul sooree. Rosa gallica. (S

Rose, China, كته گلاب kut'h gulab Rosa Chinensis. (S)

Rose, damask, ادنا گلي adna gulee, گل سرخ gulsurkh, صدبرگ ssudburg. Rosa damascena. (S)

Rose, double, گل صدبرک gul ssudburuk. Rosa centifolia. (S)

Rose, many-flowered, گل رعنا gul *r*ana. Rosa multiflora. (Tr)

Rose, sweet briar, گل نسرين gul nusreen, استرون *u*sturoon. Rosa rubiginosa. (S)

Rose, white, سيوتي seeootee, صدبرگ ssudburg نسترن nusturun. Rosa glandulifera, *Rox*. (S)

Rose, wild, گل بي فرمان gul bé furman, نسرين nusreen. Rosa arvensis. (S)

Rose-apple, common, جام jam, گلاب جام gulab-jam. Eugenia jambos. (T) A pleasant fruit, as some think, but its only good quality is its fragrance, being dry, tough, and unpalatable.

Rose-apple, watery, پانياله جام paneeal'eh jam. Eugenia paniola, *Rox*. (T) The fruit is watery and insipid.

Rose-bay, oval-leaved, see Wrightia.

Rose, chesnut, Indian, ناگ كيسر nag keesur, ناگيسر angeesur. Mesua ferrea, *Will*. (T) The dried flowers are used as a medicine, as well as being esteemed for their fragrance.

Rosemary, common, حصالبان اخضر *h*ussalban akhzzur, ببريه buburee'eh, اكليل الجبل akleel *u*l jubul. Rosmarinus officinalis. (US) It has been successfully used as a cephalic medicine for headache, and to excite the mental powers. An infusion, it is said, will keep the hair in curl, and prevent baldness. It is much used in Eau de Cologne, &c.

Rottboellia, compressed, پامشرو pamshroo, R. Rottboellia (gen. ap. *Schr.*) compressa, *Linn.* (G)

Rottboellia, perforated, كركي kurkee, R. Rottboellia (gen. ap. *Schr.*) perforata, *Rox.* (G)

Rottboellia, smooth, بكشا buksha, R. Rottboellia (gen. apud *Schr.*) glabra, *Rox.* (G)

Rottlera, dyer's, پندالو pundaloo, درخت كمود durukht-u-kumood. Rottlera tinctoria. (S) The red powder covering the capsules is used to dye scarlet, and the root to give a red dye.

Rottlera indica, see Naked trewia.

Roylea, elegant, پتكري putkuree. Roylea elegans, *Dr. Wall.* (H)

Rubia cordifolia, or munjista, see Madder of Bengal.

Rubus gowry-phul, see Himalaya blackberry.

Rubus Indicus, see Wood bramble.

Rubus lasiocarpus, see Hill bramble.

Rubus pauciflorus, see Scant flowered raspberry.

Rubus rotundifolius, Round-leaved bramble.

Rubus vulgaris, see Common blackberry.

Rue, common, سداب sudab, ستري sutures سندب sundub, سذاب suzab, خيل kheel. Ruta graveolens, (US) Used in domestic medicine as "rue-tea" being acrid, and stimulant, anthelmintic and sudorific.

Rue, Syrian, حرمل *h*urmulu. Peganum harmala (H) The seed is used in medicine.

Rue, wild, اسفند asfund, سپند supund. Ruta albiflora. (US)

Ruellia, long leaved, see Long leaved barleria.

Rumex acutus, see Sharp dock, and Bladder dock.

Rumex vesicarius, see Common sorrel.

Rush, club, چچکا chuchka. Scirpus luzulæ. (G) see Bladder dock.

Rush, mat, کورا kôra. Cyperus textilis, *Thunberg.* (G) Used for making mats.

Rush, soft, لوخ lookh, قصبا *k*ussba, استوم astoom. Juncus effusus. (H)

Rye, common, کنکران kunkuran, چاودار chaoodar. Secale cereale. (G) This grain, from its easy adaptation to all soils, and ready growth, deserves attention from the agriculturist.

Sacred-bean, Indian, کمل kumul, پدما puduma, پدم puḍum, نیلوفر neeloofur, کنول kunooul, کنولکا گٹہ kunooul ka gun'eh. Nelumbium speciosum. (A) The seeds are eaten raw or roasted, and the tender shoots of the roots in curries. An attribute of Vishnoo, and peculiarly sacred to his wife Luchmee, the lotus-like, and hence the flower has become an emblem of female beauty.

Saccharum cylindricum, see Cylindrical sugar grass.

Saccharum fuscus, see Fuscous sugar grass.

Saccharum munja, see Munja sugar grass.

Saccharum officinarum, see Sugar cane.

Saccharum procerum, see Tall sugar grass.

Saccharum sara, see Sara sugar grass.

Saccharum spontaneum, see Spontaneous sugar grass.

Safflower, عصفر *a*ssfur, کوسم koosum, کسم kusum, معصر m*a*ssur, کجیره kujeer'eh, جریصس jureessus, قرطم *k*urtum, کسمبها kusumb'ha. Carthamus tinctorius. (H) The petals dried form the Safflower of commerce, and are used in dyeing rose, purple, and violet colors; the seeds are used as a laxative.

Saffron-plant, زعفران *za*fran, عبیر *a*beer, کیسر keesur. Crocus sativus. (B) Hindoo doctors prescribe it in nervous affections, typhus fever, &c.

Sage, Bengal, سیستر seestur, ولایتی کاپور oolaeetee kapoor, ولایتی کافور oolaeetee kafoor, سالبیه salbee'eh سفاقس sufa*k*us. Salvia Bengalensis, *Rott.* (S) The leaves differ in a small degree from the common sage of Europe, but have the same qualities, and are used here for the same purposes.

Sago tree, ساوکی saookee, سابوکی کاچ saboo-kee-gach. Sagus lævis *(Jack: in comp. Bot. mag.)* (P) Is the true sago tree, but I believe the native names given would equally apply to S. farinifera, *Rox.* Saguerus Rumphic, *Rox.* said by Dr. Hamilton to produce a very fine kind of sago Caryota urens; Cycas revoluta; or to C. circinalis; as they all will yield the sago of commerce to a greater or less degree.

Salep, ثعلب *sa*lub, كنده kund'eh. Orchis mascula. Tacca pinnatifida, *Will.* (Tu.) The preparation from this tuber is highly strengthening, and given by Arabian physicians in consumption. Lindley considers that this article is more likely to be the produce of O. variegata, O. taurica, or O. militaris; and Dr. Royle, that the plant yielding it in Cashmere belongs to the genus Eulophia, and this appears borne out by fact, but the specimens obtained were not sufficient to cnable the species to be identified; the substance consisting almost entirely of a chemical principle called *Bassorin;* it is said to have the property of depriving sea water of its saltness.

Salicornia Indica, see Indian glass-wort.

Salix Babylonica, see Weeping willow.

Salix rosmarini-folia, see Rose-mary-leaved willow.

Salix tetrasperma, see Four-seeded willow.

Salvadore, Indian, جال jal, ارک هندي aruk hundee, مسواک musooak, اراک irak. Salvadora Indica, *Pro. Lin.* (T) The leaves are of a purgative nature, and the fruit, which is edible, is called پيل peel, or پيلو peeloo.

Salvadore, Persian, پيلو peeloo, ارک aruk, رديق rudeek, سردب surdub, کباث kubas, خرجال khurjal. Salvadora Persica, *Pro. Lin.* Rivina paniculata, *Linn.* (T) The berry has a strong aromatic taste like cress, and the bark of the root is so acrid as to be used by natives to raise blisters. It is supposed to be the mustard tree of Scripture.

Salvia Bengalensis, see Bengal sage.

Salvinia, hooded, پانا pana. Salvinia cucullata, *Pro. Lin.* (A)

Sambucus nigra, see Common elder.

Sandal-wood tree, صندل ssundul, صندل سفيد ssundul suféd, چندن chundun. Santalum album. (T)

Sandarach tree, Ara tree, or Jointed arbor vitæ, سندروس sundroos. Thuja articulata, now Callitris quadrivalvis, *Pro. Lin.* (T) Yields the resinous substance called *Sandarach*, from which *Pounce* is made.

Sanseviera, Cingalese, مرگابي کاگده murgabee ka gud'eh, مروا muroooua, شوچي موخي shoochee mookhee. Sanseviera Zeylanica. (H) An electuary made from the root is prescribed by native practitioners in consumption. A strong hemp, fit for bowstrings, is obtained from the leaves, and a white paper may be made from it of good quality.

Sapindus detergens, see Indian soap berry.

Sapindas emarginatus, see Emarginated soap berry.

Sappan wood, see Brasiletto.

Sarsaparilla, Indian, مکوي mukooee, مگرابو mugraboo, اننت امول anunt amool, ساده بواري sad'eh booaree, R. کرل kurul. Hemidesmus Indicus, *Pro. Lin.* Periploca Indica, *Will.* Asclepias pseudosarsa, *Rox.* (Tw) Considered quite as efficient as the sarsaparilla of America as a medicine. There is another substance in the Indian bazars called اوشبا *aooshba*, usually translated sarsaparilla, but the plant that produces it is unknown.

Sassafras tree, ساسافراس sasafras. Sassafras, officinale. *Pro. Lin.* or Laurus sassafras. (T) Yielding the well-known medicine.

Saul tree, سال sal, سانکهو sank'hoo, شال shal. Shorea robusta, *Dr. Wall.* (T) An useful timber tree growing extensively in the Morung, yielding also a balsamic resin called دهونا d'hoona.

Saunders-wood, red, لال چندن lal chundun, صندال احمر ssundal a*h*mur, رکت چندن rukut chundun, صندل سرخ ssundul surukh, عندم *a*ndum, بقم bu*k*um. Pterocarpus santalanus. (T) The wood is used by the dyers.

Saussurea, cotton-like, پهاین کمل p'haén kumul. Saussurea gossypina, *Dr. Wall.* (H)

Saw-wort, anthelmintic, or purple vernonia, بکچي bukchee, سومراج soomraj. Vernonia anthelmintica, *Pro. Lin.* Serratula anthelmintica, *Rox.* Conyza anthelmintica, *Linn.* (H) The fruit is considered a very powerful medicine in worm cases, as well as the root.

Scævola, Purslane-leaved, درخت چومکهي durukht-u-choomuk'hee. Scævola lobelia. (US)

Scammony plant, سقمونيا su*k*môneea, محموده mu*h*mood'eh. Convolvolus scammonia. (Tw)

The resin, or drug is obtained from the root.

Schmidelia, aporetic, گهي كشي g'hee kushee. Schmidelia aporetica, *Pro. Lin.* Ornitrophe aporetica, *Rox.* (S)

Schmidelia, saw-leaved, راخل پهل rakhul p'hul. Schmidelia serrata, *Pro. Lin.* Ornitrophe sarrata, *Will.* (S) The ripe berries are eaten, and the root, being astringent, is used to stop diarrhœa.

Scilla maritima, see Squill.

Scindapsus, useful, گج پيپل guj peepul, وشيرا oousheera, هاته پهل hat'h p'hool. Scindapsus officinalis, *Pro. Lin.* Pothos officinalis, *Rox.* (Pa) Roxburgh says, the dried fruit is an article of some importance in Hindoo Materia Medica, but he does not inform us of the purpose to which it is applied, going by the name of *guj peepul.* It is said that a decoction is used for rheumatic complaints as a fomentation.

Sciratula anthelmintica, see Anthelmintic sawwort.

Scirpus articulatus, see Articulated clubrush.

Scirpus bispicatus, see Two-spiked clubrush.

Scirpus glomeratus, see Glomerate clubrush.

Scirpus kysoor, see Barbed seeded clubrush.

Scirpus luzulæ, see Clubrush.

Scirpus schœnoïdes see Erect clubrush.

Scirpus squarrosus, see Tufted clubrush.

Scirpus tetragonus, see Tall clubrush.

Screw pine, green spined, كيتكي keetukee, كيورا keeora, گندهول gugund'hool. Pandanus odoratissimus. (T) The immature fruit is reputed to be an emmenagogue, and the leaves are in some parts made into mats: the tender white petals of the flowers being extremely fragrant. It is the *whana* tree of Otaheite. It is offered to Mariama and Vishnoo.

Screw pine, fœtid, كيورا كانٹا keeoora kanta. Pandanus fœtidus, *Rox*. (T)

Screw tree, East Indian, مرورپهلي muroor p'hulee, مروري murooree. Helicteres isora. (S) The juice of the root is said to be of use in affections of the stomach.

Scytalia danura, see Danurine nephelium.

Scytalia lichi, see Leechee.

Scytalia longan, see Longan.

Secale cereale, see Common rye.

Secamone, alpine, سقمونيا su*k*mooneea. Secamone alpini, *Pro. Lin.* Periploca secamone, *Linn.* (Tw) A drastic, supposed, though it is but doubtful, to yield *Smyrna Scammony.*

Semecarpus anacardium, see Marking nut.

Senna auriculata, see Eared cassia.

Senna sophora, see Round podded cassia.

Senna tora, see Oval-leaved cassia.

Senna, true, سنا suna, سونامکي sôna mukee, سوناپاط soonapat. Cassia lanceolata. *Drs. Wall.* and *Royle,* C. elongata of *Lémaire,* see Lindley's Flora Medica, (S) This differs in some respects from the C. lanceolata of Forskahl, which is by many supposed to be the *Suna* (سنا) of the Arabs.

Sesbania, or Sesbana, Egyptian, جيت jét. Agati grandiflora, *Pro. Lin.* Sesbania Ægyptiaca or rather S. grandiflora. (H) The bark is a powerful bitter tonic.

Sensitive plant, لجالو lujaloo. Mimosa sensitiva. (H)

Sesamum orientale, or Indicum, see Oriental oily seed.

Shaddock, بتاوي نيمو butaoouee neemoo, چکوتا

chukoota, چکوترہ chukootur'eh, چوکوترہ chookoo-tur'eh. Citrus decumana. (T) Originally from China and Japan.

Shallot, پیاز peeaz, پیاج peeaj. Allium ascalonicum. (B) One of the most commonly found of the onion species in this country.

Shorea camphorifera, see Camphor tree.

Shorea robusta, see Saul tree.

Sida, dwarf, جنکا junka, R. Sida humilis. (H)

Sida, Mauritius, کونگونی koongoonee, کنگوی kungooee, خبازی khubazee, خطمی khu*t*mee. Sida Mauritiana. (H) Used as a substitute for mallow-leaf, and native practitioners give infusion of the root in fever.

Sida, rhomboid-leaved, بلا bula. Sida rhombifolia, S. rhomboidia, *Rox.* (S)

Sida, small-flowered, جھانپی j'ha*m*pee, R. Sida Asiatica. (H)

Silk cotton tree, common, سیمل seemul, سینبل see*m*bul. Bombax heptaphyllum. (T) The wool is used to stuff pillows, &c.

Silk cotton tree, five-stamened, سویت سیمل sooét seemul, R. Bombax pentandrum. (T)

Silver weed, veiny-leaved, بیس تارکا bees taruka, R. Argyreia nervosa, *Pro. Lin.* Lettsomia nervosa, *Rox.* (Tw)

Silver weed, white, سمودره شوکا sumoodr'ch shoka, R. Argyreia argentea, *Pro. Lin.* Lettsomia argentea, *Rox.* (Tw)

Sinapis, see Mustard.

Singara nut, see Water caltrops.

Siphonanthus Indica, see Whorl-leaved clerodendrum.

Sissoo tree, سیسو seesoo, شیشم sheeshum. Dalbergia sisoo. *Rox.* (T) The wood is dark colored, and handsome for economical purposes.

Sisum sisarum, see Skirret.

Skirret, or white potatoe, چینا الو cheena aloo. Sisum sisarum. (Tv)

Sloe, آلنج alung. Prunus spinosa, (T) Seldom met with in India.

Smilax, China, see China-root plant.

Sneeze-wort, کندس kundus. Achillea ptarmica, now Ptarmica vulgaris, *Pro. Lin.* (H) The whole plant is pungent, and provoking a flow of saliva, the dried leaves cause sneezing.

Soap-berry, emarginated, ريته reet'eh, ريشته reesht'eh, بندكي هندي bundukee hundee, اريشته areesht'eh. Sapindus emarginatus. (T) The capsule is a valuable expectorant.

Soap-berry, Indian, ريتها reet'ha. Sapindus detergens. *Rox.* (T) It is doubtful whether this is not a mere variety of S. saponaria.

Solanum decemdentatum, see Ten-toothed nightshade.

Solanum hirsutum, see Hairy nightshade.

Solanum indicum, see Indian nightshade.

Solanum insanum, see Mad apple.

Solanum Jacquini, see Jacquin's nightshade.

Solanum longum, see Cylindrical egg plant.

Solanum lycopersicum, see Tomata.

Solanum melongenum, see Common egg plant.

Solanum nigrum, see Blackberried nightshade.

Solanum pubescens, see Downy nightshade, or Wild potatoe.

Solanum rubrum, see Red nightshade.

Solanum stramonifolium, see Mad apple-leaved nightshade.

Solanum tuberosum, see Potatoe.

Sonerila, spotted, سوتلي sootlee, (in the Khassee language.) R. Sonerila maculata, *Rox.* (H)

Sonneratia, petal-less, خورا khoora, R. Sonneratia apetala, *Pro. Lin.* (T)

Sorrel, common, چوكه chook'eh, ترسه turs'eh, حماض *h*umazz. Rumex vesicarius. (H)

Sorrel, Indian red, or Indian hibiscus, انباري am*b*aree, ميستا mésta. Hibiscus subdariffa. (H)

Sorrel, yellow wood, or procumbent oxalis, انبوتي am*b*ootee, Oxalis corniculata. (B)

Sorghum vulgum, see Indian millet.

Sonchus orixensis, see Orissa sow-thistle.

Sorgmida febrifuga, see Red wood tree.

Sour gourd, Œthiopian, called also the Baobab tree, or monkies' bread tree, بمني املي bumnee imlee. Adamsonia digitata, (T). The fruit is a pleasant tasted, sub acid; and the dried leaves powdered, are found serviceable in diarrhœa and fevers. The tree is the largest in the world, the trunk having been found 30 feet in diameter. The fibres of the bark are made into rope and a coarse cloth, but it is of no use as timber.

Southern-wood, Indian, قيصوم *k*eesoom, برنجاسف burunjasuf, دونه doon'eh, بارنكبوي barunk booee, جنجك junjuk. Artemisia Austriaca, A. paniculata, *Rox.* (US) The plant is offered to Sheva, and to Vishnoo.

Sow thistle, Orissa, كامراج kamraj, بن پالك bunpaluk. Sonchus Orixensis. (H) Used as greens by natives.

Sphæranthus, Indian, مندي mundee, دقو du*k*oo, چاگل ندي chagul nudee. Sphœranthus Indicus. (H) The seeds are by Indian practitioners, considered anthelmintic.

Sphæranthus, soft, خامادروس khamadroos. Sphæranthus mollis, *Ro.* (H)

Sphærocarya, eatable, لشپو lushpoo, بن ام bun am, (Nepalese). Sphærocarya edulis, *Dr. Wall* (T) The fruit is liked by the Nepalese.

Sphenoclea Zeylanica, see Cingalese pongatium.

Spinach, tetrandrous, اسفاناج isfanaj, اسفاناخ isfanakh, چولاي choolaee, پنيس punees. Spinacia tetrandra, *Rox.* (H) Much and deservedly cultivated.

Spikenard, جهتاماسي j'hutamansee, سنبل الطيب sum*m*bul ul *t*eeb, سنبل هندي sum*m*bul hundee, چيهر chee'hur, چهر ch'hur, نرد nurd, ناردين nardeen. Nardostachys jatamansi, *D. C.* Valeriana jatamansi of *Sir W. Jones*, and *Rox.* (H) Ναρδασταχοσ or Ναρδοσινδικη of *Dioscorides*, the real spikenard of the ancients, highly esteemed alike as a perfume, and as a stimulant medicine; native practitioners esteeming it valuable in hysteria and epilepsy. Some writers doubt its identity with this, but Dr. Royle's arguments may be considered conclusive on this point, vide *Royle's Illustrations*, p. 241 to 244.

Spiderwort, axillary, باگانلا baga nula, سوتراج sootraj. Tradescantia axillaris, *Rox.* (H)

Spondias mangifera, see Hog plum.

Spurge, oleander-leaved, تہوہر t'hoo'hur, سيج seej. Euphorbia neriifolia, (S) The acrid juice of the leaves is prescribed as a purgative in the visceral obstructions consequent on long continued intermittent fever by native practitioners, and also with *margosa oil* in contraction of the limbs by ill-treated rheumatic affections.

Spurge, sheathed, مونسا سیج moonsa seej, R. منصورسیج munssoor seej, سیہند see'hund. Euphorbia ligularia, *Rox.* (T) The root mixed with black pepper is used to cure snake bites.

Spurge, spreading triangular, تدهارا tud'hara, سیہند see'hund, قالا *k*ala, نارسیج nar-u-seej. Euphorbia antiquorum. (S) The juice is used by native doctors as an external application in rheumatic affections.

Spurge, thyme-leaved, ددهي dud'hee, سویت خیروگه sooét kheroog'eh. Euphorbia thymifolea, *Linn.* (H) The leaves and seeds are given to children in worm cases, and the juice, made to a paste with flour, is a strong purgative.

Squash, or vegetable marrow, سفرا کومرا sufura koomra. Cucurbita ovifera. (Tr.)

Squill, اسقیل is*k*eel. Scilla maritima, *Pro. Lin.* (B) Having medicinal properties which are supposed to be possessed also by S. indica, *Rox.*

Squill, Indian, جنگلي پیاز junglee peeaz, عنصل *a*nssul, کاندا kanda, اسقیل is*k*eel, پیازدشتي peeaz-u-dushtee. Ledebouria hyacinthoïdes, *Pro. Lin.* Erythronium indicum, *Rott.* (B) Used as a substitute for the true squill, and chiefly given to horses.

Staff tree, hardy, شيلكول sheelkool, R. Celastrus robustus, *Rox.* (T)

Stalagmitis gambogia, see Painter's Xanthochymus.

Stalagmitis ovalifolia, or gambogioïdes, see Indian gamboge tree.

Star-anise, see Anise.

Star apple, Indian, پيتكارا pétukara. Chrysophyllum Roxburghianum, *Dr. Wall.* Ch. acuminatum, *Rox.* But distinct from Ch. acu. of *Lamark.* (T) The fruit is eaten by natives, but is indifferent.

St. John's bread, خرنوب نبتي khurnoob nub*t*ee. Ceratonia siliqua. (T) Considered to be the locust of the scriptures.

Sterculia fœtid, جنگلي بادام junglee badam. Sterculia fœtida. (T)

Sterculia, small-leaved, رام چلپاري ram julparee, R. Sterculia parvifolia, *Rox.* (T)

Sterculia, stinging, بلي bulee, R. کاتيرا kateera. Sterculia urens. (T)

Stizolobium altissimum, see **Assam bean.**

Stizolobium pruriens, see **Cowitch.**

Strychnos, axillary, هرکچلا hur kuchla. Strychnos axillaris, *Cole*. (C)

Strychnos, colubrine, کچلا لتا kuchla luta. Strychnos colubrina, *Will.* (C) Said to have virtues in the cure of snake bites.

Strychnos nux vomica, see **Poison nut.**

Strychnos potatorum, see **Clammy nut.**

Strawberry, کهج ku'huj, اساسنو asasunoo. Fagaria vesca, and F. Indica. (H) The latter is common in Assam and the Himalayas.

Storax, common, اصطرک *ussturuk*, سلاجت sulajut, ميعة mee*a*ut'eh. Styrax officinale. (S) The resin is well known as a drug, and is considered a stimulating expectorant.

Styrax benzoin, see Benzoin tree.

Succory, wild, كاسني kasnee, هندبا hindba. Cichorium intybus, (H) called C. cosnia by *Dr. Hamilton*. Used in medicine as a tonic, and in large doses as an aperient.

Sugar-cane, اوکه uook'h, ایکه *u*eek'h, آک ak, گنا guna. Saccharum officinarum. (G)

Sugar grass, cylindrical, اولو *u*ooloo, الو uloo الوا ulooa. Saccharum cylindricum, *Linn.* (G) Used for thatching.

Sugar grass, fuscous, خري khuree, R. Saccharum fuscus, *Rox.* (G)

Sugar grass, munja, مونج moonj. Saccharum munja, *Rox.* (G)

Sugar grass, sara, سر sur, سينتها seent'ha, سينتهي seent'hee. Saccharum Sara, *Rox.* (G)

Sugar grass, spontaneous, كاس kas, كاكرا kagara, R. Saccharum spontaneum, *Linn.* (G) Used to make mats, and for thatch.

Sugar grass, tall, سرپت surput, سرپتا surputa, سركرا surkura, تنگ tung. Saccharum procerum, *Rox.* (G)

Sumach, elm-leaved, سماق suma*k*, تمتم tumtum. Rhus coriaria. (T) " Does not grow in India; but I perceive that the plant has a place in the Ulfaz Udwiyeh, and is therefore known in the higher tracts of Hindoostan."—*Ainslie.* It is a powerful astringent, and a native of Persia.

Sunflower, سورج مكهي sooruj muk'hee. Helianthus annuus. (H)

Swallow-wort, coated, کلیالتا kuleea luta, چاگل پاتي chagul patee, R. ارستو arustoo. Asclepias tunicata, *Rox*. (Tw)

Swallow-wort, double, چهوتا دودهلتا ch'hota dood'hluta. Asclepias geminata, *Rox*. (C)

Swallow-wort, emetic, or Green flowered cynanchum, انتامول untamool, اتمل atmul. Cynanchum viridiflorum, now Tylophora asthmatica, *Pro. Lin.* Asclepias asthmatica, *Rox*. (Tw) Answers the same purpose as Ipecacuanha, and successfully used as such by Dr. Anderson, Physician General at Madras, and others.

Swallow wort, prickly, اترن atrun, سگواني sugooanee, ارستو arustoo, Asclepias echinata, *Rox*. Cynanchium extensum, *Linn.* and *Will*. (Tw) The leaves are anthelmentic.

Sweet briar, see Rose.

Sweet flag, see Flag.

Sweet potatoe, شکرقندالو shukur*k*und aloo, پندالو pundaloo. Convolvolus batatas. (Tu)

Sweet sop, see Custard apple.

Sweet sultan, عزیز *azeez*, شاهپسند sha'h pusund Centaurea moschata. (H)

Swietenia febrifuga, see Febrifuge mahogany tree.

Symplocos, ferruginous, دوکتیا dookuteea, R. Symplocos ferruginea, *Rox.* (T) Used for dyeing yellow.

Symplocos, prickly, بوري booree. Symplocos spicata. (S)

Symplocos, racemose, لوده lood'h. Symplocos racemosa, *Rox.* (T) The bark is used in dyeing red as a mordaunt, and the red powder thrown about at the *Hoolee* festival, is in some places made of this bark.

Tacca, small, موتي موندها mootee moond'ha. Tacca levis. *Rox.* (H) The tuberous root yields a fecula, or starch, similar to arrowroot.

Tacca pinnatifida, see Salep.

Tagetes erecta, see African marygold.

Tagetes patula, see French marygold.

Tamarisk, Indian, جهاو j'haoo, اج aj, درخت کزم durukhtu kuzhum, شوره گز shoor'eh guz. Tamarix Indica, *Linn.* (S) Dr. Royle says the galls of this, as well as of T. dioica, and T. orientalis are highly astringent, and used both in medicine and dyeing.

Tamarisk, French, گز guz. Tamarix Gallica. (T)

Tamarisk, furas, فراس furas, اثل asul. Tamarix furas, *Dr. Ro.* (T)

Tamarind tree, املي imlee, امبلي imbulee, تمرهندي tumur hundee. Tamarindus Indica. (T)

Tapioca, see Cassava tree.

Tare, hairy, مسور musoor. Ervum hirsutum. (C)

Tea, Indian, see White Basil.

Tea tree, چا cha. Camellia viridis and C. bohea, or Thea viridis, and T. Bohea, *Linn.* (S)

Teak tree, ساج saj. ساگون sagoon. Tectona grandis. (T) Yielding a strong and durable timber, reckoned superior to any other for ship-building.

Tectona grandis, see Teak tree.

Terminalia catappa, see Indian almond.

Terminalia, hairy, آسن asun. Terminalia tomentosa. (T) The tree on which one species of the tussur silk worm feeds.

Terminalia belerica, see Belleric myrabolan

Terminalia chebula, see Chebulic myrabolan.

Terminalia, winged, عنس *ans*, ارجن arjun. Terminalia alata, *Pro. Lin.* Pentaptera tomentosa, *Rox.* T) The bark is astringent and febrifugal.

Ternströmia, saw-leaved, والوا ooalooa. Ternstromia serrata, *Pro. Lin.* or perhaps rather Eurya Chinensis, *Pro. Lin.* (T)

Tetragonolobus edulis, see Winged pea.

Tetranthera, petalless, كوكري چيتا kookree cheeta. Tetranthera apetala, *Pro. Lin.* (T)

Thea viridis, and bohea, see Tea tree.

Thistle, prickly globe, اونت كتارا *u*oont kutara, كتارا kutara. Echinops echinatus, *Rox.* (H) A native of Mysore, camels are fond of it.

Thistle, yellow, or prickly poppy, see Mexican argemone.

Thorn apple, downy, كنك kunuk. Datura metel. (H)

Thorn apple, purple, دهتورا d'hutoora, كالادهتورا kala d'hutoora, جوزماثل jooz masul, گوزگیاه gooz geea'eh, بنج دشتي bunj dushtee. Datura fastuosa. (H) Pieces of the plant are smoked in cases of asthma, and a powder of the root is given in epileptic cases by Mahomedan practitioners; the fresh leaves making a poultice for scrophulous diseases, and cancer, with the Hindoos. Its strong narcotic principle has caused it to be ranked among poisons.

Thunbergia, great-flowered, ميل لتا mél luta. Thunbergia grandiflora. (Tw)

Thyme, garden, اپار ipar, ارپا irpa, حاشا *h*asha. Thymus vulgaris. (US)

Toadstool, فطر fu*t*ur. Limacium carnosum. (Fungus) The native name applies to all *noxious* plants of the family.

Tobacco, Virginia, تماکو tumakoo, تنباکو tumbakoo, بجربهانگ bujurb'hang. Nicotiana tabacum. (H)

Tomato, or Love apple, گوت بيگن goot bégun, ولايتي بيگن oolaeeté bégun. Solanum lycopersicum. (H)

Toon, see East Indian bastard cedar.

Tooth-ache tree, Budumgan, بدرنگ budrung, (Sylhet). Xanthoxylum budrunga, or Fagara budrunga, *Rox*. (T) The seeds are aromatic, and used medicinally by the natives.

Tooth-ache tree, peppery, شهنيز shu'hneez.

Xanthoxylum piperitum. (T) Used in China, and Japan as an antidote against poisons.

Tooth-ache tree, winged, درمر durmur. Xanthoxylum alatum, *Rox.* (T)

Tradescantia axillaris, see Axillary spiderwort.

Tragia, hemp-leaved, کانچکوري kanch kooree, کاسگهني kasug'hunee. Tragia canabina. (Tr)

Travancore arrow root, see East Indian arrow root.

Tilia rubra, see Common lime tree.

Thuja articulata, see Sandarach tree.

Trapa bicornis, see Chinese water caltrops.

Trapa bispinosa, see Two-spined water caltrops.

Trefolia, Indian, بن میتهي bun mét'hee. Trifolium Indicum. (H)

Trewia, naked, پندالو pund-aloo, پيتالي peetalee. Trewia nudiflora, *Will.* or Rottlera Indica of *Gœtt.* (T)

Trianthema, five-stamened, بس کهپرا bus k'hupra. Trianthema pentandra. (Tr) Used by native medical men.

Trianthema, purslane-leaved, ناسرجنكي nasur

jungee, پنرناوي punurunaoouee. Trianthema monogyna. (Tr) The root is slightly cathartic.

Trianthema, trailing گدابني guda bunee. Trianthema decandra. (Tr)

Trichosanthus dioica, see Dioceous snake gourd.

Trichosanthus palmata, see Palmated snake gourd.

Trichosanthus anguina, see Common snake gourd.

Tribulus lanuginosus, see Downy caltrops.

Trifolium pratense, sec Common clover.

Tribulus terrestris, see Small caltrops.

Trigonella comiculata, see Horse shoe fenugreek.

Trigonella fænugræcum, see Common fenugreek.

Triphasia, three-leaved, چيني نارنگي cheenee narungee. Triphasia aurantiola. (S)

Triticum œstivum, see Summer wheat.

Trophis aspera, see Ramoon tree.

Truffle, کم kum, کما kuma. Tuber cibarium, (Fungus.)

Trumpet-flower, Indian, سون soon. Bignonia Indica. (T)

Trumpet-flower, tree, پارل parul. Bignonia suaveolens. (T)

Tuber cibarum, see Truffle.

Tuberose, common, شب shubu, گل شب بو gul shub boo. Polianthes tuberosa. (Tu)

Tulip, common, شقایق shu*k*aee*k*, لاله lal'eh, شقر shu*k*ur. Tulipa gesneriana. (B) Is little known in India, though originally from Persia, and taken thence to England in 1559.

Tulip-tree, large-flowered, دولي چمپا doolee chumpa, R. Liriodendron grandiflora. *Rox.* (T)

Turmeric, common, پیترس peetrus, حماما *h*umama, زردچوب zurd choob, هرد hurd, حلدي huldee. Curcuma longa, Amomum curcuma, *Gmelin.* (H) Forming a prominent part of all curries, and useful as a common yellow dye. Bitter, aromatic, stimulant, and tonic; and used in debilitating ferns, &c. also by natives for cleansing foul ulcers.

Turmeric, grey, نیل کنته neel kunt'h, کالاهلدي kala huldee. Curcuma cæsia. (H)

Turnip, a, شلغم shul*g*um, سلجمي suljumee, لفت luft. Brassica rapa. (F)

Turnsole, Indian, هتي‌شورا hutee shoora, سرياري sureearee, بهوروندي b'hoo roondee, كاسني kasnee. Heliotropium indicum. (US) The juice of the leaves is applied by native practitioners to gum boils.

Turpentine tree, بطم bu*t*um, سكر sukur. Pistacia terebinthus. (T) It furnishes the Cyprus turpentine by wounding the bark.

Tylophoræ asthmatica, see Emetic swallow-wort.

Typha elephantina, see Elephant, or cats' tail grass.

Ulex nanus, see Dwarf fern.

Ulnus, see Elm.

Unona, bushy, طوباي‌چاره *t*oobaee char'eh. Unona dumosa, *Rox*. (C)

Unona, long-leaved, كلاكرا kulakura, R. Unona longifolia, *Pro. Lin*. (T)

Urena, angular-leaved, بن‌وكرا bun ookra, I Urena lobata. (US)

Urena, cut-leaved, کنگویا kungooeea, R. Urena sinuata. (US)

Urtica crenulata, see Notched nettle.

Urtica globulifera, see Round nettle.

Urtica interrupta, see Stinging nettle.

Utricularia, see Hooded milfoil.

Uvaria longifolia, see Mast tree.

Valerian, جال لکري jal lukree, فو foo. Valeriana villosa. (H) Found in Deyra Dhoon, but common in the Hills.

Valeriana jatamansi, see Spikenard.

Valisneria, alternated, جانجي janjee, جاجي jajee. Valisneria alternifolia, *Rox.* Hydrilla of *Hamilton.* (A) Is used in refining sugar, to supply the moisture requisite to separate the molasses.

Valisneria, octandrous, سوار soouar. Valisneria octandra, *Will.* (A)

Vanguiera, prickly, مدن mudun, مين پهل meen p'hul. Vanguiera spinosa. (S)

Vateria, lance-leaved, موال mooal. Vateria lancecœfolia, *Pro. Lin.* (T) Produces the balsam called گوند *goond* by the Brahmins.

Vegetable, marrow, see Squash.

Ventilago, Madras, رکتپته ruktuput'eh. Ventilago Madraspatana, *Gært.* (C)

Verbascum thapsus, see Common mullein.

Verbesina, Ceylonese, پیلابهنگره peela b'hungur'eh, کشوریا kushooreea, بهنگره اسفر b'hungur'eh asfur. Verbesina calendulacea. (H) The whole plant is aromatic, and considered deobstruent.

Verbesina, climbing, بهرنگراج b'hrungraj. Verbesina scandens. (C)

Vernonia, purple, see Anthelmintic saw-wort.

Vervain, creeping, تان tan, بهوی‌وکرا b'hooee ookra, Zapania nodiflora, now Lippia nodiflora, Verbena nodiflora, *Linn.* (Tr)

Vetch, bean-like, کشنه kushn'eh, کلوله kulool'eh. Vicia faba. (Tw) This is the horse bean cultivated in Nepal.

Vetch, chickling, کساری kusaree, کسور kusoor. Lathyrus sativus. (C) The plant is good fodder for cattle, and the seeds are used as food by natives.

Vetch, common, ارده arud'eh, انکاری ankare انکری *u*nkree, عدس *a*dus. Vicia sativa, (Tw) Cattle are fond of it.

Vetchling, yellow, مسورچنا musoor chuna. Lathyrus aphaca. (C)

Vicia faba, see Garden bean, also Bean-like vetch.

Vicia sativa, see Common vetch.

Vinca rosea, see Madagascar periwinkle.

Vine, bearded, تاگوره tagoor'eh. Vitis barbata, *Dr. Wall.* (C)

Vine, black grape, درخت وین durukht ôveen. Vitis vinifera, (C) *var.*

Vine, broad-leaved, گويلا goouееla. Vitis latifolia, *Rox.* (C)

Vine, common, تاک tak, رز ruz, کرم kurm, انگور angoor. Vitis vinifera. (C) Vitis parvifolia, *Rox.* is described as having the same habit, and is a native of the eastern part of Bengal.

Vine, Indian, امدهوکه amd'hook'eh. Vitis indica. (C)

Vine, red-leaved, راجگاگي rajgagee. Vitis rubifolia. *Dr. Wall.* (C)

Vine, white grape, ناهر na'hur. Vitis vinifera, (C) *var.*

Viola tricolor, see Pansy.

Violet, shrubby, رتن پورس rutun poorus. Viola suffruticosa, *Will.* (H) The leaves and tender stalks are demulcent, and are used in decoction by natives.

Violet, sweet, بنفشه bunufsh'eh. Viola odorata. (H)

Viscum album, see Mistletoe.

Vitex negunda, see Quadrangular chaste tree.

Vitex trifolia, see Three-leaved chaste tree.

Vitis, see Vine.

Vitis vinifera, see Corinthian grapes.

Volkameria infortunata, see Long flowered clerodendron.

Volkameria, smooth, سنگ کوپي sung koopee, کندالي kundalee, بنجوما bunjooma. Volkameria inermis, *Linn.* (S) Occasionally employed in medicine on account of its slightly bitter, sub-astringent quality. *Ainslie* says, that Hindoo doctors prescribe the juice of the root in scrophulous affections.

Wall flower, قرنفل *k*urunful, لهواشبو lu'hoos shuboo, خيري kheeree. Cheiranthns cheiri. (H

Walnut, اخروت akhrôt, جوزدرختي jooz durukhtee, اخروط akhroot, چارمغز charmugz, خسف khusuf. Juglans regia. (T)

Wampee tree, Chinese, وامپي ooampee, وامپيچ ooampeech. Cookia punctata. (T) Affording a small fruit of sub-acid taste, juicy, and very refreshing to persons suffering from the parching thirst attending fever.

Water caltrops, Chinese, سنگهارا sung'hara. Trapa bicornis. (A) Not much used in India, but in Japan the seed is put into soups, &c.

Water caltrops, two-spined, پاني پهل panee p'hul, R. سنگهارا sung'hara. Trapa bispinosa, *Pro. Lin.* (A) The nut is eaten.

Water cress, ديوكاندر deeookandur, سزاب suzab, پاني كا هالم panee ka halum, پندو pundoo, رواس rooas, كبيكج kubeekuj. Nasturtium officinale. (A)

Water hemlock, creeping rooted, پان تراسي pan turasee, R. Phellandrum stoloniferum, *Rox.* (H)

Water lily, ابج abju, كوي kôee, نيرفر neerufur, امبج umbuj, سارنگ sarung, بارج baruj, نيلوفر neeloofur. Nymphæa lotus. (A) Common in pools.

Water lily, eatable, كمد kumud. Nymphæa esculenta. (A) The tuberous root is eaten and held in esteem by natives.

Water melon, see Melon.

Water weed, upright, کاست kast. Chara verticillata, *Rox.* (A)

Webera, climbing, گجیرقوتا gujér *k*ota, R. کارا kara, Webera scandens. (C)

Webera, corymbose, کنکارا kunkara. Webera corymbosa. (S)

Webera tetrandra, see Small flowered canthium.

West coast creeper, کنجه لتا kunj'eh luta, R. Asclepias odorotissima, *Rox.* (Tw)

Wheat, summer, گیهون geehoon, بر bur, گوم goom, R. گندم gundum, حنطه *h*um*t*'eh. Triticum æstivum. (G) Several varieties are grown in the cold season.

Willow, four-seeded, بید béd, پاني چوما panee chooma. Salix tetrasperma, *Rox.* (T)

Willow, rosemary-leaved, بید مشک béd mushk, بان ban. Salix rosmarinifolia. (S)

Willow, weeping, غرب *g*urub, کبود kubood, بید béd. Salix babylonica. (T)

Willughbeia, eatable, لتي ام lutee am, R. Willughbeia edulis, *Rox.* (C) The fruit is eaten by natives, it also furnishes birdlime.

Windflower, garden, بوستان افروز boostan afrooz. Anemone hortensis. (B) Found only in Persia, and some of the mountains.

Winter-cherry, clustered, اسگندہ *u*sgund'eh, اسگند asgund, بهمن b'ehmun. Physalis somnifera, or flexuosa. (US) The leaves steeped in oil are applied to inflammatory tumours; it is said to be narcotic, diuretic, and alexipharmic, and supposed to be the Στρυχνος υπνωτικος of Dioscorides.

Winter-cherry, Peruvian, or eatable, called also the Country gooseberry, طپریا *t*upureea, پوپتہ poopt'eh, Physalis Peruviana. P. angulata *Linn.* (US) It is cultivated for its fruit which is of pleasant subacid flavor.

Wolf's bane, wild, ویش ooésh, بیخ békh, or beekh, خانق الذیب khanu*k* *u*lzeeb, بیش beesh, بیشما beeshma. Aconitum ferox, *Dr. Wall.* (H) From the root is extracted the virulent poison used for arrows by the Nepalese.

Wood apple, see Elephant apple.

Wormwood, Indian, دونا doona, افسنطین afsun*t*een, گلو guloo, جنجک junjuk, گندمار gundmar, مستارو mustaroo. Artemisia indica, (H) The leaves are slightly aromatic and bitter, and considered in India an antispasmodic, and deobstruent; it is the αψινθιον of the Greeks.

Wrightia, or Rosebay, oval-leaved, see Medicinal oleander.

Wrightea, common, چهيلپاني ch'heelpatee. Wrightea caryotoïdes. (T)

Xanthium, Indian, گهاگهرا g'hag'hra. Xanthium Indicum of *König. Roxburgh* thinks it the same as Xanthium orientale. (H)

Xanthophyllum, green, گوندي goondee, R. Xanthophyllum virens, *Pro. Lin.* (T)

Xanthoxylum alatum, see Winged tooth-ache tree.

Xanthoxylum budrunga, see Farunga budrunga, or Budrungan tooth-ache tree.

Xanthoxylum piperitum, see Peppery tooth ache tree.

Xantochymus ovalifolius, see Indian gamboge tree.

Xantochymus, painter's, تمال tumal, دهي پهل du'hee p'hul, R. عصارارپوند *a*ssara reeoound. Xa..

thochymus pictorius, Stalagmitis gamboja, *Rox.* (T) The juice when inspissated yields a kind of indifferent gamboge.

Ximenia, Egyptian, هنگن hungun. Ximenia Ægyptica, *Juss.* (T)

Xylocarpus, granular, پصور pussoor, R. Xylocarpus granatum, *Pro. Lin.* (T) Extremely bitter.

Xyris, Indian, چيناغازا cheena *g*aza, R. دابي دوبا dabee dooba. Xyris Indica, *Linn.* (A) The natives of Bengal consider it a cure for ringworm.

Yam, fasciculated, سوتهني soot'hnee. Dioscorea fasciculata, *Rox.* (Tu)

Yam, prickly stemmed, چوتاپندالو chôta pund aloo. Dioscorea aculeata, (Tu :) This a very delicate and valuable species.

Yam, Winged-stalked, رتالو rutaloo. Dioscorea alata, (Tu)

Zapania, knot-flowered, see Creeping vervain.

Zea mays, see Maize.

Zedoary, long, زرنباد zurunbad, کچور kuchoor, کاخار kakhar. Curcuma zerunbet. (H)

Zedoary round, جدوار judooar, زدوار zudooar, نربسي nurbusee, انبي هلدي ambee huldee, بار bar. Curcuma zedoaria. (H) Employed in heartburn, colic, cramp, and torpor of the intestinal canal; the Hindoos use the root as a perfume.

Zinziber officinale, see Ginger.

Zizyphus jujuba, see Jujube.

Zizyphus nitida, see White jujube.

Zizyphus lotus, see Lote tree jujube.

USEFUL TERMS.

اب ab, Water.

ابادي or اباد abad or abadee, Cultivation.

ابانا *u*bana, To sow, or plant.

ابر abur, A cloud.

ابرد abrud, Cold.

ابسال absal, A vineyard.

ابكيشي abkeeshee, Barren.

اب وهوا ab-ô'huooa, Climate.

ابي abee, Aquatic.

اپبن apubun, A grove.

اپجاو apjaoo, Fertile.

اتال atal, A stack.

اتوي atooee, A forest.

اجاره ajareh, Farm, or rent.

اجوره ajoor'eh, Wages.

ادكهلا adk'hoola, Half blown.

ادهپكه ad'h puk'eh, Half ripe.

ادهكچا ad'h kucha, Half ripe.

ارام aram, A grove.

ارس arus, Juiceless.

ارنا arna, To prop.

اروا arooa, A prop.

اره ar'eh, A saw.

استيصال isteessal, Eradicating.

اسمان asman, The sky.

اشجار ashjar, Trees.

اشن *u*shun, Warm.

اصل سطبر *u*ssul suttubur,

اقليم i*k*leem, Climate.

اکھا ak'ha, A sieve.

اکھلي *u*k'hlee, A wooden mortar.

اگي or اگا aga or agé, Before, or in front of.

التمغا iltum*g*a, A royal grant.

الچھنا *u*lch'huna, To drain.

امل amul, Acid.

امود amood, Fragrance.

انتھا intu'ha, End.

انڈا anda, An egg.

انکورا ankoora, A sprout.

اوسرا *u*oosra, Barren.

اولا or اول aool, or aoola, Hail.

اھلو or اھلا a'hla, or a'hloo, The inundation.

ايرم بلي aeerum bulee, Box-leaved, arum.

بابني babnee, A snake hole.

باد bad, Wind.

بادل or بادر badur, or badul, A cloud.

باده bad'h, Stubble.

بارادري baraduree, A summer house.

باران baran, Rain.

باري baree, An enclosed garden.

باغ ba*g*, An enclosed garden.

باغيچه ba*g*eech'eh, A small garden.

باو baoo, Air.

بٹپ butup, A tree.

بچالي bichalee, Straw.

بچھو bich'hoo, A scorpion.

بداھنا buda'hna, To harrow, or plough in seed.

بدق buduk, A duck.

برابر burabur, Eve[n] alongside.

برسکال buruskal, Rain.

برق bur*k*, Lightning.

برلا burla, A wasp.

بزن buzun, A harrow.

بستوي bustooee, A lizard.

بشتي bishtee, Rain.

بطير butteer, A quail.

بقله bu*k*l'eh, A plant.

بکلا or بکل bukul, or bukla, Bark, rind, &c.

بگلا bugla, A paddy-bird, or stork.

بلو buloo, Sand.

بلوا bulooa, Sandy.

بيلي or بلي bulee, or beelee, A climber.

بمني bumunee, A red-tailed lizard.

بزر bu*z*ur, Seed.

بندهنا bund'hna, To tie.

بنور bunoour, A creeper.

بو boo, Smell, or odour.

بوارا boara, Seed-time.

بوستان boostan, A flower garden.

بونا bona, To sow, or plant.

بها لو کولا b'haloo kôla, Hyena.

بهرانا b'hurana, To fill.

بهن bu'hun, Seed.

بهندلي b'hundlee, The palmer worm.

بهنور b'hunoor, A nursery, or seed plot.

بهوات b'hoolut, Earth.

بهوين b'hooeen, Earth.

بهوين b'hooeen, A hairy caterpillar.

بهيتي or بهيتو b'heetoo, or b'heetee, Stalk, or stem.

بهيکه b'heek'h, A toad.

بيا beea, Seed.

بيار bee ar, A nursery, or seed plot.

بيجي beejee, A mungoos, or weasel

بيچهو beech'hoo, A scorpion.

بيخ beekh, A root.

بير beer, A well.

بيگا béga, Crooked.

بيگها beeg'ha, A Beegah, in Bengal 14,400 square feet.

بيل bél, A creeper.

بيل بوتا beel boota, A shrub.

بيلکbeeluk, A mattock.

بينج beenj, Seed.

بينگ béng, A frog.

پات pat, A leaf.

پاني panee, Water.

پاوس paoos, The rainy season.

پتيت or پتت putut, or puteet, Fallow.

پتاري putaree, A weavil.

پتاو putaoo, Irrigation.

پختهکرنا pukht'eh kurna, To ripen.

پرات purat, Dawn.

پراگ purag, Pollen.

پربت purbut, A mountain.

پربهات purb'hat, Dawn.

پرتي purtee, Waste land.

پرديسي purdésee, Exotic.

پشپ pushup, A flower.

پشه push'eh, A gnat.

پک puk, The Indian cuckoo.

پکا puka, Ripe.

پکهال puk'hal, A water-bag.

پکهري puk'hree, A peta

پکهيروpuk'heeroo, A bir

پگار pugar, A mound.

پلنا pulna, To thrive, to be nourished.

پلو puloo, A sprout, or spray.

پلو puloo, A worm.

پنا puna, A leaf.

پناه puna'h, Shade.

پنج punj, A heap.

پندک punduk, The turtle dove.

پندوري pundooree, A falcon.

پن کوکري pun kookree, A snipe.

پن کول pun kool, A snipe.

پنگت pungut, A row.

پنيا puneea, Water.

پودها pood'ha, A sapling.

پورا poora, Full, complete.

پورب poorub, East.

پوروا poorooa, A village.

پوري pooree, A gate.

په p'eh, Dawn.

پهاتک p'hatuk, A gate.

پهاتنا p'hatna, To rend, or split.

پهار pu'har, A mountain, or hill.

پهال p'hal, A ploughshare.

پهاورا p'haoora, A mattock.

پهل or پهر p'hur, or p'hul, Fruit.

پير peer, A tree.

پهرسا p'hursa, An axe.

پهلکا p'hulka, A flower.

پهلواري phulooaree, A flower.

پهت کري p'hut kuree, Alum.

پهنگا p'hunga, A grasshopper.

پهنگي p'hungee, A sprout.

پهوٹا p'hoota, Broken.

پهوڑنا p'hoorna, To burst.

پهول p'hool, A flower.

پهولنا p'hoolna, To blossom.

پهوني پهوهي or پهونهار p'hoonee, p'hoo'hee, or p'hoon'har, Small rain.

پهيلنا p'heelna, To spread.

پهينک دينا p'hénk déna, To throw away.

پيچ péch, A twist, or coil.

پيچهي or پيچهو pee-ch'hoo, or peech'hee, Behind.

پيدري peedree, A tom-tit.

پيزنه peezn'eh, A sieve.

پيشتر péshtur, Sooner.

پيش رس peesh rus, Early, as applied to fruit.

پيغار pégar, A ditch.

پيلک peeluk, The large black ant.

پينالا pénala, A spout, or gutter.

پينچنا pénchna, To winnow.

پيند peend, A roller.

پيوند peeound, A scion.

تاب tab, A twist, or coil.

تابستان tabustan, Summer, or hot weather.

تابش tabush, Heat.

تات tat, Canvas.

تازه tazu'h, Tender, or fresh.

تالاو or تالاب talab or talaoo, A pond.

تانبيل tambeel, A tortoise.

تبر tubur, An axe.

تبل tubul, An axe.

تپن or تپ tup, or tupun, Heat.

تپري tupree, A mound.

تتري tutree, The sand piper.

تتي tutee, A screen.

تخته tukht'eh, A bed of flowers.

تخم tu'hum, Seed.

تدا tuda, A grasshopper.

تداگ tudag, A pond.

تدي tudee, A locust.

تر tur, Moist.

ترو or تر turu, or turoo, A tree.

تراب turab, Earth.

تراي turaee, A marsh.

ترش turush, An acid.

ترشح turushuh, Small rain.

تراشنا turashna, To prune.

تركا turka, Dawn.

تركاري turkaree, Esculent vegetables.

ترمتي turmutee, A hawk.

تفسيده tufseed'eh, Cracked from heat.

تكتكي tuktukee, A lizard.

تل tul, A hillock.

تليهه tulee'h'eh, A turtle dove.

تليا tuleea, A pond.

توندي or تندي tundee, or toondee, A broken branch.

توتي or توتا tôta, or tootee, A parrot.

توترو tootro, A turtle dove.

توردالنا tôrdalna, To break down.

توردينا tôrdéna, To break.

تورلينا tôrléna, To break off, or gather

توسي toosee, A bud.

توکرا tôkra, A basket

تول تال tôl tal, Weighing, or measuring.

تونوا toonooa, A hawk.

تهالي or تهالا تهال t'hal, t'hala, or t'halee, A large branch.

تهالا t'hala, A bason round a tree to hold water.

تهليا t'huleea, A water pot.

تهندي or تهندا t'hunda, or t'hundee, Cold.

تهني tu'hnee, A large branch.

تهورا t'hôra, A little.

تهونتهي t'hoot'hee, Stubble.

تهيک t'heek, Exact.

تهيکا t'heeka, Hired, or contract labor.

تيتا teeta, Bitter.

تيتر teetur, A partridge.

تيتري teetree, A butterfly.

تيرا teera, The trunk of a tree.

ترچها or تيرچها teerch'ha, or turch'ha, Crooked.

تيرمار teermar, A viper.

تيرها tér'ha, Crooked.

تيري teeree, A locust.

تيکن or تيک teek, or teekun, A prop.

تيکها teek'ha, Pungent.

تيگرا teegra, Rising ground.

تيوکي teeookee, A prop.

ثابت sabut, Firm.

ثعلب *sa*lub, A fox.

ثمر *s*umur, Fruit, also gum.

جادج jaduj, A path.

جاگو jagoo, Place or space.

جال or جالا jala, or jal, A cobweb, or net.

جهالرا j'halra, A spring.

جبل jubul, A mountain.

جتاي jutaee, A rable.

جر jur, A root.

جروت juroout, The trunk of a tree.

جره jur'eh, A hawk.

جعفري jafree, Lattice-work.

جگنو jugnoo, A fire-fly.

جگه jug'eh, Place or space.

جل jul, Water.

جلا jula, A lake.

جلدي juldee, Quick.

جمنا jumna, To germinate.

جنبو jumboo, A jackal.

جنگله or جنگل jungul, or jungl'eh, A forest, or waste.

جنوب junoob, South.

جوي or جو joo, or joo-ee, A brook.

جوتار jôtar, A husbandman.

جور joor, Joining.

جور joor, Cold.

جونک jônk, A leech.

جوه joo'eh, A yoke.

جهابر j'habur, A marsh.

جهار j'har, Underwood.

جهانپ j'hamp, A shutter, or screen of mat.

جهانجها j'hanj'ha, The caterpillar of the cabbage butterfly.

جهانکر j'hankur, Underwood.

جهانولي j'hanoolee, Hot wind.

جهبوا j'hubooo, Bent.

جهر j'hur, Rain.

جهلار j'hular, A thicket, or waste.

جهلي j'hulee, A cricket.

جهيل j'heel, A lake.

جهينگر j'heengur, A cricket.

جيوري jéooree, A worm.

چار char, Turf.

چاس chas, A ploughing.

چاسا chasa, A ploughman.

چتاي chutaee, A mat.

چتكا chutka, Thunder.

چتكي chutkee, Sunshine.

چتي chutee, A snake.

چرا chura, Thunder.

چري or چرا chura, or churee, A sparrow.

چراگاه churaga'eh, A meadow.

چران churan, A meadow.

چرپرا churpura, Acrid.

چرز churuz, A bustard.

چرغ churg, A hawk.

چركين churkeen, Dung.

چريا chureea, A bird.

چفت chuft, A prop.

چفته chuft'eh, An arbour.

چقال chukal, A jackal.

چك chuk, An estate, or farm.

چكارك chukaook, A lark.

چكني متي chuknee mutee, Clay.

چكني صنتي chuknee suntee, Potter's clay.

چكهرن chuk'hurun, A weed.

چگير chugeer, A flower pot.

چلپاسه chulpaseh, A lizard.

چلني chulnee, A sieve.

چمتي chumtee, An ant.

چمچرخ chumchurukh, A bat.

چمرا chumra, Tough.

چمربگلي chumrubgulee, A bittern.

چمسا chumsa, Glutinous.

چمگدري or چمگيدر chumgeedur, or chumgudree, A bat.

چمن chumun, A parterre, or bed.

چند chund, The moon.

چندرانا chundrana, Withered.

چو choo, A ploughshare.

چوا chooa, A pod.

چوا chooa, A windfall.

چواي chooaee, A hurricane

چوٹ chôt, Bruise.

چورا chôura, Wide.

چوربالو choorbaloo, A quicksand.

چورس chôrus, Leaved.

چوري choouree. A summer-house.

چوک chook, Acid.

چوکيدار chôkeedar, A watchman.

چوگرا choogura, A hare.

چونا choona, Lime.

چيونٹي or چونٹا choonta, or cheeontee, The large black ant.

چونٹي choontee, An ant.

چوها choo'ha, A rat, or mouse.

چوهي choo'hee, A mouse.

چه chu'h, A well.

چهادان ch'hadan, Water bags.

چهار ch'har, A clod.

چھال ch'hal, Bark, rind, &c.

چھانو or چھان ch'han, or ch'hanoo, Shade.

چھاي ch'haee, Ashes.

چہبچہ ch'hubchu'h. A well.

چھپر ch'hupur, A thatched roof.

چھپري ch'hupree, Puddle, or caked mud.

چھپکلي or چھپکي ch'hupkee, or ch'hupkulee, A lizard.

چھترانا ch'hutrana, To scatter.

چھتکانا ch'hutkana, To scatter.

چھتنا ch'hutna, A sieve.

چھرکاو ch'hurkaoo, A watering.

چھري ch'huree, A knife.

چھلکا ch'hulka, Bark, rind, &c.

چھنکنا ch'hunkna, To winnow.

چھوي ch'hooee, Chalk.

چھيمي ch'heemee, A pod.

چھينتنا ch'heentna, To scatter.

چيتل cheetul, A spotted deer.

چيک cheek, Mud.

چيل cheel, A kite.

حاصل *h*assul, Produce.

حب حبه *h*ub or *h*ub'eh, A berry.

حديقه *h*udee*k*'eh, An enclosed garden.

حربا *h*urba, A chameleon.

حرث *h*urs, A ploughshare.

حکم *h*ukum, An order.
حلوان *h*ulooan, A kid.
حوض *h*ôzz, A reservoir.

خار khar, A thorn, or bramble.
خاربندي khar bundee, A fence of thorns (temporary.)
خاک khak, Ashes.
خالي khalee, Empty.
خراطين khura*t*een, A worm.
خرگوش khurgoosh, A hare.
خرمن khurmun, Harvest.
خريف khuree, Autumn.
خزان khu*z*an, Autumn.
خوشبوي khooshbooee, A fragrance.
خوشه khoosh'eh, An ear of corn, or spike of flowers.

خيابان kheaban, A bed of flowers.

داس das, A sickle.
دادر dadur, A frog.
داغي da*g*ee, Spotted.
دالي dalee, A large branch.
دامن damun, Lightning.
دانتهي dant'hee, Stubble.
دانه dan'eh, Grain, or seed.
دبلا dubla, Thin, or weak.
دتها dut'ha, A stalk.
دخ dukh, Smoke.
دکهن or دچهن duk'hun, or duch'hun, South.
دراج duraj, A partridge.
درانتي durantee, A sickle.
درخت durukht, A tree.
درم durum, A tree.

درمس durmus, A rammer.

درو duroo, Reaping.

درونه duroon'eh, The core, or heart.

دره dur'eh, A valley.

دريا dureea, The sea, or a large river.

دريرا dureera, Heavy rain.

دساور dusaoor, Climate.

دشت dusht, A desert, or forest.

دگهي dug'hee, A large tank.

دل dul, A leaf.

دلا dula, Cold.

دلدل duldul, A quagmire, or bog.

دلدلي duldulee, Swampy ground.

دميدگي dumeed ugee, Blowing of a flower.

دميده dumeed'eh, Vegetated.

دن dun, Day.

دند dund, A staff, or stick.

دوار dooar, A gate.

دوادو dooadoo, Labor, or fatigue.

دود dood, Milky juice.

دهالي d'halee, A large branch.

دهريانا d'hureeana, To winnow.

دهسان d'husan, A quagmire, or bog.

دهگار d'hugar, A heap.

دهلک d'huluk, Rolling.

دهندهلا d'hund'hula, Misty.

دهول d'hool, Dust.

دهوم d'hoom, Smoke.

دهوند d'hoond, A capsule, or seed vessel.

دهوند هرا d'hoond'hra, Foggy.

دهونوا d'hoonooa, Smoke.

دهيلا d'héla, A clod.

دهينكي d'heenkee, A water-lifting machine.

ديارا deeara, A white ant hill, a land deposited.

ديلا déla, A clod.

دينا deena, A large branch.

ديوک deeook, A white ant.

دهيها or ديها dee'ha or d'heeha, Rising ground.

رات or راتر ratur, or rut, Night.

راخ rakh, A white ant hill.

راستا rasta, A road, or path.

راسو rasoo, A mungoose, or weasel.

راغ ra*g*, A meadow.

راكه rak'h, Ashes.

راندا randa, Barren.

راه ra'h, A road, or path.

ربيع rubee*a*, The spring.

رج ruj, Pollen.

رس rus, Juice.

رسن rusun, Cord.

رسري or رسي rusee, or rusree, Cord.

رسي rusee, A Rope.

رطب ru*t*ub, Verdant.

رطب ru*t*ub, Moist.

رگ rug, Fibre.

رنس runs, A sun-beam.

رنگ rung, Color.

رنگت rungut, A Vulture.

رو roo, Germinating.

روباه rooba'eh, A fox.

روپ roop, A shrub.

روپنا roopna, To sow or plant.

رود rood, A small river.

رورا roora, A stone.

روز rôz, Day.

روش or روس roos, or rooush, An avenue.

روشن rôshun, Light.

روضه roozz'eh, A garden.

روکنا rôkna, To stop.

روکه rook'h, A tree.

رونپنا roompna, To plant.

روندنا roondna, To trample.

روي rooee, Vegetating.

رويدگي rooeedugee, Vegetation.

ريت reet, Sand.

ريشه reesh'eh, Fibre.

ريگ reeg, Sand.

ريگهاري reeg'haree, A furrow.

زاغ zag, A crow.

ژاله zhal'eh, Dew.

زراعت zuraaut, Agriculture.

زرد رنگ zurd rung, Yellow.

زرعنا zurana, To sow, or plant.

زغن zugun, A kite.

زلزله zulzul'eh, An earthquake.

زلو zuloo, A leech.

زمستان zumustan, Winter.

زمين zumeen, Land.

زميندار zumeendar, A landholder.

زمينداري zumeendaree, A large estate.

زنبوره or زنبور zumboor, or zunboor'eh, A hornet.

زور zoor, Force, or strength.

زهر zuhur, A bud.

زير zeer, Below.

ساته sat'h, With, together.

سار sar, Manure.

ساق sak, A trunk of a tree.

ساكهه sak'h'eh, A large branch.

سال sal, A year.

سانپ samp, A snake.

سانت sant, A flail.

سانجه sanj'h, Evening.

سايار saeear, Shade.

سباس subas, Fragrance.

سبرت subrut, A hare.

سبز subz, Verdant.

سبزه subz'eh, Herbage.

سبزي subzee, Esculent vegetables.

سبل subul, An ear of corn, or spike of flowers.

سبيرا subeera, Dawn.

سپهل sup'hul, Fruitful.

سپيده دم supéd'eh dum, Dawn.

ست sut, Sap.

ستكاري sutkaree, Tapering.

ستلي sutlee, Twine.

سحاب suhab, A cloud.

سحر suhur, Dawn.

سخت sukht, Hard.

سرا sura, Rotten.

سراون suraoon, A harrow.

سرت surut, A lizard.

سر چشمه surchushm'eh, A spring.

سرحد surhud, A boundary.

سرخاب surkhab, A widgeon.

سرد surd, Damp, cold.

سرک suruk, A road, or path.

سرنگ surung, A precipice.

سرور suroor, A pond.

سسا susa, A hare.

سگند sugund, Fragrance.

سل sul, A stone.

سلي sulee, A trunk of a tree.

سلي sulee, A teal.

سمر sumur, A pond.

سمسم sumsum, A fox.

سمن sumun, Flower.

سمور sumoor, A mungoos, or weasel.

سنبل sumbul, Flower.

سوا sooa, A parrot.

سوپابينا soopabéna, A swallow.

سوت sôt, A spring.

سوت soot, A stamen.

سوتلي sootlee, String.

سوکها sook'ha, Dry.

سوندا soonda, A weavil.

سويري suooéree, Early morning.

سيال or سيار seear, or seeal, A jackal.

سيچنا seechna, To irrigate.

سير seer, Agriculture.

شاخ shakh, A bough.

شاخچه shakhch'eh, A spray.

شاخسار shakhsar, An enclosed garden.

شاداب shadat, Verdant.

شب shub, Night.

شبنم shubnum, Dry.

شکوفه shukoof'eh, A flower.

شگفتن shuguftun, To blossom.

شوره shoor'eh, Marshy ground, or saltpetre.

شهباز shu'hbaz, The royal falcon.

شيره sheer'eh, Irrigated.

صاف ssaf, Clean.

صباح ssuba*h*, Dawn.

صمغ ssum*g*, Gum.

طلب *t*ulub, Wages.

طوفان *t*ôfan, A tempest.

ظليل zuleel, Shady.

عود *a*ooud, Timber wood.

غنچه *g*unch'ch, A bird.

فاخته fakht'eh, Turtle dove.

فجر fujur, Morning.

فرع fur*a*, A bough.

قدم *k*udum, A pace.

قشر *k*ushur, Bark.

قصيبات *k*usseebat, A creeper.

كارا kara, A black snake.

كاگ or كاك kak, or kag, A crow.

كالا kala, Black.

كانن kanu*m*, A forest.

كبوتر kubootur, A pigeon.

كتها kut'ha, A kotta'h of measure the $\frac{1}{20}$ part of a beegah.

كدالي kudalee, A hoe.

كراري kuraree, An axe.

كرم kurum, A worm.

كرمك kurmuk, A fire-fly.

كفتار kuftar, A hyena.

كلسي kulsee, A water pot.

كلهاري kul'haree, Axe.

كلي kulee, A bud.

كملي kumlee, A blanket.

كمبهير or كمهير kum'heer, or kum*m*b'heer, An alligator.

كن kun, A weavil.

كند kund, A well.

كنبت kunbut, Agriculture.

كنده kund'eh, An earthen pot.

كنولاپات kunoolapat, A shoot.

كوا kuooa, A crow.

كودال kôdal, A hoe.

كول kol, A creek.

كونتهي koont'hee, Stubble.

كوندها koond'ha, Lightning.

كهاد k'had, Dung.

كهاي k'haee, A ditch.

كهت k'hut, Mire.

كهتا k'huta, Sour.

كهري k'huree, Chalk, or pipe-clay.

كهرپي k'hurpee, A weeding knife.

كهوسا k'hoosa, Rind, or bark.

كهولنا k'hôlna, To open.

كهونتي k'hoontee, A peg.

كهيتي k'hétee, Agriculture.

كهينچنا k'heenchna, To pull.

كياري keearee, A bed of flowers.

كير keer, A worm.

كيرا keera, A sapling.

كيل keel, A sprout.

گاچ gach, A tree.

گاري garee, A cart.

گام gam, A village.

گانو ganoo, A village.

گتهلي gut'hlee, A kernel.

گچپچ guchpuch, Mire.

گر gur, A mountain.

گرگٹ gurgut, A lizard.

گرم gurum, Warm.

گده gud'eh, A large root.

گوبر gôbur, Dung of the cow in particular.

گوجر goojur, A centipede.

گورو gooroo, An ox.

گوند goond, Gum.

گهاس g'has, Grass.

گهريال g'hureeal, A crocodile.

گهوا gu'hooa, A carpenter insect.

گيدهار geed'har, A jackal.

لبن lubun, Milky juice.

لچرا luchra, A spider.

لمها lum'ha, A hare.

لوكتي looktee, A fox.

لومري loomree, A fox.

متي or ماتي matee, or mutee, Earth.

ماس mas, A month.

مالي malee, A gardener.

مثمر musmur, Fruitful.

مج muj, Ripe.

مچهر much'hur, A musquito.

مچهي much'hee, A fish.

مرگابي murgabee, A teal.

مرگ murg, A deer.

مري muree, A border.

مشک mushuk, A water bag.

مشكل mushkul, Difficult.

مشموم mushmoom, Fragrance.

موشک mooshuk, A rat.

معافي ma'afee, Rent free.

معموره mamoor'eh, Cultivation.

مغرب mugrub, The west.

مغز mugz, A kernel.

مکري mukree, A spider.

مکهي muk'hee, A fly.

مکهورا muk'hoora, A large black ant.

مگس mugus, A fly.

ملانا mulana, To mix.

ملخ muluk, A locust.

مندوا mundooa, An arbour.

منجر munjur, A blossom.

موتکي mootkee, A mattock.

مور moour, A peacock.

موسا moosa, A mouse.

موسلا moosla, A tap root.

مهن mu'hn, Rain.

ميوه meeoo'uh, Fruit.

ميه méh, Rain.

موي or ميي mee'ee, or môee, A harrow.

ناکا naka, An alligator.

نانگل or ناگل nagul, or nangul, A plough.

نالي nalee, A drain.

نبات nubat, Vegetation.

نبات nubat, A shrub.

ندي or نديا nudeea, or nudee, A small river.

نره nur'eh, A trunk of a tree.

نسي nusee, A ploughshare.

نسيم nuseem, A gentle breeze.

نضيج nusseej, Ripe.

نظر nuzur, Sight, o view.

نکہت nuk'hut, Fragrance.

نگ nug, A mountain.

ننانوي nunanooee, A thrush.

نو or نوا nuooa, or nuoo, New, or young.

نوده noodu'h, A shoot.

نہاروا nu'harooa, A guinea worm.

نہال nu'hal, A shoot.

نیچان neechan, A valley.

نیرانا neerana, To weed.

نیراني neeranee, A weeding knife.

نیول neeool, A mungoos, or weasel.

ورد oourud, A petal, or flower.

ورق oouruk, A leaf.

وس oos, Dew.

هاته hat'h, A cubit.

هانس hans, The duck, &c.

هدا huda, A wasp.

هدهد hud'hud. A hoopoe

هر hur, Every.

هل or هر hur, or hul, A plough.

هرا hura, Verdant.

هرب hurub, Verdant.

هردا hurda, Mildew.

هرن hurun, A deer.

هريلا hureela, Verdant.

هزارا huzara, A double flower.

هسوا or هسيا huseea, or husooa, A sickle.

هميشه humésh'eh, Always.

هندار hundar, A wolf.

هندي hundee, An Earthen pot.

هير heer, Pith.

هينگا hénga, A harrow.

يكيلا ékeela, or ékéla, Alone

يوز eeooz, A panther.

NAMES OF PLANTS.

الراغیس a'argees, Nepal berberry.

ابج abuj, Water lily.

ابج abuj, Angular barringtonia.

ابجو abjoo, Water melon.

ابخست ab khust, Water melon.

ابخور abkhoor, Cucumber.

ابدان abdan, Water melon.

ابرود abrood, Oriental hyacinth.

ابطنا abu*t*na, Elegant artemisia.

ابل abul, Cardamum tree.

ابلم ablum, Sabre podded dolichos.

ابنوس abnoos, Smooth date plum, Indian ebony tree.

ابهال ab'hal, Chinese juniper.

اپار ipar, Garden thyme.

اپراجتا apra juta, Wing-leaved clitoria, Crow's beak.

اتا or آت at, or ata, Custard apple.

اتاجام atajan, Indian olive.

اترج *u*truj, Citron.

اترن atrun, Prickly swallow wort.

اتسي atusee, Common flax.

انمل atmul, Emetic swallow wort.

اتوسا atuoosa, Indian birch.

اتيس atees, Linseed or flax.

اثل asul, Furas tamarisk.

اثل كيابي *u*sul keeabee, Three-leaved chaste tree.

اج aj, Indian tamarisk,

اجاس ijas, Damson.

اجمود ajmood, Parsley.

اجوان خراساني ajooan khôrassanee, Common henbane; applied also by some to Common parsley.

اجواين ajooaén, Lovage.

اچ ach, Dyeing morinda.

اچلياجا *u*chuleeaja, Large leaved itea.

احداق المرضي a*h*da*k* ul-murzzee, Chamomile.

اخروت or اختوط akhrôt, akhtoo*t*, Walnut.

اخگور akhgoor, Wildpear.

ادرک adruk, Ginger.

ادمبر adumbur, Round-headed fig tree.

ادناگلي adna gulee, Damask rose.

ادها برني ad'ha burnee, Thyme leaved herpestes.

اذاراقي azara*k*ee, Poison nut.

اراه ara'h, Mastich tree.

ارتچک artuchuk, (cor.) Garden artichoke.

ارپا irpa, Garden thyme.

ارجتا arjuta, Indian annual phyllanthus.

ارجن arjun, Winged terminalia.

ارجون *u*rjoon, Arjun pantaptera.

اردج arduj, Ebony tree, Chinese juniper.

اردندا ardunda, Indian caper.

ارده arud'h, Common vetch.

ارز aruz, Rice.

ارزن arzun, Spiked millet, Italian millet, Bengal millet.

ارس arus, Chinese juniper, Willow-leaved justicia, Oriental plane tree.

ارستو arustoo, Coated swallow wort, Prickly swallow wort.

ارسطا arus*t*a, Common henbane.

ارسه *u*rus'eh, Downy night-shade.

ارک aruk, Persian salvadora.

ارک iruk, Indian salvadora, Curl flowered calotropis.

ارکان *u*rkan, Henna plant.

ارک هندي aruk hundee, Indian salvadora.

ارنبين arunbeen, Purple stalked dragon plant.

ارند arund, Castor-oil tree.

ارو aroo, Nepal cherry, Peach.

ارود arood, Green gram, Black gram, Small fruited bean.

اروس aroos, Malaba nut.

اروروت *u*roo root, (cor.) True arrow-root.

اروي arooee, Egyptian arum, Water lily leaved caladium.

ارهر ar'hur, Pigeon pea.

اريشته areesht'eh, Emarginated soap-berry.

ازاددرخت a*z*ad durukht, Evergreen cypress.

ازان الدب *u*zan *u*ldub, Common mullein.

ازنل فيل a*z*unul feel, Air living bryony.

ازوفا *uz*oofa, Common hyssop.

اس as, Myrtle.

اسارمل isarmul, Indian birth-wort.

اسارون asaroon, Common asarabacca.

اساسنو asasunoo, Strawberry.

اسپست aspust, Common clover.

اسپرمول ispurmool, Indian birth-wort.

اسپغول ispu*g*ool, Flea-wort.

استرنگ *u*sturung, Mandrake plant.

استرون *u*sturoon, Sweet-briar rose.

استوم astoom, Soft rush, Bull rush.

اسخر askhur, Lemon grass.

اسريويل isreeooeel, Indian birth-wort.

اسطفين is*t*ufeen, Garden parsnip.

اسفاناج isfanaj, Spinage.

اسفاناخ isfanak'h, Tetrandrous spinach.

اسفست asfut, Common clover.

اسفراج isfuraj, Common asparagus.

اسفند asfund, Wild rue.

اسقيل is*k*eel, Squill, Indian squill.

اسگنده or اسگند asgund, or asgund'eh, Clustered winter cherry.

اشوک or اسوک asook, or ashook, Jonesia.

اسوگ asoog, Mast tree, Long-leaved uvaria.

اسل asul, Bull rush.

اسن asun, Hairy terminalia.

اسواته *u*sooat'eh, Sacred bean.

اسوي asooee, Waterlily-leaved caladium.

اسير *u*seer, Scented grass.

اش پهل ashp'hul, Longan.

اش شورا ash shoora, Five-leaved limonia.

اشق ashu*k*, Ammoniac dorema.

اشنه ashn'eh, Rock lichen.

اشنه ashn'eh, Common moss.

اسام که کيواچ assam k'eh keeooach, Assam cowitch.

اصف assuf, Prickly caper, Common caper.

اصطرک *u*ss*t*uruk, Common storax.

اصل السوس *u*ssul asoos, Hairy liquorice.

اطروغا *ut*roo*g*a, Citron.

اغار a*g*ar, Cork tree.

اغاره a*g*ar'eh, Common lime tree.

اغاريقون *agareekoon*, Agaric, Bolete.

افتمون *uftumoon*, Bent-back dodder.

افسنطين afsun*t*een, Indian wormwood.

افيس *u*fees, Sessile fruited oak.

افيم afeem, White Poppy.

اقتي *uk*tee, Common elder.

اقحوان a*kk*hooan, Chamomile.

اقلبار a*k*ulbar, Common Indian shot.

اک ak, Curl flowered calotropis, Sugar cane.

اكاركانتا akarkanta, Six-petalled alangium.

اكاس پون akas pooun, Bentback dodder.

اكاس نيم akas neem, Sad cymbidium.

اكتمكت akutmukt, Oval leaved nicker tree.

اكراكانتا akrakanta, Six-petalled alangium.

اكسپون akuspoon, Spotted air plant.

اكليل الجبل akleel *u*l-jubul, Common rue.

اكليل الملک akleel *u*l muluk, Hooked milk-vetch, Upright melilot.

اكندا akunda, Curl-flowered calotropis.

اكول akool, Six-petaled alangium.

اكاري or اكارا agara, or agaree, Rough achyrenthum.

اگتي *a*gutee, Large flowered agati.

اگست agustu, Large flowered agati, Large

flowered æschynomene.

اگر ugur, Sweet flag, Aloes wood, or Agila wood.

اگمکی agumukee, Bristly bryony.

اگھن گاس ug'hun gas, Lemon grass.

ال al, Broad-leaved morinda, Umbelled Merinda.

الاچی ilachee, Cardamum tree.

الحاج alhaj, Prickly stemmed manna plant.

السی ulsee, Linseed.

القنبیط alkumbeet, Cauliflower.

الکوشی alkooshee, Itching mucuna.

الگسی algusee, Round-headed dodder.

الگوچ algooch, Tessalated cymbidium.

النگ alung, Sloe.

الذیون alneeoon, Elecampane plant.

الو aloo, Bell-shaped arum, Damson, Common plum, Potatoe, and applied generally to edible tubers.

الوا or الو uloo, or ulooa, Cylindrical sugar-grass.

الوچه alooch'eh, Common plum.

الوگاچه aloo gach'h, Cassava tree.

الوی بخارا alooee bukhara, Damson.

ام am, Mango tree.

امادا amada, Mango ginger.

اماکا *u*maluka, Shrubby myrobalan.

امب amb, Mango tree.

امبشتا ambushta, Procumbent oxalis.

امبج *u*mbuj, Water lily.

امبرا ambura, Hog-plum.

امبلي imbulee, Tamarind tree.

امب هلدي amb huldee, Mango ginger.

امبه amb'h, Mango tree.

امدهوکه amd'hook'eh, Indian vine.

امر *u*mur, Hooded amoora.

امرا amra, Hog plum.

امرکلي *u*mur kulee, Red flowered ardisia.

امروت amroot, White guava.

امرود amrood, Common pear.

امرول amrool, Procumbent oxalis.

امغيلان am *g*eelan, Gum acacia.

امله or املا amla, or aml'eh, Shrubby myrobalan.

املتاس amultas, Purging cassia.

املج *u*mluj, Shrubby myrobalan.

امله aml'eh, Myrobalan plum.

املي imlee, Tamarind tree.

امرس amoos, Lovage.

انار anar, Pomegranite.

انناس پهل anas phul, Star anise.

انباري کي بهاجي am*b*aree

kee b'hajee, Indian red sorrel, Hemp leaved hibiscus.

انبربارس ambur barus, Holly-leaved berberry.

انبرباري amburbaree, Nepal berberry.

انبوتي *um*bootee, Procumbent oxalis.

انبي هلدي *am*bee huldee, Round zedoary.

انتامول *u*ntamool, Emetic swallow wort.

انتر گنگا *u*ntur gunga, Floating pistia.

انجدان anjudan, Assafœtida plant.

انجره anjur'eh, Notched nettle.

انجير *u*njeer, Common fig

انجل anjul, Common marsh mallow.

انچو anchoo, Few flowered raspberry.

اند and, Castor-oil tree.

اندراون indraooan, Bitter cucumber.

اندراين or اندراوند indraoond, or *u*ndraeen, Bitter cucumber.

اندرجو indurjoo, Medicinal oleander.

اندرني andrunee, Quadrangular chaste tree.

انزروت *u*nzuroot, Heart-leaved penæa.

انكري or انكاري ankaree, or *u*nkree, Common vetch.

انكاره angar'eh, Musk melon.

انكلينه anguleen'eh, Garden angelica.

انگورسگ angoorusug Jackquin's nightshade.

اناناس anunas, Pine-apple.

اننت امول anunt am-ool, Indian sarsapa-rilla.

انولا anoola, Shrubby myrobalan.

انيسون uneesoon, Common anise.

انيسون aneesôn, Parsley.

اوچه aooch'eh, Broad leaved morinda.

اوچيا uoocheea, Spiked bitter gourd.

اورن aoorun, Chinese juniper.

اشبا aooshba, See Indian sarsaparilla.

اوکه aook'h, Sugar cane.

اول uool, Bell-shaped arum.

اولا aoola, Shrubby myrabolan.

اولو uooloo, Cylindrical sugar-grass.

اونت کتارا aoount kutara, Prickly globe thistle.

اويش aooeesh, Marjoram.

ايا پناه aeea puna'h, Spreading eupatorium.

ايدع رومي aeeda roomee, Drag n' blood plant.

ايرسا ueersa, Florence iris.

ايکه aeek'eh, Sugar cane.

ايلوا ueelooa, Spike-flowered aloe, Common aloe.

اينانوشت aeenanooousht, Purple stalked dragon plant.

بابيرنگ babérung, Currant fruited embelia.

بابونه baboon'eh, Chamomile.

باتو batoo, Purging croton.

باجرا bajra, Spiked millet.

بادام فارسي badam-u-farsee, Persian almond.

بادام گوتي badamg ootee, Indian chesnut.

بادام هندي badam - i-hundee, Indian almond.

بادرنجبويه badrunjbooc'eh, Common balm.

بادرنک badrunk, Common balm.

بادرنگ badrung, Cucumber.

بادنجان or بادنگان badungan, or badunjan, Common egg-plant.

باديان badeean, Panmorium fennel, sweet fennel, common anise.

باديان خطي badeean khutee Star anise.

بار bar, Round zedoary.

بارج baruj, Water lily.

بارنگبوري barunkbooee, Indian southern wood.

باسرکه basook'eh, Malabar nut.

باغالتا baga luta, Palmated moonseed plant.

باکلا bakla, Garden bean, Dwarf kidney bean.

باکس or باکر bakur, or bakus, Malabar nut.

باکس bakus, Willow-leaved justicia.

باگنولا baganula, Axillary spider-wort.

باگہا چارہ bag'ha char-'eh, Prickly pisonia.

بالا or بالہ bala or bal'eh, Scented grass, Twisted hibiscus.

بالنگو balangoo, Sweet basil, Indian dragon's head.

بامن‌هتي bamun'hutee, Whorl-leaved clerodendrum.

بامنهني bamu'hnee, Heart-leaved moon seed plant.

بان ban. Benzoin tree, Ever green bead tree, Compact moringa, Rosemary-leaved willow.

باندا banda, Variegated cymbidium, Tessalated cymdium, Epidendron.

باندتي bandutee, Scarlet ixora.

باندور پالا bandoor pala, Polystachine aglaia.

بانس bans, Common bamboo.

بانسپتا bansputa, Black amaranth.

بان مالیکا ban muleeka, Narrow leaved jasmine.

باوچان baoochan, Hazel-leaved psoralia.

باي برنگ baee burung, Currant fruited embelia.

باير baeer, Jujube.

ببوي or ببي bubee, or bubooee, Cillated basil.

ببريه buburee'eh, Common rosemary.

ببوري buhooree, Gum acacia.

ببول bubool, Gum acacia.

بيينا bubeena, White-leaved mussænda.

بت but, Indian fig.

بتاس butas, White blossomed robinia.

بتاني butanee, Common pea.

بناري نيمو butaoouee neemoo, Shad lock.

بتهوا but'hooa, White goose foot.

بتيارنگ buteea rung, Colored justicia.

بتيوا buteeooua, Pinnate-leaved millingtonia.

بجرا bujra, Bullrush.

بجربهانگ bujur b'hang, Virginian tobacco.

بجيا bujeea, Hemp plant.

بچ buch, Sweet flag.

بچتوا buchtooa, Garden orache.

بچهاتا buch'hata Stinging nettle.

بخكله bukhkul'eh, Hazel nut.

بدرنگ budrung, Budrungan toothache tree.

بدرنگا budrunga, Ash-leaved fagara.

بدر وگي ابيز budroogee abeez, White basil.

بدسي زبيب budusee zubeeb, Corinthian grapes.

بديانه هتايا budeen'eh hutaceeh, Star anise.

بر bur, Indian fig.

براپياز or براپياج bura peeaj or bura peeaz, Common onion.

براجال كانتي burajal gantee, Bristly panic grrss.

براجواني bura jooanee, Tall clubrush.

برا چوچا bura choocha, Tall cyperus grass.

براچوکما bura chookma, Pointed oak.

براچولي bura choolee, Indian buckbean.

براکريلا bura kuréla, Spiked bitter gourd.

براکونده bura koond'eh, Woody jasmine.

براکيشتي bura keeshtee, Water ageratum.

براگوتهوبي bura gotôt'hoobee, Tufted kyllinga.

براگوکهرو or براگهوکرو bura g'hookuroo, or bura gook'huroo, Prickly fruited pedalium.

برالسورا bura lusoora, Broad-leaved cordia.

برامان‌دا bura manda, Two colored loranthus.

برانربشي bura nurbushee, Glomerate clubrush.

بربتي burbutee, Small fruited dolichos.

برتهي burut'hee, Upright cyperus grass.

بردي burdee, Ancient papyrus.

بردي burdee, Bullrush.

برسنگا bursunga, König's bergera.

برقوق bur*kook* Apricot.

برگ تامبول burg tambool, Betle pepper.

برما برمي or برن burma, burmee, or burun, Smooth garlic pear.

برن burun, Three-leaved caper tree.

برنج burunj, Rice.

برنجاسف burunjasuf, Indian southern wood.

برنچندلا burun chundla, Moving plant.

برو buroo, Karka reed.

بروق buroo*k*, Daffodil, Club-seeded asphodel.

برهل bur'hul, Bread fruit tree.

بري الاچي buree ulachee, Large cardamum.

بري تور buree toour, Pigeon pea.

بري كروندي buree kuroondee, Jasmine flowered caranda.

بزر قطونا bu*z*ur *k*u*t*oona, Flea-wort.

بزرک bu*z*ruk, Linseed.

بسباس busbas, Sweet fennel.

بستج bustuj, Frankincense tree.

بسترا bustura, Large-leaved callicarpa.

بستيتاج رومي busteetaj roomee, Small caltrops.

بسفايج busfaeej, Fern.

بس كهپرا dus k'hupra, Five stamened trianthema.

بصل bussul, Common onion.

بصل القي bussul *ulk*ee, Emetic nut.

بطا butta, Java rattan.

بطم bu*t*um, Turpentine tree.

بطيخ bu*t*eekh, Musk melon.

بقلت bu*k*lut, Garden bean.

بقلة الحمقا bu*k*lut'h-ul-*h*um*k*a, Small purslane.

بقله الفرستم bu*k*l'eh *u*lfurustum, Common balm,

بقلة المبارک bu*k*lut'eh alumbaruk, Creeping purslane.

بقلة الملک bu*k*l'eht *u*l-muluk, Common fumitory.

بقم bu*k*um, Narrow-leaved brasiletto, Red saunders wood.

بکارجا bubarja, Evergreen bead tree.

بکاین bukaeen, Evergreen bead tree, Margosa tree.

بکچی bukchee, Purple vernonia, Torn fleabane, Anthelmintic saw-wort.

بکشا buksha, Smooth rottboelia.

بکل bukul, Pointed-leaved mimusops.

بگرینڈی bugreendee, Angular-leaved physic nut.

بلا bula, Belleric myrobalan.

بلا bula, Rhomboid-leaved sida.

بلاخ bulakh, Holm tree.

بلادر buladur, Marking nut.

بلب bulb, Bengal quince.

بلبوس bulboos, Garlic.

بل‌تار bul tar, Fan-leaved palm, Palmyra.

بلر bulur, Black seeded dolichos.

بلسان bulsan, Balm of Gilead tree.

بلسی bulsee, Half-serrated myrsine.

بلمبو bulumboo, Bilimbi tree.

بلنجاسف bulunjasuf, Indian pellitory.

بلوط buloo*t*, Indian chesnut, Lance-leaved oak.

بلوط الملک buloot ul mu-luk, Barbary oak.

بلي bulee, Stinging sterculia.

بليلج or بليله buleel'eh, or buleeluj, Belleric myrobalan.

بمني املي bumnee im-lee.

بن bun, True coffee tree.

بن اچ bun ach, Exsert stamened morinda.

بن ادا bun ada, Wild ginger.

بن ال bun al, Exsert sta-mened morinda.

بن ام bun am, Eatable sphœrocarya.

بنب bumb, Single styl-ed bitter gourd, Great flowered bryony.

بن بربتي bun burbutee, Pointed kidney bean.

بنبو bumboo, Common bamboo.

بن بهانتا bun b'hanta, Common egg-plant.

بن پالک bun paluk, Oris-sa sow thistle.

بن تراي bun turaee, A-cute-angled cucumber, Clubbed luffa.

بنج bunj, Common hen-bane.

بنج دشتي bunj dushtee, Purple thorn-apple.

بن جام bun jam, Night-shade-like ardisia.

بن جماعت bun jumaat, Smooth clerodendrum.

بنجوما bunjooma, Smooth. volkameria.

بن چلتا bun chul ta, Curl ed leea.

بن چندر bun chundur, Indian flagellaria.

بندعل bund*a*l, Luffa bindaul.

بندق bundu*k*, Filbert, Hazel nut.

بندكي هندي bundukee hundee, Emarginated soap berry.

بن سيم bun seem, Black seeded dolichos.

بنفشه bunufsh'eh, Sweet violet.

بن ميتهي bun mét'hee, Indian trefoil.

بن نارنگي bun narungee, Fasciculated gelonium.

بن نركلي bun nurkulee, Glandulous ardisia.

بن وكرا bun ookra, Angular-leaved urena.

بونت or بوت boot or boont, Common chick-pea.

بوتا boota, Maize.

بودنک boodunk, Penny-royal.

بورا bôra, Small fruited dolichos.

بورنک boorunk, Sweet basil.

بوري booree, Prickly symplocos.

بوستان افروز boostan af-rooz, Garden wind flower.

بوصير boosseer, Common mullein.

بوعلي سينا or بوعلي boo-*a*lee seena, or boo-*a*lee, Downy-leaved avicenna.

بولي سوا boolee sôa, Heart-shaped androsace.

بول کوکري bool kookree, Chesnut-like adelia.

بولس bôlus, Roxburgh's engelhardtia.

بوند boond, True coffee tree.

بونگرا boongra, Trailing eclipta.

بهاگبت b'hagbut, Curved justicia.

بهانتا b'hanta, Common egg-plant.

بهانگ b'hang, Hemp plant.

بهانگ گندنا b'hang gunduna, Indian chive.

بهانگن b'hangun, Common egg-plant.

بهتا b'huta, Maize.

بهت کتائي b'hut kutaee, Jacquin's nightshade.

بهر بهاند b'hur b'hand, Mexican argemone, Yellow thistle, or prickly poppy.

بهرنگراج b'hrungraj, Trailing eclipta, Climbing verbesina.

بهلا وين b'hulaooeen, Marking nut.

بهمتان bu'hmutan, Daurian lily.

بهمن buhumun, Clustered winter cherry.

بهمي b'humee, Sweet common peach.

بهنگرا b'hungra, Trailing eclipta.

بهنگره اسفر b'hungureh asfur, Ceylonese verbesina.

بهوا bu'hooa, Irregular cyperus grass.

بهوادا b'hoo ada, Scarlet garland flowers.

بهوار bu'hooar, Smooth-leaved cordia.

بهوت بهيروي b'hoot b'hee-rooee, Entire-leaved premna.

بهوتراج b'hoot raj, Winding adder's tongue.

بهوج b'hooj, Tapering birch.

بهوجپتر b'hooj putur, Indian birch.

بهوجنسي b'hoojunsee, Nepal coriaria.

بهورا b'hoora, Common mangrove.

بهوروندي b'hooroondee, Indian turnsole.

بهومي پات b'hoomee pat, Creeping dentella.

بهومي كومره b'hoomé koomr'eh, Panicled butatas.

بهومي نيم b'hoomee neem, Serrated hedge hyssop.

بهوا چنپا or بهون چنپا b'hoon chum*m*pa, or b'hooua chu*m*pa, Round-leaved galangale.

بهويا b'hooeea, Handsome leucomeris.

بهوي بلو b'hooee buloo, Small-leaved myrsine.

بهوي جام b'hooee jam, Herbaceous premna.

بهوين مورا b'hooeen moora, Hardy phillyrea.

بهوي وكرا b'hooee ookra, Creeping vervain.

بهيندي or بهندي b'hundee, or b'heendee, Eatable hibiscus.

بهيرا bu'heera, Belleric myrobalan.

بهيلا b'heela, Marking nut.

بهين اونله bu'heen aoonl'eh, Indian annual phyllanthus.

بهيند b'heend, Marshy æschynomene.

بهين كوبت bu'heen koobutu, Elephant, or wood apple.

بياردهمور beearud'eh moor, Spotted air plant.

بيت bét, Cane, Rattan.

بيجا beeja, Spotted justicia.

بيه béh, China quince.

بيخ bék'h, or beek'h, Wild wolf's bane.

بيد béd, Cane Rattan, Four-seeded willow, Weeping willow.

بيدانجير béd unjeer, Castor oil plant.

بيدروكهرا béd rook'hura, Six stamened Pareira brava root.

بيد مشك béd mushk, Rosemary-leaved willow.

بيربكي beer bukee, Arched arum.

بيري beeree, Jujube.

بيس كچو bees kuchoo, Arched arum.

بيس تارك bees taruk, Veiny-leaved silver weed.

بيساكهي bésak'hee, Citron.

بيش كچو beesh kuchoo, Poisonous calla.

بيشما or بيش beesh or beeshma, Wild wolf's-bane.

بيگن bégun, Common egg-plant.

بيل bél, Religious cratæva, Arabian jasmine, Bengal quince.

بيلزار beelzar, Ash-leaved Murray's tree.

بيل كي بجلي beel kee buchlee, see Malabar nightshade.

بيما beema, Many-leaved paris.

بينا beena, Downy-leaved avicenna, Scented grass.

بينا جوني béna jônee, Diandrous bent grass.

بينج beenj, Common henbane.

پاپرا papra, Broad-leaved gardenia.

پات pat, Bristly-leaved corchorus.

پاتي patee, Water cyperus grass.

پادم padum, Nepal cherry, Bird cherry.

پارس or پارس پيپل parus-peepul or parus, Poplar-leaved hibiscus.

پارل parul, Trumpet flower tree.

پارمي كل parmee kulu, Indian damasonium.

پاژو pazhoo, Common beet.

پاكر or پاكريا pakur, or pakureea, Vein-leaved fig.

پالک paluk, Bengal beet, Horse-shoe fenugreek

پالک جوهي paluk joohee, Waving ixora, White flowering justicia.

پاله pal'eh, Box-leaved ehretia.

پامشرو pamshuroo, Compressed rottboellia.

پان pan, Betle pepper.

پانا pana, Hooded salvinia.

پان ترا سي pan turasee, Creeping rooted water hemlock.

پانک کي متر pank kee mutur, Winged pea.

پان کلي pan kulee, Nodding limodorum.

پان مهري pan mu'huree, Pamory dill.

پان مهري pan mu'huree, Sweet fennel.

پانياله جام paneeal'eh jam, White rose apple.

پاني پهل panee p'hul, Two spined water caltrops.

پاني چوما panee chooma, Four-seeded willow.

پانيچي paneechee, Plyandrous date plum.

پاني کاهالم panee ka 'halum, Water cress.

پاني کانشيرا panee kansheera, Willow-leaved commelina.

پاني کلا panee kula, Upright mint.

پاني کلي panee kulee, Indian damasonium.

پاني کي شنبالي panee kee shunbalee, Three-leaved chaste tree.

پاني مرچ panee muruch, Flaccid persicaria.

پاني ملنگه panee mulung'eh, Runing cyperus grass.

پپيا pupeea, Pupaw tree.

پت پاپرا put papra, Two-flowered Indian madder.

پتپتي چيچکا putputee cheechka, Articulated clubrush.

پتپپره putpupr'eh, Common fumitory.

پتکري putkuree, Elegant Poylea.

پتنگه putung'eh, Narrow-leaved brasiletto.

پتهرچرو put'hur choor, Aromatic plectranthus.

پتهرکا پهول put'hurkap'hool, Rock lichen.

پدما or پدم pudum, or pudma, Indian sacred bean.

پراس puras, Downy branched butea.

پرتاب سنگ که سیم purtab sung k'eh seem, see Pertab Sing's Dolichos.

پرسیا وشان purseeaooushan, Woolly brake.

پرگاچه purgach'h, Epidendron.

پرور puroour, Dioceous snake gourd.

پرولاکیندي puroola keendee, Egyptian bitter gourd.

پره pur'eh, White poplar.

پسته pust'eh, Pistachia-nut tree.

پصور pussoor, Granular xylocarpus.

پلاس pulas, Downy branched butea.

پلپل pulpul, Pimenta tree.

پلطیپتي pal*t*eeputee, Double stemmed phrynium.

پلوساگ puloo sag, Hemp leaved hibiscus.

پلول puloonl, Dioceous snake gourd.

پنج انگشت punj angusht, Quadrangular chaste tree.

پنجنگشت punjungusht, Three-leaved chaste tree.

پنجولي punjoolee, Many-flowered phyllanthus.

پندالو pundaloo, Dyer's rottlera, Sweet potatoe, Naked trewia.

پندو pundoo, Water cress.

پنرناوي punur naoouee, Purslane leaved trainthema.

پنکه punk'eh, Chrystalline oldenlandia.

پنوار punooar, Blunt-leaved cassia.

پنيالا puneeala, Paneola plum, Many spined flacourtia.

پنيرک puneeruk, Round-leaved mallow.

پنيرکا کاچه puneer ka gach'eh, Great-flowered guettarda.

پنيس punees, Spinage.

پوپايه poopaee'eh, Papaw tree.

پودينه pôdeen'eh, Common mint, Penny-royal.

پوراکوي poorakooee, Five-petalled honey berry.

پوژه درخت poozh'eh durukht, Common moss.

پوست poost, White poppy.

پوناگ چمپا poonag chumpa, Nodding alpinia.

پونه گتي poon'eh gutee, Sessile knot-grass.

پويا or پوي pooee, or pooeea, Malabar nightshade.

پوي pôee, Shining malabar nightshade.

پوي ساگ pôee sag, Red malabar nightshade.

پهاري بورا pu'haree bôra, Chinese dolichos.

پهالسا p'halsa, Asiatic grewia.

پهاها pu'ha'ha, Linseed.

پهاين كمل p'haeen kumul, Cotton-like saussurea.

پهلتي كوبي p'hultee kô-bee, Kale, or bore-cole.

پهنس p'hunus, Jack tree.

پهوت p'hoot, Momordic cucumber.

پهوتي or پهوت p'hoot, or p'hootee, Musk me-lon.

پهول كوبي p'hool kôbee, Cauliflower.

پيار peear, Broad-leaved buchanania.

پياج or پياز peeaz, or peeaj, Shallot.

پيازدشتي peeaz-u-dush-tee, Indian squill.

پياسال peeasal, Hairy pentaptera.

پيال peeal, Broad-leaved buchanania.

پيال peeal, Pleasant fla-vored chironia.

پيپل peepul, Sacred fig.

پيپلي peeplee, Peeplee pothos.

پيپل or پيپلي peeplee, or peepul, Long pep-per.

پيتالي peetalee, Naked trewia.

پيترس peetrus, Com-mon turmeric.

پيت سال pét sal, Emar-ginate-leaved ptero-carpus.

پیتکارا pétukara, Indian star apple.

پیتلي پاتي peetulee patee, Overlapped phrynium.

پیتنگا peetunga, Racemose randia.

پیرالو peeraloo, Marshy psogucria.

پیل peel, See Indian salvadora.

پیلابهنگره peela b'hungur'eh, Celonese verbesina.

پیلگوش peelgoosh, Chinese iris.

پیلو pee loo, Carey's tree, Persian salvadora see Indian salvadoro.

پیولي peeoolee, Silky crotalaria.

تاج خروش taj-u-k'huroos, Common cock's-comb.

تار tar, Fan-leaved palm, Palmyra.

تارا tara, Cingalese alpinia, Taliera palm.

تارکا taruka, Cingalese alpinia.

تاغ tag. Common poplar, Pomegranite.

تاک tak, Common vine.

تاگوره tagoor'eh, Beard-vine.

تال tal, Fan-leaved palm, Palmyra.

تالس پتري talus putree, Many-spined flacourtia.

تال مکهانا tal muk'hana, Long-leaved barleria.

تال مولي tal moolee, Narrow leaved curculigo.

تان tan, Creeping vervain.

تانبول tanbool, Betle pepper.

تپیا tupeea, Smooth garlic pear.

تج tuj, Cassia tree.

تدهارا tud'hara, Spreading triangular squrge.

توري or تراي تري turaee, turee, or tooree, Acute angled cucumber, Egyptian bitter gourd.

ترب turub, Common radish.

تربد turbud, Square stalked ipomea.

تربز turbuz, Water melon.

ترسه tursch, Sorrel.

ترمس turmus, Egyptian lupine.

ترمش turmush, Common blackberry.

ترنج turunj, Citron.

ترنجیبن turunjeebun, See prickly stemmed manna plant.

ترور turoor, Eared cassia.

ترولتا turoo luta, Wing-leaved ipomea.

تره تیزک tureh tézuk, Common cress.

تریپتا treeputa, Square stalked ipomea.

تشمیز خ tushmeezkh, Four leaved cassia.

تفاح tufah, Apple.

تفاح ارمني tufah armunee, Apricot.

تکت راج tukt-u-raj, Rotuk amoora.

تکرا tukura, Square stalked ipomea.

تکري tukree, Spreading hogweed.

تکھر tuk'hur, East Indian arrow root.

تل tul, Oriental oilyseed.

تلخ دانه tuluk'h daneh, Slender darnel.

تلسي tulsee, Purple stalked basil.

تلي tulee, Common blackberry.

تماکو tumakoo, Virginian tobacco.

تمال tumal, Painter's xanthochymus.

تمتم tumtum, Elm leaved sumach.

تمرهندي tumur hundee, Tamarind tree.

تن tun, East Indian bastard cedar.

تنباکو tu*m*baco, Virginian tobacco.

تندرکا tundooka, Polyandrous date plam.

تنگ tung, Tall sugar grass.

تنبی tu*m*bee, Eatable perlomis.

توار tooar, Pigeon pea.

توت toot, Indian mulberry.

توکاپانا tooka pana, Floating pistia.

تولا لوده toola lôd'eh, Colored rondeletia.

تومري or تومرا toomra, or toomree, Bottle gourd.

تون toon, East Indian bastard cedar.

تهوهر thoohnr, Oleander-leaved squrge.

تيت کنگا teet kunga, Green-flowered hoya.

تيسي teesee, Common flax.

تيکهي وکوا teek'hee ookra,

Corchorus-leaved melochia.

تيلا téla, Oriental oily seed.

تين teen, Common fig.

تيندو teendoo, Smooth date plum, Ebony tree.

تيوري teeooree, Square stalked ipomea.

ثعلب salub, Salep, plant.

ثوم soom, Garlic.

جاتي jatee, Catalonian jasmine.

جاتي پهل jatee p'hul, Nutmeg tree.

جاجي jajee, Alternated valisneria.

جارل jarul, Oblong-leaved lagerstrœmia.

جاري jaree, Sweet, or great millet.

جاسون jasoon, Chinese hibiscus.

جال jal, Indian salvadora.

جالج jalj, Forked chara.

جال کا نتي jal gantee, Hairy panic grass.

جال لکري jal lukree, Valerian.

جال موت jal-u-môrt, Variegated ceratostema.

جام jam, White guava, Rose apple.

جامرول jamrool, Malay apple.

جامون or جامن jamun, or jamoon, Narrow-leaved eugenia, Java plum.

جانجي janjee, Fasciculated hooded milfoil.

جانجي janjee, Alternated valisneria.

جاورس jaoourus, Spiked millet.

جاوزالقي jaooz al*k*ee, Poison uut.

جاوشير jaoosheer, Rough parsnep.

جاهي ja'hee, Catalonian jasmine.

جاي پهل jaee p'hul, Nntmeg tree.

جبه jub'eh, Native barley.

جپا jupa, Chinese hibiscus.

جپل سيند jupul seend, Indian cactus.

جتا or جت jut, or juta, Common cockscomb.

جتحي jut*h*ee, Auriculated jasmine.

جتيما ده juteemad'eh, Hairy liquorice, prickly liquorice.

جدوار judooar, Round zedoary.

جرا مانس jura manus, Common anise.

جردكلمى jurud kulmee, Involucrated bindweed.

جروک jurook, Lime.

جريصس jureessus, Safflower.

جزر juzur, Carrot, Garden parsnep.

جل پاپارا julpapara, Three leaved mollugo.

جلپاي julpaee, Saw-leaved olive.

جل جلان juljulan, Common fenugreek.

جل نيم jul neem, Thym leaved herpestes.

جليف juleef, Slender darnel.

جمال گوتا jumal goota, Purging croton.

جناح junah, Elecampane.

جنار junar, Common poplar.

جنبهيري jumb'heeree, Lime.

جنتيانا junteeana, Depressed gentian.

جنجک junjuk, Indian southernwood.

جنجک junjuk, Indian wormwood.

جنکا junka, Dwarf sida.

جنگلي اجواين junglee ajooaén, Spreading lovage.

جنگلي ارندي junglee arundee, Angular leaved physic nut.

جنگلي ام junglee am, Hog plum.

جنگلي بادام junglee badam, Fœtida sterculia.

جنگلي پياز junglee peeaz, Indian squill.

جنگلي دال junglee dal, Bearded leersia.

جنگلی کاندا junglee kanda, Dog's tooth violet.

جنگلی کندي junglee kundee, Purple stalked dragon plant.

جنگلی منگی junglee mungee, Senna hedysarum.

جنيوا juneeooa, Thread-like bent grass.

جنيوا juneeooa, Doop grass.

جو joou, Native barley.

جوا jooua, Chinese hibiscus.

جوار jôar, Indian millet.

جوارا jooara, Maize.

جواسي jooasee, Prickly stemmed hedysarum, Prickly stemmed manna plant.

جوانا jooana, Various-leaved jasmine.

جوتاكنشيرا jootakunsheera, Common commelina.

جودوپالنگ jôdoo palung, Indian glass wort.

جوزالطيب jooz ulteeb, Nutmeg tree.

جوزالقي jooz alkee, Emetic nut.

جوزالكوثل jooz alkoosul, Emetic nut.

جوزبوا درخت jooz booa durukht, Nutmeg tree.

جوزماثل jooz masul, Purple thorn apple.

جوزدرختي jooz durukhtee, Walnut.

جوگانی چوکر jooganee chookur, Tree gmelina.

جول پالک jool paluk, Sharp dock.

جوم joom, Wind-leaved garuga.

جوندري ,جوندي or جونري joondreee, joondee, or joonree, Indian millet.

جوهي پانا joo'hee pana, White flowering justicia.

جوي jooee, Auriculated jasmine, Tomentos ixora.

جهانپي j'ha*m*pee, Small-flowered sida.

جهانج j'hanj, Forked chara.

جهانكر j'hankur, Hill bramble.

جهاو j'haoo, Indian tamarisk.

جهتامانسي j'hutamansee, Spikenard.

جهنجهن j'hunj'hun, Silky crotalaria.

جهومكا j'hoomka, Laurel-leaved passion flower.

جهينگا j'heenga, Acute angled cucumber.

جياسيم jeea seem, Black seeded dolichos.

جيت jeet, Sesban æschynomene, Egyptian sesbania.

جيت الو jeet aloo, True arrow root.

جيل مريچ jeel mureech, Cingalese pongatium.

چا cha, Tea tree.

چاب chab, Chaba pepper.

چارمغز charmu*gz*, Walnut.

چاكسو chaksoo, Four-leaved cassia.

چاگل پاتي chagul patee, Coated swallow wort.

چاگل ندي chagul nudee, Indian sphœranthus.

چاندرا chandra, Red flowered ophioxylon.

چاودار chaooudar, Common rye.

چايا chaeea, Woolly achyranthes.

چپاتي chupatee, Four-leaved pepper wort.

چتا chuta, Cingalese leadwort.

چتر مار chutur mar, Mushroom.

چترمول chutur mool, Cingalese leadwort.

چتیاشوقر chuteea shoo*k*ur, Babiana-leaved epipactis.

چچکا chuchka, Club-rush.

چچندا chuchunda, Common beet.

چچوندا chuchoonda, Common snake gourd.

چچونگا chuchoonga, Common snake gourd.

چرایته churaeet'eh, Chirayta.

چرچرا churchura, Rough achyranthes.

چقندر chu*k*undur, Common beet.

چکاتي پاتي chukatee patee, Marsh marica.

چکوتا chukoota, Shaddock.

چکوتره chukootur'eh, Shaddock, Citron.

چکوندا chukoonda, Oval-leaved cassia.

چکونر chukoonur, Oval-leaved cassia.

چل بینج chul beenuj, Clearing nut.

چلتا chulta, Rough dillenia, Large-flowered dillenia.

چلموگرا chulmoogra, Scented chaulmoogra.

چماتي پاتي chumatee patee, Pangoaea cyperus grass.

چمچرخا chumchurk'ha, Bat-winged hedysarum.

چنا chuna, Common chick pea.

چنار chunar, Oriental plane tree, Common poplar.

چنالتا chuna luta, Axil flowering fringe-tree.

چنبلي chum*m*bulee, Catalonian jasmine.

چنبک or چنپا chum*m*pa, or chum*m*puk, Sweet scented michelia.

چندن chundun, Sandal wood tree.

چندي ساگ chundee sag, Eatable amaranth.

چنسر chunsur, Common cress.

چوپالتيا choopalteea, Calycine kydia.

چوتاچاند chôta chand, Red flowered ophioxylon.

چوتي سيم chôtee seem, Sabre podded dolichos.

چوتي كروندي chôtee kuroondee, Spiny carissa

چور choor, Long-leaved pine.

چوري chooree, Field amaranth.

چوري اجواين chooree ajooaeen, Viscia cleome.

چوكاپالک chooka paluk, Bladder dock.

چوكوتره chookootureh, Shaddock.

چوكه chookeh, Sorrel.

چولاي choolaee, Creeping purslane.

چولاي choolaee, Hermaphrodite amaranth, Tetandrous spinach.

چولي choolee, Tufted buckbean, Creeping purslane.

چوتا بندالو choota bund aloo, Prickly stemmed yam.

چوناري choonaree, Hairy ixora.

چونچا chooncha, Compressed cyperus grass.

چوي chooee, Chaba pepper.

چويا chooeea, Black pepper.

چھاگل خوري ch'hagul khooree, Goat's-foot bindweed.

چھتاالکاپات ch'huta alka pat, Umbelled morinda.

چھتا کنوار ch'huta kunooar, Spike-flowered aloe.

چھر ch'hur, Spikenard.

چھريلا ch'hureela, Rock lichen.

چھوتا جام ch'hôta jam, Clove-leaved calyptranthes.

چھوتاجانجي ch'hôta janjee, Two-flowered-hooded milfoil.

چھوتا دودھ لتا ch'hôta dood'h luta, Double swallow wort.

چھوتا کلپا ch'hoota kulpa, Indian borage.

چھوتاگوتھوبي ch'hôta goot'hoobee, One-headed cyperus grass.

چھوتاماندا ch'hôta manda Round loranthus.

چهوتا مچیتا ch'hôta mu-cheeta, Many-seeded justicia.

چهہارا ch'hu'hara, Common date palm.

چهیلپاتي ch'heelpatee, Wrightea.

چیترا or چیتا cheeta, or cheetra, Cingalese leadwort.

چیترا cheetra, Nepal berberry.

چیرونجي cheeroonjee, Pleasant-flavored chironia.

چیري چیرا cheeree cheera, Slender millet grass.

چیکون cheekôn, Oriental nettle tree.

چیلان cheelan, Jujube.

چیلماري cheel maree, Four-stamened coffee.

چینه or چینا cheena, or cheeneh, Common millet, Indian millet, Bengal millet.

چینا الو cheena aloo, Skirret, or White potatoe.

چیناغازا cheena*g*aza, Indian xyris.

چیني بادام cheenee badam, Earth-nut.

چیني نارنگي cheenee narungee, Three-leaved triphasia.

چیهر chee'hur, Spikenard.

حاشا *h*asha, Garden thyme.

حباک *h*ubak, Ciliated basil.

حبق *h*ubu*k*, Common mint.

حتيان کا گوند *h*uteean ka-goond, Silky cotton tree.

حرشف *h*urshuf, Garden artichoke.

حرمل *h*urmulu, Syrian rue.

حصالبان اخضر *h*ussalban akhzzur, Common rosemary.

حلبه *h*ulb'eh, Common fenugreek.

حلدي *h*uldee, Common turmeric.

حلدي *h*uldee, Ovate gardeneria.

حليم *h*uleem, Rough achyranthes.

حماض *h*umazz, Sorrel.

حماما *h*umama, Wild amomum, Common turmeric.

حمدت الرباح *h*umudut al-rubah, Cut-leaved navelwort.

حنا *h*una, Henna plant.

حنبل *h*umbul, Dwarf kidney bean.

حنطه *h*umt'eh, Summer wheat.

حنظل *h*unzzul, Bitter cucumber.

حوک *h*ook, Sweet basil.

حور *h*oour, Common poplar.

حوررومي *h*oour roomee, Black poplar.

حيمساگر *h*émsagur, Cut-leaved navelwort.

خار khar, Common blackberry.

خامادروس khamadroo Soft sphæranthus.

خاماش khamash, White mucuma.

خانق الذيب khanu*k* ul-*z*eeb, Wild wolf's bane.

خايري khaeeree, Medicinal catechu tree.

خباري khubaree, Mauritius sida.

خباز khuba*z*, Round-leaved mallow.

خربق اسود khurbu*k* asood, Black hellebore.

خربق سپيد khurbu*k* supeed, Fœtid hellebore.

خربق سياه khurbu*k* seea'eh, Black hellebore.

خربوزه khurboo*z*'eh, Musk melon.

خرجال khurjal, Persian salvadora.

خردال khurdal, Small-seeded mustard.

خرزهره khur*z*u'hur'eh Sweet scented oleander.

خرطال khur*t*al, Common oat.

خرفه khurf'eh, Shall purslane.

خرنوب نبطي khurnoob nub*t*ee, St. John's bread.

خروع khurooa, Castor-oil plant.

خري khuree, Fuscous sugar grass.

خس khus, Garden lettuce.

خسخس khuskhus, Scented grass.

خسرودارو khusuroo daroo, Greater galangale.

خسف khusuf, Walnut.

خسک khusuk, Small caltrops.

خشب ميني khushub sseenee, China root plant.

خشخاش kushkhash, White poppy.

خشوريا khushooreea, Trailing eclipta.

خطمي khu*t*mee, Mauritius sida.

خمان khuman, Common elder.

خنانق الكلب khunanu*k* *u*l-kulb, Poison nut.

خنثي khunsee, Daffodil.

خنشي khunshee, Club-seeded asphodel.

خنوف khunoof, Common flax.

خوخ khookh, Peach.

خودي جام khoodee jam, Panicled antidesma.

خودي وكرا khoodee ookra, Plaited-leaved croton.

خورا k̤hoora, Petaless sonneratia.

خورپرست خانالايک khoor-purust khana laék, Jerusalem artichoke.

خولنجان khoolunjan, Greater galangale.

خون سياوشان khoon seea ooshan, Dragon's blood plant.

خيار kheer, Cucumber.

خيارچنبر kheear chu*m*-bur, Purging cassia.

خيارشنبر kheear shun-bur, Purging cassia.

خياري kheearee, Pansy.

خيت پاپارا khét papara, Five-leaved mollugo.

خيت پاپرا khét papura, Two-flowered oldenlandia.

خيرا kheera, Medicinal catechu tree.

خيرو kheeroo, Pansy.

خيري kheeree, Wall-flower.

خيل kheel, Common rue.

خيو kheeoo, Useful melanorrhæa.

داب dab, Meadow grass.

دابي دوبا dabee dooba, Indian zyris.

دادماري dadmaree, Vesicatory ammannia, Climbing holmskioldia.

داد مردن dad murdun, Broad-leaved cassia.

داربرين dar bureen, Jacquin's nightshade.

دار چيني dar cheenee, Cassia tree, Real cinnamon.

دارفلفل darfulful, Long pepper.

دارم darum, Pomegranite.

دانت رنگه dant-u-rung-'eh, Plain-leaved millingtonia.

دانورا danoora, Danurun nephelium.

داودي daoodee, Indian chrysanthemum.

داين daeen, Fingered aralia.

دبان شاب duban shab, Sweet basil.

دجر dujur, Dwarf kidney bean.

دخ dukh, Bullrush.

دخن duk'hun, Italian millet.

ددهي dud'hee, Thyme-leaved spurge.

درخت ابهل or درخت ابهول durukht abh'ul, or durukht ab'hool, Common juniper.

درخت اخروت durukht akhroot, Three-lobed aluerites.

درخت اقويل رومي durukht a*k*ooél roomee, Balm of Gilead tree.

درخت اندر جو durukht-indurjoo, Oval-leaved wrightia, or roseberry.

درخت انگور durukht angoor, Common vine.

درخت انگوزه durukht angooz'eh, Assafœtida plant.

درخت جاپهل durukht-u-jap'hul, Nutmeg tree.

درخت جلوز durukht julooz, Pistachio nut tree.

درخت جوز durukht-u-jooz, Hazel nut.

درخت چب چيني durukht-u-chub cheenee, China root plant.

درخت چومكهي durukht-u-choomuk'hee, Purslane-leaved scævola.

درخت خرما durukht-u-khurma, Taliera palm, Common date palm.

درخت رال durukht-u-ral Dammer pine.

درخت راوند durukht-u-raoond, Medicinal rhubarb.

درخت روغن بلسان durukht-u-roo*g*un bulsan, Balm of Gilead tree.

درخت زبيب durukht-u-*z*ubeeb, Corinthian grapes.

درخت عود durukht *a*ood, Spike-flowered aloe.

درخت کتھ durukht-u-kut'h, Medicinal catéchu tree.

درخت کشم durukht-u-kusum, Indian tamarisk.

درخت کمود durukht-u-kumood, Dyer's rottlera.

درخت گرجن durukht-u-gurjun, Terebinthine dipterocarpus.

درخت لسان العصافیر durukht-u-lusan ulassafeer, Oval-leaved wrightia, or roseberry.

درخت لونگ durukht-u-lông, Clove tree.

درخت ماپھل durukht-u-map'hul, Sessil fruited oak.

درخت منطر durukht-u-muntur, Cork tree.

درخت وین durukht ooeen, Black grape vine.

درخت هنگ durukht-u-hung, Assafœtida plant.

درختي عناب durukhtee anab, Jujube.

دردار durdar, White poplar.

درمر durmur, Winged tooth-ache tree.

درند durund, Bent back dodder.

دسبچندي dusbuchundee, Chinese morea.

دسبها dusbu'ha, Chinese morea.

دسمري dusmuree, Dwarf kidney bean.

دقو dukoo, Indian sphæranthus.

دل dul, Stagnant panic grass.

دلب dulub, Oriental plane tree, Medicinal rhubarb.

دلو duloo, Medicinal rhubarb.

دم الاخوين dumalakhooeen, Dragon's blood plant.

دمچه dumcheh, Common clover.

دند dund, Purging croton.

دنقت dun*k*ut, Slender darnel.

دنكوني dunkoonee, Decussated canscora.

دوب doop, Thread-like bent grass, Doob grass.

دوپاتي dôpatee, Balsam.

دوپاتي لتا doopatee luta, Goat's-foot bind weed.

دو پهريا doop'hureea, Scarlet-flowered pentapetes.

دوده كلمي dood'h kulmee, Square-stalked ipomea.

دودمگرا doodmugra, See sweet scented oleander.

دوده لتا dood'h luta, Esculent oxystelma.

دودهي dood'hee, Esculent oxystelma.

دوديا كلمي doodeea kulmee, Great-flowered ipomea.

دورلا doorla, Mad apple.

دورا بيارا doora beeara, Upright panic grass.

دوربا doorba, Doop grass.

دورلي doorlee, Jacquin's nightshade.

دوسراساگ doosura sag, Five-styled pharnaceum.

دوکتیا dookuteea, Ferruginous symplocos.

دولال چمپه doolal chump'eh, Sweet scented garland flowers.

دوله چری dool'eh churee, Ammanioidic bergia.

دولی چمپا doolee chumpa, Large-flowered tulip tree.

دونا doona, Indian wormwood.

دوندول doondool, Egyptian bitter gourd.

دونه doon'eh, Indian southern wood.

دهاری d'haree, Downy grilea.

دهاکها d'hak'ha, Downy branched butea.

دهان d'han, Rice.

دهان مرچ d'han muruch, Bird pepper.

دهاو dhaoo, Downy grislea.

دهتورا d'hutoora, Purple thorn-apple.

دهرتی کاپهول d'hurtee kap'hool, Mushroom.

دهنچی d'hunchee, Hemp leaved æschynomene.

دهنروس d'hunroos, Eatable hibiscus.

دهنیا dhuneea, Coriander.

دهیمنا d'heemna, Elongated cissus.

دهو d'hoou, Downy grislea.

دهوروا d'hoorooa, Field pea.

دهول شمودرا d'hool shumoodra, Long-leaved leea.

دهونا گاچ d'hoona gach, Dammer pine.

دهي پهل duhee p'hul, Painter's xantochymus.

ديبدار deebdar, Mast tree, Long-leaved uvaria.

ديتارا détara, Serrated grass.

ديس dees, Bullrush.

ديک dék, Margosa tree.

ديمهاج deem'haj, Common buglos.

ديا deeoou, Mushroom.

ديوا ورد deeoo aoourd, Deodar pine.

ديودار deeoodar, Deodar pine.

ديودارو deeoodaroo, Mast tree.

ديو داري deeoo daree, Long-leaved uvaria.

ديو دهان deeoo d'han, Sweet millet.

ديو کاندار deeoo kandar, Water cress.

راتيانج rateeanuj, Smith's pine.

راجگاگي rajgagee, Red-leaved vine.

راجگيري rajgeeree, Hermaphrodite amaranth.

راخل پهل rakhul p'hul, Saw-leaved schmidedelia.

رازيانج razeeanuj, Sweet fennel, Panmorium fennel.

رازيانه رومي razeean'eh roomee, Common anise.

رامته ramut'eh, Tape leaved cordia.

راسن rasun, Elecampane.

راسنا rasuna, Medicinal rhubarb.

راکس گده rakus gud'eh, Air-living bryony.

راگي ragee, Upright Eleusine.

رالا rala, Italian millet, Italian punic grass.

رام بيگون ram bégoon, Hairy nightshade.

رام تراي ram tur*u*ee, Eatable hibiscus.

رام جلپاري ram julparee, Small-leaved sterculia.

رام گوا ram gooa, Slender betelnut.

راندني randnee, Parsley.

راي raee, Small seeded mustard.

رايا raeea, Large white mustard.

ربزق rub*z*u*k*, Jacquin's nightshade.

رتالو rutaloo, Wing stalked yam.

رتم rutum, Portugal broom, Dwarf furze.

رتن پروس rutun puroos, Pansy, Shrubby violet.

رجل الغراب rujul *ulg*urab, Dandelion.

رديق rudee*k*, Persian salvadora.

رز ru*z*, Common vine.

رشاد rushad, Common cress.

رصوت russôt, Nepal berberry.

رعگا r*a*ga, Smith's pine.

رعلول r*a*lool, Purple stalked dragon plant.

رفيف rufeef, Daurian lily.

رکتپته ruktuput'eh, Madras ventilago.

رکت چندن rukut chundun, Red saunders wood, Yellow flowered adenanthera.

رکل rukul, Leek.

رمان ruman, Pomegranite.

رند rund, Castor oil tree.

رنگترا rungtura, Orange.

رواس rooas, Water cress.

روانس rooans, Chinese dolichos.

روباه تربک rooba'eh turbuk, Deadly nightshade

روتهني root'hnee, Water mimosa.

روناس roonas, Madder of Bengal.

روهنا or روهن roo'hun, or roo'huna, Febrifuge mahogany tree.

روهونا roo'hoona, Redwood tree.

رهلا ru'hla, Common chickpea.

ريته reet'eh, Emarginated soap-berry.

ريتها reet'ha, Indian soap berry, Emarginated soap-berry.

ريحان ree*h*an, Ciliated basil, Sweet basil.

ريشته reesht'eh, Emarginated soap-berry.

ريندي reendee, Castor oil tree.

ريوند reeoond, Medicinal rhubarb.

زخم حیات zukhum *h*eeat, Cut-leaved wort.

زدوار zudooar, Round zedoary.

زراوند zuraoond, Long-rooted birth-wort.

زرت zurut, Indian millet.

زردآلو zurud aloo, Apricot.

زرد انچو zurud anchoo, Round-leaved bramble.

زرد چوب zurud choob, Common turmeric.

زردک zurduk, Carrot.

زرنباد zurunbad, Long zedoary.

زرین قدح zureen *k*uduh, Polyanthus narcissus.

زعبل *za*bul, Cotton tree.

زعفران *za*fran, Saffron plant.

زعلوک *za*look, Leek.

زغال zu*g*al, Cornel, or dog-wood tree.

زفزوف zufzoof, White jujube.

زفیزف zufeezuf, Lote tree jujub.

زن zun, Dwarf kidney bean.

زنبق zunbu*k*, Arabian jasmine.

زنپان zu*m*pan, Common anise.

زنجبیل zunjubeel, Ginger.

زوفاي يابس zoofaee eeabus, Common hyssop.

زهرزمین zuhur zumeen, Poison nut.

زیاون zeeaoon, Slender darnel.

زیتون zeetoon, Olive tree.

زیرا zeera, Common cumin.

سابوكي كاچ sabookee gach, Sago tree.

ساج saj, Teak tree, Ebony tree.

سادا بوري sada booree, Branching asparagus.

سادا كنول sada kunool, Three flowered pancratium.

سادہ بواري sad'eh booaree, Indian sarsaparilla.

سارنگ sarung, Water lily.

ساسافراس sasafras, Sassafras tree.

ساگواني sagooanee, Prickly swallow-wort.

ساگون sagoon, Teak tree.

سال sal, Saul tree.

سالبيه salbee'eh, Bengal sage.

سالسا salsa, Shrubby ichnocarpus.

سانپ كي توپي samp kee tôpee, Mushroom.

سانچي sanchee, Three stamened achyranthus.

سانكهو sank'hoo, Saul tree.

سانوا sa*m*ooua, Wheatlike millet.

سانوان or سانوا sanooa, or sanooan, Wheat-like panic grass.

ساوان saooan, Bengal millet.

ساوكي saoọkee, Sago tree.

ساهي كانٹا sa'hee kanta, White mimosa.

سپاري suparee, Betel nut tree.

سپند supund, Wild rue.

سپندان‌تلخ supundan-u-tulkh, Flea wort.

سپیاري supeearee, Betel-nut tree.

سپیدار supeedar, White poplar.

سپیداه supeeda'eh, Oriental plane tree.

ستري suturee, Common rue.

ست‌سال sut sal, Black wood tree.

ستمولي sutmoolee, Branching asparagus.

سجالاط sujala*t*, Catalonian jasmine.

سداب sudab, Common rue.

سداسهاگن suda su'hagun, Phœnician hibiscus.

سداهزرمني suda hu*z*ur munee, Indian annual phyllanthus.

سدواري sudooaree, Three leaved chaste tree.

سدیان sudeean, Holm tree.

سذاب suzab, Common rue.

سر sur, Sugar grass.

سرپتا or سرپت surput, or surputa, Tall sugar grass.

سرپن surpun, Sweet scented calophyllum.

سرخس surkhus, Fern.

سرخک surkhuk, Cornel, or dogwood tree.

سرخم surkhum, Fern.

سردب surdub, Persian salvadora.

سرس surus, Seris mimosa.

سرسون sursôn, Bengal mustard.

سرشف surshuf, Small seeded mustard.

سرشک surshuk, Evergreen cypress.

سرکچو surkuchoo, Water-lily leaved caladium.

سرکرا surkura, Tall sugar grass.

سرل پیر surul peer, Long-leaved pine.

سرمق surmu*k*, Garden orache.

سرو suroo, Evergreen cypress, Cedar of Goa.

سروۂ جیا suroo'eh jeea, Common Indian shot.

سریاري sureearee, Indian turnsole.

سريپهل sreep'hul, Bengal quince.

سزاب suzab, Water cress.

سفاقس sufa*k*us, Bengal sage.

سفراکومرا sufura koomra, Squash, or Vegetable marrow.

سفرجل sufurjul, China quince.

سفري ام sufree am, White guava.

سفري جام sufree jam, Red guava.

سفنجه sufunj'eh, Water-melon.

سفيد پاي suféd paee, Lance-leaved eleocarpus.

سفيد تلسي suféd tulsee. White basil.

سفيد گوبهي suféd Goob'hee, Sowthistle leaved eacalia.

سفيد محمد suféd mu*h*umud, White fluggea.

سفيد موسلي suféd mooslee, Linear-leaved asparagus.

سقمونيا su*k*mooneea, Scammony plant, Alpine scammony.

سک suk, Shrubby myrobalan.

سکبینج sukbeenuj, Assafœtida plant.

سکر sukur, Turpentine tree.

سکهدرسن suk'hdursun, Poison bulb.

سکهدرسن suk'hdursun, Cingalese crinum.

سکهدرسن suk'hdursun, Cingalese amaryllis.

سگ انگور sug angoor, Deadly nightshade.

سگانگور sugangoor, Dog's bane.

سگوانی sugooanee, Prickly swallow-wort.

سلاجت sulajut, Common storax.

سلت sult, Native barley.

سلجمی suljumee, Turnip.

سلطانی چمپا sul*t*anee chumpa, Sweet scented calophyllum.

سلک sulk, Common beet.

سلیخه suleekh'eh, Cassia tree.

سماروغ sumaroo*g*, Mushroom.

سماق suma*k*, Elm-leaved sumach.

سمسق sumsu*k*, Laurel-leaved jasmine.

سمسم sumsum, Oriental oily seed.

سمن sumun, Catalonian jasmine.

سمدره شوکا sumoodr'eh shôka, White silver weed.

سن sun, Indian hemp.

سمی sumee, White mimosa.

سنا suna, True senna.

سلبالي sunbalee, Plaited-leaved croton.

سنبل sum*m*bul, Oriental hyacinth.

سنبل الطيب sum*m*bul *ul* teeb, Spikenard.

سنبل ختايي sum*m*bul khutaee'ee, Garden angelica.

سنبل هندي sum*m*bul hundee, Spikenard.

سنج sunj, Lote tree jujube.

سندب sundub, Common rue.

سندروس sundroos, Sandaraj tree, Arar tree, or Jointed arbor vitæ.

سندكه suuduk'eh, Polyandrous date plum.

سندياد sundeead, Lance-leaved oak.

سنسق sunsu*k*, Dwarf myrtle.

سنف sunf, Sweet fennel.

سنكارجتا sunkar juta, Painted doodia.

سنكهاهلي sunk'ha hulee, Needle grass.

سنكارها ر sungar'har, Square stalked nyctanthes.

سنكتره sungtur'eh, Orange.

سنك كوبي sung koopee, Smooth volkameria.

سنكهارا sung'hara, Chinese water-caltrops, Two spined water-caltrops.

سنوت sunoot, Common cummin.

سوا sooa, Common dill.

سواتي sooatee, Mountain panic grass.

سوار soouar, Octandro. valisneria.

سوارہ sooar'eh, Sweet flag.

سوپلونگ sôplông, Broad-leaved podocarpus.

سوتاپاط sootapat, True senna.

سوتراج sootraj, Axillary spider-wort.

سوت گوتھوبي soout gô-t'hoobee, One-headed kyllinga.

سوتلي sootlee, Spotted sonerila.

سوتھني soot'hnee, Fasciculated yam.

سودمسترا soodumstura, Small caltrops.

سورج مکھي sooruj muk-'hee, Sunflower.

سورن soorun, Bell-shaped arum.

سورنجان soorunjan, Common meadow saffron.

سوريامہ sooreeam'eh, Phœnician hibiscus.

سوست or سوس soos, or soosut, Prickly liquorice.

سوسن soosun, Daurian lily.

سوسام or سوسن soosun, or soosam, Chinese iris.

سوف soof, Linseed.

سوفيد پوي sôféd pooee, White Malabarnight-shade.

سوکوا توتا sookooa tôta, Monodelphous cnestis.

سوم soom, Bullrush, Hairy bitter gourd.

سومراج soom raj, Anthelmintic saw-wort, Black cumin.

سون soon, Indian trumpet-flower.

سونا soona, Purple mountain ebony.

سونامکي soonamukee, True senna.

سونف soonf, Common anise.

سونيز sooneez, Indian fennel flower.

سوواه sôooa'h, Sweet fennel.

سوي چوکا sooee chooka, Common dill.

سويت برنا sooét burna, Upright randia.

سويت بسنت sooét busunt, Indian acalypha.

سويت پاني مرچ sooét panee muruch, Downy persicaria.

سويت چمني sooét chumnee, Serrated hedge hyssop.

سويت خيروگه sooét kheeroog'eh, Thyme-leaved spurge.

سويت راي sooét raee. Grey mustard.

سويت سيمل sooét seemul, Five-stamened silk cotton tree.

سويت مرغا sôét murga, Silvery spiked cockscomb.

سهجنا su'hujna, Horse radish tree.

سهي su'hee, Evergreen cypress.

سيام لتا seeam-u-luta, Shrubby echites.

سياه دانه seea'h dan'eh, Indian fennel flower.

سياده seead'eh, Small-leaved myrsine.

سياه موسلي seeah mooslee, Narrow-leaveu curculigo.

سیب seeb, Apple.

سیپھل seep'hul, Bengal quince.

سیتا پیل seeta p'hul, Pumpkin.

سیتاپھل seeta p'hul, Custard apple.

سیتاکي پنجیري Seeta kee punjeeree, Thick-leaved lavendar.

سیتل پاطي seetulpatee, See double-stemmed phrynium.

سیتي seetee, The noble magnolia.

سیج seej, Oleander-leaved spurge.

سیکھدار seekhdar, Elm.

سیستر seestur, Bengal sage.

سیسو seesoo, Sissoo tree.

سیکران seekran, Common henbane.

سیلاپوما seela pôma, Roxburgh's engelhardtia.

سیمل seemul, Silky cotton tree.

سینادکا seenaduka, Spreading hogweed.

سینبل seembul, Silky cotton tree.

سینتھا or سینتھي seent'ha, or seent'hee, Sugar grass.

سیند seend, Madras cucumber.

سیندھي درخت seend'hee durukht, Wild date tree.

سیو seeoo, Apple.

سیوتي seeootee, White rose.

سیورا seeoora, Ramoon tree.

سیہند see'hund, Spreading triangular spurge, Sheathed spurge.

شاخسار shakhsar, Pigeon pea.

شاخک shakhuk, Upright melilot.

شاخول shakhool, Pigeon pea.

شاشدان shashdan, White poplar.

شال shal, Saul tree.

شال پاني shal panee, Oval-leaved hedysarum.

شالونچه shaloonch'eh, Three-stamened achyranthes.

شاما shama, Purple panic grass, Wheat-like panic grass, Wheat-like millet.

شاماخ shamakh, Wheat-like millet.

شام‌الو sham aloo, Damson.

شاه الو sha'h aloo, Common cherry.

شاه بلوط sha'h buloot, Barbary oak.

شاه پسند sha'h pusund, Sweet sultan.

شاه‌ترج sha'h turuj, Small flowered fumitory.

شاه‌تره sha'h tur'eh, Two-flowered Indian madder.

شاهتره sha'htur'eh, Common fumitory.

شاه دانه sha'h dan'eh, Common cherry.

شاهسفرم sha'husfurum, Sweet basil.

شبب shubu, Common tuberose.

شبت shubut, Panmorium fennel.

شربتي‌ليمو shurbutee leemoo, Lemon.

شريج shureej, Water melon.

شريفه shureef'eh, Custard apple.

شعير shaeer, Native barley.

شفتالو shuftaloo, Cassava tree, Nectarine, Peach.

شقايق shukaeek, Common tulip.

شقاقل shukakul, Wild carrot.

شقر shukur, Common tulip.

شكرقند الو shukurkund aloo, Sweet potatoe.

شكري shukuree, Asiatic grewia.

شلغم shulgum, Turnip.

شمار shumar, Sweet fennel.

شمام shumam, Sweet Ispahan melon.

شمرت shumrut, Sweet fennel.

شمشاد shumshad, Box tree.

شمليت shumleet, Common fenugreek.

شنبالي shunbalee, Quadrangular chaste tree.

شنجار shunjur, Common buglos, Upright melilot.

شنگرا shungra, Lance-leaved oak.

شنو shunoo, Evergreen cypress.

شنيز shuneez, Coriander.

شوتچمني shoohtchumnee, Thyme-leaved herpestes.

شوچي موخي shoochee mookhee, Cingalese sanseviera.

شود shood, Panmorium fennel.

شورہگز shoor'eh guz, Indian tamarisk.

شوشمیر shooshumeer, Cardamum tree.

شوکران shookran, Common hemlock.

شولا shôla, Marshy Æschynomene.

شوندیکي shoondeekee, Wild potatoe.

شوندر shunder, Carrot.

شوندري shoondree, Lesser looking-glass plant.

شویت کدم shooét kudum, Four stamened nauclea.

شہتوت shu'htoot, Black mulberry.

شہنیز shu'hneez, Peppery tooth-ache tree.

شیال خانتا sheeal khanta, Yellow thistle, or prickly poppy, Mexican argemone.

شیرخشت sheer khusht, Prickly-stemmed manna plant.

شیشن sheeshun, Sissoo tree.

شیفتہرنک sheeft'eh runk, Apricot.

شیکران sheekrab, Common hemlock.

شیلکول sheelkooul, Hardy staff tree.

شین sheen, Apple.

صاب ssab, Bitter cucumber.

صبر ssubur, Common aloe.

صد برگ ssud burg, Damask rose . White rose.

صعتر ss*a*tur, Sweet marjoram.

صندل ssundul, Sandal wood tree.

صندل احمر ssundul a*h*mur, Red saunders wood.

صندل سرخ ssundul surukh, Red saunders wood.

صندل سفيد ssundul sufḗd, Sandal wood tree.

صنوبر ssunoobur, Muricated casuarina, Fir-tree, Long-leaved pine.

صوطل ssoo*t*ul, Carrot.

صيمل sseemul, Silky cotton tree.

طابي *t*abee, Long pepper.

طاليسفر *t*aleesfur, Aromatic rhododendron.

طبيخ *t*ubeekh, Musk melon.

طپريا *t*upureea, Peruvian, or eatable winter cherry.

طرفيل *t*urfeel, Common clover.

طلكرا *t*ulkura, Thick leaved pennywort.

طوباي چاره *t*oobaee chareh, Bushy unona.

طورنج *t*oorunj, Citron.

طوليدون *t*ooleedoon, Black berried nightshade.

طهوكا *t*'hooka, Noble amherstia.

طيسي *t*eesee, Linseed.

طيطان *t*ee*t*an, Leek.

عاقرقرحا *a*,a*k*ur*k*ur*h*a. Indian pellitory, Pellitory of Spain.

عبب *a*bub, Glaucous-leaved physic nut.

عبير *a*beer, Saffron plant.

عدس *a*dus, Lentil, Common vetch.

عرعا *a*r*a*a, Evergreen cypress.

عرعر *a*r*a*r, Chinese juniper.

عزيز *azeez*, Sweet sultan.

عشر *a*shur, Curl-flowered calotropis.

عشق پيچا *a*shu*k* peecha, Wing-leaved ipomea.

عصارا ريوند *a*ssara reeoond, Painter's xanthochymus.

عصاره ريوند *a*ssar'eh reooand, Indian gamboge tree.

عصفر *a*ssfur, Safflower.

علقم *a*l*k*um, Bitter cucumber.

علقي *a*l*k*ee, Heath.

علقي *a*l*k*ee, Portugal broom.

علك *a*luk. Dammer pine.

علك بغدادي *a*luk bu*g*dadee, Mastich tree.

عنب الثعلب *a*nub *u*lsalub, Deadly nightshade.

عنبه هندي a*m*b'eh hundee, Pupaw tree.

عندم *a*nduu, Red saunders wood.

عنس *a*ns, Winged terminalia.

عنس *a*ns, Hairy pentaptera.

عنقز *a*n*k*uz, Marjoram.

عنصل *a*nssul, Indian squill.

عود *a*oo*u*d, Benzoin tree.

عود قاقاي *a*oo*u*d *k*a*k*aee, Aloes wood.

عودلوباني *a*ooud looba-nee, Benzoin tree.

عودهندي *a*ooud hundee, Aloes wood, or agila wood.

غاريقون *g*aree*k*oon, Soft playporus.

غاسول *g*asool, Joint flowering marygold.

غرب *g*urb, White poplar, Weeping willow.

غرمج *g*urmuj, Common beet.

غرمج *g*urmuj, Carrot.

غرنف *g*urnuf, Arabian jasmine.

غفا *g*ufa, Slender darnel.

غوش *g*oosh, Indian birch.

غوشه *g*oosh'eh, Indian birch.

غيزوران *g*eezooran, Cornel, or dogwood tree.

فاشرا fashura, Bristly bryony.

فافير fafeer, Ancient papyrus.

فجل fujul, Common radish.

فراس furas, Furas tamarisk.

فرسق fursu*k*, Nectarine.

فرنگيداتورا furungee datoora, Mexican argemone.

فريدبوتي fureed bootee, Hairy moonseed.

فطر fu*t*ur, Toadstool.

فقوس fu*k*oos, Cucumber.

فلفل اسود fulful *u*sooud, Black pepper.

فلفل‌سیاه fulful seea'h, Black pepper.

فنجنگشت funjungusht, Quadrangular chaste tree.

فندق funduk, Filbert.

فو foo, Valerian.

فوتنج footunuj, Common mint.

فوستاق foostak, Pistachio nut tree.

فوفل fooful, Betel-nut tree.

فوک fook, Slender darnel, Small fruited dolichos.

فول fool, Two-flowered dolichos.

فوه foo'h, Madder of Bengal.

فیشوق féshook, Eastern gaint fennel.

فیلفیل‌بره feelfeel bur'eh, Thin-leaved chaste tree.

قاپال‌اغا kapal aga, Cardamum tree.

قات kat, Eatable celastrus.

قاتهاپهاریا katha pu'hareea, Woody hippocratea.

قارپاسي karpasee, Cotton tree.

قاقله‌صغار kakul'eh ssugar, Cardamum tree.

قاقله‌کبار kakl'eh kubar, Large cardamum.

قالا kala, Spreading triangular spurge.

قت kut, Common clover.

قتاد kutab, True milk vetch.

قدرتي kudrutee, Mushroom.

قراص *k*urass, Chamomile.

قرانيا *k*uraneea, Cornel, or dogwood tree.

قرطم *k*ur*t*um, Safflower.

قرع *k*ura, Bottle gourd.

قرنفل *k*urunful, Clove tree, Gilly flowered, China pink, Wall flower.

قزيل *k*uzheel, Common blackberry.

قست *k*ust, Arabian costus.

قسط *k*ust, Beautiful costus.

قسطل *k*us*t*ul, Indian chesnut.

قشطم *k*ush*t*um, Arabian costus.

قصب *k*ussb, Bamboo, Karka reed.

قصبا *k*ussba, Soft rush.

قصب الزريره *k*ussu balzureer'eh, Chirayta.

قصب بوا *k*ussub booa, Sweet flag.

قطف *k*u*t*uf, Garden orache.

قطن *k*u*t*un, Cotton tree.

قلقل *k*ul*k*ul, Oval-leaved cassia.

قلمبا كي *k*ulumbakee, Palmated moon-seed plant.

قلمبک *k*ulumbuk, Aloes wood, or agila wood.

قلمي دارچيني *k*ulmee darcheenee, Real cinnamon.

قمريب *k*umreem, Kale or borecole.

قنب *k*unub, Hemp plant.

قندرق *k*undru*k*, Common osier.

قنس *k*unus, Elecampane.

قنه *k*un'eh, Common galbanum.

قونده or قوندم *k*oond'eh, or *k*oondum, Downy jasmine.

قهوه *k*uhoo'eh, True coffee tree.

قيصوم *k*eessoom, Indian southernwood.

قيو *k*eeoo, Arabian costus.

کابلي kaboolee, Common pea.

کاتيرا kateera, Stinging sterculia.

کاتي راجگيري katee rajgeeree, Prickly amaranth.

کاجو kajoo, Cashew nut.

کاچري kachuree, Spreading pontederia.

کاخار kakhar, Long zedoary.

کارا or کاري karee, or kara, Small flowered canthium.

کارا kara, Climbing webera.

کارتنه kartun'eh Common fenugreek.

کارجنک karjunk, Most useful cucumber.

کاردي kardee, Clingstone peach.

کارنتا karnuta, Netted oleander.

کارياري kareearee, Superb gloriosa.

کاس kas, Spontaneous sugar grass.

کاست kast, Upright water weed.

كاست kast, Forked chara.

كاسير kasmeer, Caoutchouc fig.

كاسنگهني kasung'hunee, Hemp-leaved tragia.

كاسني kasnee, Common endive, Wild succory, Indian turnsole.

كاشم kashum, Assafœtida plant.

كاغذي ليمو ka*g*uzee leemoo, Lime.

كافور kafoor, Camphor tree.

كاكـجانگها kak-u-jangeh, Hairy leea.

كاكروندا kakroonda, Coromandel celsia.

كاكن kakun, Italian millet.

كاكنج kaknuj, Blue-flowered nicandra.

كاكنه kakun'eh, Jacquin's nightshade.

كاگارا kagara, Spontaneous sugar grass.

كالابچناك kala buchnak, Tall hymenodictyon.

كالا تولسي kala toolsee, Sweet basil.

كالاجاتي kala jatee, Nervose eranthemum.

كالاجام kala jam, Java plum.

كالاجوار kalajooar, Two-colored grass.

كالاجيره kalajeer'eh, Indian fennel flower.

كالاچوكما kala chookma, Open oak.

كالا دهتورا kala d'hutoora, Purple thorn apple.

كالاكستوري kala kustooree, Musk okro.

کالامحمد kala mu*h*mud, Many-flowered phyllanthus.

کالا هلدي kala huldee, Grey turmeric.

کالپنانتھ kalupant*h*, Panicled justicia.

کالکاتھا kalukat'ha, Half-serrated myrsine.

کالي اورد kalee aoorud, Hairy podded bean.

کالي تلسي kalee tulsee, Purple stalked basil.

کالي زر kalee *z*ur, Wing-leaved clitoria.

کالي سيم kalee seem, Assam cowitch, or bean.

کالي شنبالي kalee shu*m*balee, Willow-leaved justicia.

کالي مرچي kalee murchee, Black pepper.

کامراج kamraj, Orissa sowthistle.

کاملتا kamuluta, Wing-leaved ipomea.

کاموني kamoonee, Black berried nightshade.

کانتا جاتي kanta jatee, Thorny barleria.

کانتاکچو kanta kuchoo, Armed pothos.

کانچکوري kanch kooree, Cowitch, Hemp-leaved tragia.

کانچکويلکيبينغ kanchkooeelkeebeen*g*, Cowitch.

کانچن kanchun, Taper-pointed mountain ebony.

کاندا kanda, Common onion.

کاندا kanda, Indian squill.

کاندلي kandlee, Small purslane.

کاندرلي kandoolee, Naked flowered commelina.

کانشيرا kansheera, Bengal commelina.

کانکا جريا kanka jureea, Thread like millet.

کانگو or کانگن kangun, or kangoo, Italian panic grass.

کاننهکندي kanuneh kundee, Purple-stalhed dragon plant.

کانوراقا kanoora*k*a, Bengal commelina.

کاوزبان kaoo*z*uban, Common buglos.

کاوشير kaoosheer, Rough parsnip.

کاهو ka'hoo, Garden lettuce.

کايپوتي kaeeapootee, Cajeputi tree.

کا يوپوته kaeeoopoot'eh, Cajeputi tree.

کباب چيني kubab cheenee, Cubebs.

کبابه kubabeh, Cubebs.

کباث kuba*s*, Persian salvadora.

کبر kubur, Prickly caper, Common caper.

کبود kubood, Weeping willow.

کبوترکي چهار hubootur ké-chu'har, White flowering justicia.

کبيکج kubeekuj, Water cress.

کپاس kupas, Cotton tree.

کپور kupoor, Camphor tree.

کت kut, Beautiful costus.

کتارا kutara, Prickly globe thistle.

كتايا kutaeea, Jacquin's nightshade.

كتكرنج kutkurunj, Small oval-leaved guilandina.

كتكليجي kut kuleejee, Small oval-leaved guilandina.

كتول kutoól, Cowitch.

كتهبيل kut'h bél, Elephant, or wood apple.

كتهگلاب kut'hgulab, China rose.

كتهل kut'hul, Jack tree.

كتيرا kuteera, True milk vetch.

كجيره kujeer'eh, Safflower.

كچالو kuchaloo, Egyptian arum.

كچري kuchree, Madras cucumber, Sweet melon.

كچلا kuchla, Poison nut.

كچلالتا kuchla luta, Colubrine strychnos.

كچنار kuchnar, Taper-pointed mountain ebony, Variegated ebony.

كچنال kuchnal, Variegated mountain ebony.

كچو kuchoo, Egyptian arum.

كچور kuchoor, Long zedoary.

كخج kukhuj, Heath.

كدم or كدمب kudumb, or kudum, Shady nauclea, Kudum nauclea.

كدو kudoo, Bottle gourd.

كديمه kudeem'eh, Pumpkin.

كرات kurat, Leek.

كراتةتكته kurat'eh tukt'eh, Chirayta.

كراس kuras, Leek.

كرامكا kuramuka, Betel nut tree.

كراو kuraoo, Field pea.

كرايچا kuraeecha, Oval-leaved wrightia, or rosebay, Oleander.

كرايلا kuraéla, Five-leaved cleome.

كربي kurubee, Sweet-scented oleander.

كرپد kurpud, Sweet-scented oleander.

كرپور kurpoor, Balsamic columnea.

كرتهي kurt'hee, Two-flowered dolichos.

كرسنه kursun'eh, Common pea.

كرش چرن kurush churun, Barbadoes flower fence.

كرشناكيلي kurshna kélee Marvel of Peru.

كرفس kurufus, Parsley, celery.

كركمان kurkuman, Common clove.

كركي kukree, Perforated rottboellia.

كرل kurul, Indian sarsaparilla.

كرم kurum, Common vine.

كرم جوا kurum jooa, Floribund kayea.

كرم كاساگ kurm ka sag, Cabbage.

كرم كلا kurum kula, Cabbage, Kale, or bore cole.

كرمچا kurumcha, Jasmineflowered caranda.

كرنا kurna, Citron.

كرنب kurumb, Cabbage.

كرنج kurunj, Indian galedupa, or smooth-leaved pongamia.

كرنجوا kurunjooa, Indian galedupa, or smooth-leaved pongamia.

كرندرا kurundra, Common mangosteen.

كرنوير kurnooeer, Common oleander.

كرو kuroo, Common endive.

كروز kurooz, Parsley.

كرولا kuroola, Bitter luffa.

كروندا kuroonda, Jasmine flowered corinda.

كريا kureela, Smooth gooseberry.

كريات kreeat, Panicled justicia.

كريپاك kureepok, König's bergera.

كريل kureel, Prickly caper, Common caper.

كريلا kureela, Hairy bitter gourd.

كساري kusaree, Chickling vetch.

كستوله kustool'eh Upright justicia.

كسم kusum, Safflower.

كسمبها kussumb'ha, Safflower.

كسوندي kusoondee, Round podded cassia.

كسوري kusooree, Barbed seeded clubrush.

كسوري ملنگي kusooree mulungee, Two spiked clubrush.

كسيرو kuseeroo, Cyperus grass.

كش kush, Meadow grass.

كشاخل kusha khul, Pigeon pea.

كشك kushuk, Native barley.

كشمله kushmul'eh, Wodier's odina.

كشوريا kushooreea, Ceylonese verbesina.

كشنه kushn'eh, Common pea, Bean-like vetch.

كشنيز kushneez, Coriander.

كعله kala'h, Two kernelled holly.

كعتكليجي katkuleejee, Oval-leaved nicker tree.

كفري مرچ kufree muruch, Caffree chilly pepper.

ككرمتا kukurmuta, Mushroom.

ككره kukr'eh, Early-rooted mangrove.

ككري kukree, Most useful cucumber.

كلا kula, Cabbage.

كلاي kulaee, Three-lobed kidney bean.

كلا كرا kula kura, Long-leaved unona.

كلتي kultee, Madras horse gram.

كلتهي kult'hee, Two-flowered dolichos.

كل حلوا kul *h*ulooa, Gangetic amaranth.

كلفي kulfee, White goosefoot.

كلكا جامپ kulka jamp, Woolly brake.

كلگا kulga, Hermaphrodite amaranth, Prince's feather.

كلم kulum, Cabbage.

كلمي kulmee, Creeping convolvulus.

كلمي ساگ kulmee sag, Creeping bindweed.

كلو kuloo, Freestone peach.

كلوله kulool'eh, Bean-like vetch.

كليالتا kuleea luta, Coated swallow wort.

كلي انچو kulee anchoo, Hill bramble.

كليبا kuleeba, Umbelled morinda.

كليجن kuleejun, The greater galangale

كلي كيكر kulee keekur, Gum acacia.

كم kum, True milk vetch.

كما or كم kum, or kuma, Truffle, Garden lettuce, Mushroom.

كمثري kumsuree, Common pear.

كمد kumud, Eatable water lily.

كمركه kumruk'h, Carambola tree.

كمره kumruh, Carambola tree.

كمرنگه kumrung'eh, Carambola tree.

كمرها kumru'ha, Pumpkin.

كمكما kumkuma, Aromatic didymocarpus.

كمكي kumkee, Three-flowered abelia.

كمل kumul, Indian sacred bean.

كمودني kumoodunee, Indian buck bean.

كمون kumoon, Common cumin.

كمون حلو kumoon *h*uloo, Common anise.

كميزه kumeezeh, Common clover.

كناله kunal'eh, Five-leaved cleome.

كنجان بورا kunjan boora, Narrow-leaved galangale.

كنجد kunjud, Oriental oily seed.

كنجده kunjud'eh Heart-leaved penœa.

كنجه لتا kunjeh luta, West coast creeper.

كنچنا kunchuna, Creeping jussiæa.

كند kund, Catalonian jasmine.

كندالي kundalee, Smooth volkameria.

كندانه kundan'eh, Leek.

كندر kundur, Frankincense tree.

كندري kunduree, Spreading mustard.

كندس kundus, Sneezewort.

كندوري kundooree, Great flowered bryony.

كنده kund'eh, Salep.

كنك kunuk, Downy thorn apple.

كنكا kunka, Umbelled ehretia.

كنكارا kunkara, Corymbose webera.

كنكران kunkuran, Common rye.

كنكرول kunkrool, Mixed bitter gourd.

كنكري kunkuree, Common cucumber.

كنگر kungur, Garden artichoke.

كنگني kungunee, Italian millet.

كنگوي kungooee, Mauritius sida.

كنگويا kungooeea, Cut-leaved urena.

كنگيا kunjeea, Five stamened roscoea.

كنور kunoor, Evergreen cypress.

كنول kunooul, Indian sacred bean.

كنولكا گدہ kunoonlka gud'eh, Indian sacred bean.

كنولكتا kunoolkuta, Most useful cucumber

كنه kun'eh, Mastich tree.

كنير kuneer, Common oleander.

كوا kooua, Cowa mangosteen.

كوا تهينتهي kooa t'heent'hee, Wing-leaved clitoria.

كوار kuooar, True coffee tree.

كواكانشاسته kooaka nushast'eh, East Indian arrowroot.

كوامورا kooamoora, Lance-shaped callicarpa.

كوانچه kooanch'eh, Cow-itch.

كوبي kôbee, Cabbage.

كوپي koopee, Indian acalypha.

كوته ملي koot'eh mulee, Narrow-leaved canthium.

كوچري koochuree, Four celled exacum.

كوداكاچول kôda ka chool, Punctured paspalum.

كودرو kooduroo, Wheat-like paspalum.

كودو koodoo, Kora millet.

كودو koodoo, Wheat-like paspalum.

كوڈه kôd'eh, Punctured paspalum, circular paspalum.

كودي منكوني koodee munkoonee, Herbaceous psychotria.

كورا kôra, Italian panic grass, or Italian millet.

كورا kôra, Mat-rush.

كورلي koorulee, Scape-flowered commelina.

كوري پہل kooree p'hul, Wood bramble.

كوسم koosum, Safflower.

كوشا koosha, Dog's tail meadow grass, Meadow grass.

كوكري kookree, Maize.

كوكري چيتا kookree cheeta, Petalless tetranthera.

كوكنار kooknar, White poppy.

كوكورا چوره kookoora choor'eh, Pavetta ixora.

كوكور جہوا kookoor j'hooa, Staphyl leea.

كول kool, Jujube.

كولا koola, Orange.

كولتا kooluta, Round-headed combretum.

كولسي koolsee, Indian nightshade.

كولي بيگن koolee bégun, Cylindrical eggplant.

كونچ koonch, Wild jamaica liquorice.

كوندها koond'ha, Pumpkin.

كونگوني koongoonee, Mauritius sida.

كونلا koonla, Orange.

كوني kônee, Smooth meadow grass.

كوي kôee, Water lily.

كوي پورا kôee poora, Leechee.

كويل koouëel, Wing-leaved clitoria.

كهج kuhuj, Strawberry.

كهجور k'hujoor, Common date palm, Wild date tree.

كهرسنبل k'hur sumbul, Huzar bean.

كهرني k'hurnee, Obtuse-leaved mimusops.

كهل k'hul, Knot grass.

كهيرا k'heera, Cucumber.

كهيرني k'heernee, Hexandric mimusops.

كيت keet, Elephant, or wood apple.

كيت بيل két bél, Elephant, or wood apple.

كيتكي keetukee, Green-spined screw pine.

كيراس keeras, Common cherry.

كيروج keerooj, Common rest harrow.

كيسر keesur, Square-stalked nyctanthus.

كيستو keestoo, Bitter cucumber.

كيسر keesur, Saffron plant.

كيكر keekur, Gum acacia.

كيكواش keekooash, Chamomile.

كيلا kéla, Banana.

كيل راي keel raee, Spreading mustard.

كيلي كدم kélee kudum, Heart-shaped leaved nauclea.

كيو keeoo, Beautiful costus.

كيوانچ or كيواچ keeooach, or keeooanch, Cowitch.

كيورا keeoora, Green spined screw pine.

كيورا كانٹا keeoora kanta, Fetid screw pine.

کاب gab, Polyandrous date plum.

کابانل gaba nul, Bengal reed.

گاجر gajur, Carrot.

گاچ مرچ gach muruch, Cayenne, or Chili pepper.

گالگل galgul, Citron.

گانجها ganj'ha, Hemp plant.

گاندر gandur, Scented grass.

گاو زبان gaoo zuban, Branching onosma.

گاویجک gaooeejuk, Cucumber.

گج پیپل guj peepul, Useful scindapsus.

گجگا gujga, Oval-leaved nicker tree.

گجي gujee, Climbing hedyotis.

گجیر قوتا gujér kôta, Climbing webera.

گدابني guda bunee, Trailing trianthera.

گدهاپورنا gud'ha poorna, Spreading hogweed.

گران guran, Ten stamened mangrove.

گرچ gurchu, Heart-leaved moonseed.

گردوي gurdooee, Hazel nut.

گرگر gurgur, Job's tears grass.

گرمه gurm'eh, Centaury-like chironia.

گرهل gur'hul, Althæa frutex.

گز guz, French tamarisk.

گزنه guzn'eh, Stinging nettle.

گشنیز gushneez, Coriander.

كفه guf'eh, Hazel nut.

گگندهول gugund'hool, Green-spined screw pine.

گلاب or گل gul, or gulab, A rose.

گلاب جام gulab jam, Rose apple.

گلاچين gulacheen, Acuminated plumieria.

گل اشرفي gul ashrufee, Three-styled flax.

گلبن gulbun, A rose.

گل بي فرمان gul bé furman, Wild rose.

گلنيل or گلبيل gul beel, or gul neel, Heart-leaved moonseed.

گل جعفري gul-u-jafree, French marygold.

گل چيني gul cheenee, Indian chrysanthemum.

گل خيرا gul kheera, Holly hock.

گل داودي gul daoodee, Indian chrysanthemum.

گلر gulur, Clustered fig.

گل رعنا gul rana, Many-flowered rose.

گل سرخ gul surkh, Damask rose.

گل سوري gul sooree, Bussorah rose.

گل شب بو gul shub boo, Common tuberose.

گل صدبرگ gul ssud buruk, Double rose.

گل طره gul tureh, Barbadoes flower fence.

گل عباس gul abas, Marvel of Peru.

گل عجايب gul ajaeeb. Changeable hibiscus.

گل فرنگ gul-u-furung, Madagascar periwinkle.

گلگیش gulgeesh, Various-leaved amaranth.

گل مخمل gul mukhmul, Annual globe amaranth.

گل ملنگه gul mulung-'eh, Winged cyperus grass.

گل مہندي gul mu'hundee, Balsam.

گلنار gulnar, Bird cherry.

گل نرگس gul nurgus, Copper colored day-lily.

گل نسرين gul nusreen, Sweetbriar rose.

گلو guloo, Heart-leaved moonseed, Indian wormwood.

گمار gumar, Tree gmelina.

گمي gumee, Eatable milnea,

گنج gunj, Wild Jamaica liquorice.

گندالي gundalee, Fœtid pæderia.

گندبيل gund bél, Lemon grass.

گندم gundum, Summer wheat.

گندمار gundmar, Indian wormwood.

گندنا gunduna, Leek.

گندها بادلي gund'ha badulee, Winged oldenlandia.

گندهابينه gund'ha been-'eh, Lemon grass.

گندهاگورانا gund'eha goorana, Smooth grass.

گندهراج gundu'hraj, Cape jasmine.

گندهل رنگن gund'hul rungun, Small flowered ixora.

گنگاتیه gungatee'eh, Alternate-leaved achyranthes.

گوارا gooara, Close oleaster.

گواکه gooak'eh, Betelnut tree.

گوالالاتا gooala lata, Vine-leaved cissus.

گوالیا gooaleea, Lobed cissus.

گوبرا goobra, Opposite-leaved bugle.

گوتا بیگون gôta bégoon, Madapple-leaved nightshade.

گوت بیگن goot bégun, Tomata, or love-apple.

گوتي سونا gootee soona, Fragrant panax.

گوجه gooj'eh, Various-leaved jasmine.

گوراچاند gôrachand, Moving hedysarum, Moving plant.

گورخي goorkhee, Red nightshade.

گوردل سیم goordul seem, Black seeded dolichos.

گورکناته gooruk nat'hu, Sweet scented garland flowers.

گورگیا goorgeea, Lemon grass.

گوروما goorooma, Bearded apluda grass.

گوري gooree, Grass-leaved leucocephalia.

گوري gooree, Tufted clubrush.

گوري پهل gooree p'hul, Himalaya blackberry.

گوزبان goozuban, Oleander-leaved cacalia.

گوز گیاه gooz geea'eh, Purple thorn-apple.

گوشاد gooshad, Kuroo gentian.

گوشگاسوا gooshuga sooa, Slender hedyotis.

گوک شورا gook shoora, Long-leaved barleria.

گوکرو gookuroo, Long-leaved ruellia.

گوکهرو gook'huroo, Long-leaved barleria. Downy caltrops.

گوگرو googroo, Small caltrops.

گوگل googul, Camphoric amyris.

گولاموهني goola moo'hunee, Berry-bearing deeringia.

گولاميتهي goola mét'hee, Naked cyperus grass.

گولشام goolusham, Nervose eranthemum.

گولر goolur, Downy fig.

گولک چاکلي gooluk chakulee, Hare's foot doodia.

گوم goom, Summer wheat.

گوما or گوم goom, or gooma, Ladies' bed straw.

گومپوکيلا goompoo kéla, Nepal plantain.

گومچي goomchee, Wild Jamaica liquorice.

گومرا goomra, Eatable phlomis.

گونجا goonja, Wild jamaica liquorice.

گونجي goonjee, Five-leaved limonia.

گوندني goondnee, Elephant grass, Sloping cordia.

گوندي goondee, Green xanthophyllum.

گويلا gooueela, Broad-leaved vine.

گهاگهرا g'hag'hra, Indian xanthium.

گهمرا g'humra, Cingalese phlomis.

گهنچي g'hunchee, Wild jamaica liquorice.

گهوگرو g'hooguroo, Small caltrops.

گهول g'hool, Small purslane.

گهويان g'hooeean, Egyptian arum.

گهي g'hee, Coromandel quillwort.

گهيا g'heea, Bottlegourd.

گهيا توري gheea tooree, Egyptian bitter gourd, Five-stamened luffa.

گهيتوراي g'heetooraee, Furrowed cucumber.

گهيچو g'heechoo, Simple stalked aponogeton.

گهي كشي g'hee kushee, Aporetic schmidelia.

گهيكوار gheekooar, Aloe.

گيژ geezh, Fir tree.

گيلا geela, Climbing mimosa.

گيندا or گيند geend, or geenda, African Marygold.

گيهون gee'hoon, Summer wheat.

لاجونتا lajoounta, Unarmed mimosa.

لادن ladun, Cretan rock rose.

لاده lad'eh, Black pepper.

لاسورا lasoora, Sloping cordia.

لاککري lak kuree, Floribund ash.

لاکوچا lakoocha, Bread fruit tree.

لاکهچنا lak'h chuna, Sensitive oxalis.

لاکي lakee, Acacia, soft.

لال‌جام lal jam, Two-edged ardisia.

لال‌چتا lal shuta, Rose colored leadwort.

لال‌چندند lal chundund, Red saunders wood.

لال‌چيته lal cheet'eh, Rose colored leadwort.

لال‌ساگ lal sag, Gangetic amaranth.

لال‌سفري‌ام lal sufree am, Red guava.

لال‌سيم lal seem, Black seeded dolichos.

لال‌لوتيا lal looteea, Round nettle.

لال مرچي lal murchee, Cayenne, or Chili pepper.

لال‌مرغا lal murga, Common cock'scomb.

لاله lal'eh, Common tulip.

لانکلي lankulee, Willow-leaved commelina.

لانگليا languleea, Cingalese nama.

لانگلي لتا langulee luta, Palmated ipomia.

لبان luban, Benzoin tree, Frankincense tree.

لبان‌لتا luban luta, Lesser pergularia.

لبخ lubukh, Smooth-leaved cordia.

لبيرا lubeera, Smooth-leaved cordia.

لپتا lupta, Upright panic grass.

لتكن lutkun, Heart-leaved arnotta.

لتكو lutkoo, Palatable pierardia.

لتمن lutmun, Berry bearing deeringia.

لتي ام lutee am, Eatable willughbeia.

لجالو lujaloo, Water mimosa.

لجالو lujaloo, Sensitive plant.

لسان الثور lusan *ul*soor, Common buglos, Oleander-leaved cacalia.

لسان العصافير lusan-*ul*-*a*ssafeer, Spreading hound's tongue.

لسورا lusoora, Smooth-leaved cordia.

لسون lusôn, Garlic.

لشپو lushpoo, Eatable sphærocarya.

لفت luft, Turnip.

لوبان looban, Benzoin tree.

لوبها loob'ha, Chinese dolichos.

لوبي loobee, see Small fruited dolichos.

لوبيا loobeea, Chinese dolichos.

لوبي كي پهلي loobee kee p'hulee, Tranquebar bean.

لوخ lookh, Bull-rush, Soft-rush.

لود lood, East Indian bastard cedar.

لوده lood'eh, Racemose symplocos.

لونا loofa, Air-living bryony.

لوکا looka, Sheathed pontederia, Bottle gourd.

لونا lôna, Bullock's heart.

لونیا or لونا loona, or looneea, Small purslane.

لونگالتا loongaluta, Climbing limonia.

لونگان lôngan, Longan.

لہرا lu'hura, Spiked millet.

لہسن lu'hsun, Garlic.

لہواشبو lu'hooa shuboo, Wall flower.

لیچی leechee, Leechee.

لیل leel, East Indian indigo.

لیمو leemoo, Lime.

لیمون leemoon, Citron.

لینبو leemboo, Lime.

مات کي بهاجي mat kee b'hajee, Round leaved amaranth, Eatable amaranth.

ماتو لونگا matoo lônga, Citron.

مادوکا madooka, Long-leaved basil.

ما د هولتا mad'hoolta, Clustered Gærtnera.

مارچوبا marchooba, Common asparagus.

مارسیسقا marseeska, Citron.

مارگیه margee'eh, Common asparagus.

مازریون mazreeoon, Mezereon daphne.

ماسونیتها masoo neetuha, Stuart's primrose.

ماش mash, Hairy podded kidney bean.

ماش mash, Black gram.

مال انکري mal ankree, Indian eleusine.

مالتي malutee, Clove-leaved echites, Catalonian jasmine.

مالتي لتا maltee luta, Clustered gærtnera.

ماندار mandar, Indian coral tree.

مايري maeeree, Sweet fennel.

متر mutur, Common pea.

مترنجه mutrunj'eh, Hoary callicarpa.

متره mutur'eh, Hoary callicarpa.

متكي mutkee, Bean-shaped dolichos.

متياچاندا muteea chanda, Rose-colored ixora.

متيا چيتا muteea cheeta, Pouched birthwort.

متيالاتا muteealata, Auriculated hedyotis.

مجيته mujét'h, Madder of Bengal.

محاتيتا mu*h*a teeta, Panicled justicia.

محموده mu*h*mood'eh, Scammony plant.

محوط mu*h*oot, Rough achyranthes.

مخال muk'hal, Bitter cucumber.

مخال mukhal, Palmated snake gourd.

مدار mudar, Curl-flowered calotropis.

مدعت mud*a*t, Emetic nut.

مدن mudun, Prickly vanguiera.

مرچا murcha, Capsicum.

مرچاي murchaee, Capsicum.

مردمگيا murdum geea, Mandrake plant.

مرزنجوش murzunjoosh, Marjoram, Sweet marjoram.

مرسا mursa, Eatable amaranth.

مرکا murka, Upright eleusine.

مرکابي کاگدہ murgabee ka gud'eh, Cingalese sanseviera.

مروا murooa, Thick spiked eleusine.

مروا murooua, Sweet marjoram, Mugwort, Cingalese sanseviera.

مرورپهلي muroor phulee, East Indian screw tree.

مروري murooree, East Indian screw tree.

مرہ mureh, Bitter cucumber.

مستارو mustaroo, Indian Wormwood.

مصطاقي mus*t*a*k*ee, Mastich tree.

مسواک musooak, Indian salvadora.

مسور musoor, Hairy tare.

مسور musoor, Lentil.

مسورچنا musoor chuna, Yellow vetchling.

مسينا museena, Common flax.

مشمش mushmush, Apricot.

مصنبر mussu*m*bur, Common aloe.

مصوري mussooree, Lentil.

معاد m*a*ad, Thick spiked eleusine.

معصفر m*a*ssfur, Safflower.

معفر m*a*fur, Aromatic rhododendron.

مغيلان mu*g*eelan, Gum acacia.

مکرا جالي mukra jalee, Egyptian eleusine.

مکرجالي mukur jalee, Prickly panic grass.

مکو mukoo, Ten-toothed nightshade.

مکوي mukooee, Indian sarsaparilla.

مکهانا muk'hana, Prickly euryale.

مکهانا muk'hana, Spinous anneslea.

مکهسبزه muk'eh subz'eh, Common balm.

مکهن سيم muk'hun seem, Sabre-podded dolichos.

مکي جاري muké jaree, Maize.

مگرابو mugraboo, Indian sarsaparilla.

مگريلا mugreela, Indian fennel flower.

ملتهي mulut'hee, Hairy liquorice.

ملکک mulkuk, Round-leaved mallow.

منا muna, Laburnum-leaved crotalaria.

منجيهته munjee'eht'eh, Madder of Bengal.

مندار mundar, Misletoe.

مندي mundee, Indian sphæranthus.

منروا or منروي munrooa, or munrooee, Dog's tail grass.

منروي munrooee, Upright eleusine.

منصورسيج munssoorseej, Sheathed spurge.

منگي mungee, Horse-raddish tree.

موال mooal, Lance-leaved vateria.

موبرج mooburuj, Holly-leaved berberry.

موت môut, Aconite-leaved kidney bean.

موتها moot'ha, Rush-leaved cyperus.

موتها moot'ha, Round stemmed cyperus-grass.

موتيا mooteea, Arabian jasmine.

موتي موندها mootee-moond'ha, Small tacca.

موچا moocha, Banana.

موچا كوندا moocha koon-da, Various-leaved pterospermum.

مورد moord, Myrtle.

مورموري moor mooree, Erect clubrush.

مورنگ الاچي môrung alachee, Morung cardomum.

موز moouz, Banana.

موژان moozhan, Poly-anthes narcissus.

موستا moosta, Rush-leaved cyperus.

موس مسه moos museh, Globe-fruited bryony.

موفلون moofloon, Up-right melilot.

موكتپاطي mooktupatee, Double stemmed phrynium.

موگرا moogra, Arabian jasmine.

مول mool, Indian bœo-botrys.

مولسري moolsuree, Pointed-leaved mimusops.

مولي moolee, Common radish.

مونج moonj, Munja sugar grass.

موندلاارو moondla aroo, Nectarine.

مونسا سیج moonsa seej, Sheathed spurge.

مونگ moong, Green gram.

مونگ پهل moong p'hul, Earth nut.

مونگ پهلي moong p'hulee, American earth-nut.

مهوا muhooa, Long-leaved bassia.

مهي muhee, Long-leaved bassia.

میتهي meet'hee, Common fenugreek.

میتهي کدو meet'hee kudoo, Pumpkin.

میخک meek'huk, Clove tree.

میدپهل meed p'hul, Emetic nut.

میراد meeradoo, Wild-milkwort.

میستا mésta, Indian red sorrel.

میعة meeaut'eh, Common storax.

میل لتا mél luta, Great-flowered Thunbergia.

مین پهل meen p'hul, Emetic nut, Prickly vanguiera.

مینهدي mén'hdee, Henna plant.

ناتاکرنجي nata kurunjee, Oval-leaved nicker tree.

نار nar, Pomegranite.

نارجبل narjubul, Cocoa-nut tree.

نارجیل or نارجیلي narjeel, or narjeelee, Cocoanut tree.

نارده narduleh, Broke[n] panic grass.

ناردين nardeen, Thick-leaved lavender, Spike-nard.

نارسيج nar-u-seej, Spreading triangular spurge.

نارفيل narfeel, Common galbanum.

نارنج narunj, Orange.

نارنگي narungee, Orange.

نارون naroon, Elm.

ناريل nareel, Cocoanut tree.

نازبو nazboo, Ciliated basil.

نازبوي nazbooee, Hairy basil.

نازک بدن nazuk budun, Jujube.

ناژ nazh, Evergreen cypress.

ناسا بهاگا nasa b'haga, Double calyxed justicia.

ناسرجنگي nasur jungee, Purslane-leaved trianthema.

ناشپتي nashputee, Common pear.

ناغ na*g*, Elm.

ناکدون nakdoon, Common asparagus.

ناگبيل nagbél, Betle pepper.

ناگ دونا nag doona, Mugwort.

ناگر موته nagur mote'h, Rush-leaved cyperus.

ناگرموتها nagur moot'ha, Slender cyperus.

ناگ فنا nag funa, Indian cactus.

ناگ کيسر or ناگيسر nageesur, or nag keesur, Iron mesua, or Indian rose chesnut.

نال nal, Karka reed.

نانخواه nankhooa'eh, Lovage.

ناهر nahur, White grape vine.

ناي naee, Karka reed.

نخج nukhuj, Heath.

نخل nukhul, Taliera palm.

نخود nukhood, Common chick pea.

نحبوع nu*h*boo*a*, Dwarf kidney bean.

نر nur, Karka reed.

نربسي nurbusee, Round zedoary.

نربشي nurbushee, One-headed kyllinga.

نرجس nurjus, Polyanthes narcissus.

نرچا nurcha, Bristly-leaved corchorus, Heart-leaved corchorus.

نرد nurd, Thick-leaved lavender, Spikenard.

نركت nurkut, Karka reed.

نسترن nusturun, Common clover.

نسترن nusturun, White rose.

نسرين nusreen, Polyanthes narcissus.

نسرين nusreen, Wild rose.

نسندها nusundha, Three-leaved chaste tree.

نسوت nusoot, Square stalked ipomea.

نعناع nan*a*a*a*, Common mint, Peppermint.

نقمبا du*k*umba, Glaucous-leaved physic nut.

نک چکني nuk chuknee Green-flowered hoya

نک چلني nuk chulnee, Ramoon tree.

نلر nulur, Square-stalked cissus.

نمج numuj, Bullrush.

نمشک numshuk, Coriander.

نواکوتي nôakootee, Panicled eria.

نوالتا nooaluta, Climbing dalbergia.

نوا ملکا nooua mulka, Woody jasmine.

نوج nooj, Long-leaved pine.

نوريا nooreea, Climbing achyranthes.

نوشت nooursht, Purple-stalked dragon plant.

نوکا nooka, Sheathed pontederia.

نونيا nooneea, Small purslane.

ني nee, Sweet flag.

نيتا or نيتها neetuha, or neeta, Sarmentose.

نيتها neetuha, Toothed primrose.

نيرفر neerufur, Water lily.

نيرملي neermulee, Clearing nut.

نيسند ي neesundee, Quadrangular chaste tree.

نيکاري neekaree, Indian chesnut.

نيل neel, East Indian indigo.

نيل کلمي neel kulmee, Blue ipomea, Purgative pharbitis

نيلکنته neel kunt'h, Grey turmeric.

نيلکنته neel kunt'h, Horse-radish tree.

نیلوفر neeloofur, Indian sacred bean, Water lily.

نیمب or نیم neem, or neemb, Margosa tree.

نیبو or نینبو neemboo, or neeboo, Lime.

نیمدا neemda, Indian buddlea.

وارکار ooarkar, Most useful cucumber.

وارنک ooarunk, Cucumber.

والکه ooaluk'eh, Thick-leaved lavender.

والوا ooalooa, Saw-leaved ternstromia.

وامپیچ ooampeech, Chinese wampee tree.

وارچي ooaoochee, Hazel-leaved psoralia.

وتیس ootees, Tapering birch.

وج oouj, Sweet flag.

وچاسوا oocha sooa, Ovate gardneria.

ودارا oodara, Many-spined flacourtia.

ودو جاتي oodoo jatee, Long-spiked justicia.

ورد oorud, Rose.

ورکار oorgar, Common blackberry.

وریهتي ooree'hutee, Indian nightshade.

وزر oozur, Panicled justicia.

وشنه ooshn'eh, Bird cherry.

وشیج oosheej, Floribund ash.

وشیرا ousheera, Useful scindapsus.

وغل oo*g*ul, Slender darnel.

ولايتي اغاتي oulaeetee a*g*ätee, Broad-leaved cassia.

ولايتي اماي oulaeetee umlee, Gamboge mangosteen.

ولايتي اننناس oulaeetee anunas, Cantula agave.

ولايتي بيگن oulaeetee bégun, Tomato, or Love apple.

ولايتي جاو oulaeetee jaoo, Common oat.

ولايتي كافور oulaeetee kafoor, Bengal sage.

ولايتي مندي oulaeetee mundee, Myrtle.

ولايتي مونگ oolaeetee moong, American earthnut.

وله ooul'eh, Double stemmed phrynium.

ونده oond'eh, Common cress.

وياكول ooeeakool, Indian nightshade.

ويش ooésh, Wild wolf's-bane.

هاپرمالي hapurmalee, Two-stamened echites.

هاتهاجوري hat'ha jooree, Club moss.

هاتهپهول hat'h p'hul, Useful scindapsus.

هاتيسوره hatee sooreh, Indian turnsole.

هاتي كان hatee kan, Spear-leaved clerodendrum.

هارجورا or هار harjoora, or har, Square-stalked cissus.

هارچاره harchareh, Indian flagellaria.

هاریم‌هرا hareem hura, Rotuk amoora.

هاقوچ ha*k*ooch, Hazel-leaved psoralia.

هال کهوسا hal k'hoosa, Cingalese phlomis.

هالم halum, Common cress.

هتي‌شورا hutee shoora, Indian turnsole.

هدس hudus, Myrtle.

هجلي‌بادام hujlee badam, Common cashewnut.

هجلي مينهدي hujlee-mén'hdee, Bracteate eugenia.

هرا hura, Chebulic myrobolan.

هربهري hurbu'hree, Common chick pea.

هرپهاريوري hurphareeooree, Long-leaved cicca, Cheramel phyllanthus.

هرد hurd, Common turmeric.

هرسنگار hur sungar, Square stalked nyctanthes.

هرف hurf, Chinese cress.

هرفاليوري hurfaluooree, Long-leaved cicca.

هركت hurkut, Holly-leaved acanthus.

هركچلا hur kuchla, Axillary strychnos.

هركوچ كانتا hur kooch kanta, Holly-leaved acanthus.

هركي hurkee, Long-leaved echites.

هرلا hurla, Chebulic myrobolan.

هرهر hur hur, Viscid cleome.

هرهفت hur'huft, Polyanthes narcissus.

هريا كدو hureea kudoo, Bottle gourd.

هرياكيكر hureea keekur, Oval-leaved coral tree.

هري مونگ huree moong, Rayed-leaved kidney bean.

هزار دانه huzar dan'eh, Daisy.

هكتي hukutee, Large flowered coronella.

هلدا hulda, Chebulic myrobolan, Myrobolan plum.

هلده huld'eh, Chebulic myrabolan.

هلسي hulsee, Greater ægiceras.

هل كسا hul kusa, Cingalese phlomis.

هل هل hul hul, five-leaved cleome.

هليلج كاربلي huleeluj karbulee, Chebulic myrobolan.

هليله كالن huleel'eh kulan, Chebulic myrobolan.

هليم huleem, Chinese cress.

هليون huleeoon, Common asparagus.

همار humar, Bullrush.

همسود humsood, Lote tree, jujube.

هندبا hundba, Wild succory, Endive.

هندوانه hundooan'eh, Water melon.

هنگ hung, Eastern giant fennel.

هنكتشا hungtsha, Creeping enhydra.

هنكتشا ساگ hungtsha-sag, Creeping meyera.

هنگن hungun, Egyptian ximenia.

هوبر hoobur, Persian Iris.

هوگلا hoogla, Elephant grass.

هويت hoοét, Water centrostachys.

هير heeur, Hairy moon-seed.

هيشر heeshur, White poppy.

هيل بوا heel booa, Cardomum tree.

هيل كلان heel kulan, Large cardomum.

ياسمن eeasmun, Arabian jasmine.

يراميع eerameea, Common asparagus.

يشوي لانگلا eeshooee langula, Superb gloriosa.

يقطين uéktееn, Bottle gourd.

يو eeoo, Native barley.